A Third Rutan Family Index

. . . .

James J. Keegan

HERITAGE BOOKS
2010

HERITAGE BOOKS
AN IMPRINT OF HERITAGE BOOKS, INC.

Books, CDs, and more—Worldwide

For our listing of thousands of titles see our website
at
www.HeritageBooks.com

Published 2010 by
HERITAGE BOOKS, INC.
Publishing Division
100 Railroad Ave. #104
Westminster, Maryland 21157

Other books by the author:
A Rutan Family Index
A Second Rutan Family Index

International Standard Book Numbers
Paperbound: 978-0-7884-2113-6
Clothbound: 978-0-7884-8492-6

Contents

INTRODUCTION

In my "Second Rutan Family Index" I provided some information on the Rutan/Rutant family in France. The source of this was genealogical work commissioned by Charles Hercules Rutan, the Boston architect, about 1906. I recently received from Dan Gamber information that supplements the earlier material and which is summarized below. I am grateful to Dan for sharing this important information.

Abraham B. Rutan (1658-1713) was the son of Daniel Rutan (c1620-1669) and Anne De Bize bc 1618. They were married at Metz, Lorraine, France in 1642 and where Daniel was born and died.

Daniel Rutan was the son of Claude Rutan (c1590-1658) and Sarah Bigene. They wed in Metz in 1613. Claude was born at St. Mihiel, Meuse, France and he died in Metz.

Claude Rutan was the son of Claude Rutan (c1565-c1613) and Katherine Coubeue (1562-c1593). They were married about 1584 and Katherine died at St. Mihiel. Claude married Anne _____ at St. Mihiel in 1593.

Dan's research also indicates that the Rutant family originated in Neuchatel en Bray, Normandie.

I have loved history, particularly American history, since I was a teen-ager. I graduated from Holy Cross College, Class of 1959, with an A.B. in History. I had originally majored in Pre-Law but several American History courses my junior year under Professor William J. Grattan convinced me that I really wanted to concentrate on history, and I did.

So when in 1993 I became involved in the genealogy of the Rutan family I soon realized that genealogy is history on a personal basis. Not just the discovery of names and dates, gravestones and dim images on microfilm, genealogy, when looked at from a historical context, provides an opportunity to get a feeling for one's ancestors that, to a degree, lives and breathes. Genealogists and family historians strive to "flesh out" their ancestors.

Looking at the Rutan family, or any family, from the perspective of what was happening at the time they were alive, results in a better assessment of what they were like, how they lived, what they believed in---who they were.

The Rutans were colonial settlers, they farmed, pioneered the frontier, fought in the major wars (often opposing one another) they lived in cities and on the edge of civilization, they were merchants, preachers, inventors, lumbermen and builders of buildings. They held office, invested in real estate, were architects and bankers, made whiskey, grew grapes for wine and owned taverns. No doubt a few were scoundrels.

Some stayed near where they were born. Others were not averse to picking up and moving into the Virginia mountains before the American Revolution or to southwest Pennsylvania when Washington was president or into the Northwest Territory at the beginning of the 19th century or to Minnesota during the Sioux Uprising or to California before the Gold Rush was over.

And when they named their children after Theodore Frelinghuysen, an 18th century American Dutch Reformed preacher, or James Madison, or Thomas Hart Benton, Senator from Missouri before the Civil War, some conclusions can be drawn as to their religious or political views. If you find they voted for George B. McClellan in 1864 or were members of the underground railroad or were active in the prohibition movement you have an inkling as to their outlook.

If you read, for example, "The Revolutionary War in the Hackensack Valley" by Adrian C. Leiby (see bibliography) which, by the way, mentions members of the Rutan family, you can gain an appreciation for the dangers, fears, living conditions and the motivation of farm families living in the "neutral ground" between patriot and British/Loyalist forces in that area of New Jersey just west of New York City during the period of British occupation of the City.

The Rutan family was not unique. Research on most families that were in American in the 17th or 18th centuries would disclose that family members were, for the most part, uneducated or at least undereducated. Often illiterate, with no special renown, they lived their lives simply and left no particular mark on history. Yet they are interesting for collectively they are a part of the fabric of America and what it means to be an American. The impetus to try to know as much about them as possible seems obvious.

It has been five years since "The Second Rutan Family Index" became available and since then, with a great deal of help from others, I have gathered a mountain of new information relating to the Rutan family. As I started work on the present volume I thought to myself that I had really gotten a handle on placing many Rutans in to their proper place on the family tree. Now that the book is almost finished I am vividly aware that much remains to be done. There are many of individuals still unattached.

Certainly progress has been made, but mysteries remain. The Rutans of Sullivan Co. NY came from Hackensack, NJ but who are their antecedents? The Retans of Bradford Co. PA and surrounding neighborhoods, as well as those in Michigan, came from Seneca Co, NY but where did *they* originate? The Retons of Bergen Co, NJ just sort of appear---whose family are they? How about the Rutans in South Dakota or Washington State? Yes, a lot remains.

Having compiled voluminous records it is possible to draw some conclusions about family migrations before 1845. Abraham Rutan and Marie Petilon had twelve children, six sons and six daughters. Of the sons five survived childhood and four married: Daniel, Paul, Peter Abraham and Samuel. The following is a general summary showing how the some of the families of the sons of Abraham and Marie relocated.

Daniel   (Bergen County, NJ)

- Sussex Co. NJ (about 1778)
- Steuben Co, NY (about 1815)

Paul (Bergen County, NJ)

- Westchester County, NY (about 1735)
- Ontario Canada (Loyalists) 1783
- New York City 1800

Peter Abraham Rutan (Morris County, NJ)

- Hampshire County, (W) VA   1750

- Sussex Co. NJ (about 1780)
- Washington Co. PA   1793
- Garrett Co. MD (about 1790)
- Champaign Co. OH (about 1810)
- Carroll Co. OH (about 1810)
- Trumbull Co. OH (about 1805)
- Tippecanoe Co. IN (about 1820)

Samuel Rutan (Essex County, NJ)

- Staten Island (Richmond Co.) NY (about 1815)
- Kings County NY (about 1845)

I would like to correct some historical inaccuracies I slipped in the introduction to "A Second Rutan Family Index" wherein I stated that the Dutch colony of New Netherland passed to Great Britain after the Glorious Revolution of 1688. I was wrong, twice.

New Netherland never passed anything to Great Britain since it was not until 1707 that England and Scotland unified into Great Britain. After a series of maritime wars between the Netherlands and England covering 1652-1674, which the English won, New Netherland was finally ceded to England in 1674 and New Amsterdam became New York City.

The "text" of this book has been extracted from my database. In the course of researching the Rutan family genealogy I have gathered a good deal of information that, because of space limitations cannot be included. Yet, there still remains information yet to found.

In the early phase of my research I visited many archives and libraries, mainly in the northeast but as far west as Seattle, Las Vegas and Honolulu and found pertinent material from books, microfilm and the like. I always found something new. The second phase encompassed information from Rutan family members or researchers. Some of this information was probably unavailable from any other source. The third phase relates to information garnered off the Internet. I have gotten to the point where working the three phases has merged and I now soak up new material wherever I can find it.

Regarding the Internet, while more than a little of the available information looks and feels suspicious, the very fact that data is coming

ing to light that might not otherwise be discovered in one's lifetime makes it potentially valuable source.

This, of course, leads to my usual kind advice. The material in this book emanates primarily from secondary sources and its reliability should not be accepted without some skepticism. This book is intended to be a guide, a sign-post suggesting a direction to take and nothing more. Based upon comments I have received regarding the previous editions I think this course has been successful.

Have we located all the Rutans who lived in North America from 1658-1925? No. I find new ones frequently. With the availability of the 1930 federal census and other sources coming on-line we may reach a point in the near future where we have identified all the Rutans in whom we are interested but we will probably never be able to connect them all.

Since I started serious work on this project in June 2001 I have continued to unearth new Rutan information. It is sitting unanalyzed in folders until I could find time to give it a thorough sifting. Now might be a good time.

I would like to extend my thanks to all the gracious people with whom have traded Rutan material over the past several years. Their names have been shown as sources in the text. I know I have missed a few names like Stella Platt Hughes of Rapid City, SD; Patti Gamin; Donna Mohney of Ligonier, PA; Robert Rutan of Miami, FL; and, Emily Cattruna of Secaucus, NJ. Special thanks is extended to Norman Rutan of Kearny, NJ; Janet Rutan Bowers of Ft. Lee, NJ; and, my friend Elsie Garris of Newton, NJ, now in her 96th year. To those I have unintentionally omitted I beg forgiveness.

This is dedicated to those who lost their lives on September 11, 2001, and their families as well as to the memory of

Carmine Philip Capobianco (1910-2001) my father-in-law ..... Quite a guy.

James J. Keegan
Sound Beach NY
May 2002

RUTANS IN THE NORTHEAST UNITED STATES
1658-1799

Abraham B. Rutan - (1658-1713) p/Daniel Rutan-
Anne de Bize of Metz, Lorraine, France,
settled in New Paltz NY c1675; m Marie
Petilon (c1662-1713); moved to New Barbad-
oes, Bergen Co. NJ c1699; both died at New
Barbadoes Neck (Rutherford) NJ; Note: he
is identified as Abraham Boudat Rutan in
"Kinship of Claudin Rutan" by John Wesley
Sexsmith

Abraham Rutan - (1711-1798) p/Daniel Rutan-
Antje Hanse Spier m Sarah Van Gelder b 1710
of Ramapo, Bergen Co. at Aquackanonck Ref
Church in 1734; they were living at Rempug
NJ from that time until at least 1743; LDS;
MACK; PCHSP; FH

Abraham Rutan - b 1712 m Joanna Elset before
1735; PCHSQ; NJW

Abraham Rutan - (1709-c1770) p/Paulus Rutan-
Engletje Davidse of Phillipsburg Manor,
Westchester Co. m Sarah DeForest d 1788 of
Bergen Co.; MACK; GSNJ; DARLDC

Abraham Rutan - b 1721/22 p/Abraham Rutan m
Sarah DeForest d 1788; GSNJ

Abraham Rutan - (c1732-1790) p/Abraham Rutan-
Sarah De Forest m Aeltie Van Tassel bc 1731
of Tarrytown. He was probably born at
Schraalenburg, Bergen Co. NJ and died at Mt.
Pleasant, Westchester Co. NY; MACK

Abraham Rutan - m Elizabeth Dupuw; PCHSQ

Abraham Rutan - Sgt. in Major Timpany's Co.
4th Battalion (Loyalist)(from the muster roll)

Abraham Rutan - (1754-1845) p/John Rutan-Aeltie
Van Horn of Paramus; identified by Abraham A.
Rheutan as the father of the sons who married
the Courter sisters; PDRC; EARDP; AAR

Abraham Rutan - b 1754 p/John Rutan-Aeltie Van
Horn m Elizabeth _____ ; MACK

Abraham Rutan - b 1791 p/Abraham Rutan-Elizabeth
Dupuw m Rachel Garrison, mentioned in the
will of her father, Abraham Garrison of
Clarkstown, Rockland Co. NY in 1830; NCPL;
PCHSQ

Abraham Rutan - (1769-1829) p/Peter Rutan-Jannet-

je Ackerman m Catherine Dingman (1786-1861)
Note: there is a record that they were wed in
NYC in 1786 so her birthyear may be incorrect;
PPDLN; VWR; RUTT

Abraham D. Rutan - Rheutan (1798-1872) p/John
Rutan-Rachel Vanderbeek m. Mary Storms
(1801-1893) in 1818 at West New Hempstead;
both from Campgaw NJ: blacksmith living in
Hackensack, Bergen Co. in 1850 and in Newburgh, Orange Co. NY in 1860; both buried at
Old Hook Cemetery, Westwood NJ; Note: PCHSP
names him as Abraham I. or P. Rutan and the
son of Daniel Rutan-Jannitje Brower; he
deliberately changed the spelling of the surname to **Rheutan** since there were so many
Abraham Rutans in the vicinity; GSBC; BCGI;
PDRC; 1850C; 1860C; WYCK; PCHSP

Abraham Rutan - (1788-1864) m Ann Courter
(1793-1875) at Vernon Twp, Sussex Co. in
1809; both bur in Vernon Cemetery; Note:
there are some records that identify him as
the son of Abraham D. Rutan-Rebecca Kasine
(see below) AAR says that this Abraham was
the son of Abraham Rutan and Elizabeth Dupuw
(see below); FH; GMNJ; DARLDC; EG; AAR

Abram D. Rutan - (1763-1848) p/Daniel Rutan-
Willemina Bogert m (1) Rachel Kasine (2)
Lydia Vanderbeek (1792-1879) at the Ponds
(Oakland) NJ in 1798; RW soldier also fought
in War of 1812; living in Paterson NJ in
1841; Note: no mention of a first wife named
Kasine or the three sons he allegedly had
by her in his RW pension file so this first
marriage is highly suspect; NGS; DARP; FH;
PCHSP; DRCNYC

Abraham Rutan - (1776-1871) p/Daniel Rutan-
Sarah _____; m Anna Coss (1781-1824) in 1806
(2) Susannah Coss Hazen in 1825 (3) Margaret
Coss (1800-1871) in 1849; he was from Newton
and she from Sandyston (from their wedding
announcement in the *Warren Journal* of Belvidere, Warren Co. NJ; CBRF; JS

Abraham Ruton - (1796-1856) died in Astoria,
Queens Co. NY (Obit in N.Y. Post 2 Dec. 1856)
QBPL

Abraham J. Rutan - b 1779 p/Jacobus Rutan-Will-
empje Bogert m (1) Maria _____ b 1773 (2)
Melvina (Wyntje) Hopper at Clarkstown DRC,
Tappan, Rockland Co. NY in 1795; living in

Harrington Twp, Bergen Co. NJ in 1800; Note: LDS has the marriage to Wyntje as 1798; ZAB; NCPL; LDS; DAVIS; TAPDRC; PCHSQ

Abraham Retan - m Effy Wenman bc 1793 at Trinity Church in NYC in 1817 or 1820; Note: the records of this church has data on two Effys, born in 1793 and 1796 and two marriage dates

Abraham Ruton - b 1794 p/William Ruton-Rachel Brower of Tarrytown, Westchester Co. NY (see Abraham Ruton, above) GSNJ; PCHSP; MACK

Abraham Rutan - (1770/76-1871) p/Daniel Rutan-Sarah _____; Note: PCHSQ has his mother as Susan Kymer who has been confirmed as the wife of Samuel Rutan; JS; PCHSQ

Abraham Rutan - (1774-1804) p/"Elder" Abraham Rutan m Hannah Shipman bc 1779 of Morristown they lived in Springfield (now Union Co.) he was a cabinet maker and is bur at the Presbyt Chyd, New Providence; after his death Hannah m Stephen Pierson in 1822 (church records) LITT

Adaline Rutan - m Stephen Hedden; they were both from Pequannock, Morris Co. NJ; MCMR

Alethea Rutan - (see Letty Rutan below); BFG; CDRC

Alethea Rutan - m Isaac Brower in NYC in 1810; LDS

Alise Retan - resident of NYC in 1810; 1810C

Alletta B. Rutan - **Lottie** (1782-1861) p/Daniel Rutan-Jannitje Brower m Ralph Benjamin Romaine (1772-1860) they are both bur at Crooked Pond Cem, Oakland NJ; PCHSP

Ally Rutan - p/Barent Rutan-Annantje Van Rype m (1) Tobias Van Gelder in 1807 at the Bapt Ch of Wantage (2) Joseph Simonson; Note: Barbara Moore has a record of Ally Van Gelder in Steuben Co. NY in 1870 so the marriage order may be reversed although in her father's 1829 will he identifies her as the wife of Joseph Simonson; CCNEW; SCMR

Ann Rutan - p/Samuel Rutan, Jr.-Mary Brown m Peter Lucas Coeyman (Cooman) (1792-1869) in 1812; both from Bloomfield Twp, Essex Co. NJ; Note: their marriage registered at the Salem Ch of the Evangelical Assn of Lancaster, PA; they are bur at the Coeyman Cem in Belleville (Peter's data from Judith Watt) FH; ECMR

Anna Rutan - (1784-1851) p/Daniel Rutan-Jannit-

3

je Brower m Daniel Sturr; she is bur at the
Sturr Family Cem, Florida, Orange Co. NY;
GSNJ

Anna Rutan - b 1797 p/Barent Rutan-Annantje
Van Riper; AAR

Barnet Rutan - (1790-1870) p/Barent Rutan-
Annantje Van Rype; m (1) Sarah Drew (1789-
1846) at the Baptist Ch of Wantage in 1808;
moved to Hammondsport, Steuben Co. NY in
1815; (2) Anna Fitzsimmons (1809-1880) all
three are bur at the Depew Cem, Urbana Town,
Steuben Co. and their dates are from cemetery
records; 1850C; FH; STUCHS; SCMR

Betsy Rutan - (1772-1865) she died at Paramus
(Pat Wardell)

Cattrina Rutan - b 1780 p/Samuel Rutan, Jr.-
Mary Brown of Belleville, Essex Co. NJ; m
Peter Cooman; Note: Another record has her
sister Ann married to Peter Cooman; they may
the same person; CRC

Catherine Rutan - m Joseph T. Powers in Essex
Co. NJ in 1805; SRDC

Catherine Rutan - b 1792 p/John Rutan-Jane
Blauvelt; she was alive at time of her
mother's pension application in 1842; unm;
BFG; ARWPF

Catherine Rutan - b 1794 p/John Rutan-Elizabeth
Lake of Passaic m. Peter Van Dewater of
Belleville in Newark in 1810 or 1811; they
lived in Jersey City, NYC and later Barry
and Lenawee Cos. MI; the marriage confirmed
in her father's will; Note: another record
has the wedding in Lodi, Bergen Co. NJ; she
died before 1860 (Honi Jo Curtis); USARCH;
EARDP; ADRC

Catherina Rutan - b 1795 p/Daniel Rutan-Rachel
Berdan m William Joline (c1785-c1840) at
NYC in 1819; he was born in Staten Island and
died at Ft. Lee; Note: an LDS record says she
was born in 1802: NYCMM

Catherine Reton - resident of Mamakating Town,
Sullivan Co, NY in 1820; 1820C

Catherine Retan - bc 1755 of New York; m _____
Bateman/Bakeman; AGBI

Charity Rutan - b 1759 p/"Elder" Abraham Rutan
m John Miller; Note: another record has her
born in 1773; LITT

4

Conrad Rutan - (1733-1815) p/Daniel Rutan-
Catharina _____ m Claartjie Van Houten in
1758; both were from Pompton, (now) Passaic
Co. NJ; Conrad referred to as **Conrad**
Lines (alias Rutan) in several sources and
was adopted by Conrad Lein, his mother's
second husband; Conrad and Clorche Lines of
Wyoming PA sold property in Bergen Co. in
1784; Conrad's dates from Judi Crockett; LDS;
DAVIS

Cornelius Rutan - (1773-1804) p/Samuel Rutan-
Margrietje Banta m Hettie Fellow; resident
of NYC in 1800; Note: according to the
Conover Genealogy Hettie was Hester Valleau;
BARB; 1800C

Cornelius Rutan - d 1803; resident of Cross St.
NYC; he died of yellow fever 10 Aug 1803
(129 NYGBR:18)

Cornelius Rutan - W1812 soldier; drummer, 1st
Regt (Sitcher's) Artillery, N.Y. Volunteers
(War of 1812 Muster Rolls)

Cornelius Rutan - resident of Paterson in 1820;
1820C

Daniel Rutan - b 1729 P/Daniel Rutan-Armtie
Hanse Spier m (1) Susan _____ (2) Santie
_____; identified by AAR as Daniel D. Rutan;
Note: because of the birthdate he may be a
son by the second wife; LDS; PCHSQ; AAR

Daniel Reton - (1787-1845) p/Daniel Reton-Rach-
el Berdan m Sarah (Sally) Moore (1788-1852)
in 1810 at the English Neighborhood (Ridge-
field) True Ref Ch; he was a resident of
NYC; Sarah was living with her sons in NYC
(18th Ward) in 1850; both are bur at Ft.
Lee, NJ; Note: AGBI says he died in 1865;
BCMR; FH; PCHSQ; 1850C; SUSESS

Daniel Rutan - (1792-1820) p/Joseph Rutan-
Hannah Baker of New Providence m Jane
Cauldwell (1790-1849) in 1811; she died in
Newark and he is bur at the Presbyt Chyd at
New Providence (church records); LDS; LITT;
FH

Daniel Rutan - (1756-1820) p/Johannes Rutan-
Aeltie P. Van Horn m Jannitje Brower (1762-
1858) in 1789; Jannitje (Jenny) was the
daughter of his father's second wife Antye
Nix Brower; Note: according to AAR this is
the correct relationship; PCHSP; EARDP; AAR

Daniel Rutan - (1756-1825) p/Johannes Rutan-
Aaltjie Van Horn m Rachel Berdan b 1757 at
Hackensack NJ; Note: conflict between this,
the preceding and next two entries; DARLDC;
PCHSP; EARDP

Daniel Rutan - (c 1754-1826) bur at DRC Belleville NJ born in Paramus m. Jannetje Brouwer b 1756 at Tappan NY; as a widow she
married (2) Johannes Rutan at the Ref Ch in
NYC; EARDP

Daniel Rutan - (1755-1828) RW soldier, Private
in the Essex Co. Militia; bur at DRC Belleville (Shaw:36) Note: despite some conflict-
ing data the last four entries appear to
apply to the same individual; BHS

Daniel Ruttan - a carpenter employed by the
British forces at Horn's Hook, New York City
August 1781; NYHS

Daniel Rutan - bc 1711 p/Daniel Rutan-Armtie
Hanse Spier of New Barbadoes; m Catherine
_____; Note: AAR identifies Daniel D. Rutan
b 1729 as the son of this couple; LDS; AAR

Daniel Rutan - m Catherine _____ bc 1710; she
was born at Ramapo, Bergen Co.; after his
death she m Conrad Lein (c1703-1763) from
Darmstadt, Hesse, Germany who died at Saddle
River; LDS; FH

Daniel D. Rutan - bc 1723 at Paramus, Bergen Co.
m Susan _____ in 1748; Note: this may be the
Daniel D. Rutan b 1729 identified by AAR as
the son of Daniel Rutan-Armtie Hanse Spier;
EARDP; LDS; AAR

Daniel Rutan - m Susan Kymer (Cymer) of Sussex
Co. Note: family bible records at GSNJ show
that Susan Kymer married Samuel Rutan and
thus this record should be rejected; PCHSQ;
GSNJ

Daniel Rutan - b 1769 p/Abraham Rutan-Aeltie
Van Tassel of Westchester Co. NY; MACK

Daniel Rheutan - m Jane _____ (1770-1858)
(from Storm Family Bible records); PCHS

Daniel Rutan - (1798-1891) p/Peter C. Rutan-
Charity Corselius of Sussex Co. m Mary A.
Mattox (1798-1884) in 1821; living in Darke
Co. OH in 1880; he died in Madison Twp,
Butler Co. OH; MEACH; CBRF; 1880C
in 1880; 1880C

Daniel Rutan - b 1799 p/John Rutan-Susanna Storm
at the Ref Ch in NYC; PCHSQ; LDS

Daniel Reton - resident of the 6th Ward, NYC
in 1810 (see John Reton, below); 1810C
Daniel Reton - W1812 soldier, 2nd Regt (Ward's)
N.Y. Militia (muster roll)
Daniel Reton - resident of the 8th Ward, NYC
in 1820; 1820C
David Abraham Rutan - (1688-1775) p/Abraham
Rutan-Marie Petilon, unm; he died in Morris-
town, NJ and is bur at the Presbyt Chyd
(church records)
David Rutan - b 1740 p/Paulus Rutan-Elizabeth
Foshay m (1) Caterina Bord b 1743 (2) Hille-
gond Webbers; he was b in Paramus and later
lived in Acquackanonk; EARDP; LDS; PCHSP;
MACK; PDRC
David Ruton - b 1769 p/Abraham Rutan-Aeltie Van
Tassel; resident of New Castle, Westchester
Co. NY 1810-1830; 1810C; 1820C; 1830C
David Ruton - resident of Westchester Co. 1820-
1830; not in 1840C; prob son of David Ruton;
1820C; 1830C
David J. Ruton - resident of Windsor Twp,
Cumberland Co. NJ (see Jonathan Ruton); 1790C
Derreck Rutan - **Derick** b 1777 p/Johannes Rutan-
Maria _____ of Schraalenburg; witnessed a
deed involving John Rutan of new Barbadoes
in 1798 (see Richard Rutan); DMD; SDRC; DAVIS
Dority Rattan - of Scotch Plains NJ died 1781;
SPBC
Dorothy Retan - (1726-1781) m Nathaniel Drake
(1727-1891) of Plainfield NJ; after her death
Nathaniel m Elizabeth Bishop (Drake Genealogy)
Dorothy is bur at Scotch Plains Baptist Chyd
(NJ Genealogies:5840; Nathaniel was b at
Plainfield NJ or in Sussex Co. (see prior
entry); NJHS; ARMS

Elinor Rutan - **Neeltje** (1785-1856) p/John
Rutan-Elizabeth Lake m. John C.F. Rummel/
Rommel (1764-1829) at Essex Co. in 1803;
he was born in Kassel-Hesse, Germany and d
in Jersey City; she d in So. Trenton, NY
(see her father's entry for an additional
source) PCHSP; NYGBS
Eliza Rutan - **Anna Eliza** (1799-1804) p/Abraham
Rutan-Hannah Shipman; she is bur at the
Presbyt Chyd, New Providence, NJ; LITT; LDS;
GSNJ
Elizabeth Rutan - bc 1721 p/Paulus Rutan-

Elizabeth Foshay m (Angle) William Hoff, Jr.
b 1714 of Hopewell, Dutchess Co. NY at
Tarrytown Ref Ch in 1739; Note: one record
has a first marriage to Matthew Vanderlinden
in 1733 and that Elizabeth was b in 1716;
(the first name: "Angle" from Sue Desort)
CMAC; EARDP

Elizabeth Rutan - b 1733 p/William Rutan-Maria
Demarest of Schraalenburg m Matthew Van
Orden (1723-1790) of Hackensack in 1750/2;
Loyalists, emigrated to Canada; some records
call him Martin Van Orden; MHILL; GSNJ; RUTT

Elizabeth Rutan - **Eliza Ann** b 1794 p/Joseph
Rutan-Hannah Baker m Barnabas (Barney) Earl
b 1802 of Westport MA; dismissed from the
Westfield NJ Presbyt Ch to Village Presbyt Ch
in NYC in 1827; moved to Kalamazoo MI and
were living in Cooper MI in 1860 ("The
Huguenot")("Daniel Perrin History") LDS; GSNJ;
BPL

Elizabeth Rutan - b 1767 p/Paul Rutan-Jannetje
Bord m (1) Johannes Toers (2) Thomas Van
Horn b 1749 at Acquackanonk Ref Ch in 1797/98;
he was b in Slooterdam NJ and they lived in
Wagarow NJ; Elizabeth was Thomas'third wife;
Note: this marriage was registered at the
Salem Ch of the Evangelical Assn of Lancaster,
PA; LDS; FH; ADRC; ROOTSW; NJW; PCHSP

Elizabeth Rutan - **Eliza** b 1787 p/John Rutan-Jane
Blauvelt; Note: this is from a DAR application and is incorrect (see next entry) NSDAR

Elizabeth Rutan - (1787-1842) p/John Rutan-
Elizabeth Lake m Rev. Thomas Roberts (1783-
1856) of Denbighshire, N. Wales in 1805 or
1806 at Schuyler's Mines, Barbadoes Neck;
Note: several sources show her mother as
Jane; FH; GSNJ; SIHS; NJBI

Elizabeth Rutan - (1773-1826) p/"Elder"Abraham
Rutan-Elizabeth _____ m Abraham Caldwell b
1768 in 1791; Note: LITT has her born in
1788; NJGS; LITT

Elizabeth Rutan - (1758-1839) of Essex Co. m
Andrew Poe at Green Twp, Beaver Co. PA or
Williamsport (now Mononghela) PA (Earl
Bake)(see PA listing) LDS; CRC

Elizabeth Rutan - (1758-1780) b in Essex Co. NJ;
(see prior entry); according to MEACH she
may be the daughter of John Rutan-Sarah
Manning; LDS; MEACH

Esther Rutan - b 1757 p/Abraham Rutan-Aeltie
Van Tassel of Tarrytown NY; she was bpt at
the First Ref Ch of Tarrytown; LDS; GSNJ

Eva Rutan - **Evaatje** b 1734 p/Paulus Rutan-
Elizabeth Foshay of Hackensack m Peter
Helmich (Helmerich Van Houten) (1709-1771)
of Slooterdam, Bergen Co. about 1745; they
moved to Wawayanda, Sussex Co. in 1771;
Note: LDS has the wedding in 1753; FH; LDS;
PCHSP; NSDAR

Geesje Rutan - **Casia/Keziah** b 1775 p/Barent
Rutan-Annantje Van Riper of Acquackanonk m
Rem Onderdonk (1763-1833); Rem born in New
West Hempstead, Rockland Co. and died in
Saddle River NJ; he was first married to
Helena Blauvelt (1771-c1792) of Orange Co.
NY (Sandy Rankin) DARLDC; ECMR; MEACH; ECMR

Hannah Retan - m Alexander Pelton at Madison
Ave. Ref Ch, NYC in 1817; LDS

Hannah Ruttan - (c1765-1829) she died in Warren
OH; NYEP

Hannah Rutan - (1761-1797) p/"Elder" Abraham
Rutan m John J. Caldwell (1755-1801) in
1783; their families moved to OH although
this couple may have stayed in Morris Co. and
died there (NSDAR appl #76484 Olive Colwell
Blose) Hannah was born in Elizabethtown and
died at New Providence (Patricia Elliot
Meyer) NJW; LITT; LDS

Hannah Rutan - b 1840 m Phineas J. Inslee b
1734 at Woodbridge NJ ("Long Island Ancestry
of William Jones") PNJHS; ROOTSW

Harmon Rutan - (1768-1832) p/John Rutan-Altje
Van Horn m Chloe Lobdell (1777-1843) of
Oyster Bay, Nassau Co. NY in 1797; he was
born at Ft. Lee NJ and died in NYC; both are
bur at River Road Burying Ground, Edgewater
NJ; PCHSQ; MACK; DRCNYC; BCGI

Harmanus Rutan - a porter in NYC mentioned in
"The History of the NYC Fire Department"
as a foreman in 1799

Harriet Ruton - (1797/99-1878) p/William Ruton-
Rachel Brower of Tarrytown, Westchester Co. NY;
Note: another record has her born in 1801;
GSNJ; MACK

Henry Retan - d 1799 he was a porter living at
36 Church St, NYC died of yellow fever (NYGBR
v131 p122-Apr 2000)

Henry Rattan - resident of NYC 1800; 1800C
Henry Seguine Rutan - (1790-1833) p/Henry Rutan
of Belleville, Essex Co. NJ; m Rachel Kingsland (1794-1875) in 1813; moved to Staten
Island NY; bur at Woodrow M.E. Ch; Note:
according to Vicki Furth Rachel was born in
1795; ECMR; BAYL; KFH; LDS; SIHS

Isaac Brower Ruton - (1790-1852) p/William
Ruton-Rachel Brower m Margaret Baker (1791-
1860 at St. John's Methodist Church in NYC
in 1809; living in Yonkers, Westchester Co.
in 1820; known as **"Captain"** he was a Hudson
River shipmaster of the schooner "Emmeline"
(Scharf); kept the "Indian Queen Inn" in
Yonkers c1823; (Allenson:145); living in NYC
1830-40 as a grocer in partnership with his
brother Alexander B. Ruton; Note: per Maher
he died in 1857: MACK; CDIR; MAHER; MYCMM;
1820C; 1830C; 1840C; NCPL
Isaac Rutan - W1812 soldier, Pvt.43rd Infantry
Regt of N.Y. (Volker)

Jacob Rutan - b 1714 p/Paulus Rutan-Engletje
Davidse; he was bpt at the First Ref Ch of
Tarrytown: he was alive in 1753; MACK
Jacob Rutan - b 1784 m Mary Sayre bc 1786 of
Somerset Co. NJ Co. NJ; moved to Washington
Co. PA; Note: GSNJ records have a Jacob Rutan
to Elinor Sayres in Greene Co. PA; MEACH;
GSNJ
Jacob William Rutan - (1753-1811/15) p/William
Rutan-Maria Demarest of Schraalenburg, Bergen
Co. m Margaret Haring; EARDP; SDRC; LDS;
RUTT; PPDLN
Jacob Rutan - b 1766 p/Daniel Rutan-Margaret
Stegg; he was bpt at Acquackanonck Ref Ch;
Note: another record has him b 1767; ADRC
James Rutan - W1812 soldier, Swartswood's Regt,
N.Y. Volunteers (Muster Roll)
James Rutan - m Mary Predmore (1793-1874) of
Newton, Sussex Co.; LDS
James Rutan - (1790-1877) p/Daniel Rutan-Sarah
_____ of Sussex Co. NJ; m Martha _____;
MEACH
James Rutan - m Anna Shoemaker in Chemung Co.
NY c1812; ROOTSW
James Rutan - b 1799 m Mary _____ b 1796, both
born in NJ; living in Garnavillo Twp, Clay-

ton Co. IA in 1850; 1850C

Jane Rutan - p/Paul Rutan-Metje Spier m Barney
Spier (1777-1844) at Acquackanonk in 1807;
Barney was a W1812 soldier; they lived in
Belleville, Essex Co. NJ; Note: one record
has her the daughter of Paul Rutan-Jannetje
Bord (they were her grandparents); NJW; ECMR

Jannetje Rutan - b 1772 p/Daniel Rutan-Catherine Bord; she was bpt at Acquackanonk Ref
CH; ADRC

Jannetye Rutan - b 1778 p/Paulus Rutan-Metje
Spier of Totowa, Bergen (now Passaic) Co.
NJ; LDS

John Rutan - (1792-   ) p/Paul Rutan-Metje
Spier m Catherine Coon b 1796 at the First
Presbyterian Church of Paterson NJ in
1813; referred to as Major John Rutan in
PCHSP; Note: John was dead prior to 1852
because Catherine had married Charles
Hartley before that date, consequently the
report that he had been killed at the
Battle of Bull Run is incorrect; NJHS;
PCHSP

John Reton - m Susanna Helling; she was first
married to Abraham Quackenbosch; their
child Jacomyntie was born in Tappan in 1735;
PCHSB

John A. Rutan - (1752/3/60-1828) m Elizabeth
Lake b 1750/60 at Totowa; he was in the
weaving business per his will; Elizabeth was
from Marlboro NJ; he died in Essex Co.; Note:
his parents in the Huguenot Society of NJ
appl of Lester R. Dunham (NYGBS); PCHSQ;
MACK; SRDRC

John Retan - (1787-1846) m Margaret Smith
(1794-1864) of NJ; he died in Waterford MI;
(Barbara Bombassei)

John Retan - resident of Parma, Monroe Co. NY
in 1830; 1830C

John Retan - resident of Prattsburg, Steuben
Co. NY in 1840; 1840C

John Rutan - b 1772 p/Abraham J. Rutan-Santie
Banta m Rachel Vanderbeek b 1771; living
in Manchester Twp, Passaic Co. in 1850;
AAR; PCHSP; 1850C

John Rutan, Sr. - (1726-1761) p/Peter A. Rutan-
Geertruy Vanderhoef m Sarah Manning (c1726-
1760) c1743; he owned property in Hampshire
Co. VA (dates from Kim Vierra); NJW; FH; RER

John Rutan - b 1775 p/Daniel Rutan-Rachel
Berdan m (1) Susanna Storm(s) at the New
Amsterdam Ref Ch in 1797 (2) Martha
(Maria) Frost; NJGS; PCHSQ; GENEX; GSNJ

John Reton - W1812 soldier, 2nd Regt (Ward's)
N.Y. Militia; served with Daniel Reton
(W1812 Muster Rolls)

John Rutan - (1749/51/60-1803) p/Johannes
Rutan-Aaltje Van Horn of Paramus; m Jane
Blauvelt (1767-1845) at the Ponds (Oakland)
NJ; he was a RW soldier; Jane from Tappan,
Rockland Co. NY who lived in NYC as a widow;
SRDC; EARDP; NGS; DARP; ARWPF; MACK; LDS

Johannes Rutan - (1725-1787) p/Daniel Rutan-
Antje Hanse Spier of Rosendael m (1) Aaltje
(Prevost) Van Horn bc 1728 of Wesel in 1746;
at the Acquackanonk Ref Ch; (2) Antje Nix
Brower b 1758 in 1781; Note: one record says
he was alive in 1792; MEACH; ARWPF; NGS;
DMD; PCHSP; MACK; LDS; SDRC

Johannis Rutan - b 1786/87 p/John Rutan-Jane
Blauvelt; SDRC; ARWPF

John Rutan - RW soldier, Pvt. Bergen Co. Militia (Capt. Dey's Co.; Capt. Samuel
Demarest's Co.) ROOTSW

John A. Rutan - property-owner of Franklin Twp;
he sold property in Saddle River Precinct,
Bergen Co. in 1800; DAVIS;

John D. Rutan - on 1779 Tax List for Bergen Co.
NJ; GMNJ

John D. Rutan - b 1792 p/Daniel Rutan-Jannitje
Brower m Sally Ann Webb; stone mason; W1812
soldier of Bergen Co., Pvt, 42nd N.Y. Infantry; moved to Cincinnati in 1818; held a
land warrant for property in IL (see IL and
IA entries) AAR; USARCH; GSNJ; PCHSP; SDRC

Johannis A. Rutan - b 1752 p/Abraham Rutan-
Sarah Van Gelder of Paramus m Elizabeth
_____; MACK; SDRC; PCHSQ

John Ruttan - carpenter employed by the British
forces at Horn's Hook, NYC, Aug 1781; NYHS

John Rutan - b 1792 a blacksmith living in
Rockaway Twp, Morris Co. NJ in 1850; 1850C

Johannes Ruton - b 1755 p/Abraham Rutan-Aeltie
Van Tassel of Tarrytown; he was bpt at the
First Ref Ch, Tarrytown; GSNJ; DARLDC; LDS

Johannes Rutan - b 1773/74 p/David Rutan-Catar-
ina Bord; PCHSQ; DARLDC

John Rutan - W1812 soldier, 3rd Regt (Freling-

huysen's) N.J. Militia (mustered as Ruton)
(muster roll)

John I. Rutan - member of the N.J. State Militia in 1793 (Norton)

John Rutan, Jr. - (1744-1833) p/John Rutan-Sarah Manning m Catherine _____ and may have had a second wife, Hannah Frazer of NJ; he was a scout on the frontier, settled in Westmoreland Co. PA, served in the PA Militia during the RW; he died and is bur at Trumbull Co. OH (see PA and OH entries) FH; RER; SXHS

Johannes Rutan - m Jannetje Brower at the Ref Ch in NYC; she was formerly wed to Daniel Rutan (1754-1826); Note: CMAC identifies her as Jacomyntje Brower and there is an LDS record of a marriage to Jakkomeintje Brouwer at Schraalenburg in 1782; EARDP; CMAC; LDS

John Rutan - m Jacomyntje Quackenbush b 1735; she was also wed to Isaac Brower; QFH

John Reton - resident of the 5th Ward, NYC in 1820; 1820C

John Reton - resident of the 6th Ward, NYC in 1820; 1820C

Jonathan Ruton - resident of Windsor Twp, Middlesex Co. NJ in 1790 (see David J. Ruton, above) 1790C

Joseph Rutan - (1769-1809) p/"Elder"Abraham Rutan of Morris Co. NJ; m (1) Hannah Baker (1770/1-1804) in 1791 (2) Rachel Hole in 1805; one record refers to her as Rachel Stanbury Hole; after Joseph's death she wed Samuel Frazee; Joseph and Hannah are bur at the Presbyt Chyd, New Providence NJ where they had been married (church records); JS

Joseph Retan - member of the Morris Co. Militia in 1783; he was from Morris Twp and served with Peter Retan; LDS

Joseph Ruttan - bc 1735 in Connecticut ("Rolls of Connecticut Men in the French & Indian Wars", Bates)

Katherine Rutan - b 1795 p/Daniel Rutan-Rachel Berdan m William Joline; EARDP; ROOTSW

Lea Rutan - bc 1730 m Jan W. Vanvoorhees b 1730 at Bergen Co. c1752 (Judy Ullman) LDS

Lea Maria Rutan - (1761-1850) p/John Rutan-Aaltje Van Horn m Samuel Thomas Moore b 1754; she d

at Ft. Lee, Bergen Co. NJ; Note: one record
claims that Samuel T. Moore m Lea Rutan the
daughter of William Rutan-Maritje Demarest
Leeu Reton - (see Magdalena Reton, below)
Lena Rutan - p/Daniel Rutan-Antje Hanse Spier m
Hannes Meyer b 1714 of Hackensack in 1745;
Note: EARDP gives her birth year as 1744 which
incorrect; she was b in Second River and he at
Paramus; at the time of her marriage she was
living at Rosendael; HDRC; EARDP
Magdelena Reton - (1778-1847) m Thomas Van Orden
(1776-1847) she was born in Hackensack and he
in NYC; both died in Hackensack and are bur
at the New York Lutheran Cem in No. Bergen;
PCHSQ; ROOTSW
Magdelena Rutan - (c1782-1861) m John Huyler
(1810-1884) both bur at the New York Cem,
Hackensack; (see prior entry) BCMR
Margaret Rutan - b 1793 p/Cornelius Rutan-Hester
Valleau m (1) Joshua Slidell at Christ Ch, NYC
in 1812 (Conover Genealogy) (Valleau Webpage);
(2) Cornelius Meyers; ROOTSW; FH; WENP
Margaret Ann Rutan - (1747-1835) m (1) John
Penny (1740-1826) of Ireland; he was a RW
soldier who lived in Mansfield MA (2) Samuel
Power d in 1840 of VA; all three died in PA
(see PA listing); CVHM; WCCL; LDS
Margrietje Rutan - b 1772 p/Daniel Rutan-Marg-
aret Stegg; she was bpt at Acquackanonk Ref
Ch (church records); EARDP
Maria Rutan - b 1701 p/Abraham Rutan-Marie Petilon m Thomas Teunisse (S)pier (1705-1796)
at Hackensack Ref Ch in 1721 (Lorine M.
Schulze) Note: his death year from the Huguenot Society of NJ appl of Helen G.H. Wright
(1974); according to Jane V. Bauch they wed
in 1729; LDS; FH; NYGBS; HDRC
Maria Rutan - **Maritje** b 1720 p/Paulus Rutan-
Elizabeth Foshay of Phillipsburg (Tarrytown)
m Johannes Mangel from Germany in 1737;
their children bpt at Tappan Ref Ch, Rockland Co. in 1738 and 1740 (Cole); Note:
according to the Huguenot Society of NJ appl
of Roderick M. Horne (1962) Johannes was
later known as John Roll; he died in 1782
HDRC; PPDLN; NYGBR; NCPL
Maria Rutan - b 1736 p/William Rutan-Marytjia
Demarest m Hermanus Gardiner b 1727 at Collegiate Ref Ch in NYC in 1756; he was from

Tarrytown; VWR; FH; RUTT; PCHSQ; LDS; ROOTSW

Maria Ratan - b 1774 p/John Ratan-Maria _____ of
Belleville; SRDRC; LDS

Maria Rutan - b 1797 p/Cornelius Rutan-Hester
Valleau; Maria was bpt at Broadway/71st
Christ Episcopal Ch in NYC; LDS; PCHSP

Maritje Rutan - b 1749/51 p/Daniel Rutan-Susan
_____; she was bpt at Paramus Ref Ch in 1751;
LDS; EARDP; PCHSQ; AAR

Martha Rutan - (c1767-1816) p/"Elder"Abraham
Rutan m Moses Camp (1765-1845) (DeCamp, Van
Campen, LeCompte) at New Providence in 1787;
they moved to Washington Co. PA; LITT; LDS

Mary Rutan - m John Van Gelder in 1802 (see
Nancy Rutan, below) DFH

Mary Rutan - bvc 1779 p/Daniel Rutan-Sarah _____
of Sussex Co. m Michael Mattox in 1797 and
they moved to Madison Twp, Butler Co. OH in
1810; JS; CoMR

Mary Rutan - m Elisha Frazee b 1743 of Essex Co.
NJ at Turkey (New Providence) Ref Ch, Morris
(now Union) Co.; Elisha prob died in Allegany
Co. MD before 1800 (Kathleen Beaver) Mary was
probably the daughter of John Rutan-Sarah
Manning; PCTU

Mary Rutan - p/John Rutan-Sarah Manning (from
his will probated in 1762)

Mary Rutan - (1764-1838) p/"Elder"Abraham Rutan-
Elizabeth _____ m Matthias Roll (1762-1831)
of Elizabethtown at New Providence in 1785;
they moved to Washington Co. PA and later to
OH; they died in Butler or Hamilton Co. OH
Note: his dates from the NSDAR appl #111915
of Georgia Cram Nerborvig; ROOTSW says she
died at McGonigles, Hamilton Co. OH; NJW;
LDS; LITT; PCTU; MAR; ROOTSW

Mary Reton - m David Emmy at the First Presbyt
Ch in NYC in 1817 (see Polly Rutan, below)
LDS

Mary Retan - m David Concklin at the Madison Ave
Ref Church, NYC in 1816; LDS

Mary Ruton - **Polly** (1792/6-1840) p/William
Ruton-Rachel Brower of Tarrytown NY; m James
Requa (1789/90-1870) at the John St. Meth.
Ch in NYC in 1811; they lived in Brooklyn;
upon Mary's death he wed her sister Letitia
(Seabring Collections) Mary is bur at the
Bedford St. M.E. Chyd in NYC; he died at
Chatfield MI; LDS; NYCMM; GSNJ; WHIT; MACK

Mary Rutan - p/Henry Rutan-Frances Toers of
Belleville, Essex Co.; MCRC

Mary Rutan - (1772-1859) p/Peter Rutan-Jannetje
Ackerman of Ramapo, Bergen Co.; she was bpt
at the Evangelical Lutheran Ch; m Thomas E.
Mathews (1766-1819); they were Loyalists and
she died at Brougham, Renfrew, Ontario (Mark
Ruttan); RUTT; LDS; VWR

Mary Rutan - (1795-1829) she died in NYC; NYEP;
LISTAR

Melvina Reton - m James Howe in NY in 1811;
Note: another record calls her Alvina Retan;

Nancy Rutan - (1784-1855) poss daughter of Bar-
ent Rutan-Annantje Van Riper; m John Van
Gelder (1777-1864) at Sussex Co. in 1802 per
Van Gilder family bible; JS; NJGS; FH; CCNEW

Nathaniel Ruton - resident of Greenwich Twp,
Cumberland Co. NJ in 1810; 1810C

Neelyte Ratan - (see Elinor Rutan)

Paulus Rutan - b 1685/6 p/Abraham Rutan-Marie
Petilon of New Paltz NY m (1) Engletje
(Angelique) Davidse b in Canada d in 1716
in 1708 (2) Elizabeth Foshier (Foshay) b 1686
both marriages in Tarrytown NY; Paulus was
living in Ossining, Westchester Co in 1707
and in Hackensack, Bergen Co. NJ in 1723;
CMAC; VWR; LDS; NYGBR

Paulus Rutan - (1744-1795) p/William Rutan-
Maria Demarest m Jannetje Bord of Ringwood
d 1814 in 1762; they lived in Harrington; as
a widow Jannetje wed Nicholas Van Blarcom at
Acquackanonk in 1795; Note: GSBC record says
that Paul died in 1812 and is bur at Schraal-
enburg; another record has Paulus m to Jennie
Mabie sister to John Mabie the husband of
Leah, the sister of Paulus; NJW; SDRC; EARDP;
POCGS; ADRC

Paul Rutan - resident of Brooklyn NY in 1826;
CDIR

Permilia Rutan - (1798-1836) p/Abraham D. Rutan-
-Lydia Vanderbeek m Garrabrant Van Houten at
Paramus Ref Ch in 1820; one record has the
wedding at Saddle River Landing; as a widower
he married Esther Mills; PDRC; LDS; BCMR

Peter Ratten - resident of Albany NY; 1790C

Peter Rutan - RW soldier 2nd Lieut, Canada Regiment (American) in 1776; HAMER

16

Peter C. Rutan - (c1770-1848) p/Daniel Rutan-
Sarah _____ m Charity Corselius b 1771 at
at Stillwater Ref Ch in Sussex Co. in 1797;
they moved to OH about 1818; in 1860 Charity
was living in Lawrence Twp, Tippecanoe Co. IN;
SCMR; DARLDC; JS; EG; BOGGS, MEACH; 1860C
Peter Ruttan - (1742-1822) p/William Rutan-Maria
Demarest of Schraalenburg; served in Staten
Island and in the Southern Campaign as a
Captain in the N.J. Volunteers (Loyalist)
during the RW and he moved to Ontario about
1783; m Jantjie Ackerman (1751-1810/2) of
Paramus; he is bur at Hay Bay Cem; Note: one
record has his death year as 1829; SDRC; LDS;
VWR; RUTT; MEACH; LLC
Peter Rutan - (c1749-1801) p/Peter Rutan-Sarah
_____ m Frances Usher (1758-1800) of Bristol
RI in 1783; RW soldier served in Lieut. Living-
ston's Regiment (Index of Official Register:
92) and in the 1st Canadian Regt; served
under General Gates at Saratoga and in Rhode
Island; living in Albany in 1790 and Bristol
RI in 1800; they are bur at Juniper Hill Cem,
Bristol (cem records); JS; NSDAR; 1790C;
1800C; USARCH; ROOTSW
Peter Retan - m Clannsa (Clarissa?) _____ of NJ
they are the parents of John R. Retan who d
in Kent Co. MI; MDI
Peter Rattan - RW soldier, prisoner of the Brit-
ish aboard HMS Jersey in NYC (Society of Old
Brooklynites)
Peter Abraham Rutan - (1691-1774) p/Abraham
Rutan-Marie Petilon m (1) Geertruy Vander-
hoef b 1691 from Albany in 1713; (2) Eliza-
beth Sickles (1691-1740) about 1734; he moved
moved to New Providence about 1736 and to
Long Hill, Morris Co. in 1738; he died in New
Providence or Morristown (NJHS Genealogy:4762)
FH; NJW; LITT; NJHS; PCTU; MEACH; RUTT
Peter Rutan, Jr - (c1720-1754) p/Peter Abraham
Rutan-Geertruy Vanderhoef m Sarah Thompson
of Long Hill; Sarah moved from Morris Co. to
Frankford Twp, Sussex Co. by 1774; Peter was
Sarah's second husband; she m (1) James Enos
(3) Samuel Van Sickle; EG; NJW; FH; CBRF;
MEACH
Peter Rutan - resident of Southeast Twp, Dutch-
ess Co. NY in 1790; 1790C
Peter Rutan - living in Amenia, Dutchess Co NY

in 1810 ("The Dutchess" 1:18)
Peter Retan - bc 1775 m Polly Hatt (1793-1871)
living in Ovid Twp, Seneca Co. NY in 1850;
they moved to Lenawee Co. MI; 1850C; LHRL
Peter Rutan - RW soldier from NY, he served in
Third Regt of the Line (muster toll)
Peter Reton - RW soldier from NY, he served in
the Levies (Pawling) (muster roll)

Rachel Rutan - b 1747 p/William Rutan-Marytjia
Demarest of Schraalenburg or Waldwick; m
(1) William Dobs (c1740-1784) their children
were bpt at Tappan Ref Ch, Rockland Co. NY
(Cole) (2) Richard Mount (c1760-1828) who
was born in VA; Note: LDS has him bc 1745;
ROOTSW; RUTT; LDS; CoMR; SDRC
Rachel Rutan - (1790-1876) p/Daniel Rutan-Rachel
Berdan m William Rotherie; she is bur at the
Reton Historic Cem, Ft. Lee, Bergen Co. (from
cemetery records)
Rachel Rutan - bc 1791 in NJ; resident of Staten
Island, NYC in 1850; Note: this is probably
Rachel Kingsland widow of Henry Seguine Rutan
1850C
Rachel Rutan - (1797-1852) bur at the Presbyt
Chyd, Westfield, Union Co. NJ; (cemetery
records) Note: this is probably **Lockey Meeker**
the wife of Samuel Rutan; NEHGS
Rebecca Sarah Rutan - (1793-1853) p/Barnet Rutan-
Annantje Van Rype m William Drew (1791-1871)
at the Baptist Ch of Wantage, Sussex Co.;
they lived in Amity, Orange Co. NY and are bur
at the Longwell Cem, Vernon Twp, Sussex Co.;
CCNEW; SCMR; FH
Richard Rutan - b 1749; resident of Weehawken,
Bergen Twp, Hudson Co. NJ; 1830C
Richard Rutan - **Rattan** W1812 soldier, Ranger,
U.S. Volunteers (muster roll)
Richard Rutan - p/John Rutan-Elizabeth Lake m
Catherine Vandewater (c1787-1832) in 1803 at
Essex Co. NJ; Note: some info from the will
of his father and the marriage is registered
at the Salem Ch, Lancaster PA; she is bur at
Bayonne, Hudson Co.; SDRC; ECMR; LDS
Robert Rutan - (c1787-1852) PCHSQ
Robert Rutan - (1794-1858) p/Abraham Rutan-Reb-
ecca_____ of Sussex Co.; Robert died in Pat-
erson; PCHSQ
Robert Rutan - (c1796-1858) buried at Longwell

Cem, Vernon Twp, Sussex Co.; LVLC

Robert Rutan - p/Abraham D. Rutan-Rebecca _____
m Mary Courter in 1810; farmer, New Milford,
Passaic Co. NJ; both bur at Longwell Cem,
Twp, Sussex Co.;Note: The last three entries
pertain to the same person. Robert was the
son of Abraham but it is improbable that his
father was the Abraham D. who m Lydia Vanderbeek; according to AAR Robert was the son of
Abraham Rutan (1754-1845) the son of John
Rutan; 1850C; PCHSP; AAR

Roseannah Rutan - (1765-1823) p/"Elder" Abraham Rutan-Elizabeth _____ m Thomas Parrot
(1767-1840) in 1786; he m (2) Abigail Meeker
(1769-1846) in 1824; they lived at Long Hill,
Morris Co. and all are bur at the Methodist
Chyd, New Providence NJ; LITT; JS; PCTU

Saartje Retan - b 1770 p/Daniel Retan-Margaret
Stegg; she was bpt at Acquackanonk Ref Ch
(church records)

Samuel Rutan, Sr. - (1710-1777) p/Abraham Rutan-
Marie Petilon m Maria Stoughtenburg (1712-
1779) in 1733; he was a RW soldier, Essex Co.
Militia; both died in Belleville; Note: some
supplementary info from Clinton Rutan's memb-
ership appl to the Huguenot Society of NJ
(1954) at the NYGBS; GSNJ; NJW; FH; CDAR; FH;
MEACH

Samuel Rutan, Jr. - (1752-1814) p/Samuel Rutan-
Maria Stoughtenburg m Maria Bruyn (Mary
Brown) (1754-1834) in 1775; Samuel a RW
soldier in the Essex Co. Militia; he was born
in Poversham, Essex Co. and she in neighbor-
ing Second River; both died in Belleville;
CDAR; NJGS; FH

Samuel Rutan - (1799-1827) p/Joseph Rutan-Hannah
Baker m Rachel (Lockey) Meeker (1803-1858) of
Scotch Plains, Union Co, NJ in 1827; he died
at Long Hill, Morris Co. and is bur at the
Presbyt Chyd, New Providence; she is bur in
Westfield NJ (some information from her will
and from the Windemuth Family webpage); LITT;
LDS; NJHS

Samuel Rutan - bc 1752 p/John Rutan-Aeltie Van
Horn m Margaret (Gretei) Banta b 1748 of
Spring Valley; as a widow Margaret later wed
Isaac Stegg (1747-1843) about 1778; MACK; FH;

19

EARDP
Samuel H. Rutan - (1776-1864) p/Henry Rutan-Ann-
atie Joralemon m (1) Sarah Joralemon (1771-
1806) in 1798 at Second River (2) Hannah Winne
in 1808; Note: both weddings registered at the
Salem Ch, Lancaster PA; ECMR
Samuel S. Rutan - (1782/8-1834) p/Samuel Rutan-
Mary Brown m Hannah Garrabrant (1788-1855);
Samuel known as **"Black Sam"** was born and died
in Springgarden and she died in Newark; they
are both bur in Springgarden; CDAR; LDS; FER
Sarah Rutan - (1779-1818) p/Daniel Rutan-Sarah
_____ of Sussex Co. m Jacob Struble (1776-
1857) in 1799 at the Old Clove Ch, Wantage Twp
Sussex Co.; he was born at German Valley,
Morris Co. and died at Sterling Town, Cayuga
Co. NY; she died at Litchfield, Bradford Co.
PA (Mark Grassman) LDS; ROOTSW; MCRC; EG
Sarah Rutan - **Sally** b 1756 p/"Elder"Abraham Rutan
m Simeon Simpson, a RW soldier, 1st Penna Regt
Continental Line; they moved to Washington Co.
PA; ROOTSW; JS; LITT; PCTU
Susanna Rutan - b 1705 p/Abraham Rutan-Marie
Petilon m Johannes Teunisse (S)pier (1688-
1763) in 1724; he was a resident of Hanover
Twp, Morris Co.; she was alive in 1760 when
his will was prepared; he died in Morris Co.
(some data from Jane V. Bauch and Bob White)
FH; LDS
Susanna Rutan - b 1736 p/Abraham Rutan-Sarah
De Forest m (1) Julian Demarest b 1739 of
Schraalenburg in 1761 (2) Abraham Vanderbeek
at Schraalenburg; she was living in Paramus
at the time of her first marriage; Note:
Julian sometimes known as Jillian or Gillian
and one record has Susanna's mother as Sarah
Van Gelder (they may be the same person); FH;
HDRC; CRC; PCHSQ; VHFH; MACK
Susannah Rutan - (1796/1800-1889) m Stephen Roy
b 1796; they lived in Papakating and Wantage
Twps, Sussex Co.; LDS; STICK

Thomas Rutan - **Rattan** W1812 soldier, Ranger,
U.S. Volunteers (muster roll)
Thomas Rutan, Sr. - (c1763-1822) p/John Rutan-
Aaltje Van Horn m Christina (Tyne) Berdan at
Schraalenburg; EARDP; DRCNYC

Vaartje Rutan - b 1767 p/Jacobus Rutan-Willemtie

Bogert; she was born in Paramus; Note: this
may be Saartje Rutan

William Rutan - (1759-1843) p/William Rutan-
Maria Demarest m Margaret Steel (1764-1844)
of Ireland at the Ref Ch in NYC in 1782; he
was a Loyalist who went to Ontario after the
American Revolution; they are both bur at the
Anglican Cem, Adolphustown, Ontario; SDRC;
LLC; LDS; PPDLN

William Ruton - b 1797 p/William Ruton-Rachel
Brower of Tarrytown m (1) Sepronah Winston
(1803-1848/54) at Westerlo NY ("Descendants of
Thomas Stanton of Connecticut") he was living
in Northeast Town, Dutchess Co. NY 1843-1850
(2) Charlotte Dewey (1809-1886) in 1855;
Charlotte was bur at Grosvenors Corners
Cem, Schoharie Co. (Roberts Bible-NSDAR)
ARWPF; PCHSP; 1810C; 1850C

William Ruton - (1760-1828) p/Abraham Rutan-
Aaltje Van Tassel of Tarrytown m (1) Rachel
Cox (Cocks) (c1763-1783) in 1782 (2) Rachel
Brower b 1770 at Mt. Pleasant, Westchester
Co. NY in 1789; RW soldier, Third Regt, West-
chester Militia captured by the British and
imprisoned in NYC; Rachel was living in Coble-
skill, Schoharie Co. NY in 1843; he is bur at
the Hannacroix Cem near Dormanville, Westerlo
Town, Albany Co. NY (cemetery records); Note:
GSNJ identifies the second wife as ‾‾‾‾‾‾
Batchelor which is incorrect; also ‾A‾R‾W‾P‾F‾ says
the first wife was Rachel Van Wart; WHIT;
DARLDC; SLHOLOW; DRCNYC; MACK; PCHSP; ARWPF

William Retan - p/John Retan-Margaret Smith m
Tryphena Mead of MI; LDS

William Retan - resident of Harrington Twp,
Bergen Co. in 1780 (from local census records)

William Reton - resident of the Third Ward in NYC
in 1840; 1840C

RUTANS IN THE NORTHEAST BORN AFTER 1799

Abby A. Rutan - bc 1848 p/Richard Rutan-Mary A.
Fort of Fallsburgh, Sullivan Co. NY; she is
not in the 1860C; 1850C; 1855C

Abel Ruton - resident of Springfield Twp,
Burlington Co. NJ; 1850C

Abigail Rutan - b 1815 p/Samuel Rutan-Susanna
Cymer of Sussex Co. m David Hazen at Jeffer-
son Twp, Lackawanna Co. PA in 1833; Note:
LDS has her born in 1816; LDS; GSNJ; MEACH;
NJG

Abner D. Rutan - (1892-1961) p/Albert Rutan-
Catherine _____ m Florence Eccles (1890-1977)
he was a jewelry salesman living in Nutley,
Essex Co. NJ; he is bur at Vincent Memorial
Cem Nutley; NYTO; CDIR; PCHSQ; SSA

Abraham Reton resident of Boston MA in 1825;
CDIR

Abraham Rutan - resident of Newtown, Queens Co.
NY in 1840; 1840C

Abraham Rutan - (1840-1918) p/Henry Abraham
Rutan-Harriet Burnett of Newark NJ and Kings
Co. NY m Sarah Maria Stewart b 1841; brick
mason and builder in Brooklyn in 1870; living
in Farmingdale, Nassau Co. NY in 1908 per his
brother Thomas' CW pension file; Sarah a
widow in the 1920C; 1850C; 1870C; CDIR;
1900C; 1920C; USARCH

Abraham Rutan - b 1817 p/Abraham Rutan-Leah
_____ (probably Lydia)(see next entry) PDRC

Abraham Rutan - (1817/18-1847) p/Abraham
Rutan-Lydia Vanderbeek; PCHSP; PDRC

Abraham Rutan - b 1839 p/Abraham G. Rutan-Harriet Hicks of Brimfield MA (from Brimfield
VRs)

Abraham Rutan - (1844-1900) p/Albert Rutan m
Mary C. Bradford (1852-1911) both bur at
Valleau Cem, Bergen Co. NJ; AFH

Abraham Rutan - bc 1863 living with his mother
Ellen J. Rutan in Kearny, Hudson Co. NJ;
1880C

Abraham Rutan - (1864-1915) bur at Arlington Cem
Kearny NJ (cem records); this is probably the
son of Samuel Rutan and his second wife Ellen
of Belleville (see prior entry)

Abraham Rutan - m Catherine Smith; living in
Kearny in 1898 (from his son James M. Rutan's
death certificate) (see prior entry)

Abraham Rutan - p/Samuel Rutan-Jane Meyers of
   Belleville; Note: Jane was Samuel's first
   wife) (see prior entry) PCHSQ
Abraham Rutan - (1898-1899) bur at Arlington Cem
   Kearny NJ (cemetery records)
Abram Rheutan - p/John W. Rheutan-Ann Welch;
   GSNJ
Abraham Rheutan - resident of the 16th Ward, NYC
   in 1840; 1840C
Abraham A. Rutan - (1806-1844) p/Abraham J.
   Rutan-Wyntje Hopper; bpt at Collegiate Ref Ch
   in NYC; bur at M.E. Ch Cem, Saddle River,
   Bergen Co. (Little Zion) Cem; ZAB; JS; PCHSQ
Abraham A. Rutan - m Jane _____; she was a widow
   in NYC 1869-1885; CDIR
Abram A. Retan - m Jane Haney 29 Dec 1836 at the
   Greene St. Methodist Ch NYC (see prior entry)
   NYCMM
Abraham A. Rheutan - (1837-1913) p/Abraham
   Rheutan- Mary Storms m Mary Hoyt Young of NYC
   in 1861; he was a superintendent in Worcester
   MA in 1891; he died there: GSNJ; CDIR; PCHSQ;
   AAR
Abraham Courter Rutan - (1823-1911) p/Abram
   Rutan-Ann Courter m (1) Catherine Anne Rhodes
   (1823-1853) in 1847 at Glenwood, Sussex Co.
   (2) Ellen C. Drew (1833-1904) in 1865; he was
   a freeholder and farmer (Wintermute Family
   History) JS; LDS; FH; MEACH
 Abram D. Rutan - (1862-1863) p/Abraham C.
   Rutan-Ellen C. Drew of Vernon Twp; he is bur
   at Warwick Cem, Orange Co. NY (cemetery
   records)
 Abraham George Rutan - (c1814-1873) of Paterson
   NJ m (1) Harriet E. Hinman (1815-1837) of
   Willmington CT in 1834; she is bur at Brook-
   line CT (Brimfield MA VRs) (2) Harriet Hicks
   (1817-1881) at Ludlow MA in 1838; lived in
   Brimfield MA per son Rynier's CW pension
   file; moved to Brown Co. OH; CW soldier 175th
   OVI; Note: middle name George is not confirm-
   ed; LDS; CVMR; CVHM; USARCH
Abraham P. Rutan - b 1818 in NJ m Mary Ann
   Phelps in 1860 and moved to IA in 1863; he
   may be the son of Abraham Rutan-Lydia
   Vanderbeek although there is a hint that he
   died in 1847 (Yvonne Rutan Reed) HMCI
Abraham R. Rutan - (1822/25-1900) p/Robert
   Rutan-Mary Courter m (1) Fannie May (1832-

1874) in 1850 (2) Minnie Wallow (1868-1933);
Minnie a "chorus girl" from St. Lawrence Co.
NY about 1888; Abram a carriage builder/
undertaker who lived in Orange Co. NY in
1850, Newburgh NY in 1860 and Paterson after
1875; his will was subject to a dispute
covered in the New York Times; he and Minnie
are bur at Cedar Lawn Cem, Paterson; her
gravestone says she was born in 1859; CDIR;
PCHSP; NYT; 1900C; NJBI; HONEY; 1850C

Abram W. Rutan - (1848-1922) p/John D. Rutan-
Anna Perry of Lafayette Twp, Sussex Co. m (1)
Anna Elizabeth "Lizzie" Case (1849-1893) in
1865 (2) Mary Chant (1846-1914) of Leicster-
shire England in 1893; he was a wagon-maker
living in Port Jervis, Orange Co.; he is bur
Laurel Grove Cem, Port Jervis; NYDC; CDIR;
EG; SXHS; 1900C

Abram Wilson Rutan - (1855-1931) p/Martin Rutan-
Hannah Jane Wilson m Kate Ayers b 1865 in
1881 at Greenville M.E. Ch; living in
Sandyston Twp, Sussex Co. in 1900; Note:
SXHS has him born in 1844 and that at some
time he lived in Port Jervis however it appears that that info relates to the prior
entry EG; METC; SCMR; 1860C; 1900C; NYMC;
NYGBS

Adaline Ruton - b 1874 p/George N. Ruton-Sarah
Souder; living in No. Hempstead, Nassau Co.
NY in 1900; 1900C

Adam Rutan - m Elizabeth _____ (1849-1893) from
her Obit in the *Port Jervis Register* 26 Jan
1893

Adam C. Rutan - (1818-1881) p/Daniel Rutan-
Hannah Corselius m Lauretta Conklin b 1826 by
1847; he was a farmer in Papakating, Frankford Twp, Sussex Co. he was living with
Catherine (his aunt) bc 1789 there in 1850;
later he was a tavern-keeper at Mt. Pisgah
near Branchville; 1850C; 1860C; MCRC

Adam Thomas Rutan - b 1818 a carpenter in
Blairstown, Warren Co. m Abigail Tinsman b
1814; they moved to Susquehanna Co. PA in
1865; he may be the brother of Charles Stuart
Rutan of Warwick, Warren Co.; LEE; 1850C

Adelia Ann Rutan - bc 1822 p/John Rutan-Catherine ?Coon; bpt at Bloomfield (NJ) Presbyt Ch;
(from church records); GSNJ

Agnes Rutan - (1893-1975) p/Harry Rutan-Nellie

Sheridan of Rochester NY m Edward Welch
(1887-1966) TMR

Agnes Anne Rutan - (1886-1916) p/Harvey R. Rutan
-Emily Bergmann of NYC m (1) Percy Vinton (2)
Nicholas Rickert in NYC; Note: she is listed
as Annie A. Rutan in 1900C; SML; 1900C

Albert Rutan - (1805-1808) p/John J. Rutan-Maria
Terhune; he is bur at the First Ref Chyd
onthe-Green, Hackensack (cemetery records)
ZAB

Albert Reton - d 1847 p/Daniel D. Reton-Ellen
_____ (see next entry) GENEX

Albert R. Reton - (1841-1856) p/Daniel D. Reton-
Ellen _____; RET

Albert Hurd Retan - b 1845 p/Almeran Retan-Zylla
Longwell of Steuben Co. NY; he may be an
adopted son (see AR listing) MEACH; STUCHS

Albert Rutan - (1850-1910) p/Theodore Rutan-
Elizabeth Dunham of Piscataway, Middlesex Co.
NJ; he is bur in Plainfield; Note: his fath-
er's CW pension file says he was b in 1848;
his death certificate says he was b in 1853;
NYDC; USARCH

Albert Corwin Rutan - (1852-1910) p/Amzi Rutan-
Letitia Garrabrant of Belleville m Adeline
Vermule of Plainfield; living in Milburn,
Essex Co. in 1880 and Goshen, Orange Co. NY
in 1900; he was a stationary engineer; bur in
Plainfield (from his Obit in the *Port Jervis
Union*; Note: info on these two Alberts
appears to be mixed; NYDC; 1900C

Albert C. Rutan - m Katherine M. _____; she was
a widow in Nutley in 1928; CDIR

Albert Terhune Rutan - (1867-1933) p/Samuel B.
Rutan-Mary Louisa Fitzgerald m Emma Jane Shaw
b 1869 of Paterson at Middletown, Orange Co.
in 1895; he was a grocer; he died in Brooklyn
NY; 1880C; BDC; 1900C

Alberta Rutan - (1898-1985) p/Abram W. Rutan-
Kate Ayers of Sussex Co. m Edward P. Snook
(Alberta Moore) 1900C; EG

Alexander Rutan - (1878-1954) p/Cornelius Rutan-
Elsie Terwiliger m Lucy Calhoun (1885-1950)
at St. Joseph's Ch, Forestburg, Sullivan Co.;
in 1903; he was born at Port Jervis, Orange
Co. and they were living in Wurtsboro in
1920; he was an interior designer in Silver
Lake, Wallkill Town, Orange Co.; Note: the
marriage certificate gives her birth year as

1882; NYDC; NYMC; 1880C; 1900C; 1920C

Alexander Batchelor Ruton - (1804-1884) p/William Ruton-Rachel Brower of Tarrytown NY; m Sarah J. Sayre (1799-1843) of Bottle Hill, Morris Co. NJ in 1826; he was a coffee-merchant and grocery man in NYC (1836-1841) MACK; SFH; CDIR; PCHSP

Alfred Rutan - b 1843 p/Daniel Rutan-Lucy Compton; he may have moved with his family to Wayne Co. PA; MCRC

Alfred Arthur Ruttan - (1875-1928) p/Charles David Ruttan-Martha A. Duetta m (1) Addie M. Dulmager (1877-1903) in 1902; Gertrude Franklin (1883-1961) in 1904; Alfred a "stockkeeper" in Rochester NY in 1901 and worked for Eastman-Kodak; he is bur at Holy Sepulchre Cem, Rochester; RUTT; CDIR; NYMC; NYDC

Alfred Farley Ruttan - (1873-1951) p/Christopher Ruttan-Mary J. Farley m (1) Rebekah Parks (1865- 1936) at Akron Valley, Erie Co. NY in 1900 (2) Hazel Baker d 1979 in Los Angeles; was b in Houseys Rapids, Ontario and d at Ryde Twp; he served as a Pvt in the 10th Infantry during the SpAm War; he is bur at Mickles Memorial Cem, Gravenhurst, Ontario; NYMC; RUTT

Alfred M. Rutan - (1895-1973) born in MA he died in Los Angeles; CADRI

Alice Rutan - bc 1875 p/Jacob Rutan-Nancy Rollison of Sussex Co.; 1880C

Alice Rutan - b 1885 p/Henry K. Rutan m _____ Ehner; JRB; 1900C

Alice Rutan - m William Beemer d 1930; CVAN

Alice Rutan - (1917-1993) p/George D. Rutan-Henrietta Hepp of Newark; 1920C; JRB

Alice Conklin Retan - (1902-1969) she died at Honeoye Falls, Monroe Co. NY; NYDC

Alice E. Retan - (1863-1950) p/Nelson Retan-Esther Ball of Steuben Co. NY; m Clarence L. Fox of Italy NY in 1882; she died in Penn Yan, Steuben Co. (Rich MacAlpine) 1880C; PUH; MEACH

Alice Hazard Ruton - (1877-1965) p/William V. Ruton-Laura L. Hazard of East Orange, Essex Co, NJ m Alfred Ranney Bunnell (1867-1954) he was b in NYC and died in East Orange; she d in Belvidere, Warren Co. and is bur at Rosedale Cem, Orange NJ (Pam Walling) 1880C

Alice R. Rutan - member of the Davenport and

Fergusonville M.E. Ch, Delaware Co. NY in 1877 (church records)

Almeran Retan - **Mead** (1811-1885) p/Barnet Retan-Sarah Drew of Sussex Co. m Zylla Longwell b 1813; living in Steuben Co. in 1850 (some info from his son's death certificate) Note: MEACH has him b in 1810 and she in 1811; STUCHS; MEACH; 1850C

Alonzo Rutan - (1854-1854) p/Melancthon Rutan-Eliza J. Smith; he is bur at Bethel M.E. Cem, Staten Island (cemetery records)

Alonzo Rutan - m Helen Brace (1884-1948) of Lambs Creek PA; they lived in Addison, Steuben Co.; NYDC

Alta Maude Ruttan - (1903-1904) p/Alfred A. Ruttan-Addie Dulmager of Rochester; NYDC

Alvin L. Rutan - b 1871 p/James R. Rutan-Hannah Machette; produce man in Newark in 1909; meat purveyor in Morristown in 1923; he died in ME CRC; CDIR

Amanda Rutan - (1859-1887) p/Peter Rutan-Jane Sherman of Sullivan Co. NY m Luther F. Warner at Midland MI (see MI listing) MCRC; CAREY

Amelia Rutan - a nurse in Fitchburg MA in 1888-1890; CDIR

Amy Newton Rutan - b 1843 p/Hezekiah Rutan-Matilda Hayes m James A. Gault; FER

Amzi Rutan - (1819-1894) p/Abraham Rutan-Margaret Ennis m Letitia Garrabrant (1823-1902) in 1842; stone-mason of Belleville (Rutan & Johns in 1890); CDIR; 1860C

Amzi Rutan - (1848-1856) p/John Rutan-Susan Walker of Newark; he is bur at Mt. Pleasant Cem in Newark (cemetery records) 1850C; GSNJ

Ann Reton - p/Daniel Reton-Sarah Moore m _____ Wallace (see Ann Moore Reton, below) GENEX; GSNJ

Ann Retan - bc 1848 p/James Retan-Urania Conover of Seneca Co. NY and later MI; (Jonathan Gushen) 1850C

Ann Reton - bc 1827 resident of NYC, 16th Ward in 1850; 1850C

Ann Ruton - m Joseph Wade in NYC (Wade Genealogy)

Ann Rutan - b 1828 p/John Rutan-Catherine Coon; PCHSP

Anna Ruton - resident of Vetran, Chemung Co. NY in 1850; 1850C

Ann A. Rutan - (1878-1878) p/Thomas B. Rutan-

Annie Powers Heningham; bur at Greenwood Cem
Brooklyn   (her Obit in the *Brooklyn Eagle*)

Ann Eliza Rutan - (1811-1880/89) p/Samuel S.
Rutan-Hannah Garrabrant m Peter Van Riper;
Ann died in Harrison, Hudson Co. NJ and is
bur at Springgarden. Essex Co.; DRCSHP; FER;
GSNJ

Ann Maria Reton - m Abraham Carlock in NYC in
1832; LDS

Ann Mary Rutan - (1840-1845) p/John D. Rutan-
Anna E. Perry; bur at the Sturr Family Cem,
Campgaw, Franklin Twp, Bergen Co. (cemetery
records) PCHSQ; GSNJ

Ann Matilda Rutan - (1846-1870) p/Charles S.
Rutan-Margaret Vanover of Hardwick Twp, Warr-
en Co. m Philip Teeter in 1863 she is bur at
Hainsburg Cem, Warren Co. (Jan Raub) SXHS;
MEACH; 1850C

Ann Maude Rutan - b 1889 p/Charles G. Rutan-Mary
Abbot m Joseph Way; LDS

Anna Rutan - b 1813 p/Samuel Rutan-Susanna Cymer
of Sussex Co. m _____ Kellum/Kellam of Long
Island NY; MEACH; MCRC

Anna Allerton Rutan - (1883-1970) nurse of Rochester NY; NYDC

Anna Belle Rutan - b 1885 p/Abram W. Rutan-Kate
Ayers m Frank Linford Newell at Beemerville,
Sussex Co.; records having her married to
Fred Wilson are incorrect (Alberta Moore)
1900C; EG

Anna Eliza Rutan - (1841-1845) p/Peter C. Rutan-
Maria Compton; MCRC

Anna Jane Rutan - (1852-1920) p/John Rutan-
Elizabeth Snook m Amzi Merring in 1868; bur
at Baleville Cem, Sussex Co.; Note: another
record has her 1860-1933; may be the daughter
of John and his first wife, Mary Ann Struble;
JS; NJGS; EG

Anna Louise Rutan - b 1892 p/James D. Rutan-Emma
Murray m Harry Bradner (1889-1976) of Bell-
vale NY in 1913; they lived in Pine Island,
Orange Co.; Note: her bc calls her Anna
Murray Rutan; 1900C; SSA; NYBC; POCGS

Anna May Retan - (1879-1936 p/Nelson Retan-Ester
Ball of Steuben Co. NY m Ray Gibson b 1879 of
Catawba NY at Pulteney in 1902; Note: MEACH
has her born in 1880; NYMC; USARCH; 1880C

Anna Ray Rutan - (1882-1976) p/David Rutan- Mary
E. Westervelt m John G. Goode, Jr. (1881-

1958) PCHSP; DARLDC

Anne Rutan - b 1801 p/Paul Rutan-Margy Speer of
  Bloomfield NJ; she was born in Scotch Plains;
  DRCSHP; LDS

Anne E. Rutan - bc 1903 p/Moses Rutan-Ida M.
  Rose of Port Jervis, Orange Co. NY; 1920C

Anne M. Rutan - **Anna** bc 1878 p/William H. Rutan-
  Julia Dunning of Port Jervis m Harry Melber
  and living in Jersey City in 1909 (from her
  father's Obit) 1880C; PJUGO

Anne Moore Rutan - b 1811 p/Daniel Rutan-Sarah
  Moore; bpt at English Neighborhood Ref Ch;
  m _____ Wallace per her father's will; NJGS

Annie Rheutan - p/Daniel Rheutan-Rosina Duff of
  Orange Co. NY; AAR

Annie Ruttan - b 1877 p/Peter Ruttan-Sarah See
  of Sydenham Ontario m Horace G. McCabe at
  Watertown in 1896; NYMC

Annie A. Rutan - b 1886 p/Harvey R. Rutan (see
  Agnes A. Rutan, above)

Annie F. Rutan - (1889-1972) of MA she died in
  Los Angeles; probably Annie F. Keegan wife of
  William H. Rutan of Boston; CADRI

Archie James Ruttan - (1899-1985) p/George
  Almond Ruttan-Elizabeth M. Wright of Dexter,
  son Co. NY; RUTT; FMLWT

Archie N. Rutan - (1868-1924) p/David C. Rutan-
  Harriet Perry m Mary Elizabeth Gray b 1867 at
  Elmira NY in 1887; "air brake inspector" in
  Elmira; he died in Washington DC and is bur
  at Woodlawn Cem, Elmira; 1900C; CDIR; CHEMHS

Arnold Robert Rutan - (1900-1969) p/Josiah T.
  Rutan-Laurietta Birck of Brooklyn m Rose
  Ellen Mulligan (1899-1974) at St. Paul's RC
  Ch, Binghamton in 1939; WWI soldier, he was a
  sales manager; they both died at Staten Is-
  land and are bur at the Moravian Cemetery;
  MRUT; SSA

Arthur Ruttan - (1908-1976) of Oswego NY; SSA

Arthur C. Rutan - b 1922 p/Phay B. Rutan-Mary
  C. Cromer of Elmira NY m Marianne Palme b
  1929; (Arthur C. Rutan)

Arthur Edwin Reton - p/John T. Reton-Frances
  Dewey of Kansas City (from her DAR appl
  #59336) Note: SSA has a Fannie Reton
  (1873-1971) of Monrovia Los Angeles Co. CA;
  RET; SSA; NSDAR

Arthur H. Rutan - (1880-1895) p/Levi Rutan-
  Emmagen Hubbard of Rome NY; he is probably

the son of Levi's first wife, Amelia Spear;
NYDC

Arthur L. H. Ruttan - (1887-1906) p/Peter Ruttan
-Sarah E. See; he was a bricklayer, unm born
in Canada and died in Watertown, NY; RUTT;
NYDC

Augustus M. Rutan - (1849-1903) p/Abraham Ruttan
-Mary Ann See m Annabelle McDonald born in
1849; he was a carpenter born in Canada and
living in Watertown NY in 1902 where he died;
RUTT; NYDC; CDIR; 1900C

Austin Retan - bc 1819 m Bathia Frost of Carmel
NY Putnam Co. NY (Underhill:643) (see PA
listing) LDS

Austin Retan - b 1824 and was from Matinecock or
Mattituck, L.I. NY; LDS

Barnet D. Retan - (1822-1852) p/Barnet Retan-
Sarah Drew m Deborah _____ (1827-1895) living
in Urbana Twp, Steuben Co. in 1850; he is bur
at West Urbana Cem; as a widow she wed Joseph
Steward by 1856; Note: cemetery records say
he was bur at the Depew Cem in Urbana and bur
with him is his wife Mary C. _____ (1822-
1848) MEACH; 1850C; STUCHS

Barnet L. Retan - (1836-1910) p/Almeran Retan-
Zilla Longwell m (1) Catherine H. Brundage at
Pleasant Valley in 1857 (2) Euphemia Barrett;
living in Urbana Twp, Steuben Co. in 1900;
she is bur at Mahopac Falls Bapt Chyd, Putnam
Co. NY (Buys:166); 1850C; STUCHS; 1900C;
NYDC; CoMR; NYMC

Beatrice Rutan - bc 1912 p/Earl Rutan-Mary E.
Stratton; 1920C

Beatrice S. Rheutan - (1895-1971) m Frank
Markle; she was born in IL and d in
Glastonbury CT (State Death Index)

Beekman Retan - (see Harmon Beekman Retan,
below)

Bella Ruton - b 1856; sister of William E.
Ruton of NYC; 1920C

Belle Rheutan - p/Daniel A. Rheutan-Rosina Duff
of Orange Co. NY; AAR

Belle K. Rheutan - living in Newark, 4th Ward in
1870 (see David Rheutan, below); 1870C

Belle Rutan - **Isabelle** (1860-1934) p/William D.
Rutan-Kate C. Dodd of Newark m James Dade
Bailey (1846-1926) a physician from Rock-
ville, Montgomery Co. MD; GSNJ; 1900C

Belle Rutan - b 1859 p/Rynier S. Rutan-Adeline
   M. Griggs of Brimfield MA; m _____ Murray
   (info from Rynier's CW pension file) USARCH
Belle Rutan - b 1890 p/Harry Rutan-Nellie
   Sheridan of Rochester NY; m Frank McClain b
   1889;   (Thomas M. Rutan) 1900C
Bernadette Rutan - bc 1917 p/Francis Rutan- Mary
   _____; 1920C
Benjamin Reuton - bc 1808 m Clarissa Moody in
   1832; he was from Schoharie Co. NY; LDS
Benjamin Ruton - resident of Woolwich Twp,
   Gloucester Co. NJ in 1840 (see Moses Ruton,
   below) 1840C
Benjamin A. Rutan - (1872-1943) p/Peter D. Rutan
   -Sarah Spangenburg m (1) Mary E. Pittenger b
   1881 at Newton, Sussex Co, in 1904; they had
   a son, Clyde b 1899 so he may have married
   earlier or Mary had been married earlier;
   Note: Mary E. Hardy named as his wife in his
   Obit in the *Sussex Independent* Feb 4, 1943;
   GSNJ; SXHS; 1880C
Benjamin B. Ruton - (1806/07-1882) p/William
   Rutan-Rachel Brower of Tarrytown NY; m Joanna
   Maria Vermilye d 1877 at Brick Ch NYC in 1838
   he was a cabinet-maker in NYC in 1840; she is
   bur at Mt. Pleasant Cem, Newark (cemetery
   records) LDS; NYEP; MAHER; CDIR; PCHSP
Benton Thomas Rutan - (1863-1923) p/Thomas B.
   Rutan-Johanna M. Harsen m Jeanne May Ludlow
   (1864-1957) of Bridgehampton, Suffolk Co. NY;
   where they lived; he was a custom-house
   guard; he died in Southampton; BBC; NYDC
Benton T. Rutan - b 1892 p/Josiah T. Rutan-
   Laurietta Birck; 1900C
Bert A. Ruttan - (1881-1939) p/William H. Ruttan
   -Gertrude A. Ruttan m Mary J. Potter (1882-
   1954) in 1907 at Adams Center, Jefferson Co.
   NY; he was a farmer b in Lyme NY and d at
   Hounsfield, NY; RUTT; NYMC
Bertha Rutan - (1863-1915) bur at Branchville
   Cem. Sussex Co. (cemetery records)
Bessie Ruton - d 1890 bur at Hillside Cem,
   Rutherford NJ (cemetery records)
Bishop Rutan - b 1867 p/Hudson Rutan-Mary Jane
   Bell of Hamburg, Sussex Co. (from Hudson's CW
   pension file) probably Simeon B. Rutan (see
   MI entry) USARCH
Brice Perry Rutan - (1838-1903) p/John D. Rutan-
   Anna E. Perry m Corcelia Elizabeth Elston

(1845-1928) at Greenville M.E. Ch in 1867; he
was a farmer in Westtown, Orange Co. NY, b
in Vernon Twp, Sussex Co. NJ and died at
Slate Hill NY; she was b and d at Unionville;
they are bur at Unionville Cem; Note: cemetery records diclose that she d in 1927; LDS;
CMOR; CRC; OCD; 1920C

Calvin Rutan - (1841-1909) p/John S. Rutan-Mag-
dalena Duncan m Rachel Elizabeth Stager
(1845-1905) in Bloomfield, Essex Co. NJ in
1865; they lived in Belleville and Nutley;
CW soldier 26th N.J. Infantry; he was a
"market-gardener" in Belleville in 1890; he
is bur at Bloomfield Cem, Bloomfield, Essex
Co. (cemetery records) CDIR; PCHSQ; USARCH;
LDS

Carl Rutan - b 1883 p/Charles Rutan-Emma _____ m
Lucy Emma "LuLu" Paine (1884-1962) at Oneida,
Madison Co. NY in 1922; he was an accountant
and she City Clerk; she is bur at Lakewood
Cem, Cleveland NY; CDIR; NYDC; 1900C

Caroline Rutan - (1821-1908) p/Abram Rutan-Ann
Courter m Jonas W. Rhodes (1821-1891) at
Glenwood, Sussex Co. in 1843; they moved to
Somers WI; (Windemuth Family Org.) DARLDC;
LDS; GSNJ; JS

Caroline Rutan - b 1843 p/Henry A. Rutan-Harriet
Burnett of Brooklyn; m George Dottin b 1836;
living in Philadelphia in 1908 per her brother Thomas' CW pension file; USARCH; LDS

Caroline Rheutan - p/Daniel Rheutan-Rosina Duff
of Orange Co. NY; AAR

Caroline Rutan - (1870-1899) p/Frank Rutan-Lena
Seitler of Newark (Janet Rutan Bowers) NJHS

Caroline Elizabeth Rutan - (1817-1887) p/Harmon
Rutan-Chloe Lobdell of NYC m Daniel Nichols
Bates (1816-1843) in NYC in 1837; he was a
China Trade ship's captain who died in Canton
China; she d at Warwick RI; LDS; PCHSQ

Carrie Lillie Rutan - b 1862/9 p/Samuel B. Rutan
-Mary L. Fitzgerald of West Milford, Passaic
Co. NJ; LDS; 1880C

Catharine Retan - d 1886 bur at Pleasant Valley
Cem, Urbana, Steuben Co. NY (cemetery
records) MEACH

Catherine Rutan - p/Harmon Rutan-Chloe Lobdell
of NYC; PCHSQ

Catherine Rutan - b 1802 p/Daniel Rutan-Rachel

Berdan of NYC; LDS

Catherine Rutan - (1808-1859) p/Peter Rutan-Jane ?Sherman; PCHSP

Catherine Rutan - (1812-1908) p/Abraham D. Rutan -Lydia Vanderbeek; Note: PDRC has a Trientje Rutan b 1815 in Paramus, unm, d at Mt. Tabor; bur at Cedar Lawn Cem, Paterson (cemetery records) PCHSP; PDRC

Catherine Rutan - (1813-1881) p/John Rutan-Catherine Coon m Ellis E. Collins in 1835 in Essex Co.; they moved to IA (see IA listing) PCHSP; ECMR

Catherine Rutan - b 1831 m John Hartley in 1852; lived in Bloomfield NJ; Note: this may be bad info and it refers to Catherine Coon b 1796, the widow of John Rutan; PCHSQ; LDS

Catherine A. Rutan - d 1908 in Vernon Twp, Sussex Co. she is bur at Warwick Cem, Orange Co. NY (cemetery records)

Catherine Acelia Rutan - (1854-1941) p/Charles S. Rutan-Margaret Vanover of Warren Co. m Hiram France (1836-1918) in 1871; 1860C; LDS; 1870C; MEACH

Catherine Ann Reton - m Andrew John Blauvelt b 1817 in NYC in 1838; MCNY; BFH

Catherine Matilda Retan - (1808-1872) m Capt. Prince Snow (1804-1861) who was lost at sea; she is bur at Wyckoff Cem, Bergen Co.; Note: another record says she was bur at the Old Burial Ground, Edgewater NJ; BCMR; NYCMM; FH; GSBC

Catherine Maria Rutan - (1841-1879) p/Albert Z. Rutan-Alida Van Blarcom m Theodore Kingsland in 1858 at the Saddle River Ref Ch; after her death he m Jane Post in 1882; HKING; 1860C; ZAB; LDS

Catherine S. Rutan - (1825-1882) p/Paul Rutan-Lydia Speer m (1) Stephen Parsells (1818-1846) in 1842 (2) Arthur Lathrop (1821-1885); she was b in CT and d at Cuyahoga Co. OH; bur at Woodland Cem, Cleveland (cemetery records) MHIL; FH

Cecelia B. Reton - p/John T. Reton: RET

Charity Rutan - (1813-1850) p/Abraham J. Rutan-Wyntje Hopper m John Zabriskie Goetschius (1809-1884) at Second Ref Ch of Paterson in 1831; she is bur at Saddle River Methodist (Little Zion) Cem; ZAB; MZB; FH; DARLDC; PCHSQ

BHS; 1900C

Charles Ruttan - (1853-1891) painter of Rochester; NYDC

Charles Ruton - resident of Trenton, Mercer Co. NJ in 1850; 1850C

Charles Ruton - seaman residing at 295 W. 11th St. NYC in 1890; CDIR

Charles Rutan - b 1894 in Canada; living in Hamilton, Morehouse Town NY in 1900; 1900C

Charles Ruttan - m Josephine Marie Mitchell (1891-1947); she is bur at St. Paul's Cem, Oswego NY; NYDC

Charles Rutan - (1897-1980) m Hazel Tilley (1891-1989; he was b in OH; they lived in Old Lyme, CT (see OH listing) SSA

Charles Rutan - (1919-2000) p/Chauncey Rutan-Mabel D. Sigafoos of Bayonne NJ; m Catherine Christopher d 1993; he was a WWII veteran, a POW and later a laborer in Wilson PA (from his Obit in the *Allentown Morning Call* 27 Sept 2000) 1920C; LIZR

Charles Arthur Rutan - (1886-1932) p/Charles E. Rutan-Emma M. Haight m Elizabeth Mae Wilson (1892-1979); living in Oneida in 1910 and Cortland in 1920; he d at Solon NY; Note: RUTT has him 1866-1953; his Obit says he died in 1932; RUTT; 1900C; 1920C; COCHS

Charles D. Ruton - b 1856 p/Charles Ruton-Martha E. Smith; he was a "steamboat clerk" in 1870 in Poughkeepsie and in the produce business in NYC 1897-1917; 1860C; CDIR; 1870C

Charles D. Ruttan - b 1890 p/Peter Ruttan-Sarah See of Sydenham Ontario; m Belle Roushon b 1889 at Watertown NY in 1909; NYMC

Charles David Ruttan - (1851-1918) p/David W. Rutan-Nancy Davis of Northport Ontario; m Martha A. Duetta (1853-1924) of South Bay; emigrated to the U.S. in 1893; Methodist minister in Rochester; he d at Sparta, Livingston Co. NY and is bur at Union Cem; she died at Avoca, Steuben Co.; Note: MEACH identifies him as Thomas D. Ruttan; RUTT; MEACH

Charles E. Rutan - (1855-1911) p/Henry Rutan-Sarah Courter m Mary Louisa/Laura Bissell (1855-1911) at Grace M.E. Ch, Paterson in 1876; Note: another record has Mary Laura Rutan living in Paterson in 1900; PCHSQ; FH; 1870C; 1880C; 1900C

Charles Edwin Ruttan -(1884-1934) p/Charles D.
Ruttan-Martha A. Duetta m Della Elvira Brown
(1885-1978) in Rochester in 1903; he was an
artist; NYMC; RUTT

Charles G. Rutan - m Mary Abbot; LDS

Charles H. Rutan - (1858-1862) p/William H.
Rutan-Hannah Winters of Paterson; METC

Charles H. Rutan - (c1869-1875) p/Thomas B.
Rutan-Annie Heningham of Brooklyn; he is bur
at Green-Wood Cem, Brooklyn (cemetery records) 1870C

Charles Hart Rutan - (1891-1968) p/Peter C.
Rutan-Jeannette Hart of Port Jervis NY; he
was Jeannette's son by a first marriage and
adopted by Peter; "newspaper man" in Los Angeles (from Peter's Obit) (see CA listing)
PJUGO

Charles Hartley Rutan - (see FL listing)

Charles Heningham Rutan - (1886-1960) p/Josiah
T. Rutan-Emma Laurietta Birck m Violet
Sherman/Sheran (1885-1965) of Holyoke MA; he
was a construction superintendent in New
Rochelle NY; WWI soldier; both bur at Pine-
lawn Cem, Suffolk Co. NY; 1900C; NYDC; MRUT

Charles Hercules Rutan - (1851-1914) p/Nicholas
W. Rutan-Sarah Marsh of Newark NJ; m Sarah
Ellen Brower in 1874; he was a noted
architect (Shepley & Rutan) in Boston who
commissioned the genealogy of the Rutan
family about 1908; WWW; FER; NYTO

Charles H. Rutan - (1885-1886) p/Charles H.
Rutan-Sarah E. Brower; Note: PCHSQ has him
(1875-1876)

Charles Jefferson Rutan - (see Jay Rutan, below)

Charles Longwell Rutan - b 1839 p/Peter Rutan-
Hetty Longwell; he was a "harness-maker" who
moved to CA (Bob Longwell) (see CA listing)
PCHSP; FH

Charles Lyon Retan - (1879-1963) p/Orsamus Retan
-Emma Lyon of Steuben Co. NY and Vail IA; m
Blanche Edna Early b 1888 at Jerusalem, Yates
Co. NY in 1908; he died at Bath, Steuben Co.;
he is bur at Nondaga Cem (cemetery records)
NYMC; NYDC

Charles M. Ruttan - (1874-1960) p/Martin Rut-
tan-Amanda Mabee of Ontario m Ida M. Abbott
(1877-1972) he was a stationary engineer for
Niagara-Mohawk; both bur at the Rural Cem,
Oswego NY; NYDC

Charles May Rutan - **Cuffy** (1854-1892) p/Abraham R. Rutan-Fannie May m Jennie Lee (1856- 1886) in 1877; "Undertaker/Artist"; Pvt. in the Paterson Light Guard (NJNG) in 1883; both bur at Cedar Lawn Cem, Paterson; Note: his gravestone says he was born in 1853 (cemetery records) GSNJ; PCHSP

Charles May Rutan, Jr. - (1880-1880) p/Charles M. Rutan-Jennie Lee; he is bur at Cedar Lawn Cem, Paterson (cemetery records)

Charles P. Ruton - (1830-1919 p/Isaac B. Rutan-Margaret Baker m Martha Elnora Smith (1828-1904) at the Bedford St. Methodist Ch in NYC in 1852; they were living in Poughkeepsie NY until at least 1870; he was a "boatman"; she is bur at St. Johns Cem, Yonkers, Westchester Co. NY; he died in Jamaica, Queens Co. NY (Peggy Gaertner) 1850C; NYCMM; 1870C

Charles R. Ruttan - b 1866 in Canada m Jennie Ayrhart b 1863 in Canada; living in Brownsville Town, Jefferson Co. NY in 1900; 1900C

Charles Stuart Rutan - b 1822 in Hartwick, Warren Co. m (1) Margaret Vanover bc 1820 (2) Sarah Jane Osenbaugh bc 1842 in 1875; SCMR; EG; 1850C; MEACH; 1870C; 1880C

Charles W. Rutan - b 1860 m Mary E. Roosa b 1862; they lived in Port Jervis (from son's birth certificate); NYBC

Charles W. Rutan - b 1867 p/William H. Rutan-Julia Dunning of Libertyville, Sussex Co. m (1) Fanny O. Sheels (1865-1920) of Barryville NY (2) Clarissa E. McIntyre d 1927; he was a foreman in Port Jervis; all are bur at Laurel Grove Cem (cemetery records) NYDC; EG; 1880C; 1900C; CDIR

Charlotte Rutan - b 1833 p/Daniel Rutan-Lucy Compton; may have moved with her family to Wayne Co. PA; MCRC

Charlotte Ruton - resident of Cobleskill, Schoharie Co. NY; 1860C

Charlotte Rutan - b 1895 p/Edward P. Rutan-Adeline _____ ; 1900C

Charlotte Amelia Retan - (1850-1916) p/Gilbert Retan-Melecta Drew m Edward Willeby Clark (1849-1944) in 1871 at Steuben Co. NY (Rose Alexander) MEACH; LDS

Chauncey Rutan - (1883-1933) m Mabel Diana Sigafoos (1889-1931) in 1918; he was born in Phillipsburg, Warren Co. and she in Easton

PA; living in Warren Co. in 1900 and in
Bayonne, Hudson Co. in 1920 with his mother
Alice; (marriage date from Carol Haner);
LIZR; 1900C; 1920C

Christiana Reton - m John Brazee 30 May 1841 in
NYC; NYCMM

Christopher Martin Rutan - (1850-1910) p/Amzi
Rutan-Letitia Garrabrant m Susan E. _____
(c1853-1931); Susan born in Poughkeepsie NY;
died in Westfield NJ; one daughter per her
Obit; he was working for U.S. Express Co. in
1890; he is bur at Vincent Mem Cem, Nutley;
(cemetery records) 1860C; NYTO; CDIR

Clarence Reton, Jr. - (1897-1982) p/Clarence
Reton-Grace S. _____; he lived in Patchogue,
Suffolk Co. NY; 1900C; SSA

Clarence Rutan - (1888-1965) he died in Rochester NY; SSA

Clarence Retan - (1889-1889) p/Robert Retan-Ida
Beers of Urbana, Steuben Co. NY; NYDC

Clarence Rutan - bc 1918 p/Cody Linn Rutan-Addie
Kelly; 1920C

Clarence Brush Rutan - (1846-1894) p/John Rutan-
Susan Walker of Newark; "hat-manufacturer" in
West Orange NJ; unmarried per probate records
he is bur at Mt. Pleasant Cem, Newark (cemetery records) NYTO; GSNJ

Clarence Dewey Retan - (1898-1935) p/John H.
Retan-Catherine Lepper of Palmyra NY; m Marg-
aret Alice Conklin b 1902 of Batavia, Genesee
Co. NY; he was an insurance agent in Rochest-
er and earlier a telegrapher in Jersey City
(Tanya White) NYMC; NYDC

Clarence E. Rutan - (1861-1940) p/William H.
Rutan-Julia Dunning m Annie H. Hennessey b
1879 at Middletown NY in 1897; they were living there afterwards; the city directory
calls him Clarence C. Rutan; in 1920 they
were living in San Francisco and he died in
Los Angeles; Note: one record calls her Annie
Henning and his death certificate gives his
mother's surname as "Janes"; CADRI; CDIR;
LDS; NYMC; 1920C

Clarence Eugene Rutan - (1888-1965) p/William H.
Rutan-Adelaide L. Rice m Miriam Tanger and
lived in Rochester NY; 1900C; NYDC; 1920C

Clarence G. Reton - b 1897 in NYC; NYCBC

Clarence I. Retan - b 1898 (see Clarence Dewey
Retan, above); 1900C

Clifford S. Rutan - (1867-1940) p/James R. Rutan
-Hannah Machette m (1) Cora C. Smith (1864-
1900) (2) Rose Nichols (1872-1937) he was a
"green-grocer" in Morristown, Morris Co.; all
were bur at Evergreen Cem, Morristown
(cemetery records) he is listed as Clifford
T. Rutan in 1900C; 1900C; 1920C

Clifford S. Rutan - (1903-1979) p/Herbert W.
Rutan-Lillian Neary; he died in Morristown;
SSA; 1920C; PCHSQ

Clinton Norman Rutan - (1918-1986) p/Norman E.
Rutan-Althea Smith Edwards of Irvington,
Essex Co. NJ; compiler of the Clinton Rutan
Collection at the NJHS, Newark; CRC; SSA

Clyde Rutan - (1899-1933) p/Benjamin A. Rutan-
Mary E. Pittenger of Sussex Co.; m Helen M.
Burkacky (1905-1988) in 1923 in PA; he died
in Scranton PA and is bur at the North Hardy-
ston Cem, Sussex Co. (cemetery records) SSA;
1920C

Cody Linn Rutan - (1887-1932) p/Linn Rutan-Juliette Coykendall m Adelaide Kelly (1891-1965)
in 1909; he was a carpenter living in Newark
in 1920 and in Belleville at the time of his
death; he was killed in an auto mishap; she
died in El Paso TX; both are bur at Fairview
Cem, Sussex Co. (cemetery records) CDIR; EG;
GSNJ; TXDR; NYTO

Cody Linn Rutan, Jr. - (1927-1990) p/Cody L.
Rutan-Adelaide Kelly; he died in El Paso TX;
TXDR

Coe C. Rutan - (1836-1839) p/Peter C. Rutan-
Maria Compton; MCRC

Cora Amelia Rutan - b 1878 p/Charles E. Rutan-
Mary Laura Bissell; bpt at Grace M.E. Ch,
Paterson; PCHSP; 1880C

Cora B. Rutan - b 1895 p/William A. Rutan-Grace
B. Stanaback m Emil Block (1897-1968) of
Lyndhurst NJ; SSA; CVAN

Cornelius Rutan - bc 1842 p/Cornelius Rutan-Caty
Van Alen; he is not mentioned in his mother's
1859 will; PCHSP; 1850C

Cornelius Rutan - (1849-1917) p/Richard Rutan-
Mary Ann Fort of Fallsburgh, Sullivan Co. NY;
m Elsa Ann Terwiliger (1859-1923) they lived
in Phillipsport, Sullivan Co. NY and he died
in Wurtsboro; JS; 1860C; NYDC; 1900C

Cornelius J. Rutan - (1800-1863) m Catherine
(Caty) Van Alen/Valen (c1809-1859) at the

Paramus Ref Ch in 1826; he was a mason living
in Manchester Twp, Passaic Co. in 1850; TDRC;
BCMR; 1850C; PCHSP

Cynthia A. Retan - (1849-1914) p/John Retan-
Rachel Shuart of Steuben Co.; m Frank Carman
at the Presbyt Ch of Hammondsport, Steuben
Co. NY in 1885; she died in Bath Village and
is bur at Glenview Cem, Pulteney (her Obit
appeared in the *Steuben Courier* 13 Nov 1914)
(Alice W. Matson) CoMR; MEACH

Cynthia A. Rutan - b 1853 p/Peter Rutan-Jane
Sherman of Sullivan Co.; she died young and
does appear in the 1855C; CAREY; 1855C

Cyrus Ellsworth Rutan - b 1864 (see Ellsworth
Rutan, below)

Cyrus Franklin Ruttan - (1884-1966) p/John A.
Ruttan-Edith E. Switzer of Harrowsmith Ontario; m Emma Pauline Burley (1896-1938) he died
in Oneida NY; Note: her mother was Levina
Adelia Ruttan; RUTT; NYDC

Damon Edgar Ruttan - (1879-1942) p/James Miles
Ruttan-Alice A. Peters m Marion B. Dennison
(1881-1946) at Port Leyden, Lewis Co. NY in
1904; he died in Boonville, Oneida Co. NY;
Note: his death certificate says his mother
was Almira; NYMC; RUTT; NYDC

Daniel Ruton - resident of Martinsburgh, Lewis
Co. NY (see Daniel H. Ruttan, below)

Daniel Rutan - m Lovina Louisa Folts of Herkimer
NY; they lived at Cranesville NY (from their
daughter Maria's death certificate)

Daniel Rutan - (1806-1890) p/Samuel Rutan-Susanna Cymer of Sussex Co. NJ m Lucy Compton
(1807-1882) in 1829; living in Texas Twp,
Wayne Co. PA in 1860; CBRF; NJG; SCMR; JS;
MCRC; 1860C

Daniel Routan - resident of Amsterdam, Montgomery Co. NY in 1860; 1860C

Daniel A. Rheutan - b 1825 p/Abraham Rheutan-Mary
Storms m Rosina B. Duff of NYC in 1845; GSNJ

Daniel A. Rheutan - (1848-1861) p/Daniel A.
Rheutan-Rosina B. Duff; his Obit in *The Whig
Press*, Middletown, Orange Co.; DARLDC; AAR

Daniel A. Rutan - (1850-1929) p/Daniel H. Ruttan
-Melissa Arthur b Atlanta m Alida Swackhammer
(1859-1929) he was a coachman and they lived
at Cleveland, Oneida Co. NY; Note: sometimes
they were known as Ruttan; NYDC; 1900C

Daniel D. Rutan - (1804-1851) p/Daniel Rutan-
Jannetje Brower m Maria Ackerman b 1812 at
the Ponds in 1826; both born at Campgaw NJ;
he was a blacksmith who died at Oakland and
bur at Wyckoff Chyd; she died in KS; CRC;
1830C; PCHSP; BCMR

Daniel D. Rutan - (1829-1889) p/Daniel Rutan-
Maria Ackerman m Keziah Eve Zebriskie (1832-
1902) at the Ponds (Oakland) NJ in 1851; both
born in NY; he was a blacksmith and was killed from the kick of a horse he was shoeing
(Yvonne Rutan Reed) Note: LDS identifies her
as Eliza Zebriskie of Bergen Co, NJ; they
later lived in Will Co. IL and Seward Co. NE;
dates from a family bible; PCHSP; CRC; AFH;
LDS

Daniel D. Reton - (1824-1865) p/Daniel Rutan-
Sarah Moore m Ellen _____; lived in New Barbadoes, Bergen Co. per his probate papers;
Ellen was a widow in NYC in 1869 and in Jersey City in 1889-1893; CDIR; RCFL

Daniel Reton - (1851-1852) p/Daniel D. Reton-
Ellen _____; RET; GENEX

Daniel E. Rutan - (1849-1933) p/Daniel Rutan-
Lucy Compton (see PA listing)

Daniel G. Rutan - (1910-2000) p/Alexander Rutan-
Lucy Calhoun of Sullivan Co. NY; m Marie Mc
Cade d 1980 of Middletown; he was a fuel oil
delivery driver born in Wurtsboro and he died
in Walkill; she died in NV and both are bur
at Walkill Cem, Philipsburg, Orange Co.
(Hilda Walrath) 1920C; SSA

Daniel H. Rutan - (1827-1887) p/Abraham Rutan-
Susanna Hazen m Charlotte A. Rollison b 1831
at the Clove Ch in 1851; they were living in
Frankford Twp, Sussex Co. in 1860 and moved
to Hollisterville, Monroe Co. PA in 1871;
they are bur at the Maplewood Cem, Scranton
PA; EG; LDS; 1860C; CBRF; MCRC

Daniel H. Ruttan - (1818-1897) p/Daniel Ruttan-
Rhoda B. Haight of Ontario; m Melissa Arthur
(1815-1880) of Martinsburgh NY; Daniel lived
in Georgia in the early 1850's and he served
as a CW soldier in the 14th N.Y. Infantry;
Note: his CW pension file disclosed that he
was born in Lewis Co. NY, was living in
Evansville AR, 1886-1888; Valley Springs,
Boone Co. AR in 1890, in Indian Territory in
1891 and in Port Leyden, Lewis Co. in 1896;

he died at Bath, Steuben Co. NY (some info from June Matthys) USARCH; RUTT; NYDC

David Retan - (1827-1845) p/Barnet Retan-Sarah Drew of Steuben Co.; he is bur at West Urbana Cem, Steuben Co. (Bob Longwell) PUH

David Rheutan - living in the 4th Ward, Newark NJ with Belle K. Rheutan (see above) in 1870; 1870C

David Rutan - p/Daniel Rutan-Sarah _____ m Caty Russell of Wantage Twp, Sussex Co. in 1806; SCMR; SUSESS

David Rutan - died in 1850 in Sussex Co.; CRAWN

David Ruttan - (1869-1942) m Delina Cassidy (1864-1942) he was a carpenter in Ogdensburg NY and died in Buffalo; both bur at Holy Cross Cem; Note: the 1900C has him as David F. Rutan b 1861; NYDC; 1900C

David Briton Rutan - (1827-1849) p/Abraham Rutan-Susanna Hazen m Elizabeth Jane Cassidy in 1848 at Stillwater Presbyt Ch; Note: Briton Rutan and David may be two different individuals; CRAWN; CBRF; PCHSQ; JS; SCMR

David C. Rutan - (1838-1922) CW soldier living in Millport Town, Chemung Co. NY in 1890; farmer in Big Flats in 1868; bur at Woodlawn Cem, Elmira NY; 1890C; CHEMHS; CDIR

David E. Rutan - (1838-1922) p/Peter Rutan-Maria Compton of Sussex Co. NJ) m Harriet Perry (1835-1917) lived in Catlin Town, Chemung Co. NY; Note: in family correspondence he is referred to as David Compton Rutan (see prior entry) MEACH; 1900C; MCRC

David F. Rutan - b 1886 p/David F. Rutan-Mary E. Westervelt m Etta _____; they lived in CO and in 1920 were in Los Angeles CA; PCHSP; 1920C

David H. Rutan - (1886-1949) p/Calvin Rutan-Sarah Combs of IN m Luella Halliman (1885-1968) in 1918; they lived in IN (see IN listing) and Bloomfield, Essex Co. NJ where he died; PCHSQ; ACPL

David Henry Rutan - (1838-1905) p/Layton Rutan-Dorothy Hull; called Henry Rutan in 1850C, at Dingmans Twp, Pike Co. PA at that time; he also lived in Coles Co. IL; SXHS; 1850C

David William Ruton - (1826-1853) p/William Ruton-Sophronia Winston m Margaret Becker (1827-1907) (Shafer Bible-NSDAR) (NSDAR appl. # 78811 of Sophronia Ruton Shaffer) Note: this source has him dying in 1852

Deborah Roseannah Retan - (1848-1895) p/Gilbert
Retan-Matilda Drew of Steuben Co. (Rose Alexander) 1860C; MEACH; STUCHS

DeForest Francis Ruttan - (1908-1936) p/Damon E.
Ruttan-Marion B. Denison; he was a lineman
"killed in a fall from a telephone pole"; bur
at Port Leyden, Lewis Co. NY; NYDC; RUTT

Delilah Rutan - b 1810 in Springwater, Livingston Co. NY; LDS

Delilah Rutan - m Ira Freeman in NY in 1827; LDS

Dell Rutan - laborer in Watertown NY in 1902;
CDIR

Dennis S. Rutan - (1849-c1925) p/Adam T. Rutan-
Abigail Tinsman m Lois Arminda Shay (1856-
1911 in 1878 at Susquehanna Co. PA; she was
from Fairdale PA and d at Union, Broome Co.
NY; 1850C; LEE; LDS; 1850C; NYDC; 1900C

Diana Ruton - (1919-1999) of Bohemia, Long Island NY (her Obit was in *Newsday* 18 Jan 1999)

Donald Rutan - WWII Vet, SSGT USAAC, captured 25
July 1943, imprisoned at Stalag 17B,
Grieschendorf, near Kress Austria (WWII POWs)

Donald Purdy Rutan - (1923-1997) m Phoebe Parr;
he was born in Orange and lived in Montclair,
Essex Co. NJ; he served in WWII and later
lived in Newton; LDS

Donald Ray Rutan - (1927-2000) (his Obit was in
the *Orange County Record* 1 Feb 2001)

Dorothea Rutan - (1903-1989) p/John E. Rutan-
Mary L. Hardy of Brooklyn NY; m William
Droge (1904-1965) she died at Sag Harbor,
Suffolk Co. NY; 1920C; EOVB; SSA

Dorothy Rutan - bc 1897 m _____ McMaster and
lived in Evanston IL; she is the sister of
William A. Rutan b 1897; she d in Cook Co. IL
PCHSQ

Dorothy Elizabeth Rutan - (1898-1987) p/Joseph
V. Rutan-Dorothy M. Davis of Brooklyn m Harry
Souder Mecray (1895-1950) of Cape May NJ at
the Bronx, NYC in 1935; she died in Los
Angeles (Russ Hauver) NYT; GSNJ; BBCI; 1900C

Dullcina Rose Ruttan - b 1883 p/William Ruttan-
Hannah M. Hazard m (2) Andrew J. A. Rose b
1878 in Rochester NY in 1907; RUTT

E. G. Rutan - d 1893; bur at Warwick Cem, Orange
Co. NY (cemetery records)

Earle Arthur Ruttan - (1880-1956) p/Charles E.
Ruttan-Emma M. Haight of Sophiasburg Ontario;

m Mary Etta Stratton (1888-1968) in Utica NY;
he was a dairy farmer; they lived in Syracuse
and he died in Madison Co. NY; he is bur at
Glenwood Cem, Oneida; COCHS; NYDC; RUTT

Ebenezer Retan - (1825-1904) p/Barnet Retan-
Sarah Drew m Phoebe Clark bc 1828; living in
Pulteney Town, Steuben Co. in 1850; moved to
Elgin Twp, Will Co. IL before 1870; STUCHS;
1850C; MEACH; 1900C

Edgar W. Rutan - b 1857 p/Rynier Rutan-Adelaide
Griggs of Danbury, Fairfield Co. CT; TMR;
1870C

Edith Rutan - b 1879 p/Samuel B. Rutan-Maria L.
Fitzgerald m Henry S. Sturr b 1880; living in
Paterson in 1910; 1910C

Edith Rutan - (1905-1995) p/George W. Rutan-Anna
Rockafellow m (1) Clyde E. Hood (1899-1964)
of Delancey NY in 1923 (2) Zealiah "Zeke"
Eighmey (1908-1980) of Delhi NY; she is listed as a student in Colchester, Delaware Co.
NY in 1915/16 (see Emma Rutan, below) she is
bur in Delaware Co.; CoMR; SSA; 1920C

Edith A. Rutan - (1885-1960) p/William E. Rutan-
Emma Jane Hopper m David Christie Zabriskie
(1879-1955) at Westwood, Bergen Co. in 1907;
Edith was born in NYC; both buried at the So.
Schraalenburgh Ref Chyd, Bergenfield NJ;
Note: PCHSQ has a second husband _____
Eisenhart which appears that appears to be
incorrect; LDS; ZAB; PCHSQ

Edith Margaret Rutan - b 1867 p/George W. Rutan-
Clara J. Cowles of Springfield MA; she died
in infancy; CVHM; LDS

Edward Rutan - m Alice Allison (1909-1949) of
CT they lived in Elmont, Nassau Co. NY; NYDC

Edward Ruttan - bc 1865 m Louise Humes b 1876;
living in Newark; (see Edward Norman Rutan,
below) 1920C

Edward Rutan - bc 1910 p/Frank E. Rutan-Candace
Johnson; CRC; 1920C

Edward Rutan - (1909-1982) resident of Denville,
Rockaway Twp, Morris Co. NJ; SSA

Edward Rutan - (1923-1998) resident of Port Jervis, Orange Co. NY; SSA

Edward A. Rutan - (1919-1952) p/Phay B. Rutan-
Mary C. Cromer; he was an industrial engineer
unm (Arthur C. Rutan) NYDC; 1920C

Edward Allen Rutan - (1859-1939) p/William H.
Rutan-Julia Dunning m (1) Susan Jane Dimon

(1863-1906) in 1883 (2) Louise Wollner Doerr
(1864-1940) in 1909; living in Port Jervis
1897-1920 and Gardena CA in 1937; all are bur
at Laurel Grove Cem, Port Jervis (cemetery
records); LDS; CDIR; EG; PJPL; 1900C; NYGBS;
NYMC

Edward J. Rutan - booking agent in NYC 1903;
probably the son of James B. Rutan-Mary Curry
of Queens Co. NYC; CDIR

Edward John Rutan - (1866-1916) p/Abraham W.
Rutan-Anna E. Case m (1) Susan Boyes d 1895
of Liverpool, England (2) Marguerite E. Vogel
b 1876 at Port Jervis in 1896; he was a
carpenter; Susan is bur at Laurel Grove Cem
(from her Obit in the *Port Jervis Union*)
CDIR; NYMC; NYGBS

Edward Norman Rutan - (1864-1924) p/Hudson Rutan
-Mary J. Bell of Sussex Co.; m Nellie Louise
"LuLu" Humes b 1876; he was an insurance
agent in Newark in 1909; they are bur at the
East Ridgelawn Cem, Clifton NJ.; Note in the
1920C he is listed as Edward N. Ruttan (Norman Rutan) 1875C; CDIR; NJBC; NYDC

Edward William Rutan - p/Reynier Rutan-Adelaide
Griggs of Springfield MA; TMR

Edward Wilson Rutan - (1869-1931) p/John Rutan-
Eunice Carman m (3) Rosetta Newell Bennett
(1869-1955) in 1884; (Alberta Moore)

Edythe Rutan - (1906-1969) p/Clifford Rutan-Rose
Nichols m _____ Douglas; living in Glastonbury CT in 1940 (from her father's Obit) she
died in Glastonbury; SSA

Effie Rutan - b 1802 p/Peter Rutan-Charity
Corselius (see OH listing) CBRF

Effie D. Rutan - (c1900-   ) p/Edward N. Rutan-
Louise Humes m Joseph Murphy after 1924; she
was living in Newark in 1924 before her marriage (Norman Rutan) CDIR

Effy Ruton - resident of NYC in 1860; 1860C

Eleanor Rutan - bc 1919 p/Layton Rutan-Ella R.
March of Port Jervis, Orange Co. NY; 1920C

Eleanor C. Rutan - (1843-1919) p/Peter Rutan-
Jane Sherman of Sullivan Co. NY; m Squire
Whitaker Breese (1835-1906) of Horseheads,
Chemung Co. NY in 1861; they died in Grey
Eagle MN; CAREY; 1850C; 1855C; MCRC

Eleanor L. Rutan - (1916-1967) p/Phay B. Rutan-
Mary C. Cromer, unm, she was a nurse; bur at
Woodlawn Cem, Elmira NY (Arthur C. Rutan);

NYDC

Eleanor Mary Rutan - b 1880 p/Charles H. Rutan-
Sarah Brower of Boston; m Willard Puckney;
FER; MCRC

Eleanor V. Rutan - (1876-1947) p/Samuel Rutan-
Sarah Everett of Brooklyn; m Benjamin Murphy
(1876-1928) in 1903; bur at St. John's Cem,
Middle Village, Queens Co. NY; BBC; CDAR;
EOVB

Eliza Retan - d 1840 m Janna Osgood b 1794 of
Barrington NY in 1817; he m (2) Susan Stein-
beck (3) Sarah J. Knapp ("Osgood Descendants")

Eliza Rutan - (1809-1856) m James Puff (1798-
1880) perhaps of Newfield NY (NSDAR appl #
119899 of Adah Puff Horton)

Eliza A. Rutan - b 1872 p/Cornelius Rutan-Elsa
A. Terwiliger m Warren H. Dunn b 1869 of
Mountaindale at Philipsport, Sullivan Co. NY
in 1891; Note: the 1880C has her b in 1876;
1880C; NYMC

Eliza A. Rutan - (1885-1960) (See Edith Rutan,
above); DFH

Eliza A. Rutan - (1885-1960) m David Christie
Zabriskie (1879-1955) in 1907; she was born
in NYC and he in River Edge NJ; she died in
Westwood NJ (see Edith A. Rutan, above) she
is bur at the So. Schraalenburg Chyd; Note;
another record says she was b in Kings Co.
NY; DFH

Eliza D. Retan - b 1832/33 p/Barnet Retan-Sarah
Drew m James Edwin Benedict b 1824 in 1854;
they moved to Lyon, Ionia Co. MI that year
("The Genealogy of the Benedicts in America")
Note: one record has her the daughter of Gilbert Retan-Melecta Drew which seems to be
incorrect; PUH; STUCHS; 1850C; MEACH

Eliza Jane Rutan - b 1835 p/Abraham G. Rutan-
Harriet Hinman of Brimfield MA; Note: LDS
has her mother as Harriet Hicks (Abraham's
second wife) but his CW pension file confirms
the above; LDS; USARCH

Eliza Jane Rutan - m Robert A. Martin in Essex
Co. NJ in 1842; NJHS; LDS

Elizabeth Rutan - b 1806 p/Peter C. Rutan-Charity Corselius of Sussex Co. NJ; moved with
her family to Butler Co. OH; BOGGS

Elizabeth Rutan - (1826-1915) p/Abram Rutan-Ann
Courter m William Farber in 1850; both bur at

the Longwell Cem, Vernon Twp, Sussex Co.
(cemetery records) MEACH; DMDV; DARLDC

Elizabeth Rutan - (1859-1909) p/Robert J. Rutan-
Adelia Lanterman of Sparta, Sussex Co.; m
Samuel Raynor; she died in NYC; 1860C; GSNJ;
CoDR

Elizabeth Rutan - (1830-1853) p/Daniel Rutan-
Lucy Compton; she may have moved with her
family to Wayne Co. PA; MCRC

Elizabeth Retan - p/Gilbert Retan-Melecta Drew;
she is mentioned in Gilbert's will and is
probably **Charlotte Elizabeth Retan**; MEACH

Ella M. Rutan - bc 1852 m Henry Monroe Whitfield
b 1852; lived in Belleville NJ; PCHSQ

Elizabeth Rutan - (1859-1901) m _____ Raynor;
she died in NYC; NYDC

Elizabeth R. Ruton - (1829-1854) p/William Ruton
-Sepronah Winston of Cobleskill, Scoharie Co.
NY m Jared Patrick in 1850; 1850C; DARLDC

Elizabeth M. Rutan - **Lizzie** b 1875 p/Albert C.
Rutan-Allie Vermule m Franklyn Greene b 1869
in 1890; they were living in Goshen NY in
1910 (from her father's Obit); Note: 1880C
has her born in 1872; 1880C; NYMC

Elizabeth Shoemaker Rutan - (c1825-1862) prob
daughter of James Rutan-Anna Melvina Shoemaker of Catlin NY; m John Truesdell Carpenter
(1808-1876) at Horseheads, Chemung Co. NY in
1849; he was born at Cornwall, Orange Co. NY;
both died at Horseheads (Geneanet)

Elizabeth Y. Rutan - author of "Before the In-
vasion" mentioned in "Americans in Process",
Boston, 1902; she is probably the wife of
William Lincoln Rutan (see below and CA listing)

Ella May Rutan - (1879-1896) p/Thomas B. Rutan-
Annie Heningham of Brooklyn; she died at
Cairo NY and is bur at Green-Wood Cem, Brook-
lyn (cemetery records) NYDC

Ella U. Ruttan - b 1875 p/Peter Ruttan-Sarah See
of Sydenham, Ontario; m Robert Forsythe b
1876 at Watertown NY in 1897

Ellen Reton - (1901-1977) of Boynton Beach FL;
SSA

Ellen Rutan - domestic in Watertown NY in 1892;
CDIR

Ellen E. Rutan - (1849-1927) p/Richard Rutan-
Mary Ann Fort of Fallsburgh, Sullivan Co. NY;
m Lewis Edgar Skinner (1857-1916) at West-

brookville; she died at Deerpark and he at
Cuddebackville, both Orange Co. NY; Note: LDS
has her born in 1836; LDS; GENFORUM

Ellen H. Rutan - bc 1906 p/Alexander Rutan-Lucy
Calhoun of Orange Co. NY; 1920C

Ellen M. Rutan - (1843-1919) p/Peter Rutan-Jane
Sherman (see Eleanor C. Rutan, above) PCHSB

Ellen Shandley Rheutan - b 1866 p/Abram A. Rheutan-Mary Hoyt Young of NYC; m George E. Ryan
at Worcester MA; (from her NSDAR appl #49465)
GSNJ

Ellsworth C. Rutan - (1865-1929) p/Sedgewick
Rutan-Hannah _____ m Martha Cortright (1866-
1929) of NJ; living in Minisink Twp, Orange
Co. NY in 1900; both bur at Unionville Cem;
(cemetery records) Note: DAR records have him
(1864-1927) (see Cyrus Ellsworth Rutan,
above) 1900C; MAV; PCHSQ

Ellsworth G. Rutan - (1854-1927) of Orange Co.
NY; SHBC

Elmer Rutan - bc 1861 p/William H. Rutan-Julia
Dunning (see Clarence E. Rutan, above)

Elmer Rutan - bc 1879 p/Albert Rutan-Allie
Bermule of Millburn, Essex Co. NJ; m Elizabeth _____ b 1881; living in Buffalo NY in
1920; (some info from his father's Obit)
1880C; 1920C

Elsie Rutan - (1894-1980) p/Samuel Rutan-Freda
_____ m Raymond Reilly (Janet Rutan Bowers)

Elsie Rutan - (1902-1926) p/George H. Rutan-
Lillian Britchford of Newark; she was the
step-daughter of Sydney Goldsmith; 1920C;
METC

Elsie Canady Rutan - b 1899 p/John L. Rutan-
Laura B. Conklin of Orange Co.; 1900C; NYBC

Elton Edgar Rutan - b 1891 p/William E. Rutan-
Emma J. Hopper; he was a resident of Hackensack NJ working in NYC in 1917; in 1940 he
was living in Allendale, Bergen Co. (Ree Hopper) 1900C; LDS; ZAB; CDIR

Elveretta Rutan - (1855-1907) p/Melancthon F.
Rutan-Eliza J. Smith of Staten Island, NYC, m
John Lindeman Dailey (1853-1921) at Tottenville. S.I. in 1881; he was born at Fleming-
ton, Hunterdon Co. NJ; LDS

Elwood Edward Rutan - (1879-1899) p/William H.
Ruttan-Hannah M. Hazard; he was a teamster;
drowned at Dexter NY; FMLWT; NYDC

Emily Caroline Rutan - b 1894 p/Harvey R. Rutan-

Emily Bergmann of NYC; m Henry Isaac Raymond
Harper; SML; 1900C
Emily Holmes Rutan - (1892-1949) p/William V.
Ruton-Laura L. Hazard; she was a clerk at
the General Council of the Presbyterian Ch in
the U.S.A. in NYC in 1933; Emily died in East
Orange and is bur at Rosedale Cem, Orange NJ;
(Pam Walling) CDIR; 1880C
Emma Reutan - b 1833 p/Benjamin Reutan-Clarissa
Moody of Amherst, Hampshire Co. MA; LDS
Emma Rutan - (1859-1860) of Newark NJ (Mortality
Schedule) 1860C
Emma Rutan - m Jefferson H. Price c1880; BFH
Emma Rutan - student at Colchester, Delaware Co.
NY in 1915/16 (from school records) (see
Edith Rutan, above)
Emma Rutan - m Delbert Howe at Delaware Co. NY
in 1922; CoMR
Emma Rutan - (1848-1901) p/John S. Rutan-Eliza-
beth Coles of Hainesville, Sussex Co. m Hiram
Transue/Transo b 1835 in 1870; he m (1) Abby
Ann Shay (1842-1868) Emma and Hiram lived in
Layton, Sussex Co.; she died (as a widow) in
Sandyston Twp and is bur at Bevans (Judy
Cochrane) SXHS
Emma Jane Rutan - bc 1848 p/Adam C. Rutan-Lor-
etta Conklin of Sussex Co.; 1860C; MCRC
Emma E. Rutan - (1838-1860) p/John Rutan-Abigail
Allen; she was a milliner who died at Mendham
Twp, Morris Co. NJ; her death noted in the
Genealogical Magazine of NJ v 73/2 and her
Obit in the *True Democratic Press* of Morris-
town 9 June 1860; 1860C
Emma G. Rutan - (1872-1900) p/Thomas B. Rutan-
Annie Hemingham of Brooklyn; m Joseph Jones;
Note: another record has her born in 1862;
1900C
Emma Irene Rutan - (1864-1934) p/Abram C. Rutan-
Ellen C. Drew m Walter I. Drew; living in
Vernon Twp, Sussex Co. in 1900; MEACH; GSNJ;
1900C
Emma Irene Rutan - bc 1863 p/Adam C. Rutan-Laur-
etta Conklin; 1880C; MCRC
Emma L. Ruton - (c1840-1911) p/Benjamin B. Ruton
-Joanna Vermilye; living with William V.
Ruton in East Orange NJ in 1888-90; she is
bur at Mt. Pleasant Cem, Newark (cemetery
records) CDIR; 1880C
Emmett H. Rutan - bc1912 p/Benjamin A. Rutan-

Mary E. Pittenger; 1920C; GSNJ

Enos Rutan - bc 1835 m Nancy J. Sayre bc 1841 of
OH at Elmira NY in 1865 (from the marriage
certificate of their daughter) Enos was born
in NJ; NYMC; 1880C

Enos W. Rutan - (1835-1921) p/Peter Rutan-Maria
Compton of PA; m Nellie Elwell (1849-1923) of
Luzerne Co. PA; he was a carpenter in Elmira
NY in 1900; bur at Woodlawn Cem the records
of which show Enos b 1825 and Nellie (1850-
1923); GSNJ; NEHGS: CDIR; 1920C; CHEMHS

Ernest Rutan - (1882-1940) p/Robert J. Rutan-
Emma Garrison m Sarah Elizabeth Lane (1879-
1947) at Middletown NY in 1902; both bur at
Warwick Cem, Orange Co. NY; Ernest was a
boilermaker and Sarah was born in Paterson;
EG; NYMC

Erwin Rutan - (1907-1977) of Oswego NY; SSA

Erwin Jesse Rutan - b 1876 p/James C. Rutan-
Amelia C. Breese of Elmira NY; m Helen Lang
in 1920; MCRC; USARCH

Estelle Rutan - d 1958 she m George Symington
and they lived in Astoria and Flushing,
Queens Co. NY (Jill Villatro)

Estelle May Rutan - (1872-1875) prob daughter of
Robert J. Rutan-Mary Maines; PCHSB

Esther Rutan - (1897-1974) her Obit in the
Morristown Daily Record

Esther Frances Rutan - (1834-1907) p/Abraham
Rutan-Susanna Hazen of Frankford Twp, Sussex
Co.; living in Lackawaxen Twp. Pike Co. PA in
1870 and Hainesville NJ and Port Jervis about
1885; m George Meyers d 1904 in 1854; prob a
widow by 1870; she is bur at Laurel Grove Cem
Port Jervis (from her Obit in the *Sussex
Independent* 14 June 1907) CBRF; LDS; JS;
1850C; 1870C

Ethel Rutan - b 1888 p/Robert J. Rutan-Emma
Garrison of Warwick, Orange Co.; m Martin M.
Smith b 1875; Note: PCHSP her her born in
1875; PCHSP; NYBC

Ethel Elizabeth Rutan - b 1893 p/Archie N. Rutan
-Mary E. Gray of Elmira NY; 1900C; NYBC

Ethel Emily Rutan - (1907-1988) p/Frank H. Rutan
-Katherine Schlee of Newark m Arthur Bremer
(1901-1974) at Jersey City; he was a printer;
she a retail buyer; they are bur at Princeton
Cem, Princeton NJ (Janet Rutan Bowers) 1920C

Ethel I. Rutan - (1915-1975) she was born in NY

49

and died in Los Angeles; CADRI

Ethel M. Ruttan - b 1876 p/William H. Ruttan-Hannah Maria Hazard of Picton, Ontario m Orson L. Adams b 1877 at Dexter, Jefferson Co. NY; FMLWT; NYMC; RUTT

Ethel Machette Rutan - (1896-1985) p/Melville M. Rutan-Ida Luff m J. Roscoe Wood; they were living in Summit NJ in 1920 and she later lived in East Hanover, Morris Co.; 1920C; SSA

Eugene Rutan - b 1872/76 p/John Rutan-Mary E. _____ m Eva _____ b 1877/80; he was a salesman in 1898 and a "flagman" in Montclair in 1904; 1880C; 1900C; 1920C; CDIR

Eugene Rutan - (1906-1937) p/John E. Rutan-Mary L. Hardy of Brooklyn; he was a farmer in Hempstead, Nassau Co. NY; he died in CT and bur at Evergreen Cem, Brooklyn; NYDC; 1920C

Eugene Rutan - (1910-1993) of Piscataway, Middlesex Co. NJ; SSA

Eva Rutan - (1871-1871) p/William H. Rutan-Hannah Winters of Newark; METC

Evalina Rutan - bc 1912 p/George W. Rutan-Anna Rockafellow of Sullivan Co. NY; 1920C

Evaline Rutan - b 1818 m William Beemer b 1820 in Sussex Co. NJ in 1836; Note: according to Morrow Co. OH vital records Evaline was the second wife of William Beemer, Sr. b 1784; he m (1) Elizabeth Decker in NJ in 1813; some of Evaline's children were born in Morrow Co.; LDS; CoMR

Evaline Rutan - b 1827 p/Samuel S. Rutan-Hannah Garrabrant m Thomas West in 1852; he died in Philadelphia; she was born in Springgarden, Essex Co. NJ; Note: LDS has the marriage in 1842; FER; MCRC; LDS

Evelyn Rutan - bc 1917 p/Harry Rutan-Mary _____ of Bayonne; 1920C

Everett J. Rutan - (1898/99-1975) p/John E. Rutan-Mary L. Hardy of Brooklyn NY; m Frances Schneider; living in Little Neck, Queens Co. NY in 1951 and lived in Madison CT; he died in IL (CT Death Index) Note: he may have wed a second time to Edna _____; EOVB; 1900C; SSA; PCHSQ

Everett J. Rutan - m Elizabeth M. Kern (1893-1965) she died at Huntington, Suffolk Co. NY and is buried at Linden Hill Cem, Maspeth, Queens Co. NY; NYDC

Fannie Rutan - Sarah Frances (1856-1890) p/Peter
R. Rutan-Hettie Longwell m Isaac Post (1848-
1948) of Union Valley in 1877 (per her father's will (see Sarah F., below); PCHSQ; MCNF;
PCHSP

Fannie Ruttan - b 1871 p/John S. Ruttan-Margaret
Bauter m Willie J. Flanders b 1871 in Lyme NY
in 1892; RUTT; NYMC

Fannie M. Rutan - b 1881 p/Peter R. Rutan-Frances L. Martin; 1900C

Fannie May Rutan - (1878-1915) p/Charles May
Rutan-Jennie Lee; bpt at Market St. M.E. Ch,
Paterson; m Frank Irving Ackerman (1877-1968)
in 1899; divorced in 1908; he m (2) Edith
Lorraine (Todd) Lynde at Calicoon NY in 1913
(Diane Devido) PCHSQ

Fanny A. Rutan - bc 1867 p/John H. Rutan-Elizabeth Snook of Sussex Co.; (Carol Van Buren)

Fletcher L. Rutan - he was living in Fitchburg
MA in 1888-90; CDIR

Flora Grace Ruttan - b 1883/84 p/Augustus M.
Ruttan-Annabell McDonald; living in Watertown
NY in 1902 m George E. Gould b 1883 in 1910
at Watertown; 1900C; CDIR; RUTT; NYMC

Flora Townsend Rutan - b 1879 p/James C. Rutan-
Amelia C. Breese m Edward Walling Beardsley b
1873 of Hillsdale NY in 1904; USARCH; 1880C;
MCRC

Florence D. Reton - b 1891 p/Fred S. Reton-Kate
L. Conklin; RET; 1900C

Florence E. Rutan - (1884-1886) buried at Cedar
Lawn Cem (in the A.R. Rutan plot) Paterson NJ
(from cemetery records)

Florence Irene Rutan - (1909-1984) m George
Grant Zabele (1910-1986); she was born at
Higginsville NY and he at Bennett's Corners
NY; both died at Oneida; CoMR; 1920C

Floyd Rutan - (1907-1976) p/Benjamin A. Rutan-
Mary E. Pittenger; GSNJ; 1920C; SSA

Floyd W. Rutan - b 1867 p/Sedgwick Rutan-Hannah
_____ of Wantage Twp, Sussex Co.; living
there in 1900 with step-mother Esther Crawford; LDS; 1900C

Frances Rutan - (1825-1889) p/Samuel H. Rutan-
Hannah Winne m Amos Williams at Belleville in
1854; she died at Lee, Berkshire Co. MA; LDS;
SRDRC

Frances Rutan - (1926-1997) she lived in Pleas-
antville, Atlantic Co. NJ and died in El Paso

TX; (see TX listing)

Frances Louisa Reton - m Jesse Cody in NYC in
1850; MAHER

Frank Rutan - (1894-1972) of East Orange, Essex
Co. NJ; SSA

Frank Rutan - d 1888 p/George A. Rutan-Elizabeth
A. Quimby; died in infancy; BDC

Frank Rutan - b 1895 p/Ellsworth Rutan-Martha
Cortright of Minisink Twp, Orange Co. NY;
(See Frank Ellsworth Rutan, below); 1900C

Frank C. Rutan - "Rudy" (1894-1968) p/Frank H.
Rutan-Carolina Seitler m Marion Cahill d 1978
he was a fireman in Newark in 1924 and later
a fire inspector; no children; they are bur
at Holy Sepulchre Cem , Newark (Janet Rutan
Bowers) CDIR; SSA

Frank E. Rutan - bc 1885 p/Edward Rutan of West
Orange NJ; m Condrance (Candace) Johnson b
1880 of Fredonia Twp, Sussex Co. in 1908; he
lived in Papakating Twp and South Wantage
(Betty Decamp) 1910C

Frank Ellsworth Rutan - (1896-1944) p/Ellsworth
C. Rutan-Martha Cortright of Minisink; he was
a mechanic in Unionville, Orange Co. and is
bur at Unionville Cem, Orange Co. NY; (cemetery records) MAV; NYDC; 1900C

Frank H. Rutan - b 1869 p/Henry K. Rutan-Sarah
Roe m (1) Carolina (Lena) Seitler (1870-1899)
(2) Katherine Schlee b 1863 in 1902 at the
Lutheran Evangelical & Reformed Ch of Newark;
he was a city employee there in 1924 (Janet
Rutan Bowers) CDIR; 1880C; 1900C; NJHS; 1920C

Frank S. Rutan - this is Frank C. Rutan (see
above

Franklin Rutan - (1891-1968) died in No. Plain-
field NJ; Note: this may be Franklin Guy
Rutan the son of Joel Rutan-Edith Weed of
Scranton PA; SSA

Fred Retan - (1872-1931) p/John Retan-Elizabeth
Cowley of Byron NY; he died at Rome, Oneida
Co. NY; NYDC

Fred Retan - m Myra Scrafford (1877-1959) of Ft.
Leyden NY; they lived in Cortland; Myra was
listed as a widow in the 1931 Homer city
directory; NYDC; CDIR

Fred Retan - (1911-1983) of Manlius, Onondaga
Co. NY; he may have m Doris _____ (1912-1986)
SSA

Fred S. Reton - b 1856 m Kate L. Conklin (1861-

1934) he was a secretary at Grand Central
Station in NYC in 1897 and living with Clarence G. Reton in 1900 where he was listed as
Frederick K. Reton; she was living in Manhas-
set, Nassau Co. NY at the time of her death
and is bur at Mt. Hope Cem, Westchester Co.;
CDIR; NYDC; 1900C

Frederick Rutan - (1878-1903) p/Warren Rutan-
Etta _____; he was a painter in Hawley PA and
he died in West Seneca NY; NYDC

Frederick Newman Rutan - b 1859 p/Nicholas Warr-
en Rutan-Sarah Marsh m Charlotte Crosby Starr
(1867-1961) at Monticello, Sullivan Co. NY in
1891; they were living in NYC in 1890 and in
Colonie, Albany Co. NY in 1900; he was born
in Newark NJ and was a minister; she died in
Fulton Co. NY; FER; 1900C; NYMC; CDIR; MCRC;
NYDC

Frederick Starr Rutan, Jr. (1923-1999) p/ Frederick Starr Rutan; he was born in MA and was
a 1st Lt, USAAF in WWII; captured 29 July
1944 and imprisoned at Stalag Luft 3, Sagan,
Silesia, Germany (WWII POWs) later he was a
Lt. Col who lived in Melbourne FL; he is bur
at Arlington Nat. Cemetery (cemetery records)

Frederick Wolcott Rutan - (1864-1939) p/James C.
Rutan-Amelia C. Breese of Elmira NY m Ida M.
Boone b 1868 at Horseheads, Chemung Co. NY in
1887; moved to DE (see DE listing) he was an
agent for the Pullman Co.; he died in Elmira
and is bur at Maple Grove Cem, Horseheads;
his death certificate shows his widow as Edna
Armstrong (Arthur C. Rutan) NYDC; 1880C; MCRC

G.B. Ruton - resident of Paxton, Worcester Co.
MA; 1860C

Garret Herring Rheutan - b 1842 p/Abraham Rheutan-Mary Storms m Mary Edmonston at Newburgh
NY in 1866; superintendent in Hartford in
1882 and a foreman at Stearns Mfg. Co. in
Erie PA in 1891; CDIR; PCHSQ; GSNJ

George Rutan - p/Harmon Rutan-Chloe Lobdell;
PCHSQ

George Reton - b 1827 p/Daniel Reton-Sarah Moore
of NYC; m Katherine _____ of the British West
Indies; he was a "coppersmith" living with
his mother in NYC in 1850; GENEX; 1860C; RET;
LDS

George Reton - "cooper" in NYC in 1854 and 1869;

living in NJ in 1873; CDIR

George Reton - m Catherine R. Swainson in 1853
in NYC; MAHER

George Ruton - (1826-1918) m Clara P. Pinkney
(1831-1911) both are bur at Evergreen Cem,
Morristown NJ (cemetery records)

George Rutan - bc 1849 p/Isaac Miers Rutan-
Elizabeth Aggear; 1850C; FER

George Rutan - m Ella _____ (1884-1951) of
France; they lived in Summitville, Mamakating
Town, Sullivan Co. NY; NYDC

George Rutan - (1890-1944) m Anna _____; they
lived in Delhi, Delaware Co. NY; NYDC

George Rutan - (1898-1905) p/Lemuel J. Rutan-
Rosa B. Wakefield; he is bur at Keyserville
PA; MEACH

George Rutan - (1901-1975) of Dunellen, Middlesex Co. NJ; SSA

George Ruttan - (1891-1966) of NY; he lived in
FL; SSA

George Ruton - (1912-1954) of NY; SSA

George Ruton, Jr. - bc 1913 p/George Ruton-Emma
_____; 1920C

George Rutan - p/Benjamin A. Rutan-Mary E. Hardy
of Sussex Co.; living in Perth Amboy NJ in
1943 (from his father's Obit)

George Rutan - m Cornelia Mather (1868-1928)
they lived at New Rose Gap, Mamakating Town,
Sullivan Co. NY (see George Washington Carman
Rutan, below)

George A. Ruton - m Maria J. Parker in 1866 at
Allen St. Methodist Ch, NYC; NYCMM

George A. Retan - clerk living at W. 2nd St, NYC
in 1869; CDIR

George A. Ruton - (1832-1858) p/William Ruton-
Sepronah Winston of Cobleskill, Schoharie Co.
NY (Shafer Bible-DAR); 1850C

George Almond Ruttan - (1874-1947) p/William H.
Ruttan-Hannah Maria Hazard m Elizabeth M.
Wright (1875-1954) at Sacketts Harbor NY in
1898; truck-driver and farmer; he died at
Dexter, she died at Loudonville, Albany Co.
NY; both are bur at Dexter Cemetery; NYDC;
RUTT; FMLWT

George Abraham Rutan - (See Abraham George
Rutan, above)

George B. Rutan - living in NYC in 1925; he is
related to Joseph V. Rutan; CDIR

George B. Ruton - b 1864 p/Samuel C. Ruton-Alm-

ira _____ of Huntington, Suffolk Co. NY;
1870C
George C. Rutan - b 1865 p/Hudson Rutan-Mary J.
Bell of Sparta, Sussex Co.; living in New
Brunswick NJ in 1920; 1875C; LDS; 1920C
George C. Rutan - resident of Montclair, Essex
Co. NJ in 1932; CDIR
George Dunn Rutan - (1875-1946) p/Henry K. Rutan
-Sarah Roe of Newark; m (2) Henrietta Hepp bc
1895 about 1913 (Janet Rutan Bowers) 1880C;
1920C
George Dunn Rutan, Jr. - **"Dutch"** (1915-1980) p/
George D. Rutan-Henrietta Hepp m Rita Cahill;
they are bur at Holy Cross Cem, No. Arlington
Hudson Co. NJ (cemetery records) JRB; 1920C
George E. Rutan - (1836-1861) bur in the Wood-
bridge NJ M.E. Trinity Chyd (cemetery rec-
ords) NJHS
George E. Rutan - m Sarah Martin at Rahway,
Union Co, NJ in 1859; LDS
George E. Rutan - (1916-1963) p/William H. Rutan
-Annie F. Keegan of Boston; he died in Los
Angeles; LDS; CADRI
George E. Ruton - b 1849 m Amelia Engleman b
1851; Note: mother's maiden name from son
George's death certificate; 1880C; 1900C; BDC
George E. Ruton - (1873-1945) p/George Ruton-
Amelia Engleman; factory worker who died in
Brooklyn; bur at Flushing Cem, Queens Co. NY;
1880C; BDC
George E. Ruton - (1836-1860) p/John Rutan-Abi-
gail Allen; PCHSP
George Edward Rutan - (1888-1953) p/John Henry
Roughtean-Mary Ellen Cullen of Boston; he d
in Los Angeles; LDS; CADRI
George Henry Rutan - (1872-1907) p/William H.
Rutan-Hannah Winters of Newark; m Lillian
Britchford b 1875; after George's death she
married Sidney A. Goldsmith at Newark in 1913
1880C; PCHSP; CDIR; METC; 1900C
George Henry Rutan, Jr. - (1907-1912) p/George
H. Rutan-Lillian Britchford of Newark; METC
George Hudson Rutan - bc 1912 p/Edward Rutan-
Louise Humes of Newark (Norman Rutan) 1920C
George Matthew Retan - (1889-1970) p/Olney A.
Retan-Mary Sornberger of Seeley Creek NY; a
physician m (1) Emilie Weller (1889-1944) of
Clay NY in 1909; divorced (2) Kathryn Sears
Partridge (1892-1967) in 1928; (from "Central

New York-An Inland Empire" v. 4)   he died in
Orange Co. CA; SSA; NYDC
George O. Retan - d 1944, from NY, he was a 2nd
Lieut. 101st Airborne, winner of the Bronze
Star, died in the Netherlands and is bur at
the Netherlands American Cemetery, Margraten
Holland; USARCH
George S. Ruton - b 1849 m Amelia Engleman b
1851 in NY at the Madison St. German Presbyt
CH NYC IN 1871; he was a "bookbinder" in
Brooklyn and NYC as late as 1890; CDIR; 1900C
George W. Ruttan - (1842-1914) p/Abraham Ruttan-
Mary Ann See of Ontario; m Lucilia Danley b
1831 at Lymetown, Jefferson Co. NY; he is bur
at Pt. Peninsula Cem; Note: his death certif-
icate names his mother as Mary Ann Knight;
1900C; NYDC; RUTT; MEACH
George W. Rutan - (1839-1927) p/Henry Rutan-
Sarah Courter m Sarah J. _____ b 1833; he d
at Boonton, Morris Co,; bur at Laurel Grove
Cem, Totowa, Passaic Co. NJ; PCHSP; METC
George W. Rutan - b 1874 p/Cornelius Rutan-Elsa
A. Terwiliger of Wurtsboro, Sullivan Co. NY
m Mida Rockefeller (1876-1900) of Paterson NJ
in 1895 (2) Anna Rockafellow (1881/5-1960) in
1902; he was a stonemason; Anna died at Delhi
Delaware Co.; 1880C; COMR; NYMC; NYDC; 1920C
George W. Ruton - clerk in NYC in 1849; "grain-
measurer" in 1855; CDIR
George W. Ruton - shoemaker in Albany NY in 1891
CDIR
George W. Rutan - m Clara Jane Cowles in Hingham
MI; LDS
George Washington Carman Rutan - (1876-1949)
p/Peter S. Rutan-Lydia F. Carman m (1) Ella
_____ (2) Cornelia _____ in 1920; Note: there
is a marriage certificate reporting his nupt-
ials with Blanche Mae McGuire b 1887 at Phil-
lipsport, Sullivan Co. in 1905; she was from
Napanock; CAREY; 1880C; 1900C; NYMC
Gerard Rutan - bc 1919 p/Francis Rutan-Mary
_____ of NYC; 1920C
Gerard Rutan - (1919-1972) of NY; SSA
Gideon W. Rutan - (1826-1897) p/David Rutan-Caty
Russell m Mary Ann Litts (c1823-1907) in 1843
he was a farm laborer; both bur at Sandyston
Cem, Hainesville, Sussex Co.; Note: several
records have his year of death as 1896; his
gravestone says 1897; CRC; MEACH; 1860C; SXHS

1875C; SCMR

Gilbert Retan - (1814-1859) p/Barnet Rutan-Sarah
Drew m Matilda (Melecta) Drew (c1829-1865) in
1847; he was a farmer in Pulteney Town, Steuben Co. NY; he is bur at the Drew Cem, Urbana
after Gilbert's death Melecta m Gabriel Morehouse; STUCHS; 1850C; 1855C

Gladys Ruton - b 1898 p/William E. Ruton-Eliza-
beth Daly of NYC; she was there in 1925;
1900C; CDIR

Grace Rutan - bc 1871 p/Adam C. Rutan-Lauretta
Conklin of Sussex Co.; 1880C

Grace Rutan - b 1871 p/Abram C. Rutan-Ellen C.
Drew m John Giveans Truesdell (1864-1919) in
Vernon NJ in 1898; he was in the railroad
business born in East Orange NJ; he died in
Vernon; PCHSP; LDS

Grace Rutan - (1871-1969) of NY; SSA

Grace Rutan - p/Thomas B. Rutan-Alice Standerwick of Brooklyn NY; CDIR

Grace Rutan - bc 1910 p/Harry R. Rutan-Nellie M.
Sheridan of Rochester NY; m Eugene Roth
(Thomas M. Rutan) 1920C

Grace E. Ruton - (1895-1950) prob daughter of
Joseph F. Ruton-Mercedes _____ she is bur at
Hillside Cem, Lyndhurst NJ (cemetery records)
(Norman Rutan)

Grace Olive Retan - b 1876 p/Thomas Retan-Emma-
line E. Hubbard of Jefferson Co. NY; m Fred
Edmund Sisson at Rutland NY in 1897; 1880C;
USARCH; NYMC

Greene Rutan - (1833-1833) p/Peter C. Rutan-
Maria Compton; MCRC

Gussie Rutan - p/George Dunn Rutan and his first
wife (Janet Rutan Bowers)

Halsey Rutan - b 1838 p/Samuel Rutan-Sarah Adams
of Branchville, Sussex Co. he was a farm
laborer in 1860 and later a school-teacher in
Newark; JS; 1860C; MEACH

Hannah Retan - b 1815 p/Barnet Rutan-Sarah Drew
m John M. Clark in Steuben Co.; STUCHS; PUH

Hannah Rutan - m Stephen Pierson in 1822; this
prob is Hannah Shipman, widow of Abraham
Rutan; MCRC

Hannah Rutan - b 1830 in NJ; m Phineas J. Inslee
(1834-c1902) ("L.I. Ancestry of William
Jones") Phineas was from Woodbridge; Note:
one record has her born in 1840; PNJHS;

ROOTSW
Hannah B. Rutan - (1816-1842) p/Daniel Rutan-
Jane Caldwell of Long Hill, Morris Co. NJ;
she died in Newark, unm; LITT; LDS
Hannah Jane Rutan - **Jennie** (1862-1880) p/John A.
Rutan-Eunice Carman m Charles Cortwright at
the First Presbyt Ch of Wantage in 1880; they
lived in Colesville; LDS; JS; EG
Hannah Jane Rutan - p/Isaac M. Rutan-Elizabeth
Aggear m William Young; FER
Hannah Jane Rutan - (1848-1869) she died in
Washington Twp, Bergen Co. (mortality sched-
ule) 1870C
Harmon Beekman Retan - m Frances Maria Ball in
NYC in 1840; NYCMM
Harmon E. Rutan - (1876-1913) p/Peter Rutan-
Sarah Spangenburg, he lived in Branchville,
Sussex Co.; BRVC
Harold Rutan - (1895-1896) p/Joseph V. Rutan-
Dorothy M. Davis (Russ Hauver)
Harold C. Rutan - (1918-1973) p/Chauncey Rutan-
Diana Sigafoos; LIZR; 1920C
Harold Duane Rutan - (1898-1956) p/David D.
Rutan-Almira Corrigan of Newark; m Sylva
Downs d 1969; lived in Huntington Station,
Suffolk Co. NY; Harold died in Newark and bur
at Evergreen Cem, Elizabeth NJ; GSNJ; WWW;
PCHSQ; NYTO
Harold J. Rutan - (1919-1998) p/Harry E. Rutan-
Olive Miller m Hester Davidson; IKE
Harriet Retan - living in the 11th Ward, Brook-
lyn in 1860; 1860C
Harriet Ruton - (1801-1879) p/William Ruton-
Rachel Brower of Tarrytown NY; m William
Jackson Walker (1793-1867) in 1820; they liv-
ed in Cobleskill, Schoharie Co. NY (Roscoe:
"History of Schoharie Co.") Note: DAR appls
of Beverly Mosher (1966) and Amy J. Walker
Leeds have slightly different dates; he was
from Greene Co. NY; WHIT
Harriet Rutan - b 1833 p/Daniel Rutan-Lucy Comp-
ton; she may have moved with her family to
Wayne Co. PA; MCRC
Harriet Rutan - m Archibald J. Gamble (1914-
1992) of Mahwah, Bergen Co. NJ; he was bur at
Redeemer Cem, Mahwah (from his Obit in the
Bergen Record 29 Oct 1992) he was a mechanic
Harriet C. Rutan - (1846-1927) p/Samuel Rutan-
Sarah Adams of Branchville, Sussex Co. m

Albert L. Williams (1843-1922) of Frankford
Twp in 1863; he was a stonemason; she died in
Wantage and they are bur at the Branchville
Cem; Note: his Obit in the *N.J. Herald* says
that they were married in 1865 (Mark Daley
Genealogy)

Harriet E. Rutan - b 1843 p/Abraham G. Rutan-
Harriet Hicks of Greece, Monroe Co. NY; 1850C

Harriet J. Rutan - (1874-1948) p/Samuel Rutan-
Sarah Everett m Francis Cornelius Skinner
M.D. (1865-1929) in Brooklyn in 1897; tradit-
ion says her middle name was Jane but her
daughter Virginia's SS5 says it was Josephine; BMC

Harriett P. Rutan - (1826-1917) died in Corning
NY; bur at Woodlawn Cem, Elmira; this is prob
Harriet Perry the wife of David Rutan; CHEMHS

Harriet R. Ruton - b 1861 p/Samuel C. Ruton-Alm-
ira _____ of Huntington, Suffolk Co. NY;
1870C

Harriet S. Rutan - (1857-1913) p/Henry K. Rutan-
Lucetta May Roe of Paterson NJ m Andrew P.
Haldane (1855-1921); both bur at Cedar Lawn
Cem, Paterson (cemetery records) METC; 1870C;
PCHSP

Harrison Rutan - (1896-1940) p/Harrison Rutan-
Nellie Sheridan; unm, he is bur at Holy
Sepulchre Cem, Rochester NY; 1900C; 1920C;
NYDC

Harrison M. Rutan - b 1888 p/Charles W. Rutan-
Mary E. Roosa of Port Jervis, Orange Co. NY;
NYBC

Harrison Reynier Rutan - p/Rynier S. Rutan-
Adelaide M. Griggs of Brimfield MA; m Margaret Ellen (Nellie) Sheridan (1865-1943); they
lived in Rochester; he was a compositor bur
at New Hope Cem; CDIR; 1900C; USARCH; 1920C

Harry Rutan - (1904-1967) of Broome Co. NY (see
Hiram Edward Rutan, below) SSA

Harry A. Rutan, Jr. - (1897-1926) p/Harry A.
Rutan-Leona McCabe; WWI soldier, he lived in
Oceanside, Nassau Co. NY and he died at the
Veterans Hospital, Wappinger, Dutchess Co.
NY; EOVB

Harry D. Rutan - (1878-1923) p/David Rutan-Mary
E. Westervelt; he died in CA (see CA listing)

Harry E. Rutan - b 1881 p/Daniel E. Rutan-Elizabeth Reynolds m Vinnie L. Williams b 1876 at
Binghamton NY in 1904; he was a salesman;

Vinnie was from Uniondale PA; NYMC

Harry Elmer Rutan - (1887-1946) p/Joseph Rutan-Fannie L. Martin m Olive C. Miller (1891-1958); living in Netcong, Morris Co. in 1920; he is bur at Franklin Plains Cem; SCDR; CRC; 1900C; 1920C; GMNJ

Harry Frederick Rutan - (1896-1885) p/Frank H. Rutan-Carolina Seitler m Katherine Flanagan b 1905 of Eldred PA; he was a chauffeur in Newark in 1924 and later they were both in sales both are bur at Hollywood Cem, Union NJ (Janet Rutan Bowers) 1900C; CDIR; SSA

Harry Ira Rutan - (1905-1964) p/Lemuel J. Rutan-Rosa B. Wakefield; m Dorothy Boydell; he was working in Paterson in 1928 and lived in Fairlawn NJ; PCHSQ; COCHS; CDIR; 1920C

Harry K. Rutan - (1905-1986) p/James D. Rutan-Emma Murray m Elsie Terry (1909-1977) of Cornwall NY in 1928; he was a manager who was born and died in Newburgh, Orange Co. NY; 1920C; SSA; POCGS; NYDC

Harry R. Rutan - b 1866 p/Rynier S. Rutan-Adeline M. Griggs of Brimfield MA (see Harrison Reynier Rutan, above)

Harry Rhodes Rutan - (1889-1889) p/Charles W. Rutan-Mary ?Roosa of Port Jervis; he is bur at Laurel Grove Cem, Port Jervis; NYDC

Harvey Rutan - (1837-1908) a "truckman" living with John Vanderhoff at Brookhaven L.I., NY in 1900; he died at Patchogue, Suffolk Co.; NYDC; 1900C

Harvey Joseph Rutan - (1889-1974) p/Harvey R. Rutan-Emily A. Bergmann m Lydia Lizzie Woodbury in NYC in 1910; CRC; NYMC

Harvey Raymond Rutan - (1866-1923) p/John H. Rutan-Eliza Banker of Passaic Co. NJ; m Emily ("Minnie") Agnes Bergmann (1869-1954) in NYC c1884; they were living there in 1890-1900; he was a "ferry-man" amd later a driver and delivery man; he was living in Guttenburg Hudson Co. NJ in 1920 where he died; bur at Holy Name Cem, Jersey City; SML; CDIR; 1920C

Hattie Rutan - b 1898 p/Peter R. Rutan-Frances L. Martin m _____ Kern (from her brother Henry's Obit)

Hattie M. Rutan - b 1865 p/Enos Rutan-Nancy J. Sayre m Henry W. Carmer b 1860 at Elmira in 1887; Henry was born in Litchfield PA; NYMC

Hazel A. Rutan - (1896-1942) she died in Queens

Co. NY (see PA listing)

Hazel Bertha Rutan - b 1890 p/Wilber Rutan-Jennie Babcock; NYBC; 1900C

Helen Rutan - (1855-1871) p/Daniel Rutan-Lucy Compton; she may have moved with her family to Wayne Co. PA; MCRC

Helen Rutan - living in NYC in 1933; CDIR

Henry Rutan - (1800-1847) p/Abraham Rutan-Rebecca _____ m Sarah Courter in 1821; as a widow she married Jacob Welch in Paterson in 1848; Note: according to the genealogy of Abram A. Rheutan Henry was the son of another Abraham Rutan, the son of John Rutan; AAR; PCHSP

Henry Rheutan - p/John W. Rheutan-Ann Welch of NYC; GSNJ

Henry Rutan - b 1829 p/Daniel Rutan-Hannah Corselius of Sussex Co.; m Eliza Hackett b 1849; he was a CW soldier, Pvt., Co. I, 15th NJ Infantry; he moved to Bradford Co. PA (see PA listing); NJG; NYMC; EG; 1850C; USARCH; NJCW; 1900C

Henry Rutan - (1853-1856) p/John H. Rutan-Elizabeth Ann Smith; PDRC; ZAB

Henry Reton - (1838/44-1856) p/Daniel D. Reton-Ellen _____; RCFL

Henry Rutan - m Eliza _____; NKG

Henry Rutan - (1895-1973) p/Peter R. Rutan-Frances L. Martin m Anna Holmer (1892-1987) he was a WWI soldier and later owned a coal and oil business in Dover, Morris Co.; his Obit was in the *Morristown Daily Record*; 1900C; SSA

Henry Abraham Rutan - (1810-1872) p/Abraham Rutan-Margaret Ennis m Harriet Burnett (c1814-1878) of Rockaway Twp, Morris Co. NJ; married in Paterson in 1832; lived in Newark, moved to Williamsburg, Kings Co. NY about 1845 and to Brooklyn about 1856; he was a "master mason"; CDAR; 1870C; BDC; PCHSP

Henry C. Retan - bc 1843 p/James Retan-Urania Conover of Seneca Co. NY; he later moved to MI (see MI listing) (Jonathan Gushen) 1850C

Henry C. Reton - (1892-1981) of NY and later he lived in Boynton Beach, Palm Beach Co. FL; (see next item) SSA

Henry C. Reton - (1892-1982) p/Fred S. Reton-Kate L. Conklin m Dorothy Walz; 1900C; RET

Henry C. Rutan II - (1927-2000) m Mary Flynn

about 1948; he was born in Toms River NJ and she in Franklin (from his Obit in a local newspaper)

Henry Kasine Rutan - (1818-1865) p/Robert Rutan-Mary Courter m (1) Sarah Van Giesen (2) Lucetta May Roe, a widow (1818-1882) in 1842 per her will; he was a harness-maker; she was born in Parsippany or Springfield NJ; both are bur at Cedar Lawn Cem, Paterson (cemetery records) Note: Henry's middle name was found in PCHSP but is not absolutely confirmed, an important point in connection with the Kasine controversy; FH; PCHSP; ROOTSW; METC

Henry K. Rutan - (1852-1885) p/Henry K. Rutan-Lucetta M. Roe of Paterson; bur at Cedar Lawn Cem (cemetery records) LDS; PCHSP

Henry Kingsland Rutan - (1878-1943) p/Henry K. Rutan-Sarah Hageman m Regina Clara Brawn b 1877 at Newark in 1903; resident of Bloomfield, Essex Co. NJ in 1932; CDIR; POV

Henry N. Rutan - b 1883 p/Cornelius Rutan-Elsa A. Terwiliger of Sullivan Co. NY; m Lovinia A. Munn (1886-1956) at Wurtsboro in 1904; living in Oneonta NY in 1942; he was a painter; Note: his death certificate identifies her as Lorenia (1888-1956); they died at Ballston, Saratoga Co. NY; NYMC; NYDC; SSA; 1900C; CDIR

Henry Terhune Rutan - (1841-1919) p/Daniel Rutan-Maria Ackerman; he lived in IL, IA and NE (see those listings) AFH; CRC; 1900C

Henry Walden Retan - (1897-1972) p/Olney A. Retan-Mary Sornberger m Dorothy Brooks (1900-1971) of IL; he was a physician; both are bur at Oakwood Cem, Syracuse NY; NYDC

Herbert Rutan - b 1918 p/Lucius W. Rutan-Edna _____; 1920C

Herbert Rutan - (1901-1960) m May Denninger b in Montclair NJ; he was a "Collector" for Public Service E&G and a resident of North Caldwell NJ in 1932; he died in Newark; CDIR; PCHSQ

Herbert Allen Ruttan - (1874-1967) p/Alonzo Ruttan-Eliza Jane Rankin of Shannonville, Ontario; m Clara Pearle Bishop (1881-1960) at Syracuse NY in 1899; he was a salesman who moved to TX; he is bur at Resthaven Memorial Cem, Midland TX; RUTT

Herbert M. Rutan - bc 1881 p/James R. Rutan-Han-

nah Machette m Lillian Neary (1876-1939) of
Verona NJ; he was a purveyor of meats in
Morristown in 1923; she is bur at Evergreen
Cem, Morristown (cemetery records) 1920C;
CDIR; PCHSQ

Herbert W. Rutan - (c1902-1962) p/Herbert M.
Rutan-Lillian Neary; his Obit is in the *Morristown Daily Record* 7 Sep 1962; 1920C

Hester Rutan - (1805-1883) of Sullivan Co. NY;
m Stephen James Sears (Tawni Bell)

Hester Rutan - p/Richard Rutan; she is bur at
Walkill Cem (cemetery records)(Hilda Walrath)

Hester Rutan - m George Myers in 1880; EG; CoMR

Hester Rutan - bc 1866 p/Enos Rutan-Nancy J.
Sayre; 1880C

Hettie Rutan - b 1882 p/Abram W. Rutan-Kate
Ayres of Tuttles Corner m Allen S. Knight of
Fredon Twp, Sussex Co.; EG; MCRC

Hilda Jane Rutan - Hulda b 1831 p/Abraham Rutan-
Susannah Hazen of Sussex Co.; m (1) Aaron
Beegle in Sparta (2) Samuel Hewy (Hooey) JS;
MEACH; CRAWN

Hiram Edward Rutan - Harry (1904-c1964) p/Edward
N. Rutan-Louise Humes of Newark; he served in
WWII and later lived with his aunt in Johnson
City NY; he died in Miami (Norman Rutan)
1920C

Hiram W. Ruton - b 1854 p/Charles Ruton-Martha
E. Smith; he was a "steamboat clerk" in
Poughkeepsie NY in 1870; 1860C; 1870C

Horace Rutan - "wood dealer" in NYC in 1869;
(see next entry) CDIR

Horace Rutan - b 1825 m Mary E. Smith b 1823; he
was born in NJ and was a private watchman
living in NYC in 1880 and Newark in 1900;
Note: Mary may be Mary C. Barnes, a widow
(see next entry) 1860C; 1880C; 1900C

Horace E. Rutan - (1825-1915) p/Henry Rutan-
Sarah Courter m Mary Caroline Barnes b 1836
in 1853 and 1856; NYCMM shows two separate
marriages; lived in NYC, Hempstead L.I. and
Newark NJ; he died in Hempstead or Rockville
Center L.I. NY Note: his death certificate
says his father was John Rutan; MEACH; NYCMM;
NYDC

Howard Rutan - b 1866 p/Calvin Rutan-Rachel Sta-
er of Belleville; he was a gardener there in
1890 and living in Nutley in 1920; CDIR; LDS;
1920C

Howard Rutan - p/George D. Rutan-Henrietta Hepp
(Janet Rutan Bowers)
Hulda Rutan - b 1871 moved from NJ to Northampt-
on Co. PA; 1900C
Huntington Rutan - b 1907 p/Frederick N. Rutan-
Charlotte C. Starr; GSNJ

Ida Rutan - d 1929 p/John A. Rutan-Eunice Carman
m Lewis Decker; she died at Phillipsburg NJ
(from her Obit)
Ida Ellen Rutan - (1874-1909) p/William H.
Rutan-Julia Dunning of Port Jervis, Orange Co
NY m William H. Wagner b 1873 at Port Jervis
in 1909; he was an architect in NYC and they
were living in Brooklyn when she died there
at the German Hospital; CoDR; 1880C; PJUGO;
NYMC
Ida Jeannette Rutan - (see Jeannette Ida Rutan,
below)
Ida M. Retan - (1855-1910) p/Mathew K. Retan-
Margaret A. Mitchel of Millerton PA; she died
at Elmira; NYDC
Ida M. Rutan - (1863-1864) p/James C. Rutan-Ame-
lia C. Breese of Horseheads, Chemung Co. NY;
Note: her gravestone identifies her as Ida A.
Rutan (Arthur C. Rutan) MCRC; NYDC
Ida M. Rutan - b 1877 and living in Port Jervis
in 1900; 1900C
Ida M. Rutan - (1892-1917) prob daughter of
Peter Rutan-Lydia Carman; bur at Poplar Grove
Cem, Phillipsport, Orange Co. NY; BHS
Ira M. Rutan - (see Harry Ira Rutan, above)
Irene Rutan - (1885-1928) p/Samuel Rutan-Sarah
Everett of Brooklyn NY; m Robert Grist Kittle
(1884-1954) a lighting salesman; she is bur
at St. John's Cem, Middle Village, Queens Co.
NY; he died at Riverhead, Suffolk Co. NY and
is bur at Cold Spring NY (Nick Roach) EOVB;
1900C
Irene Rutan - (1903-2001) her maiden name was
Marks (her Obit in the *Ballston Spa Daily
Gazette* (NY) 3 Jan 2001)
Irvine Dennison Ruttan - b 1911 p/Damon E. Rutt-
an-Marion B. Dennison of Oneida Co. NY; RUTT
Irving Ruttan - (1911-1976) he was born in NY
and died at Long Branch, Monmouth Co. NJ;
(see prior entry) SSA
Irwin Rutan - (see Erwin Jesse Rutan (above)
Isaac Rutan - b 1845 p/Abram Rutan-Mary L. See

of Canada m Sylvia S. Sammons b 1850 at
Watertown NY in 1885; he was a mechanic;
NYMC

Isaac Rutan - a carpenter in Rochester in 1891;
CDIR

Isaac Lewis Rheutan - b 1867 p/Abram A. Rheutan-
Mary Hoyt Young m Gertrude Rich Everett b
1870 in 1893 at Worcester MA ("Genealogy of
Richard Rich") GSNJ; 1900C; CDIR

Isaac Miers Rutan - b 1815 p/Samuel S. Rutan-
Hannah Garrabrant m Eliza(beth) Aggear; he
was a ship's carpenter in Newark in 1840;
living in NYC in 1847 and Vallejo CA in 1860;
(see CA listing) FER; 1850C; 1860C

Isabel Mary Rutan - b 1890 p/Harrison R. Rutan-
Nellie Sheridan m Frank Oliver McLain b 1889
in Rochester NY in 1910; NYMC

Isabella Rutan - **Isabelle** (1848-1931) p/Richard
Rutan-Elizabeth Wager; living in Newark in
1887; NDIR; PCHSP; 1850C

Isabelle Rutan - p/Reynier S. Rutan-Adelaide
Griggs of Brimfield MA (Thomas Rutan)

J.B. Ruttan - b 1865 m Rozella Edwards; LDS

Jacob Rutan - (1812-1892) p/John Rutan-Rachel
Vanderbeek m Helena (Ellen) Ackerman (1813-
1887) in 1832 at Stonehouse Plains Ref Ch,
Bloomfield, Essex Co.; they lived in Pater-
son; he was a stonemason and a constable in
Manchester Twp, Passaic Co. (info from his
will and her dc) they are bur at Cedar Lawn
Cem, Paterson (cemetery records) 1850C;
PCHSP; BCMR; 1880C

Jacob Rutan - stonemason in NYC in 1844; CDIR

Jacob Reton - b 1822 p/Daniel Reton-Sarah Moore
m Kate _____ from PA; GENEX; LDS; GSNJ

Jacob Rutan - resident of Bloomfield, Essex Co.
NJ in 1830; 1830C

Jacob Rutan - resident of Phelps, Ontario Co. NY
in 1850; 1850C

Jacob W. Rutan - (1858-1931) p/Martin Rutan-
Hannah Jane Wilson of Sussex Co.; he was living with his mother in Montague Twp in 1900;
he was born and died in Frankford Twp and was
bur at Beemerville Cem (from his Obit) Note:
the 1900C has him born in 1865; EG; 1860C;
1900C

James Retan - (1825-1896) p/Peter Retan-Polly
Hatt of Seneca Co. NY; m Urania Conover (1822

-1915); they were living in Lodi, Seneca Co.
in 1850 and moved to Lenawee Co. MI before
1858; Note: in the 1850C the surname is
Rattan (Jonathan Gushen) (see MI listing)
LHRL; 1850C

James Rutan - m Catherine Fox at Essex Co. NJ
in 1824; the marriage was registered at the
Salem Ch of the Evangelical Assn, Lancaster
PA; ECMR

James Reton - (1831-1856) p/Daniel Reton-Sarah
Moore; he was a coppersmith living with his
mother in the 18th ward of NYC in 1850;
GENEX; SUSESS

James Rutan - (1898-1970) of Balmville, Orange
Co. NY; (see James Dudley Rutan, Jr., below)
SSA

James Rutan - (1909-1972) of Providence RI; SSA

James Rutan - m Sarah E. _____ (1822-1848) in
NJ; NJHS

James Rutan - (1909-1972) a resident of South
Providence RI; SSA

James Rutan - (1918-1970) of MA; SSA

James A. Rutan - (1898-1963) p/Harrison Rutan-
Nellie Sheridan of Rochester NY; WWI soldier,
26th Infantry; unm; he is bur at Holy Sepulchre Cem, Rochester; NYDC

James B. Rutan - b 1852 p/James Rutan-Charlotte
Merrick of NJ; m Mary Curry b 1857 in Ireland
he was an engineer living in NYC in 1890 and
Queens Co. NY in 1900; LIZR; 1900C; CDIR

James C. Rutan - (1838-1911) p/Peter Rutan-Jane
Sherman m Amelia M. Breese (1841-1911) in
1861; they lived in Elmira, Chemung Co. NY;
he was a CW soldier, Sgt. Co. A 179th N.Y.
Volunteer Infantry; he lived in Minnesota and
Dakota Territory in 1868; Berks Co. PA in
1898 and Philadelphia in 1900 where he died;
he was a builder and cabinet-maker; both are
bur at Maple Grove Cem, Horseheads NY; Note:
LDS identifies him as James R. Rutan and some
records call her Amelia Brees; CAREY; 1850C;
1880C; 1890C; USARCH; LDS; 1900C

James Dudley Rutan, Jr. - (1898-1970) p/James D.
Rutan-Emma Murray m Alice R. Walsh; he was a
butcher in Newburgh, Orange Co. NY; bur at
Calvary Cem, New Windsor NY; 1920C; NYDC

James Diercks Ruttan - (1867-1947) p/Christopher
Ruttan-Mary J. Farley m Margaret B. (Maggie)
Jones (1868-1951) living in Buffalo NY in

1890, Shelby, Orleans Co. in 1892 and Lock-
port Cottage, Niagara Co. in 1900; he was a
miller; both died at Cohocton; Note: the
1892C of Orleans Co. has him age 28 and the
1900C has him born in 1863; RUTT; 1892C;
NYDC; 1900C

James H. Rutan - (1849-1851) bur at Cedar Lawn
Cem, Paterson NJ (cemetery records) METC

James M. Rutan - (1898-1955) p/Abraham Rutan-
Catherine Smith of Kearny, Hudson Co. NJ; he
died in a fire at Waterloo NY and is bur at
Maple Grove Cem, Waterloo (cemetery records)
NYDC

James W. Rutan - (1844-1864) p/Martin Rutan-
Hannah J. Wilson; CW soldier, Cpl, Co. M.,
2nd N.J. Cavalry; died of illness at Memphis
TN in July 1864; bur in Beemerville Cem;
Note: there is a record of his burial at the
National Cemetery, Memphis; USARCH; NJCW; EG;
SXHS; 1860C

James W. Retan - (1902-1965) p/Fred Retan-Myra
Scrafford; he was a "wire-drawer" living in
Cortland NY, unm, he is bur at the Rural Cem,
Cortland; NYDC

Jane Rutan - b 1800 prob daughter of Daniel
Rutan-Jannitje Brower m Jonathan Fox of NYC,
a W1812 soldier; AAR

Jane Rutan - (1804-1877) m Jeremiah K. Haight;
she is bur at the Stanton (Centennial) Cem,
Wurtsboro, Sullivan Co. NY (cemetery records)
NYGBS

Jane Rutan - resident of Springfield MA in 1850;
1850C

Jane Rutan - p/Adam C. Rutan-Lauretta Conklin m
Carlos A. Utter; Note: she is probably **Emma
Jane** Rutan; EG

Jasper Rettan - resident of Warwick, Orange Co.
NY in 1860; 1860C

Jay Rutan - Charles Jefferson (1893-1993) p/
Lemuel J. Rutan-Rosa B. Wakefield m Greta
Sherer (1898-1961) of Homer NY; they lived in
Forkstone PA (per her Obit); he worked for
Public Service E&G and died in Grand Junction
Co; MEACH; COCHS; 1920C; PCHSQ; SSA

Jay Sloat Rutan - b 1882 p/Wilbur Rutan-Jannie
Babcock m Grace Helen Markert (1885-1963) in
1906 at Corning, Steuben Co. NY; she is bur
at Hope Cem; CDIR; 1920C; NYMC; NYDC

Jeanette Retan - bc 1914 of Corning, graduate of

Mansfield PA High School in 1932 (school records)

Jeanette Ida Rutan - b 1879 p/Abraham Rutan-Sarah M. Stewart of Brooklyn NY m Norman Powell b 1874 at Simpson M.E. Ch, Farmingdale, Nassau Co. NY in 1905; Note: the marriage certificate has her Ida Jeanette b 1872; 1880C; NYMC

Jefferson Rutan - (1863-1911) bur at Arlington Cem, Kearny, Hudson Co. NY (in plot owned by Annie A. Rutan)(cemetery records)

Jennie Rheutan - b 1870 p/Garret H. Rheutan-Mary Edmonston; Jennie was born in Portsmouth NH and m Thomas Mathis in Chicago; AAR

Jennie Ann Ruton - p/George N. Ruton-Sarah M. Souder; she was born in NYC and lived in Yonkers NY in 1880 and in No. Hempstead, Nassau Co. NY in 1900; 1880C; USARCH; 1900C

Jennie M. Rutan - (1873-1941) p/Peter Rutan-Lucy Babcock m Milton Adams (1869-1939) at Elmira NY in 1910; she was a "dress-maker" in Elmira NYMC; CDIR

Jennie M. Ruttan - b 1874 p/Peter Ruttan-Sarah L. See of Ontario; m Bernard Halliday b 1875 of Worth Center NY in 1899; Note: FMLWT calls her mother Mary Ann See; RUTT; FMLWT

Jennie Rutan - (1868-1868) p/William H. Rutan-Hannah Winters of Newark NJ; METC

Jennie Evelyn Rutan - (1893-1965) p/Abram W. Rutan-Kate Ayers m Fred Wilson (Alberta Moore) SCMR; GSNJ; 1900C; MCRC

Jennie Lee Rutan - **Jane** (1882-1945) p/Charles M. Rutan-Jennie Lee m George Whitney Flewwellin (1880-1954) she died at Paterson and he at New Castle, Westchester Co. NY; both bur at Kensico Cem, Valhalla NY; PATB; PCHSP

Jenny M. Rutan - b 1871 p/James C. Rutan-Amelia M. Breese of Elmira NY; m Jacob Cole at Hankow, China in 1917; USARCH; 1880C; MCRC

Jeptha Retan - (1835-1903) p/John Retan-Rachel Shuart m Susan Elizabeth Longwell (1838-1918) of Vernon Twp, Sussex Co. NJ in 1858; he was a CW soldier in the 161st N.Y. Infantry and after the war a vineyardist in So. Pulteney, Steuben Co. NY; as a widow she wed James B. _____ (Bob Longwell) they are bur at Glen View Cem; 1850C; NYDC; STUCHS; CDIR; PCHSQ;

Jesse Rutan - b 1855 p/Adam C. Rutan-Lauretta Conklin of Frankford Twp, Sussex Co. NJ; LDS;

MCRC

Jesse Rutan - m Anne Mary _____ (1819-1892)
    DARLDC

Jesse Rutan - m Lillian Mager (1885-1959) she is
    bur at Mt. Ida Cem, Troy, Rensselaer Co. NY;
    NYDC

Jesse D. Rutan - (1865-1939) p/Thomas B. Rutan-
    Annie Powers Heningham m Lauretta Birck bc
    1867; he was a warehouse clerk in Brooklyn
    bur at Green-Wood Cem, Brooklyn (see Josiah
    T. Rutan) CRC; BDC; 1920C; CDIR

Joel Rutan - (1821-1869) p/Samuel Rutan-Susanna
    Cymer of Sussex Co.; m (1) Catherine Ann
    Smith (1824-1863) (2) Esther Quick (1834-
    1886) in 1864; Esther was the widow of Jonat-
    han Lilly; Joel was a carpenter living in
    Lackawaxen Twp, Pike Co. PA in 1850; MEACH;
    1850C; NJG; MCRC; SXHS; PPDLN; ROOTSW

Joel Rutan - b 1846 p/Daniel Rutan-Lucy Compton;
    may have moved with his family to Wayne Co.
    PA; MCRC

Joel W. Rutan - (1845-1929) p/Peter Rutan-Maria
    Compton of PA; m Violetta Young bc 1847; they
    lived in Southport Town, Chemung Co. NY and
    later moved to IL (see IL listing) both bur
    at Woodlawn Cem, Elmira NY; LDS; 1900C; NYDC

John Reton - m Charlotte Lavinia _____ (1805-
    1858) she is bur at St. John's Cem, Yonkers,
    Westchester Co. NY (cemetery records) Note:
    he may be John Jackson Ruton b 1801, the son
    of Isaac B. Ruton; BHS

John Rutan - b 1871 p/Cornelius Rutan-Mary ?Haw-
    kins; Note: spelled Ruthan in the 1900C

John Rutan - a carpenter residing at 156 Frank-
    lin St. NYC in 1847; CDIR

John Rutan - b 1808 p/Peter C. Rutan-Charity
    Corselius of Sussex Co.; he may have moved
    with his family to Butler Co. OH; BOGGS

John Retan - living in Parma, Monroe Co. NY in
    1830; 1830C

John Retan - (1809-1870) p/Barnet Retan-Sarah
    Drew m (1) Polly Lemy dc 1834 (2) Rachel
    Shuart (1811-1884) they were both born in
    Sussex Co. NJ and were living in Steuben Co.
    NY by 1850; John was a suicide (info on Polly
    from Bob Longwell) PUH; 1850C; MEACH

John Rutan - b 1811 p/John Rutan-Susannah Storm
    of NYC; LDS

John Rutan - d 1898 bur at Laurel Grove Cem,

Port Jervis NY (cemetery records) NYGBS

John Reton - m Anna Maria Van Orden in NYC in 1824; NYCMM

John Rutan - (1900-1979) p/Henry Rutan; he lived in Spencerport, Monroe Co. NY (see John Alfred Rutan) SSA

John Rutan - (1922-1997) of Spencerport, Monroe Co. NY; SSA

John Rutan - (1905-1987) of West Orange, Essex Co. NJ; SSA

John Rutan - died in 1937; he is bur at Mt. Pleasant Cem, Newark (cemetery records)

John Rutan - (1905-1987) prob son of John R. Rutan-Alliene N. Marley; SSA

John Retan - m Elizabeth Cowley of NJ (Tanya Retan Smith-White)

John Rutan - (1838-1871) he died near Deemerville, Sussex Co. (*Orange County Press*, 21 Nov 1871)

John A. Rutan - (1850-c1915) p/Adam T. Rutan-Abigail Tinsman m (1) Ethelyn Gaylord d 1894 (2) Marta M. _____; he was born in Warren Co. NJ and moved to Susquehanna Co. PA; Note: there is a marriage certificate for John A. Rutan and Myrtle Aldrich Knapp b 1876 at Binghamton NY in 1903 showing him born in 1863 and the 1910C has him born in 1854 and living with Marta; 1869C; NYMC; 1910C; LEE

John A. Rutan - (1840-1872) p/Martin Rutan-Hannah J. Wilson m Eunice Carman (1840-1910) in 1861; he was a farm laborer; after his death she wed Philip S. Tims; Note: an article in *The Jerseyman* says she married Philip S. Timms of Morris Co. in 1860; she was from Baleville; John is bur at Old Beemerville Cem and she at Newton Cem (Nancy Pascal) LDS; EG; 1860C

John A. Rutan - m Ethel _____; he was a civil engineer in Brooklyn NY in 1933; CDIR

John Alfred Rutan - (1900-1979) p/Harrison Rutan -Nellie Sheridan of Rochester NY; m Eleanor Reynolds (1902-1977); he worked for Eastman-Kodak (Thomas M. Rutan) NYBC

John Allen Rutan - b 1880 p/William H. Rutan-Julia Dunning m Lillian L. Kadel at Port Jervis in 1909; he was an auto salesman there in 1924; NYMC; 1900C; CDIR

John B. Reton - p/John T. Reton; RET

John C. Reton - died in 1855; MAHER

John D. Rutan - (1812-1881) p/Abram Rutan-Ann
Courter m Anna Perry (1813-1914); they lived
in Sussex Co.; she was a second cousin to
Commodore Oliver Hazard Perry (per her Obit
in the *N. Y. Times*) he was a farmer in Minisink Town, Orange Co.; both bur at Howell's
Cem, Howell NY; Note: another record has them
bur at Westtown Presbyt Chyd, Orange Co. NY;
1870C; 1880C; NYTO; PCHSQ; WPCC

John Everett Rutan - (1872-1927) p/Samuel Rutan-
Sarah Everett of Brooklyn NY; m Mary Louise
"Minnie" Hardy (1871-1929) both died in Rich-
mond Hill, Queens Co. NY (some info from the
Huguenot Society of N.J. appl of their daugh-
ter Muriel Rutan Sweeney; NYGBS; BMC; QCDI

John E. Rutan - b 1836 (see John P. Rutan,
below)

John H. Retan - (1829-1882) of Morristown NJ; a
widower he died at Brighton, Monroe Co. NY;
bur at Mt. Hope Cem, Rochester NY; NYDC

John H. Retan - b 1817 m Henrietta Hatt (1821-
1848) at Seneca Co. NY; she is bur at the Mc-
Neil Cem, Ovid NY (from their son Albert's CW
pension file) Note: in the pension file she
is called Henrietta Huff and she is buried
among Huffs; NYGBS; USARCH

John H. Rutan - m Catherine _____; John was a
carpenter living in Ho-Ho-Kus, Washington Twp
Bergen Co. NJ; living in NYC in 1890; GSBC;
CDIR

John H. Retan - (1875-1938) p/John Retan-Elizabeth Cowley of Jersey City m Catherine Lepper
(1878-1951) of Sodus Point NY; he was a
freight agent in Rochester NY; they are both
bur at Riverside Cem, Rochester (Tanya White)
Note: according to his birth certificate he
was born aboard the canal boat "Dorsett" at
the foot of Pavonia Ave, Jersey City; NYMC;
NYDC

John H. Rutan - d 1908 of Vernon Twp, Sussex Co.
bur at Warwick Cem, Orange Co. NY (cemetery
records) (see Catherine A. Rutan, above)

John H. Reutan - resident of the 5th Ward,
Newark NJ; 1850C

John Harry Rutan - (1995-1959) p/John Henry
Roughtean-Mary Ellen Cullen of MA; he died
in Los Angeles CA; CADRI

John Henry Rutan- (1843-1892) p/Jacob Rutan-
Ellen Ackerman m (1) Ada Snyder (1855-1876)

(2) Emma A. Vanderhoof b 1853 in Newark; he
was a stonemason in Paterson in 1861 and a CW
soldier, Co. K, 1st N.Y. Engineers; Note: Ada
was from Wyckoff NJ and Emma's maiden name
sometimes cited as Vanderhoff; John was living Newark in 1891; Ada was originally bur at
Sandy Hill Cem but was reinterred at Cedar
Lawn Cem (cemetery records) CDIR; USARCH;
1850C; 1880C

John Henry Rutan - p/Charles S. Rutan-Margaret
Vanover of Warren Co. NJ; MEACH

John Hewet Rutan - (1835-1898) p/Daniel Rutan-
Maria Ackerman m Annie Eliza Banker (1839-
1905) at the Ponds (Oakland NJ) in 1855, they
were both of Paterson as reported in *The
Christian Intelligencer* 15 Feb 1855; he died
in Kearny, Hudson Co. NJ; both bur at Cedar
Lawn Cem, Paterson (cemetery records) SML;
1850C; CRC

John J. Reton - died in 1854; MAHER

John Jackson Ruton - (1801-1832) p/William Ruton
-Rachel Brower of Tarrytown NY; m Eliza Ann
Requa (1804-1861) he was a physician whose
Obit appeared in the *N.Y. Evening Post*; Note:
Elizabeth A. Ruton listed in the NYC direct-
ory for 1836 and the 1855C; WHIT; GSNJ; CDIR;
MACK

John James Snyder Rutan - (1844-1917) p/John
Rutan-Susan Walker m Laura H. Bull bc 1850
from PA; he was a jeweler who lived in Newark
and later in Madison NJ; his Obit in *The Madison Eagle* and *The Asbury Park Evening Press*
5 Nov 1917; he is bur at Mt. Pleasant Cem,
Newark (cemetery records) 1850C; CDIR; GSNJ;
1880C; 1900C

John Lanterman Rutan - (1855-1924) p/Robert J.
Rutan-Adelia Lanterman of Ogdensburg, Sussex
Co. NJ; m Laura Hulse Conklin (1870-1948) of
Cold Spring, Dutchess Co. NY at Goshen,
Orange Co. in 1895; he was a butcher who had
moved to Goshen about 1875; they are bur at
Slate Hill Cem (cemetery records) 1860C; LDS;
NYMC; GSNJ; NYDC; CDIR; POCGS; 1900C; 1920C

John Melvin Retan - (c1820-c1877) he was born in
NJ and moved to Shiawassee Co. MI before 1843
(see MI listing) CLA

John P. Rutan - died in 1910 in Newark; prob son
of Peter Rutan-Hettie Longwell; his Obit in
the *Sussex Register* 6 Nov 1910

John R. Retan - (1807-1881) m Catherine Emmons
in NY in 1841 at the First Ref Ch in Ovid,
Seneca Co. NY; moved to Kent Co. MI in 1843;
Note: Church records have him John Rutan (see
MI listing) KCH

John R. Rutan - b 1872/8 p/John J.S. Rutan-Laura
H. Bull m Alliene Nichols Marley (1881-1954)
he was a jeweler in Glen Ridge, Essex Co. NJ;
they are bur at Mt. Pleasant Cem, Newark
(cemetery records); CDIR; 1920C; GSNJ; LDS

John S. Rutan - b 1818 p/Samuel Rutan-Hannah
Winne m Magdalena Duncan b 1818 in England in
1839; John was a farmer in Belleville in 1891
1850C; CDIR; BDRC; FER; SRDRC

John S. Ruttan - b 1837 p/Abraham Ruttan-Mary
Ann See of Leeds, Ontario; m Margaret Bauter
(1825-1905) of Lyme, Jefferson Co. NY; they
died in Watertown; she was a widow in 1890;
CDIR; NYDC; RUTT

John S. Rutan - m Elizabeth Coles and they lived
in Sussex Co. NJ (from daughter Emma's 1901
death certificate)

John T. Reton - p/John Reton-Sarah A. Frost; RET

John T. Rutan - m Emma _____ he was a clerk in
Brooklyn in 1922; CDIR

John W. Rheutan - b 1822 p/Abraham Rheutan-Mary
Storms m Ann Welch b 1821 of NYC in 1842; he
was a machinist living in NYC in 1850; CDIR;
1850C; GSNJ

John W. Rutan - b 1855 p/Peter Rutan- Jane Sherman of Sullivan Co. NY; m Flora Townsend (see
MI listing) CAREY

Joseph Rutan - (1807-1844) p/Joseph Rutan-Rachel
Hole m Sally Anne Fornote of Rahway in 1826,
his second wife; LITT; NJW

Joseph Retan - resident of Barrington, Yates Co.
NY in 1825; 1825C

Joseph Rettan - resident of Warwick, Orange Co.
NY (see Jasper Rettan, above) 1860C

Joseph Rutan - (1901-1984) of the Bronx, NYC;
SSA

Joseph Rutan - bc 1917 p/Frank E. Rutan-Candace
Johnson; CRC; 1920C

Joseph Rutan, Jr. - (1836-1838) p/Joseph Rutan,
bur at the First Presbyt Chyd, Newark; Note:
his Obit in the *N.J. Eagle* says he was the
only son of Henry Rutan; GMNJ; NJHS; ECDR;
NEHGS

Joseph Archer Ruton - (1893-1967) of Lyndhurst

NJ prob the son of Joseph F. Ruton-Mercedes
E. ____ ; he is bur at Hillside Cem, Lynd-
hurst (cemetery records) SSA
Joseph B. Retan - resident of Southport, Tioga
Co. NY in 1830; 1830C
Joseph B. Rattan - resident of Prattsburg Town,
Steuben Co. NY in 1835 (county archives)
Joseph F. Rutan - (1855-1922) p/Gideon Rutan-
Mary Ann Litts m Fannie L. Martin (1860-1922)
in Jersey City; they lived in Frankford Twp,
Sussex Co. NJ; CRAWN; SXHS; SCDR; CRC; 1860C;
1875C; 1900C
Joseph F. Rutan - (1906-1978) of NJ; SSA
Joseph F. Ruton - (1853-1922) m Mercedes E.
____ (1854-1938) of Providence RI; they were
living in Rutherford NJ in 1920; both bur at
Hillside Cem, Lyndhurst (cemetery records)
Note: the cemetery has him Joseph H. Ruton
(Norman Rutan) 1920C
Joseph Louis Rutan - (1906-1978) p/Frank H.
Rutan-Katherine Schlee of Newark; he was a
florist; unm, bur at Christ Chyd, Bordentown
NJ (Janet Rutan Bowers) SSA; 1920C
Joseph Volney Rutan - (1878-1931) p/Volney Rutan
-Elizabeth Merkle m Dorothy **Marie** Davis
(1876-1941) of Australia; she died at Wood-
bury, Orange Co. NY and is bur at Woodlawn
Cem, NYC; BDC; NYDC; 1900C
Josephine Retan - (1852-1862) p/Gilbert Retan-
Melecta Drew of Steuben Co. (Rose Alexander)
STUCHS
Josiah T. Rutan - (1864/6-1939) p/Thomas B.
Rutan-Annie Heningham of Brooklyn; m Emma
Laurietta Hopley Birck (1866-1942) he was a
cement worker in Brooklyn; he evidently was
the son of Annie and her first husband Josiah
T. Heningham (1839-1865) Thomas' business
partner; Josiah went by the name of Jesse D.
Rutan (see above) Laurietta died in Bridge-
port CT; CDIR; 1880C; 1900C; MRUT
Julia Rutan - p/Issac M. Rutan-Eliza Aggear; she
died in Brooklyn; FER
Julia Ann Rutan - (1870-1940) p/Brice P. Rutan-
Corcelia Elston of Unionville or Westtown,
Orange Co. NY; m Richard Allison Lain Terry
(1868-1916) at Westtown in 1891; Note: anoth-
er record has her born in 1876; LDS; NYMC;
FH; CVAN
Julia Pearl Rutan - b 1889 p/Linn Rutan-Juliette

Coykendall of Sussex Co.; 1900C

Karl Arthur Rutan - (1884-1973) p/Daniel A.
Rutan-Alida Swackhammer m Lucy E. Paine in
1908 at Oneida NY; he was a CPA who died at
Conastota, Madison Co. NY; NYDC; SSA
Karl Massey Rutan - (1911-1912) p/William Rutan-
Grace Stanaback of Unionville, Orange Co. NY;
he died at Minisink Town, Orange Co.; Note:
one record has him born in 1908 (Carol Van
Buren) NYDC
Kate Rutan - (1858-1860) p/Abraham C. Rutan-
Ellen Drew; she is bur at Warwick Cem, Orange
Co. NY (cemetery records) 1860C
Kate Rutan - b 1861 p/John H. Rutan-Catherine
_____ ; she was bpt at the English Neighbor-
hood Ch, Bergen Co., NJ; GSBC; GSNJ
Kate Rutan - b 1887 p/Abram W. Rutan-Kate Ayers
of Sussex Co.; m Norman Bensley; EG; 1900C
Kate Reton - b 1861 p/George Reton-Katherine
?Swainson; RET
Kate Adelaide Reton - of Passaic NJ; m Charles
Howell Woodhull b 1854 in 1883 (Woodhull
Genealogy)
Kate Severenson Retan - (1829-1911) of Bermuda;
she died at Northport, Suffolk Co. NY and is
bur at New Hope NY; Note: she may be Kate
Swainson the wife of George Reton; NYDC
Kenneth Rutan - (1905-1981) p/Victor Rutan-Abbie
Jones; he lived in Big Flats, Chemung Co. NY;
SSA; 1920C

Laura Rutan - (1863-1910) p/William H. Rutan-
Hannah Winters of Paterson NJ; m Joseph Edgar
Blauvelt (1856-1917) in 1882; he was a
grocer; she died in Newark; METC; BFH
Laura Rutan - (1885-1906) p/Linn Rutan-Juliette
Coykendall (from Linn's Obit) she is bur at
Beemerville; SXHS
Laura Elizabeth Retan - (1866-1948) p/Jeptha
Retan-Susan E. Longwell; may have married
Spencer H. Cole; Note: MEACH has her wed to
Green Cole (1859-1934) in 1884 as do county
marriage records; STUCHS; MEACH; CoMR
Laura L. Rutan - bc 1862 p/Richard Rutan-Mary A.
Fort of Sullivan Co. NY; CAREY
Lavinia Catherine Rutan - **Rheutan** (1833-1917)
p/Abraham D. Rutan-Mary Storms m Jacob Van
Valer d 1907 of English Neighborhood, Bergen

Co. in 1850; she was born in NYC and died at
Richmond Hill, Queens Co. NY; he died in
Brooklyn; they are bur at Cypress Hills Cem,
Queens Co. (R.L. Van Valer) PCHSP

Lawrence Rutan - (1890-1963) of NJ; SSA

Lawrence O. Rutan - bc 1919 p/Blase M. Rutan-
Flora M. Cassidy; 1920C

Layton Rutan - (1808-1888) p/David Rutan-Caty
Russell in Dingmans Twp, Pike Co. PA; m Doro-
thy Hull (1812-1890) about 1829; both died in
Coles Co. IL (see IL listing) and are bur at
Pleasant Grove Cem, Coles Co. (cemetery rec-
ords (1830C; 1850C; SXHS

Layton Rutan - m Elsie Brigge (1890-1967) they
lived in Middletown, Orange Co. NY; she is
bur at Bloomingburg Rural Cem, Orange Co.;
NYDC

Layton Dimon Rutan - (1886-1974) p/Edward A.
Rutan-Susan J. Dimon; m Ella R. March (1888-
1958); he was born in Hammondsport, Steuben
Co. NY and a pipe-fitter in Port Jervis NY;
both bur at Laurel Grove Cem, Port Jervis;
EG; SSA; 1920C; NYDC; NYGBS; PJPL; CDIR

Layton D. Rutan - m Florence Elizabeth Robertson
(1889-1962) she is bur at Laurel Grove Cem,
Port Jervis, Orange Co. NY; NYDC

Leah Rutan - b 1811 p/Daniel Rutan-Jannetje
Brower m John Hewet of NY; they lived in
Belleville, Essex Co. NJ; Note PCHSP identif-
ies her mother as Jannetje Ackerman; PCHSP;
AAR

Leah H. Ruttan - b 1891 p/James D. Ruttan-Maggie
B. Jones; Note: this appears to be a census
error and refers to Leo Harold Ruttan, see
below; 1900C

Leah Jane Rutan - b 1837 p/Daniel Rutan-Maria
Ackerman of Paterson NJ; m Lucius Tuttle in
IL in 1860; LDS; AFH; CRC

Lee Rutan - (1910-1984) prob Leander Rutan son
of Cody L. Rutan-Addie Kelly; SSA

Lee C. Rutan - of Tioga Co. NY m Lillian Bisch-
off (1911-1970) she is bur at Vestal, Tioga
Co.; NYDC

Lemuel Jefferson Rutan - (1850-1928/9) p/Charles
S. Rutan-Margaret Vanover of Warren Co. NJ; m
(1) Elizabeth Angeline Guile (1852-1879) of
Auburn PA at Lymanville PA in 1875 (3) Rosa
Baker Wakefield (1861-1941) of PA; they were
living in Wyoming Co. NY in 1900 and Homer NY

in 1928; he is bur in Keyserville and she at
Glenwood Cem, Homer (see PA listing) MEACH;
LDS; NYDC; ROOTSW; 1900C; CDIR; 1920C

Lena Rutan - died in 1972 and bur at Glendale
Cem, Bloomfield, Essex Co. NJ (cemetery records)

Leo E. Rutan - b 1874 p/George Rutan-Amelia
Englemann; 1900C

Leo Harold Ruttan - (1891-1959) p/James D. Rutt-
an-Margaret B. Jones of Medina NY; m Dorothy
Ackerman (1896-1964) at Brooklyn NY in 1917;
RUTT; 1900C

Leona Rutan - (1904-1904) p/Harry A. Rutan-Leona
McCabe of Brooklyn; EOVB; CRC

Leonard L. Rheutan - bc 1846 p/John W. Rheutan-
Anna Welch of NYC (see MN listing) Note: the
1850C spells the surname Retan; 1850C

Leroy Rutan - (1897-1983) he died in Dover NJ;
he was the brother of Henry Rutan (see Roy
Rutan, below) SSA

Leroy Rutan - b 1897 p/Luther M. Rutan-Virginia
Beard of Elmira NY (see CA listing) MCRC

Lester Rutan - (1894-1969) he was born in NJ and
died in Lewes, DE; SSA

Lester Richard Rutan - (1895-1948) p/Josiah T.
Rutan-Laurietta Birck of Brooklyn NY m Ada
Wells bc 1901; he was a WWI soldier and a
machinist in Middletown, Orange Co. NY in
1920; he later lived in New Paltz, Ulster Co.
NY; bur at Wallkill Valley Cem; 1900C; NYDC;
1920C; NYTO; CDIR; MRUT

Letitia Ruton - (1803-1857) p/William Ruton-
Rachel Brower of Tarrytown, Westchester Co.
NY; m James Requa at Bedford St. Meth Ch, NYC
in 1842; Note: James was previously wed to
her sister Mary (Sebring Collections) they
died in Chatfield MN; NYCMM; GSNJ; MACK;
PCHSP

Levi Rutan - bc 1918 p/Charles A. Rutan-Elizabeth Wilson of Cortland NY; 1920C; RUTT

Levi Rutan - (1844-1918) p/Daniel H. Ruttan-
Melissa Arthur of Lewis Co. NY; m (1) Amelia
Spear bc 1842 at Manorville NY in 1868,
divorced about 1876 (2) Emma L. Hubbard (1847
-1926) after 1898; he was a CW soldier in the
5th NY Hvy Arty and he lived in Richland,
Oswego Co. NY; Onondaga Co., Rome, Martins-
burg and Syracuse NY; he d in Bath, Steuben
Co. and is bur at the Bath National Cemetery;

Note: his CW pension file lists him as Rutan
and that is the way he signed his name although some records spell it Ruttan; one record
has him born in 1840; STUCM; RUTT; 1890C;
NYDC; USARCH

Lewis E. Retan - (1875-1955) p/Thomas Retan-
Emmaline Hubbard of Jefferson and Lewis Cos.
NY m Dora A. Sisson (1891-1954) of East Rod-
man NY in 1910; he is bur at North Watertown
Cem; USARCH; NYMC; NYDC

Lewis Harvey Rutan - (1896-1968) p/Joseph F.
Rutan-Fannie L. Martin of Sussex Co. NJ m
Henrietta Kiritz (1894-1986); he died at West
Hempstead NY and is bur at the L. I. National
Cemetery, Pinelawn; SSA; CRC; 1900C; NYDC

Lida Rutan - m John Phillips in NY or PA; ROOTSW

Lila May Ruttan - b 1896 p/Oliver F. Ruttan-Mary
A. Young of Lewis Co. NY; NYBC

Lillian Rutan - b 1866 p/Samuel B. Rutan-Mary L.
Fitzgerald m Joel Coleman b 1865 of Hampton-
burg, Orange Co. NY at Goshen in 1888; Note:
the 1880C has her b in 1862; 1880C; NYMC

Lillian A. Rheutan - m Earl D. Dunn at Delaware
Co. NY in 1925; CoMR

Lillian Alice Rutan - b 1888 p/Cornelius Rutan-
Elsa A. Terwiliger of Mamakating Park, Sull-
ivan Co. NY; m David O'Connell Hunt b 1885 at
Bridgeville; NYMC

Linn Cody Rutan - (1914-1926) p/Cody Linn Rutan-
Addie Kelly; 1920C

Linn Roy Rutan - (1853-1924) p/Jacob Rutan-Nancy
Rollison m Juliette Coykendall (1862-1947) at
Greenville M.E. Ch in 1878; they lived in
Montague Twp, Sussex Co.; Note: PPDLN has her
death in 1949; SCMR; SXHS; GSNJ; 1880C

Lois M. Rutan - p/Benjamin A. Rutan-Mary E.
Pittenger of Sussex Co.; GSNJ

Lorenda Rutan - **Lorinda** (1815-1868) p/Robert
Rutan-Mary Courter m Peter Nicholas Ryerson
(1814-1902) in 1833; he was a farmer and they
lived in Glenwood, Sussex Co. and later in
Florida, Orange Co. NY; he died in Union
Corners NY (Ryerson Genealogy) Note: per AAR
she was born in 1814; FH; JS; AAR

Loretta Ruth Retan - d 1976 m Frank Lee Austin
(1910-1977) he was born in Columbus MO and
died at Potsdam NY; he is bur at Bayside Cem
(from his Obit in the *Standard-Speaker* of
Hazelton PA)

Lottie Adelaide Rutan - (1878-1933) p/Peter S.
Rutan-Lydia F. Carman of Circleville, Orange
Co. NY; m Charles R. Andrews b 1887 at Thompson Ridge, Orange Co. in 1900; he was born in
Montgomery Town, Orange Co.; 1880C; CAREY;
LDS; NYMC

Lotty M. Rutan - bc 1843 p/Richard Rutan-Mary A.
Fort of Fallsburgh, Sullivan Co. NY; Note:
she is listed as **Letty** in the 1855C; 1855C;
1860C

Louis Retan - b 1849 p/James Retan-Urania Conover of Lodi, Seneca Co. NY (see MI listing)
1850C; (Jonathan O. Gushen)

Louis Rutan - bc 1873 p/Henry K. Rutan-Sarah Roe
he was living in East Orange, Essex Co. NJ in
1920; 1880C; 1920C

Louis Rutan - bc 1875 p/Thomas Rutan-Emmaline E.
Hubbard of Jefferson Co. NY; 1880C

Louis Osborne Rutan - (1907-1981) p/Edward Rutan
-Louise Humes of Newark; 1920C; SSA; METC

Louise Rutan - (1899-1985) p/James D. Rutan-Emma
Murray m Arthur Quackenbush of Bellvale,
Orange Co. NY in 1919; QFH; SSA; POCGS

Louise Retan - m _____ Nelson in RI in 1891;
AGBI

Lucetta Rutan - (1854-1917) p/Henry K. Rutan-
Lucetta M. Roe; she is bur at Cedar Lawn Cem.
Paterson NJ; METC; LDS; 1870C

Lucinda Rutan - (1824/5-1914) m Jacob Clair
Gould (1830-1903) at Lafayette Twp, Sussex
Co. in 1865 where he died; she died in Beemerville; his first wife was Catherine Mariah
Valentine (1834-1865) and Lucinda may have
had a first husband _____ Sanders; ROOTSW; EG

Lucius Washburn Rutan - (1894-1933) p/Josiah T.
Rutan-Laurietta Birck of Brooklyn; m Edna
_____ bc 1900 from NJ; he served aboard the
U.S. Navy dirigible "Akron" which crashed
into the Atlantic Ocean off Barnegat NJ in
1933; 1900C; MRUT; 1920C

Lucy Rutan - b 1841 p/Daniel Rutan-Lucy Compton;
she may have moved with her family to Wayne
Co. PA; MCRC

Luke Tronson Rutan - (1849-1889) p/Nicholas W.
Rutan-Sarah Marsh of Newark NJ; m Mary Louisa
Carmer d 1880 in 1879; FER

Luther M. Rutan - (1874-1949) p/James C. Rutan-
Amelia Breese of Elmira NY; m Virginia Beard
(1878-1965) in 1896; they d in Los Angeles;

Note: he was sometimes known as Martin L.
Rutan; 1880C; USARCH; CADRI

Lydia Rutan - b 1818 p/Peter C. Rutan-Charity
Corselius of Sussex Co.; she moved with her
family to Butler Co. OH (see OH listing)
BOGGS; CBRF

Lydia A. Rutan - m William T. Strang in NYC in
1833; NYCMM

Lyman Rutan - **Luman** b 1878 p/Lemuel J. Rutan-
Eliza A. Guile m Elizabeth Titman b 1875 in
1902; he was born in Auburn, Susquehanna Co.
PA; ROOTSW

Lyndon Smith Rutan - (1850-1911) p/John Rutan-
Susan Walker of Newark NJ; m Rachel A. _____
d 1933; they are bur at Mt. Pleasant Cem in
Newark (cemetery records) GSNJ; CDIR

Mabel Rutan - bc 1875 p/James R. Rutan-Hannah
Machette m Howard E. Wright d 1953 in Caldwell, Essex Co. NJ in 1940; she also lived in
East Orange and Asbury Park NJ (some info
from her brother Clifford's Obit) PCHSQ

Mabel Edith Ruttan - (1881-1963) p/Peter M. Rut-
tan-Mary Long; in 1908 she was a nurse at
City Hospital, Oswego NY, unm, she died at
Camillus, Onondaga Co. NY; she was bur at the
Riverview Cem, Napanee, Ontario; NYDC; RUTT

Mabel Elizabeth Rutan - b 1889 p/William E.
Rutan-Emma Jane Hopper m _____ Eisenhardt abt
1907; 1900C; PCHSQ; ZAB

Mabel Maud Ruttan - b 1887 p/Charles R. Ruttan-
Jennie Ayrhart m William G. Ladd b 1888 at
Theresa, Jefferson Co. NY in 1906; NYMC

Magdalena Rutan - (1810-1884) p/John J. Rutan-
Maria Terhune of Hackensack; m John Huyler
(1808-1870) in NYC in 1829; they lived there
and later Bergen Co. NJ; both bur at the New
York Cem, Hackensack; PCHSQ; ZAB; LDS; FH

Malcolm Rutan - b 1918 p/Jay S. Rutan-Greta
Scherer; 1920C

Malveny Rutan - (1857-1860) p/Abram C. Rutan-
Ellen C. Drew; she is buried at Warwick Cem,
Orange Co. NY (cemetery records)

Mamie G. Rutan - b 1891 p/Charles W. Rutan-Fanny
O. Sheels of Port Jervis NY; 1900C; 1920C

Marcus B. Rutan - (1872-1892) p/Rynier Rutan-
Adelaide Griggs; he was a clerk in Rochester
NY; NYDC

Margaret Ruton - (1810-1900) p/William Ruton-

Rachel Brower of Tarrytown; she was living in
Cobleskill, Schoharie Co. NY by 1850 and is
bur at the Walker Family gravesite at the
Cobleskill Rural Cem; MACK; GSNJ; PCHSP;
1850C; DARLDC

Margaret Rutan - (1812-1881) p/John J. Rutan-
Maria Terhune of NYC m Dr. Edward Valentine
Price (1812-1885) of Jersey City in NYC in
1832; he died in Passaic; they are both bur
at the New York Cem, Hackensack; BF; ZAB; FH;
LDS; NYGBR; LISTAR; JS; HDRC

Margaret Rutan - (1826-1895) p/Albert Rutan m
Cornelius Z. Berdan (1824-1897) of Fairlawn,
Bergen Co. before 1846; they are bur at Vall-
eau Cem (cemetery records) AFH

Margaret Rutan - (1834-1880) p/Henry Rutan-Sarah
Courter m James Baker b 1834 of NY; PCHSP

Margaret Rutan - b 1879 p/Linn Rutan-Juliette
Coykendall of Sussex Co.; CoBR

Margaret Rutan - (1884-1926) she is bur at Arlington Cem, Kearny, Hudson Co. NJ in a plot
owned by Percy Rutan (cemetery records) (Norman Rutan)

Margaret Rutan - bc 1918 p/Thomas B. Rutan-Alice
Standerwick; 1920C

Margaret A. Rutan - (1842-1888) p/Abraham A.
Rutan-Sarah _____; CRC

Margaret E. Rutan - (c1876-1881) p/John J.S.
Rutan-Laura H. Bull; she is bur at Mt. Pleasant Cem, Newark (cemetery records) 1880C

Margaret Maria Rutan - m John Hillikin LaTour-
ette at Bergen Point NJ in 1838; LDS

Maria Rutan - (1801-1830) p/Samuel H. Rutan-
Sarah Joralemon of Second River, Essex Co.
NJ; (Herb Kingsland)

Maria Rutan - **Mariah** (1813-1888) p/Abraham Rutan
-Anna Coss of Sussex Co.; m Isaac Layton
(1804-1897) in 1831; they moved to Steuben
Co. NY and are bur at the Depew Cem, Urbana
Town, Steuben Co. (cemetery records); CBRF;
BB; PPDLN; MEACH; CoMR

Maria Rutan - b 1810 p/Peter Rutan-Charity Corselius of Sussex Co.; moved to Butler Co. OH
(see OH listing); CBRF; BOGGS

Maria Rutan - **Marie** (1850-1918) p/Robert C.
Rutan-Elizabeth Ekings m Robert Eakins (1837-
1928) in 1873; METC

Maria Folts Rutan - (1857-1928) p/Daniel Rutan-
Lovina L. Folts; she lived in Cranesville and

Amsterdam NY, unm; she died at Utica State
Hospital and is bur at New Forest Cem, Utica
(cemetery records) NYDC
Maria Rutan - (1863-1938) she died in Brooklyn
NY; BDCI
Maria Retan - m Samuel Richardson 17 Oct 1822 in
NYC; NYCMM
Maria Rutan - (1844-1894) p/Henry K. Rutan-Luc-
etta M. Roe m Samuel McIlroy (1842-1931) of
Belfast, Ireland; he was the owner of a feed
and grain business in Paterson NJ in 1867;
both bur at Cedar Lawn Cem, Paterson (info on
Samuel from Patti Gamin) METC; PCHSP; CoMR
Maria Rutan - bc 1912 p/George Rutan of Newark
(see Marie June Rutan, below) 1920C
Maria Elizabeth Rutan - b 1852 p/Daniel Rutan-
Keziah E. Zebriskie of Franklin Twp, Bergen
Co. NJ; AFH; LDS
Marian Rutan - b 1918 p/Victor Rutan-Abbie Jones
(see PA listing) 1920C
Marian Rutan - (1895-1986) m _____ Borland
(Thrall Library database, Middletown NY)
Marie June Rutan - (c1912-1993) p/George D.
Rutan-Henrietta R. Hepp (Janet Rutan Bowers)
Marion Rutan - bc 1919 p/Thomas B. Rutan-Alice
Standerwick of Brooklyn NY; 1920C
Marion K. Rutan - bc 1913 p/Jay S. Rutan-Grace
H. Markert; 1920C
Marion Louise Ruton - b 1914 p/William V. Ruton,
Jr.-Laura E. Ware m George Bounsall (Pam
Walling)
Marjorie B. Reton - b 1894 in NYC; NYCBI
Marjorie Gertrude Rutan - (1887-1964) p/Josiah
T. Rutan-Laurietta Birck; she is bur at
Green-Wood Cem, Brooklyn (cemetery records)
1920C
Mark B. Rutan - a "matcher" in Rochester NY in
1891; CDIR
Marriah Rutan - bc 1842 p/Isaac M. Rutan-Eliza-
beth Aggear; 1850C
Martha Rutan - b 1852 p/Daniel Rutan-Lucy Comp-
ton; may have moved with her family to Wayne
Co. PA; MCRC
Martha A. Rutan - (1838-1909) of Corning Town,
Steuben Co. NY; bur at Hope Cem, Corning (cem
records) NYGBS
Martha A. Rutan - b 1844/48 p/Gideon Rutan-Mary
A. Litts m Nelson J. Willson at Hainesville,
Sussex Co. NJ in 1869; CoMR; 1850C; SXHS;

1860C

Martha Ann Rutan - (1842-1926) p/Adam T. Rutan-
Abigail Tinsman m (1) Andrew Titus (1821-
1901) in 1862 (2) Munsell Rundell (3) David
Tarbox in 1882; Andrew had three later wives
(Cornell-Titus website) FH; LEE

Martha C. Rutan - (1910-1979) bur at Evergreen
Cem, Morristown (cemetery records) her Obit
appeared in the *Morristown Daily Record*

Martha Carman Rutan - (1871-1922) p/John Rutan-
Eunice Carman m Charles Conklin (1887-1942)
Note: other records have her wed to Edward or
James E. Conklin and LDS has a record of her
death in 1931; she is bur at Old Beemerville
Cem, Sussex Co. NJ; JS; EG; LDS

Martha Elnora Ruton - (1862-1925) p/Charles P.
Ruton-Martha E. Smith of Poughkeepsie NY and
NYC m Parsells Cole (1864-c1948) a caterer
in Park Ridge; he is bur at Park Ridge Cem,
Bergen Co. NY (Peggy Gaertner) 1870C

Martin Rutan - b 1854 p/James Rutan-Martha _____
of Montague Twp, Sussex Co. (Sally Tinsman)
LDS

Martin L. Rutan - b 1874 (see Luther M. Rutan,
above)

Mary Rutan - p/Harmon Rutan-Chloe Lobdell; PCHSP

Mary Reton - b 1816 p/Daniel Reton-Sarah Moore
of NYC; m William Wallace; GENEX; PCHSQ; LDS

Mary Rettan - living in West Orange, Essex Co.
NJ (see Peter Rettan, below) 1860C

Mary Rutan - bc 1828 probably Mary Share the
wife of Peter Rutan the blind musician and
living with his parents Cornelius Rutan-Caty
Van Alen in 1850; 1850; (Georgia K. Bopp)
PCHSP

Mary Rutan - (1831-1918) p/Peter Rutan-Maria
Compton; she is bur at Woodlawn Cem, Elmira
NY (cemetery records) CHEMHS

Mary Rutan - p/Daniel Rutan-Sarah _____ m Michael Mattox after she moved with her family to
Butler Co. OH (see OH listing) SUSESS; CoMR

Mary Reton - b 1864 p/George Reton-Katherine
?Swainson m ?Clinton H. Smith; GSNJ; RET

Mary Rutan - (1881-1976) m Linn M. Nearing b
1884; both died at South Berlin NY; Note:
she may be the daughter of Lemuel Rutan-Rosa
B. Wakefield (see next entry) PCHSP

Mary Rutan - b 1893 p/Lemuel Rutan-Rosa B.
Wakefield; she lived in So. Berlin NY; PCHSQ

Mary Rutan - a clerk in Brooklyn in 1933; CDIR

Mary Rutan - b 1893 p/Peter R. Rutan-Frances L. Martin of Dover; 1900C

Mary A. Rutan - b 1897 p/Daniel Rutan-Jannitje Brower m Rev. Christian Brinkerhoff and moved to Brooklyn NY; GSNJ; PCHSP

Mary A. Rutan - bc 1847 p/Adam C. Rutan-Lauretta Conklin of Sussex Co.; m Harmon Clifford in 1869; CoMR; 1860C; LDS

Mary Alice Rutan - b1860 p/Sedgwick Rutan-Easter Crawford of Wantage Twp, Sussex Co. may have wed William D. Beemer; Note: her mother may be Hannah, the first wife; LDS; SXHS

Mary Ann Rutan - (1830-1864) p/Henry Rutan-Sarah Courter m John J. Snyder (1828-1898) at the Second Ref Ch, Paterson in 1848; PCHSQ

Mary Ann Rutan - d 1879 bur at Laurel Grove Cem, Port Jervis, Orange Co. NY; NYGBS

Mary Ann Retan - m Joseph M. Swick (1821-1894) (see Polly Ann Retan, below)

Mary Ann Eliza Rutan - m Peter Van Riper in 1832 in Newark; CoMR

Mary B. Rutan - m Martin R. Drake in Greene Twp, Sussex Co. (see Mary E. Rutan, below) CRAWN

Mary C. Rutan - (1835-1885) p/Peter Rutan-Jane Sherman of Mud Hook, Sullivan Co. NY; m Joshua Budd in 1859; she died in Saginaw MI; MCRC; 1850C; CAREY; 1860C

Mary Catherine Rutan - (1831-1878) m Isaac P. Ackerman (1825-1877) in 1852; they lived in Manchester Twp, Passaic Co. NJ and are bur at Valleau Cem, Ridgewood NJ; Note: one record calls her **Margaret Catherine** Rutan) PCHSQ; LDS

Mary E. Rutan - p/Harry E. Rutan-Olive Miller m Fritz Blume (1927-2000) (Richard Ike)

Mary E. Rutan - (1844-1845) probably the daughter of Peter C. Rutan-Rebecca J. Hough; SXHS

Mary E. Rutan - b 1846 p/Peter C. Rutan-Rebecca J. Hough m Nelson Drake; they were living in Newark in 1909 (from her brother William's Obit) 1860C; PJUGO; EG

Mary E. Rutan - (1860-1931) p/Henry K. Rutan-Lucetta M. Roe; she lived in Oakland, Passaic Co. NJ and is bur at Cedar Lawn Cem, Paterson (cemetery records) 1870C; METC; PCHSP

Mary Elizabeth Rutan - (1868-1914) p/Enos Rutan-Nancy J. Sayre; she was a telephone operator in Elmira NY in 1902; bur at Woodlawn Cem,

Elmira; Note: the 1880C indicates that she
was born in 1874; CHEMHS; 1880C; CDIR

Mary Elizabeth Ruttan - (1811-1898) m Thomas Demarest Davis in 1828; FH

Mary Elizabeth Rutan - (1850/1-1907) p/Abraham
R. Rutan-Fannie May m William Clerihew d 1905
of NY at Market Street M.E. Ch, Paterson in
1872; they were involved in her father's
undertaking business (Paterson *Morning Call*
Death Roll, 1906) LDS; 1860C

Mary Elizabeth Rutan - b 1837/8 p/Peter Rutan-
Hettie Longwell m Vincent Carr (1832-1863) a
CW soldier of Vernon Twp, Sussex Co. at New-
foundland Presbyt Ch, West Milford, Passaic
Co. in 1857 (Mary Carr); LDS; FH

Mary Elizabeth Rattan - (1827-1913) m William H.
Smith in 1844; she had a sister Jane who m a
Mr. Wood (see Jane Ann Rutan, below)

Mary Emma Rutan - (1875-1878) she was born and
died in Newark; bur at Cedar Lawn Cem, Paterson (cemetery records)

Mary I. Rutan - (1861-1925) p/John H. Rutan-
Eliza Banker of Passaic Co.; she was born in
Joliet IL; m John Pullen (1848-1893) and they
lived in Kearny, Hudson Co. NJ; both bur at
Cedar Lawn Cem, Paterson (cemetery records)
SML; CRC

Mary Jane Rutan - (1818-1904) p/Henry S. Rutan-
Rachel Kingsland of Tottenville, Staten Island NY m James Johnson Winant (1815-1890) in
1836; EARDP; SIHS; LDS

Mary Jane Retan - (1842-1911) born in Canada, m
William Walter Novell (1833/5-1906) of Kent,
England at Watertown NY in 1859; they moved
to NE in the 1860's (April Robbins) she died
in Platte Co. NE and is buried at the Columbus NE Cem (cemetery records)

Mary Montgomery Rutan - m Henry Darling Hare in
NJ in 1878; LDS

Mary Montgomery Ruton - (1883-1916) p/William V.
Ruton-Laura L. Hazard of East Orange NJ; she
is bur at Rosemont Cem, Orange, Essex Co. NJ;
(Pam Walling)

Mary Riddle Rutan - b 1864 p/Robert J. Rutan-
Adelia Lanterman m Cornelius S. Martin b 1867
at Warwick, Orange Co. NY in 1897; Note:
her mother Adelia is reported to have died in
1863 so she may be the child of the second
wife; JS; LDS; NYMC; GSNJ

Matilda Retan - bc 1845 p/James Retan-Urania
Conover of Seneca Co. NY; moved to MI (see
MI listing) (Jonathan O. Gushen) 1850C
Matilda Mae Rutan - bc 1914 p/George D. Rutan-
Henrietta Hepp (Janet Rutan Bowers) 1920C
Matthew A. Rutan - (1852-1902) p/Daniel H. Rut-
tan-Melissa Arthur of Ontario; he died in
Watertown NY, a widower; Note: RUTT has him
(1853-1906) the above dates are from his
death certificate; CDIR; RUTT; NYDC
Matthew May Ruton - (1803-1869) he is bur at
Grosvenors Corners Cem, Schoharie Co. NY
(cemetery records) DARLDC
Maude Ruttan - b 1887 p/Charles R. Ruttan-Jenn-
ie Ayrhart; 1900C
Maude May Rutan - (1873-1971) p/Hudson Rutan-
Mary J. Bell of Hamburg, Sussex Co. m Alva
Crone (1874-1944) of Hainesville in 1897;
were in Newark in 1902 per Hudson's CW pens-
ion file; she was living in Johnson City NY
in 1936 and she died in Binghamton; they are
bur at Floral Park Cem, Johnson City (Norman
Rutan) MCRC; USARCH
May Ruton - bc 1883 p/William V. Ruton-Laura L.
Hazard of East Orange, Essex Co. NJ; 1880C
May Rutan - b 1886 p/David F. Rutan-Delina Cass-
dy; 1900C
May Rutan - (c1905-1969) p/Frank H. Rutan-Kate
Schlee of Newark (see Sadie Mae Rutan, below)
1920C
May H. Rutan - b 1888 p/Edward T. Rutan-Anne E.
Holloway of Brooklyn; 1900C
Melancthon Freeman Rutan - (1829-1908) p/Henry
S. Rutan-Rachel Kingsland m Eliza Jane Smith
at Tottenville, Staten Island NY in 1853; he
was a ship's carpenter; Eliza was born at
Deal Beach, Monmouth Co. NJ; she is shown as
a "dress-maker" in Tottenville in 1892; both
are bur at Bethel Cem, Staten Island (Vicki
Firth) LDS; SIHS; 1860C; CDIR
Melecta Retan - (1859-1860) p/Gilbert Retan-Mel-
ecta Drew of Steuben Co. NY (Rose Alexander)
Melissa J. Rutan - (1833-1910) p/Peter Rutan-
Jane Sherman of Mud Hook, Sullivan Co. NY; m
William Miller in 1853; she died in Elmira NY
MCRC; 1850C; CAREY
Melville Rutan - (1848-1924) p/Sylvanus J. Rutan
-Sarah I. Mansfield m Jane ____ (1856-1928)
they were living in Irvington, Essex Co. NJ

in 1900 and Jane was in Belleville when she
died; they are bur at East Ridgelawn Cem,
Clifton NJ; Note: their dates are from the
cemetery records and do not agree with the
dates in the censuses; CDIR; 1860C; 1900C

Melville Rutan - bc 1859 m Jennie _____ b 1860;
living in Newark in 1920 (see prior entry)
1920C

Melville Mansfield Rutan - (1869-1950) p/James R
Rutan-Hannah Machette m Ida Luff in 1891; he
was a grocer who died in Summit, Essex Co. NJ
NYTO; NJBI; NPL

Melvin Joseph Rutan - (1900-1984) p/Joseph V.
Rutan-Dorothy M. Davis of the Bronx, NYC; m
Lucille Winifred Lakestream (1901-1959) she
died at Newark Valley, Tioga Co. NY; he died
at Crossroads, Pinellas Co. FL; she is bur at
Owego Cem (some info from William Hauver and
Russ Hauver, his grandsons) NYDC; SSA; 1920C

Michael Quick Rutan - (1863-1936) p/John Rutan-
Eunice Carman m Cara (Carrie) Estelle Lord
(1866-1949) in 1884; he was born in Bales-
ville, Sussex Co. and was a jeweler in East
Orange; she was born in Dingmans Ferry, Pike
Co. PA; he is bur at Delaware Cem, Dingmans
Ferry; NYTO; LDS; GSNJ; JS; 1920C; EG

Mildred Rutan - bc 1916 p/Charles A. Rutan-Elizabeth M. Wilson; 1920C

Mildred Keith Ruttan - b 1905 p/Oliver F. Ruttan
-Mary A. Young of Lewis Co. NY; NYBC

Milton E. Ruton - (1895-1944) p/William E. Ruton
-Elizabeth Daly of NYC; m Mary _____; he was a
WWI vet and later an inspector of construct-
ion in NYC; they lived in Valley Stream, Nas-
sau Co. NY and he is bur at Holy Rood Cem,
Westbury NY; NYDC; 1900C

Minnie H. Rutan - (1880-1937) p/Peter B. Rutan-
Lucy Babcock m William Edward Young (1880-
1955) at Elmira in 1905; she was a stenographer in 1902; CDIR; 1900C

Molly I. Rutan - p/James R. Rutan-Hannah Machette m _____ Fenton and they were living in
Philadelphia in 1940 (from her brother Clifford's Obit) 1900C

Moses Ruton - living in Woolwich Twp, Gloucester
Co. NJ; 1840C

Moses D. Rutan - (1871-1951) p/William H. Rutan-
Julia Dunning m Ida May Rose (1877-1952) at
Port Jervis, Orange Co. NY in 1899; they app-

ear to have lived there their entire lives;
both bur at Laurel Grove Cem; Note: he is in
the 1920C as Moses I. Rutan; 1880C; NYMC;
1920C; NYDC; NYGBS

Muriel Rutan - (1905-1994) p/Robert A. Rutan-
Abbie Langstaff m George Lederer (1902-1967)
they lived in Glen Rock NJ; she died in Ft.
Myers FL; 1920C; PCHSQ; SSA

Muriel J. Rutan - (1900-1978) p/John E. Rutan-
Mary L. Hardy of Brooklyn; m Charles Anthony
Sweeney b 1898 in 1923 at Richmond Hill NY;
they lived in Mountain Lakes NJ; she died in
FL; Note: some of this info is from her 1967
Huguenot Society of NJ appl (NYGBS) EOVB; CRC

Myra Edith Retan - b 1883 p/Orsamus Retan-Emma
Lyon of Steuben Co. NY and Vail IA; m Henry
C. Werly b 1883 of Potter NY at Jerusalem,
Yates Co. NY in 1910; NYMC

Nathan B. Rutan - (1861-1863) p/Abraham Rutan-
Ellen C. Drew; he was bur at Vernon Cem and
reburied at Warwick Cem, Orange Co. NY in
1911 (cemetery records) GMNJ; LDS

Nathaniel Rutan - bc 1852 p/Richard Rutan-Mary
A. Fort of Sullivan Co. NY; 1855C

Nellie Retan - (1867-1871) p/Nelson Retan-Esther
Ball; she died at Bluff Point NY and is bur
at Glenview Cem, Pulteney Town, Steuben Co.
NY (cemetery records) PUH

Nellie Rutan - (1909-1911) p/George W. Rutan-
Blanche McGuire of Summitsdale, Sullivan Co.
NY; NYDC

Nellie Rutan - bc 1919 p/Earle A. Rutan-Mary E.
Stratton; 1920C

Nellie B. Retan - (1887-1969) p/Olney A. Retan-
Mary A. Sornberger of Syracuse NY; Nellie was
born in North Chemung NY, a teacher and unm;
she is bur at North Syracuse Cem; 1920C; NYDC

Nellie Beatrice Rutan - p/Abram W. Rutan-Kate
Ayers m Burton Wilson (1900-1991) in 1926;
they were both from Wantage Twp, Sussex Co.
NJ; MCRC; EG; 1920C

Nelson Retan - (1837-1921) p/John Retan-Rachel
Shuart of Steuben Co. NY; m (1) Esther Salle
Ball (1841-1889) in 1860 (2) Helen M. Ball
(1839-1914) in 1890 (3) Sate Lyon Tousley Depue (1842-1936) in 1917; he was a CW soldier,
161st NY Infantry; a farmer and box manufact-
uerer in Pulteney Town, Steuben Co.; bur in

Lake View Cem (some info from his CW pension
file); 1850C; NYMC; 1880C; PUH; 1900C; MEACH;
USARCH
Nettie Rutan - m Norman Powell b 1874; he m (2)
Amy Godbold (Powell Family History)
Nettie Rutan - m Lester Hill (1877-1944) she was
a sister of John Rutan (1886-1953) and lived
in Blairstown, Warren Co. NJ; a widow there
in 1953 (from John's Obit) Lester was bur at
Cedar Ridge Cem; Note: SSA has a Nettie Hill
(1888-1980) of Cherry Hill, Camden Co. NJ;
CRAWN; HACHS; SSA
Nicholas Warren Rutan - (1824-1873) p/Samuel S.
Rutan-Hannah Garrabrant m Sarah Elizabeth
Marsh (1818-1889) in 1846; he was a house-
painter in Newark NJ where he died; 1850C;
MCRC; 1860C; FER
Nicholas Winfield Rutan - (1854-1930) p/Nicholas
W. Rutan-Sarah E. Marsh m Annie L. Brown b
1857 in 1875; a painter in East Orange, Essex
Co. NJ in 1890; CDIR; FER
Norman Edward Rutan - (1892-1978) p/William H.
Rutan-Elizabeth O. Johnson m Althea Edwards
Smith (1890-1984) at Irvington, Essex Co. NJ
in 1915; he was a banker; CDIR; SSA; FER; LDS
Norman Judson Rutan - (1904-1961) p/Edward Rutan
-Louise Humes of Newark; m Grace Bauer and
was a chauffeur in Newark in 1924; he lived
in Buffalo NY from 1927; he is bur at Elmlawn
Cem, Buffalo; Note: listed as Norman S. Rutt-
an in 1920C (Norman Rutan) NYDC; 1920C
Norman Victor Rutan - b 1896 p/Josiah T. Rutan-
Laurietta Birck m Elizabeth _____; they lived
in CT; MRUT; 1900C
Norrice Rutan - b 1890 p/David F. Rutan-Delina
Cassidy; 1900C

Olive A. Rutan - bc 1908 p/Alexander Rutan-Lucy
Calhoun; 1920C
Oliver Franklin Ruttan - (1876-1938) p/Miles
Ruttan-Mary Jane Davis of Sydenham, Ontario;
m Mary A. Young b 1876 at Hainesville, Lewis
Co. NY; NYMC
Oliver Perry Rutan - (1902-1986) p/Linn Rutan-
Juliette Coykendall of Sussex Co. m Alma
Alexandra Enolm; they lived in OR (some info
from his sister Laura's Obit and from his
Obit in the *North Pacific Union Gleaner*-Sev-
enth Day Adventist Obituaries) (see OR list-

ing; 1920C; SSA; SXHS

Olney Retan - (1846-1920) p/John Retan-Rachel
Shuart m Harriet A. Hulse (1846-1919) he was
a carpenter in Pulteney Town, Steuben Co. NY;
she was bur at Dundee, Yates Co. NY; (Debbie
Warford) 1850C; STUCHS; NYMC; NYDC

Olney Albee Retan - (1858-1922) p/Olney Retan-
Harriet A. Hulse m Mary Augusta Sornberger
(1860-1922) of Seeley Creek, Chemung Co. NY;
he was a minister and in 1914 a vineyardist
at Jerusalem, Yates Co. (some info from the
DAR appl of Nellie B. Retan and from "Syracuse and its Environs") NYMC; CDIR

Ophelia Avis Rutan - (1847-1918) p/Peter C.
Rutan-Maria Hursh of Sussex Co.; m John F.
Bond (1846-1912) in Philadelphia; she died
there; SXHS

Orpha Rutan - (1820-1894) m Reuben Randolph
Predmore (1820-1894) at Baleville Christian
Ch, Sussex Co. in 1839, although LDS has the
wedding in Newton in 1846 and her born in
1824; they did live in Newton and moved to
Irvington, Essex Co. NJ in 1879; both died in
Newark; he was born in Fredon Twp, Sussex Co.
and his first wife was Emily M. Hammond (1823
-1846) (Carol Van Buren) CRAWN; LDS; EG

Orsamus S. Retan - (1847-1925) p/Barnet Retan-
Deborah _____ m Emma Lyon (1849-1921) in 1876
at South Pulteney, Steuben Co. NY; he was a
vineyardist living at Jerusalem, Yates Co. in
1892 and he died at Canandaigua, Ontario Co.
NY; she died at Jerusalem; he is bur at Penn
Yan NY; MEACH; 1850C; NYDC; CoMR; 1892C

Parthenia Rutan - bc 1848 p/James M. Rutan-Leah
Crocheron of Staten Island NY; m John C. Mc-
Allister in 1876; they lived in Philadelphia;
1850C; EARDP

Patty Rutan - bc 1800 p/Peter Rutan-Charity Corselius; according to family bible records she
was born Susan Rutan and married Robert Gilmore in Preble Co. OH in 1818 just after she
and her family moved there (see OH listing)
CoMR; CBRF; BOGGS; MEACH

Paul Rutan - (1891-1969) he was born in NY and
died in Swarthmore, Delaware Co. PA (see DE
listing) SSA

Paul Rutan - m Joan Alice Thorbahn in Ventura NJ
in 1928; ROOTSW

Paul D. Rutan - b 1914 p/John A. Rutan-Lillian
L. Kadel of Port Jervis, Orange Co. NY; 1920C
Pauline W. Rutan - (1905-1905) p/William Rutan-
Grace Stanaback of Unionville, Orange Co. NY;
Note: another record has her Pauline C. Rutan
(Carol Van Buren) NYDC
Pearl Ruttan - b 1885 p/Charles F. Ruttan-Jennie
Ayrhart m Thomas Higginbottom b 1880 at Alex-
andria, Jefferson Co. NY in 1819; 1900C; NYMC
Pearl Rutan - b 1888 p/David F. Rutan-Delina
Cassidy; 1900C
Pearl M. Rutan - bc 1918 p/Benjamin A. Rutan-
Mary A. Pittenger of Sussex Co. NJ; 1920C;
GSNJ
Pearl Minnie Rutan - (1897-1984) p/Ellsworth C.
Rutan-Martha Cortright of Minisink Town,
Orange Co. NY; m William J. Klug (1885-1980)
in 1931; he was from WV and died at Dundee,
Yates Co. NY (Monique Barnhart) 1900C
Percy A. Rutan - (1892-1929) bur at Arlington
Cem, Kearny, Hudson Co. NY (cemetery records)
(Norman Rutan)
Percy C. Rutan - carpenter in Newark in 1924
(see prior entry) CDIR
Peter Rutan, Jr. - (1813-1886) p/Peter Rutan-
Charity Corselius of Sussex Co.; moved to
Butler Co. OH (see OH listing) BOGGS; CBRF
Peter Rettan - resident of West Orange, Essex
Co. NJ; 1860C
Peter Rutan - (1808-1883) p/John Rutan of Hack-
ensack NJ m Jane Sherman (1816-1892) of Ulst-
er Co. NY in 1832; he was a distiller living
in Mamkating, and in 1855 in Fallsburgh,
Sullivan Co. NY; in 1880 they were living in
Midland Co. MI (Terri Bartley) both died in
Elmira NY and are bur at Maple Grove Cem,
Horseheads NY; Note: the 1855C shows him b in
1811; 1850C; CAREY; 1855C; MEACH; NYDC
Peter Rutan - (1815-1882) p/Robert Rutan-Mary
Courter m Mehetabel (Hettie) Longwell (1819-
1887) of Warwick, Orange Co. NY; he was a
farmer in Newfoundland, New Milford Twp,
Passaic Co. NJ; she is bur at the Methodist
Cem, Newfoundland (Bob Longwell) 1850C; FH;
1870C
Peter Rutan - resident of Crawford, Orange Co.
NY; 1840C
Peter Retan - b 1826 p/Peter Retan-Polly Hatt of
Ovid Town, Seneca Co. NY; m Thankful Skinner

b 1827 in 1852 at the Methodist Ch of Lodi
(church records) (see MI listing) 1850C

Peter Rutan - b 1828 p/Cornelius Rutan-Catherine Van Alen m Mary E. Share (1829-1907) at
Greenwich Village Ref Ch in NYC in 1849; he
was a blind musical composer and teacher and
they later lived in IN, MI, IL, NV and CA;
he died in CA (Georgia K. Bopp) 1850C; PCHSP;
LDS

Peter Ruttan - b 1837 p/Lorenzo Ruttan-Margaret
Harpel of Loughborough, Ontario; m Sarah E.
See (1846-1923) she died in Pamelia, Jeffer-
son Co. NY and is bur at the No. Watertown
Cem; RUTT

Peter Rutan - (1848-1852) p/Henry K. Rutan-Lucetta M. Roe; he is bur at Cedar Lawn Cem,
Paterson NJ (cemetery records)

Peter Rutan - (1853-1923) m Anna Kelder; NYDC

Peter Rutan - (1870-1874) bur at Cedar Lawn Cem,
Paterson; Note: he was bur the same day as
James H. Rutan (see above) (cemetery records)
METC

Peter Bedell Rutan - (1849-1934) p/Peter Rutan-
Maria Compton of Sussex Co. NJ; m Lucy Pend-
leton Babcock (1847-1917) he was the owner of
a bicycle shop in Elmira NY; both bur at the
Woodlawn Cem, Elmira (Arthur Rutan) 1880C;
NYDC; CDIR; 1900C

Peter Bernard Rutan - b 1914 p/Phay B. Rutan-
Mary C. Cromer (Arthur Rutan) 1920C

Peter C. Rutan - m Maria DePue Hursh b 1826 in
1848; he died early in the marriage; she m
(2) Moses Shoemaker of Dingmans Ferry, Pike
Co. PA; SCMR; SXHS

Peter C. Rutan - (1808-1896) p/Samuel Rutan-Susanna Cymer of Sussex Co. NJ m Mariah Compton
(1806-1887) they moved to Newton Twp, Luzerne
Co. PA about 1838, Bradford Co. PA about 1853
and Southport Town, Chemung Co. NY in 1862;
he was a milk-dealer there in 1869; both are
bur at Woodlawn Cem, Elmira (cemetery records) NGS; JS; CHEMHS; NYDC; NEHGS; GSNJ

Peter C. Rutan - m Mary ____ ; he was the father
of Elmer Rutan b 1849 and may be the Peter C.
Rutan who wed Maria D. Hursh; SCDR

Peter C. Rutan - (1869-1931) p/William H. Rutan-
Mary ____ m Jeanette (Janet) Hart (1867-
1963) a widow from Brooklyn NY in 1900; he
was the mayor of Port Jervis, Orange Co. NY

and he was an auto dealer there; he died in
an auto accident; both bur at Laurel Grove
Cem; 1880C; PJUGO; NYTO; CDIR; 1900C; NYGBS
Peter Coss Rutan - (1809-1900) p/Abraham Rutan-
Anna Coss m (1) Rebecca Jane Hough (1808-
c1887) in 1830 (2) Elizabeth L. _____ in 1894
he was a farmer in Deckerstown, Sussex Co. NJ
and is bur at Frankford Plains Cem; CoMR; EG;
CBRF; SXHS; MEACH; 1880C
Peter D. Rutan - (1850-1918) p/Adam C. Rutan-
Lauretta Conklin m Sarah E. Spangenburg (1854
-1891) living in Swartswood, Stillwater Twp,
Sussex Co. in 1880; both bur at Branchville
Cem, Frankford Twp (cemetery records); MCRC;
1860C; 1880C
Peter N. Rutan - (1907-1908) p/George W.E. Rutan
-Blanche N. McGuire of Mamakating Town, Sull-
ivan Co. NY; NYDC
Peter R. Rutan - (1852-1900) p/Peter Rutan-Hett-
ie Longwell of West Milford, Passaic Co.; m
Frances L. Martin b 1864; living in Dover,
Morris Co. NJ in 1900; FH; LDS; 1900C; PCHSP
Phay Babcock Rutan - (1885-1979) p/Peter Rutan-
Lucy P. Babcock m Mary Catherine Cromer
(1879-1962) in 1912; he was a sporting goods
dealer in Elmira NY; he died in Dundee, Yates
Co. NY; they are bur at Woodlawn Cem, Elmira;
SSA; NYDC; GSNJ; 1920C
Phoebe M. Rutan - b 1850 p/Theodore Rutan-Eliza-
beth Dunham of Piscataway, Middlesex Co. NJ;
she lived later in Plainfield; USARCH
Phoebe M. Ruton - b 1856 p/Samuel C. Ruton-Alm-
ira _____ of Huntington, Suffolk Co. NY;
1870C
Polly Ann Retan - p/Peter Retan-Polly Hatt of
Seneca Co. NY; m John Swick; LHRL

Rachel Rutan - b 1815 p/Abraham Rutan-Lydia Van-
derbeek m Levi Wilder (1807-1874) of Lancast-
er, Worcester Co. MA at Paterson NJ in 1838;
they were living there in 1855 and later
lived in Brooklyn NY; he was a music teacher
(June Matthys) PCHSP; PDRC; JS; LDS
Rachel Rutan - b 1802 p/Cornelius Rutan-Hettie
Fellow of NYC; LDS
Rachel Rutan - (1815-1840) of Fallsburgh, Sull-
van Co. NY m Nicholas Sarine b 1809; ROOTSW
Rachel Retan - (1820-1892) p/Barnet Retan-Darah
Drew of Pulteney Town, Steuben Co. NY; m

Lewis B. Longwell b 1818 in NJ; they were
living in Urbana, Steuben Co. in 1841 (Bob
Longwell) MEACH; STUCHS

Rachel Ann Rutan - (1850-1911) p/Jacob Rutan-
Ellen Ackerman of Totowa, Bergen Co. NJ; she
died in Paterson and is bur at Cedar Lawn Cem
(cemetery records) 1870C; PCHSP

Ralph E. Rutan - (1903-1972) p/Uziah Rutan-Helen
S. Henry; he was a clerk in Newark in 1929;
he died in Miami FL; CDIR; 1920C; SSA

Raymond Rutan - (1904-1977) resident of Brick,
Ocean Co. NJ; SSA

Raymond Ruton - bc 1917 p/George Ruton-Emma _____
1920C

Raymond G. Rutan - (1894-1937) p/George H. Rutan
-Lillian Britchford; a clerk in Bloomfield NJ
in 1932; he is bur at Tranquility Chyd, Sussex Co.; METC; 1920C; SXHS

Raymond W. Rutan - (1909-1999) p/William E.
Rutan-Emma J. Hopper m Gertrude Maxwell; they
lived in Westwood, Bergen Co. NJ and Chicago;
he was a missionary in India and he died in
Pinellas FL; his Obit was in the *Kansas City
Star*, 24 Jan 1999; ZAB; 1920C

R.E. Rutan - (1896-1976) (see Robert E. Lee
Rutan, below)

Rebecca Rutan - b 1816 p/Peter Rutan-Charity
Corselius of Sussex Co.; she moved with her
family to Butler Co. OH (see OH listing)
BOGGS; CBRF

Rebecca Retan - (1814-1893) p/Peter Retan-Polly
Hatt of Seneca Co. NY; m Josiah Swick (1811-
1895) at Seneca Co. in 1834; she was from
Romulus NY; LDS; LHRL

Rebecca Rutan - (1836-1887) p/Henry Rutan-Sarah
Courter m John Drew (1833-1905) in 1854 at
Manchester Twp, Passaic Co. NJ; both bur at
Cedar Lawn Cem, Paterson (cemetery records)
METC; LDS; PCHSP

Rebecca Rutan - b 1817 p/Abram Rutan-Ann Courter
m (1) Bartlett C. (Barton) Winfield (1811-
1850) in 1837 (2) David Hennion about 1838
(Judith Courter Ullman) PCHSQ

Rebecca A. Rutan - b 1836 m John Struble (1827-
1859) in 1853 (Carol Van Buren)

Rebecca Anna Rutan - b 1835 p/Abraham Rutan-Susanna Hazen m Horace J. Rollison in 1861 (see
prior entry) JS; CBRF; LDS

Reinhardt Rutan - d 1928 p/George Rutan-Claudine

Landos m Sarah Corwith of Brooklyn ("Thomas
Halsey and His Descendants in America") NYDC

Rhoda E. Ruttan - (1880-1920) p/Peter Ruttan-
Sarah E. See of Kingston, Ontario; m Charles
Flora b 1851 at Potsdam NY in 1897; they
lived in Quebec and returned to the U.S.
about 1903; they lived in Clark Co. WI and
she died in Stanley WI; she is bur at Oakwood
Cem ; Note: their marriage certificate
indicates that he was born in 1854 (Nikki
Flora) NYMC

Richard Rutan - (1818-1892) m Mary Ann Fort b
1824 of Albany NY; he was a farmer in Fallsburgh, Sullivan Co. NY and later in Sandburgh
Mamakating Town; he was a widower when he d
in an accident; CAREY; 1855C; 1860C; CDIR;
NYDC

Richard Reuton - resident of MA; 1840C

Richard Rutan - (c1895-1947) (see Lester Richard
Rutan, above)

Richard E. Rutan - (1863-1919) evidently the
step-son of Thomas B. Rutan of Brooklyn, the
son of Annie Powers and her first husband,
Josiah T. Heningham; MRUT

Richard F. Rutan - bc 1919 p/Lawrence E. Rutan-
Florence Hughson; 1920C

Richard G. Rutan - (1824-1880) p/Henry Rutan-
Sarah Courter m Elizabeth Wager (1824-1894)
in 1846; he was a carpenter in Newark 1860-
1870; CDIR; METC; 1850C; PCHSP; 1860C; 1870C

Richard G. Rutan, Jr. - (1859-1860) p/Richard G.
Rutan-Elizabeth Wager; METC

Richard M. Rutan - p/Harry E. Rutan-Olive Miller
m Alice Jordan; IKE

Richmond Ruttan - bc 1911 (see William Richmond
Rutan, below)

Rita V. Rutan - (1915-1990) bur at Holy Cross
Cem, North Arlington, Hudson Co. NJ (cemetery
records) (see Frank B. Rutan, above)

Robert Rheutan - p/Daniel A. Rheutan-Rosina Duff
of Orange Co. NY; AAR

Robert Retan - m Ida Beers at Hammondsport NY in
1888; NYMC

Robert Rutan - b 1919 p/Lucius W. Rutan-Edna
_____; 1920C

Robert Rutan - (1883-1964) of NJ; SSA

Robert Rutan - bc 1899 m Rose Ethel _____ (1899-
1974; she lived on Staten Island NY; 1920C;
SSA

Robert Rutan - (1907-1992) of NY; SSA

Robert A. Rutan - corporate officer, Coughlin-Brown, Inc., NYC living in Fairlawn NJ in 1933; CDIR

Robert C. Rutan - (1823-1912) p/Henry Rutan-Sarah Courter of West Milford, Passaic Co. NJ m Eliabeth White Ekings (1822-1895) in 1848; METC; PCHSP; 1850C; 1900C

Robert E. Lee Rutan - (1896-1976) p/Linn Rutan-Juliette Coykendall m Lillian _____; resident of Belleville in 1934 he died in Beemerville, Sussex Co.; CDIR; 1900C; SSA

Robert Felice Rutan - b 1893 p/James B. Rutan-Mary Curry of Newark; he was born in Long Island City NY; NYBC; 1900C

Robert J. Rutan - p/Robert Rutan m Mary Maines (1847-1875) of Sparta NJ at Lafayette Twp, Sussex Co. in 1867; JS; EG

Robert J. Rutan - d 1893; bur at Warwick Cem, Orange Co. NY (cemetery records)

Robert James Ruttan - (1876-1953) p/John C. Rettan-Mary E. Slack of Loughborough, Ontario he was a drill-operator, unm, and is bur at the Rural Cem, Adams NY; RUTT; NYDC

Robert Judson Rutan - bc 1919 p/Cody L. Rutan-Adelaide Kelly; 1920C

Robert L. Rutan - d 1902 p/Frank H. Rutan-Katherine Schlee of Newark; Robert died in infancy; NJHS

Robert M. Rutan - (1846-1920) p/Henry K. Rutan-Lucetta M. Roe; CW soldier, 37th N.J.Infantry harness-maker in Paterson in 1871, unm; he died in Paterson and is bur at Cedar Lawn Cem (cemetery records) 1870C; NJCW; USARCH; CDIR; PCHSB

Robert M. Rutan - p/Harry E. Rutan-Olive Miller m Alice Jordan; TKE

Robert Miller Rutan - (1941-1976) (New Jersey Biographical Index)

Robert R. Rutan - bc 1918 p/Clarence E. Rutan-Miriam Tanger; 1920C

Robert Ware Ruton - b 1927 p/William V. Ruton-Laura E. Ware (Pam Walling)

Rosina Rheutan - p/Daniel A. Rheutan-Rosina Duff of Orange Co. NY; AAR

Roy Rutan - (1897-1983) p/Peter R. Rutan-Frances L. Martin (see Leroy Rutan, above) 1900C; SSA

Roy Rutan - p/David E. Rutan-Harriet Perry of

Elmira NY; MCRC

Roy Rutan - m Mary _____; he was a clerk in NYC
in 1933; CDIR

Roy Rutan - p/George D. Rutan-Henrietta Hepp
(Janet Rutan Bowers)

Roy F. Rutan - (1890-1903) p/Archie N. Rutan-
Mary E. Gray; he died in an accident and is
bur at Woodlawn Cem, Elmira NY; 1900C; NYDC;
CHEMHS

Roy W. Rutan - (1900-1944) p/William A. Rutan-
Grace B. Stanaback m Violet (Viola) Utter
(c1900-1976) in 1920; he was a WWI vet and is
bur at Unionville Cem, Orange Co. (cemetery
records) she died in NYC (Carol Van Buren)

Royal E. Rutan - (1889-1911) p/Charles E. Rutan-
Mary L. Bissell of Paterson; 1900C; METC

Russell Rutan - (1886-1948) p/James B. Rutan-
Mary Curry of Queens Co. NY; he died in San
Francisco CA; 1900C; CADRI

Russell Rutan - (1908-1979) of NJ and Staunton
VA; SSA

Russell Conklin Rutan - (1896-1938) p/John L.
Rutan-Laura H. Conklin m Marion Borland (1895
-1986) he was a veterinary surgeon in Goshen,
Orange Co. NY; she later lived in Florida,
Orange Co.; CDIR; 1900C; NYDC; SSA

Russell E. Rutan - resident of Elizabeth NJ in
1924; CDIR

Ruth Rutan - (1921-1971) p/Chauncey Rutan-Mabel
D. Sigafoos m _____ Morrison; LIZR; ROOTSW

Ruth Rutan - bc 1918 p/Harry Rutan-Mary _____;
1920C

Ruth D. Rutan - b 1895 p/David Rutan-Minnie
Starkweather of Newark ("A Brief History of
Robert Starkweather") 1900C

Ruth E. Rutan - bc 1917 p/Harry E. Rutan-Olive
Miller m Harry A. Ike (1915-1986) IKE; 1920C

Rynier Speer Rutan - b 1806 p/Paul Rutan-Metje
Speer of Bloomfield, Essex Co. NJ; m Catherine _____ (1819-c1867); they were living in
Hartford CT in 1840 and Springfield MA in
1850; he was a silversmith there in 1854;
Note: LDS has him born in Scotch Plains,
Union Co. NJ; Springield MA records have an
unnamed Rutan female ag 49 dying there in
1867 (probably Catherine) LDS; CDIR; ABRWP;
1850C; DRCSHP; CVHM

Rynier S. Rutan - (1837-1908) p/George A. Rutan-
Harriet Hinman of Brimfield MA; he is bur in

Danbury, Fairfield Co. CT (Thomas M. Rutan)

Sadie Rutan - (1877-1915) p/William H. Rutan-
Hannah Winters of Newark; m Walter Adam Evans
(1874-1924) she died in So. Orange, Essex Co.
NJ; METC; 1880C; PCHSP

Sadie Mae Rutan - **Mae** (1904-1969) p/Frank H.
Rutan-Katherine Schlee of Newark; m Leo H.
Bilse (1905-1998) both are bur at Hollywood
Cem, Union NJ (Janet Rutan Bowers)

Sally Ann Rutan - (1820-1866) p/Robert Rutan-
Mary Courter; she died in Newark (see Sarah
Ann Rutan, below) FH; PCHSB

Sally Ann Retan - b 1829 p/Barnet Retan-Sarah
Drew of Steuben Co. NY; m Samuel Gibson bc
1829; Note: MEACH has her bc 1825; Bob Longwell has her death by 1870; STUCHS; PUH

Samuel Rutan - p/Harmon Rutan-Chloe Lobdell;
PCHSB

Samuel Rutan - (1815-1869) p/David Rutan-Catherine Russell m Sarah Adams bc 1821 in 1837; he
was a farm laborer/blacksmith in Branchville,
Sussex Co. in 1850 and living with his mother
in 1860; he is bur at Branchville Cem (cemetery records) MEACH; CoMR; 1850C; SXHS; 1860C

Samuel Rutan - (1819/20-1910) p/John Rutan-Catherine Coon of Paterson (see AL and FL listings)

Samuel Rutan - b 1841 m Jane Meyers in Belleville, Essex Co. NJ; there is a Jane Rutan
(1842-1916) bur at Arlington Cem, Kearny NJ
across the river from Belleville (cemetery
records) PCHSQ

Samuel Rutan - (1845-1912) p/Henry A. Rutan-
Harriet Burnett of Williamsburg, Kings Co. NY
m Sarah Jane Everett (1847-1894) at Brooklyn
in 1866; he was a typographer for the *N.Y.
World*; both died in Brooklyn; 1880C; NYDC

Samuel Rutan - (1887-1970) of NYC; SSA

Samuel B. Rutan - (1835-1915) p/Robert Rutan-
Mary Courter m Mary Louisa Fitzgerald (1841-
1929) in West Milford, Passaic Co. in 1860;
he was a farmer in Goshen, Chester and Wash-
ingtonville, all Orange Co. and later an
undertaker with his brother Abraham R. Rutan;
he also was a stable-owner in Paterson in
1910; he is bur at Laurel Grove Cem, Totowa;
METC; 1860C; 1880C; LDS; 1910C; POCGS; PCHSP

Samuel C. Ruton - b 1836 m Almira _____ b 1843;

he was a brickmason living in Huntington,
Suffolk Co. NY in 1870; 1870C

Samuel J. Rutan - bc 1849 p/Charles S. Rutan-
Margaret Vanover of Warren Co. NJ; 1850C

Samuel J. Retan - a machinist in NYC in 1849;
CDIR

Samuel L. Rutan - chauffeur in Paterson in 1927;
CDIR

Samuel M. Rutan - (1871-1933) p/Samuel B. Rutan-
Maria L. Fitzgerald m Mary Semer Senior (1872
-1968) in 1894; they lived in Paterson where
she was born; she died in Wayne and both are
bur at Cedar Lawn Cem, Paterson (cemetery records) 1900C; PCHSP

Samuel T. Rutan - (1839-1915) p/Layton Rutan-
Dorothy Hull; he was living in Dingmans Twp.
Pike Co. PA in 1850 and Coles Co. IL in 1900
(see IL listing) 1850C; 1900C

Sarah Reton - b 1805 p/John Reton-Susannah Storm
of NYC; LDS

Sarah Ruton - d 1888; bur at Mt. Pleasant Cem,
Newark (cemetery records)

Sarah Rutan - b 1818 p/Samuel Rutan-Susannah
Cymer of Sussex Co. NJ; NJG

Sarah Rutan - (1824-1865) of Newark NJ; CRC

Sarah Rutan - b 1853 p/Horace Rutan-Mary C.
Barnes m Arlington Bedell b 1859; METC

Sarah Rutan - (1834-1910) p/Daniel Rutan-Lucy
Compton (see PA listing) MCRC

Sarah Rutan - (1857-1905) p/Peter Rutan-Jane
Sherman of Waverly, Sullivan Co. NY; m Julius
Camp in 1876; she died at Traverse City MI;
MCRC

Sarah Ann Rutan - (1820-1866) p/Robert Rutan-
Mary Courter, unm, she died in East Newark NJ
and is bur at Cedar Lawn Cem, Paterson (cemetery records) where her gravestone says
(1821-1867); Note: AAR identifies her as Polly Ann Rutan; 1850C; PCHSP

Sarah Ann Ruttan - b 1878 p/Peter Ruttan-Sarah
E. See m (1) Horace J. McCabe of Springbrook,
Ontario in 1896 (2) Daniel G. Allan b 1873 of
Potsdam NY at Watertown, Jefferson Co. NY in
1902; NYMC; RUTT

Sarah C. Ruton - b 1868 p/Samuel C. Ruton-Amelia
_____ of Huntington, Suffolk Co. NY; 1870C

Sarah Catherine Rutan - b 1881 p/Peter S. Rutan-
Lydia F. Carman m John A. Wyatt b 1866 at the
Protestant Ref Ch of Bloomingsburg, Sullivan

Co. NY in 1899; they were both from Burling-
ham; NYMC; CAREY; CoMR

Sarah Elizabeth Ruttan - p/Jacob Ruttan-Margaret
Clapp of Fredericksburg, Ontario; m Edgar C.
Smith in 1866; they lived in Waterbury VT
(from the DAR appl #66153 of Maude C.S. Pad-
dock)

Sarah Frances Rutan - **Frances** (1856-c1885) p/
Peter Rutan-Hettie Longwell of Postville,
Passaic Co.; m Isaac Post in 1877 (Bob Long-
well) FH; PCHSP

Sarah J. Rutan - bc 1844 p/Layton Rutan-Dorothy
Hull of Green Twp, Sussex Co. NJ; 1850C

Sarah L. Retan - (1838-1891) p/Almeran Retan-
Zillah Longwell of Steuben Co. NY; m Chester
Enos Cole at Urbana in 1856; MEACH; 1850C

Sarah M. Rutan - bc 1858 p/Adam C. Rutan-Lauretta Conklin of Sussex Co.; m Henry M. _____;
1860C; MCRC

Sarah Mariah Rutan - **Sally** (1811-1835) p/Abram
Rutan-Ann Courter m John Sprague b 1803 in
1828 (Carol Van Buren) CoMR; JS

Sedgewick R. Rutan - **"Sid"** (1836/7-1918) p/Peter
Coss Rutan-Rebecca J. Hough m (1) Hannah ____
bc 1837 (2) Easter Crawford in Sussex Co. in
1868; he was a farmer in Deckerstown in 1860
and was living in Port Jervis, Orange Co. NY
in 1900; he is bur at Laurel Grove Cem, Port
Jervis (cemetery records) NYGBS; EG; 1860C;
1900C; GSNJ

Shirley Rutan - bc 1915 p/Layton Rutan-Ella R.
March of Port Jervis; 1920C

Silvanus James Rutan - (1816-1886) p/Abraham
Rutan-Margaret Ennis m Sarah Isabel Mansfield
(c1827-1865) of Dutchess Co. NY in 1842; he
was a carpenter in Belleville in 1850 and
later a merchant in Harrison, Hudson Co. NJ;
she was born in Brooklyn NY and he died in
Boonton, Morris Co. NJ; CRC; FER; 1850C

Simeon B. Rutan - b 1867 p/Hudson Rutan-Mary J.
Bell (see Bishop Rutan, above) 1875C

Simon Retton - resident of Fayette(ville) Seneca
Co. NY in 1830; 1830C

Sophia Reton - (1809-1814) buried near Boston
(NEHGR 79:52)

Sophia Rutan - (1839-1912) p/John Rutan-Susan
Walker of Newark; m Eugene Virginius Connet
(1836-1905) in 1858; he was a hat manufactur-
er and was born in Norfolk VA or Millburn,

Essex Co. NJ (Connet Genealogy) they died in
So. Orange NJ; GSNJ; LDS

Sophronia Ruton - b 1848 p/William Ruton-Sophronia Winston m John H. Shaffer b 1846 in
(from DAR appl #78820 of Nellie E. Shaffer)

Stanley Rutan - b 1913 p/Earl Rutan-Mary E.
Stratton m Cecil McArnt of Freetown NY; he
was a chauffeur in Oneida, Madison Co. NY;
she is bur at Glenwood Cem, Oneida; 1920C;
NYMC

Stella Rutan - b 1868 p/Calvin Rutan-Rachel E.
Stager of Belleville; she was living in Nutley, Essex Co. NJ in 1928, unm; CDIR; FER

Stella Rutan - p/Peter D. Rutan-Sarah Spangenburg m _____ Stevens; resident of Matawan NJ
in 1943 (from her brother Benjamin's Obit)
1900C

Stella Rutan - b 1891 p/Peter R. Rutan-Frances
L. Martin; 1900C

Stella Rutan - bc 1890 m George Symington (1885-
1949) of Manchester CT (see Estelle Rutan,
above) ROOTSW

Stephen Rutan - b 1833/35 p/Layton Rutan-Dorothy
Hull; living in Morgan Co. IN in 1900 (see IN
listing) 1850C; 1900C

Stewart Rutan - d 1891 of Walpack Twp, Sussex
Co. NJ; CRAWN

Stuart C. Rutan - (see Charles Stuart Rutan,
above)

Susan Rutan - b 1800 p/Peter C. Rutan-Charity
Corselius of Sussex Co.; she moved with her
family to Butler Co. OH (see Patty Rutan,
above) BOGGS

Susan Retan - (1831-1865) p/John Retan-Polly
Lemy of Steuben Co. NY; m Henry Smith; Note:
per MEACH she was a "half-sister to Olney
Retan"; 1850C; 1855C; MEACH; STUCHS

Susan Retan - b 1818 p/Barnet Retan-Sarah Drew
of Steuben Co. NY; m William Lounsbury b 1813
and confirmed by Barnet's will; STUCHS; MEACH

Susan Rutan - b 1839 p/Daniel Rutan-Lucy Compton
she may have moved with her family to Wayne
Co. PA; MCRC

Susan A. Rutan - b 1842 p/Peter Rutan-Hettie
Longwell m Samuel A. Cooper at Newark in
1860 (Bob Longwell) FH; LDS

Susan J. Rutan - d 1859; bur at Mt. Pleasant Cem
in Newark (cemetery records)

Susanna Rutan - bc 1815 p/Abraham Rutan-Anna

Coss m Stephen Roy (1796-1882) both bur at
Wantage Cem, Sussex Co. (cemetery records)
Note: PPDLN has her (1801-1889) CBRF; STICK;
BB; LDS; PPDLN

Sylvester L. Retan - (1840-1917) p/John Retan-
Rachel Shuart of So. Pulteney, Steuben Co. NY
m Alice Angelica Depew (1844-1922) at Urbana
in 1867; he was a CW soldier, 161st N.Y. Infantry and after the War a vineyardist in
Urbana in 1890 and Hammondsport in 1891; no
children; some info from his CW pension file;
he is bur at Elmwood Cem, Hammondsport and
his Obit appeared in the *Hammondsport Herald*,
12 Dec 1917; Note: MEACH has him born in 1837
(Alice W. Matson) 1880C; CDIR; STUCHS; 1890C;
NYMC; USARCH

Sylvia Rutan - a dressmaker in Rochester NY in
1891; CDIR

Sylvina Retan - (1844-1923) p/John Retan-Rachel
Shuart of Steuben Co. NY; m John L. Sprague
(1840-1920) of Pleasant Valley at Penn Yan,
Yates Co. NY in 1882; she died at Bath and is
bur at Glenview Cem, Pulteney Town and he at
Pleasant Valley, Steuben Co. (her Obit was in
the *Hammondsport Herald*, 2 May 1923) CoMR;
STUCHS; 1850C; PUH

Thelma Rutan - (1926-1988) p/Chauncey Rutan-
Diana M. Sigafoos of Bayonne NJ; m Carl Haner
(1915-1975) of Suffern, Rockland Co. NY; they
both died at Media, Delaware Co. PA (Carol
Haner) LIZR

Theodore Rutan - (1823-1907) m Elizabeth Dunham
at Plainfield, Union Co. NJ in 1849; he was a
blacksmith born in Belleville; CW soldier,
30th N.J. Infantry; they were living in
Plainfield in 1900; he is bur at Hillside Cem
Scotch Plains; USARCH; NJCW; 1900C

Theodore Rutan - m Mary _____; they lived in
Hunterdon Co. NJ; LDS

Theodore Rutan - b 1856 m Sarah Beverage (1869-
1949) of NYC; she is bur at Woodlawn Cem. NYC
NYDC

Theodore Rutan - b 1857 p/William Rutan-Elizabeth _____ of Plainfield, Union Co. NJ; LDS

Theodore Rutan - (1874-1945) p/Albert C. Rutan-
Adeline Vermule of Plainfield; m (1) Sarah
Black (2) Mattie Eliza Green b 1876 of Wash-
ingtonville, Orange Co. NY in 1892; he was a

pipe-fitter and mechanic in Goshen, Orange
Co.; he is bur at Woodlawn Cem, NYC (some
info from his father's Obit; Note: the order
of the two marriages is uncertain; 1880C;
NYMC; NYDC; CDIR; 1900C

Theodore Hazard Ruton - b 1913 p/William V.
Ruton-Laura E. Ware (Pam Walling)

Thomas Retan - b 1800 p/Thomas Retan-Christina
Berdan of Schraalenburg; EARDP; DRCNYC

Thomas Rutan - resident of Washington Twp, Bergen Co. NJ in 1840; 1840C

Thomas Reton - m Mary _____; she was a widow in
NYC in 1849; CDIR; AGBI

Thomas Retton - m Mary Thomas in NYC in 1821;
NYCMM

Thomas Rutan - m Elizabeth _____ (1839-1906)
ROOTSW

Thomas Retan - (1846-1932) m Emmaline Hubbard
(1854-1939) in Jefferson Co. NY; possibly related to Mary Jane Retan who wed William Novell and lived in IA; 1880C; NYMC

Thomas Benton Rutan - (1892-1949) p/Josiah T.
Rutan-Laurietta Birck of Brooklyn NY; m Alice
Standerwick (1896-1983) he was a bricklayer
in Brooklyn in 1920 and is bur at St. Charles
Cem, Pinelawn, Suffolk Co. NY; she died in
Garden City, Nassau Co. NY; Note: he is list-
ed as Thomas Fenton Rutan in the 1920C; NYDC;
SSA; 1920C

Thomas Benton Rutan - (1923-1923) p/Thomas B.
Rutan-Alice Standerwick; NYDC

Thomas D. Ruttan - (1851-1918) p/David Ruttan-
Nancy Davis of Picton, Ontario; m Martha Ann
Duetta (1853-1924) he was an ordained minister and they lived in Avoca and Rochester NY;
he died at Sparta, Livingston Co. NY and is
bur at Union County Cem; Note: see Charles
David Ruttan, above) CDIR; NYDC

Thomas H. Reton - b 1827; of NY; AGBI

Thomas K. Rheutan - bc 1845 p/Daniel A. Rheutan-
Rosina B. Duff; he m the daughter of C.M.
Leonard-Rebecca Smith bc 1845 ("Portrait and
Biographical Record of Orange Co. N.Y.")

Vanetta Rutan - m Timothy Depue at Sussex Co. NJ
in 1824; Note: she is called Van Etta Reutan
in county marriage records; GSNJ; CoMR

Violet Rutan - b 1886 p/Peter R. Rutan-Frances
L. Martin m _____ Sanders (from her brother

Henry's Obit) 1900C

Violet Rutan - (1901-1976) of NYC; SSA

Violet Rutan - (1907-1969) of MA; SSA

Virginia Ruton - hairdresser in NYC in 1873;
CDIR

Virginia Rutan - (1908-1995) p/Harry Rutan-Leona
McCabe of Brooklyn NY; m Frederick Broderick
d 1970; they lived in Sussex Co. NJ; EOVB;
CRC; 1920C

Volney Rutan - (c1849-1910) p/Henry A. Rutan-
Harriet Burnett of Brooklyn; m Elizabeth Merkle (1849-1917) of London in 1870; NYMC; NYTO

Waldemar I. Rutan - b 1889 p/Josiah T. Rutan-
Laurietta Birck of Brooklyn NY; m Matilda
_____; he was an Episcopal Priest; MRUT;
1900C

Walter Rutan - b 1868 p/John Rutan-Mary Elizabeth _____ m Mary _____ b 1868; he was a
"pressman" in Montclair and living there with
his mother in 1900; 1880C; CDIR; 1900C

Walter Rutan - bc 1874; grandson of Jacob Rutan;
1880C

Walter Rutan - (1901-1984) of Asbury Park, Mon-
moth Co. NJ; SSA

Walter Abram Rheutan - b 1874 p/Abram A. Rheutan
-Mary H. Young of Worcester MA; he died young
AAR

Walter E. Rutan - (1865-1937) he was a printer
born in Mountain Lakes NJ and died in Montclair; bur at Rosedale Cem per his Obit in
the *Montclair Times* 12 Dec 1937; (see prior
entry) CDIR; NYTO

Walter H. Ruttan - (1892-1980) p/James D. Ruttan
-Margaret B. Jones of Vernon, Oneida Co. NY;
he is bur at Cooper St. Cem, Vernon (cemetery
records) RUTT; SSA

Walter Harrison Rutan - (1891-1970) p/Harrison
R. Rutan-Nellie M. Sheridan of Rochester NY;
m Lucy M. Neidinger (1890-1981) he was a WWI
soldier, 347th Infantry; after the War he was
a mechanic; bur at Holy Sepulchre Cem, Rochester (Thomas M. Rutan) 1900C; NEHGS; NYDC;
SSA; 1920C

Walter J. Rutan - (1873-1929) p/John H. Rutan-
Lydia Snyder; living with his step-mother,
Emma Vanderhoof, his father's second wife,
in Newark in 1900; PCHSQ; 1900C

Walter J. Rutan - locksmith in Newark in 1924;

CDIR
Warren Rutan - of NJ; m Etta _____ (from his
son's death certificate (see PA listing) NYDC
Wesley Anna Rutan - b 1849/51 p/James M. Rutan-
Leah Crocheron of Tottenville, Staten Island
NY; m Benjamin Hill Warford there in 1866;
she was alive in 1908 (from his CW pension
file) 1870C; SIHS
Wilber R. Rutan - (1852-1922) p/Peter Rutan-
Mariah Compton of Sussex Co. NJ; m Jennie A.
Babcock Hunt (1860-1932) of Caton Center NY
at Elmira NY in 1881; he was a paper-hanger
and painter in Elmira in 1900; he is bur at
Woodlawn Cem; Note: his death certificate has
his widow was Jennie L. Hunt however her dc
calls her Jennie A. Babcock Rutan (Arthur C.
Rutan) CHEMHS; CDIR; 1900C; NYDC
Wilbur R. Rutan - (1875-1946) p/Peter Rutan-Lucy
Babcock m Nellie M. Wood (1878-1963) at Elm-
ira NY in 1905; he is listed as a "trainman"
in Elmira in 1900 and an engineer in 1934; he
is bur at Woodlawn Cem (cemetery records)
William Ruton - living in Cobleskill, Schoharie
Co. NY; 1850C; 1860C
William Ruton - living in White Plains, Westch-
ester Co. NY in 1850; 1850C
William Retan - bc 1830 p/Peter Retan-Polly Hatt
of Ovid Town, Seneca Co. NY; m Hulda Evans;
LHRL
William Miers Rutan - bc 1845 p/Isaac M. Rutan-
Elizabeth Aggear; living in Vallejo CA with
his father in 1860 (see CA listing) 1850C;
FER
William Rheutan - living in Newark, 4th Ward in
1870 (see David, Belle K. Rheutan, above)
1870C
William Rutan - (1863-1921) p/Henry K. Rutan-
Lucetta M. Roe m Geneva Nanny (1867-1888) at
Middletown, Orange Co. NY in 1887; she died
of blood-poisoning; they are bur at Cedar
Lawn Cem (cemetery records) PCHSP; 1880C;
METC; 1920C
William Rutan - m Ida Seaman (from child's death
certificate) Note: Cedar Lawn Cemetery in
Paterson NJ has an Ida (1873-1906) wife of a
William Rutan (see prior entry) NYDC
William Rutan - living in Caldwell, Essex Co. NJ
in 1932; CDIR
William Retan - shoemaker in NYC in 1849; CDIR

William Reton - m Ann Maria Jerbus in NYC in
1834; NYCMM
William Ruttan - (1893-1900) p/Charles D. Ruttan
-Martha Duetta; he drowned in the Erie Canal
at Rochester; bur at Riverside Cem; NYDC
William Rutan - (1904-1986) p/Harry R. Rutan-
Nellie M. Sheridan of Rochester NY; he lived
in Hilton, Monroe Co. NY (Tom Rutan) 1920C;
SSA
William Rutan - a contractor in Revere MA in
1890-1892; CDIR
William A. Rutan - (1869-1946) p/Brice P. Rutan-
Corcelia Elston of Unionville, Orange Co. NY;
m Grace Bell Stanaback (1871-1969) in 1900;
she died in the Bronx NY; both are bur at
Unionville Cemetery, Orange Co. (cemetery re-
cords) Note: her son's death certificate
calls her Grace Bell so she may have been a
widow when she wed William; LDS; MAV; SXHS;
EG; NYDC
William A. Ruttan - (1861-1923) p/Abraham Ruttan
-Elvira Gordon of Picton, Ontario; m Mary
Hicks (1862-1939) he was a salesman who came
to the U.S. in 1902; he died in Jefferson Co.
NY; RUTT
William A. Rutan - (1897-1964) of Paterson, WWI
vet and prob unm; his sister Dorothy b 1897
lived in IL; he is bur at Cedar Lawn Cem
cemetery records); PCHSQ
William Benjamin Rutan - (1888-1953) p/James D.
Rutan-Emma Murray m Myra Huston (1892-1957)
of Warwick, Orange Co. NY; NYDC
William Burton Ruttan - (1872/3-1935) p/Peter
Ruttan-Sarah L. See of Sydenham, Ontario;
Melba (Melva) Lehr in 1923; he was a painter
who died at Theresa, Jefferson Co. NY; bur at
Oakwood Cem; Note: his death certificate says
that his mother was Mary Ann See; RUTT; NYDC;
FMLWT
William C. Ruton - b 1860 p/Samuel C. Ruton-Al-
mira _____ of Huntington, Suffolk Co. NY;
1870C
William D. Rutan - coal dealer at 111 Broadway,
NYC in 1869; CDIR
William D. Rutan - hat dealer at 612 Broadway,
NYC in 1869; CDIR
William D. Rutan - bc 1916 p/Elmer Rutan-Eliza-
beth _____; 1920C
William Duane Rutan - (1835-1912) p/John Rutan-

Susan Walker m Kate Canfield Dodd (1837-1866) at Newark in 1858; he was Collector of Internal Revenue and Postmaster of Newark in the 1890's; they are bur at Mt. Pleasant Cem, Newark (cemetery records) Note: one record has his middle name as David (Robert Rutan) 1850C; CoMR; GSNJ; NPL

William Edgar Rutan - (1855-1940) p/John Henry Rutan-Elizabeth Ann Smith of Nyack, Rockland Co. NY m (1) Amanda Lavinia Hopper (1863-1882) (2) Emma Jane Hopper b 1865; living in Westwood, Bergen Co. 1917-20; he was a carpenter and was working in NYC in 1920; he and Amanda are bur at Valleau Cem, Bergen Co. (Ree Hopper) ZAB; LDS; 1860C; PCHSP; 1920C; CDIR

William Elias Ruttan - (1843-1901) p/Henry P. Ruttan-Mary Jones of Ontario; William was a newspaper reporter who died in Brooklyn NY; NYDC; RUTT

William G. Rutan - (1860-1862) p/William H. Rutan-Hannah Winters of Paterson; METC

William H. Rutan - (1831-1925) p/Henry Rutan-Sarah Courter m Hannah Winters (1836-1916) at Paterson in 1857; they moved to Newark in 1864 where he died and is bur at Fairmount Cem; he was born at Snufftown, Sussex Co.; PCHSP; METC; PCHSQ; CRC; 1880C; 1920C

William H. Rutan - (1843-1904) p/James M. Rutan-Leah Crocheron of Staten Island; m Annie Manee (1852-1907) they are bur at Bethel M.E. Cem, S.I.; BHS; 1860C; EARDP; 1900C

William H. Rutan - Supervisor, Town of Westfield Richmond County (Staten Island) NY 1858-1861 and the N.Y. State Assembly in 1864 (Clute: "Annals of Staten Island") (see prior entry) NYGBS; DARLDC

William H. Rutan - (1837-1909) p/Peter Coss Rutan-Rebecca J. Hough m (1) Mary _____ (2) Julia A. Dunning (c1839-1893) at Frankford Twp, Sussex Co. NJ in 1858; he was a farm laborer at Deckerstown in 1860; William, Julia (and perhaps Mary) are bur at Laurel Grove Cem, Port Jervis, Orange Co. NY; Note: there is a marriage certificate showing a William H. Rutan wed to Ella Van Sickle Quick at Port Jervis in 1895; and, the death certificate of his son Clarence of CA says that Clarence's mother was surnamed "Janes";

EG; NYGBS; 1860C; NYMC; CADRI; PJUGO

William H. Rutan - (1857-1929) p/Horace Rutan-
Mary C. Barnes m Adelaide L. Rice (1849-1927)
they lived in the Bronx NY where she died; he
died in Brooklyn and they are bur at Evergreen Cem, Brooklyn; METC; EG; 1900C; NYDC;
1920C

William H. Ruttan - (1855-1921) p/Abraham Ruttan
-Mary Ann See m Gertrude A. Ruttan b 1861,
his niece; he was a farmer who died in Watertown, Jefferson Co. NY; bur at Chaumont;
NYDC; RUTT

William H. Ruttan III - (1898-1963) p/George H.
Rutan-Lillian Britchford m Alice Traynor
(1904-1963) of Scotch Plains NJ in 1921; he
was an insurance agent born in Newark; they
died in a house fire at Keyport, Monmouth Co.
NJ; bur at Fairview Cem, Westfield NJ; METC;
1900C; PCHSP

William Henry Rutan - (1854-1907) p/Hudson Rutan
-Mary J. Bell of Sussex Co. NJ; m Alice
Stradworthy; moved with his father to MI
about 1884 (see MI listing) KKI; 1860C

William Henry Rutan, Jr. - b 1878 p/William H.
Rutan-Alice Stradworthy; he moved with his
father to MI; m Elsie M. Stevenson (see MI
listing) KKI

William Henry Ruttan - (1843-1902) p/Henry P.
Ruttan-Mary Ann Taylor m (1) Hannah Maria
Hazard (1843-1885) in 1871 (2) Alice Sayer
(1862-1944) of Napanee, Ontario at Three Mile
Bay, Jefferson Co. NY in 1890; he was a farmer born in Hastings, Ontario; he died in Watertown NY; RUTT; NYMC; NYDC

William Henry Ruttan - (1887-1949) p/John Henry
Roughtean-Mary Ellen Cullen of Boston MA; m
Annie F. Keegan of Framingham MA in Boston
about 1910; he died in Los Angeles: LDS;
CADRI

William Henry Ruttan - (1888-1982) p/John A.
Ruttan-Edith E. Switzer m Ethel Elizabeth
Jackson (1894-1963) he was born in Black
River NY and died at Harrowsmith, Ontario;
RUTT

William Henry Rutan - b 1910 p/Henry K. Rutan-
Regina C. Brawn of Newark; m Tina Pepe b 1914
of PA in 1937; POV

William Henry Rutan - (1911-1988) p/William H.
Rutan-Annie F. Keegan of Boston; he died in

Los Angeles; CADRI; LDS

William Lincoln Rutan - (1865-1915) p/Nicholas
W. Rutan-Sarah Marsh; m Elizabeth Young
(1865-1951) in Brooklyn in 1887; he was a
builder born in Newark NJ and was working in
Boston 1887-1905; she was a writer born in MA
they were living in Santa Clara CA in 1910;
he died in Sacramento CA and she in Marion
Co. OR; his Obit was in the *Boston Globe* 8
Jun 1915 (see CA listing) FER; 1910C; NYMC;
1910C; BPL; ORDI

William M. Rutan - (1883-1955) p/James B. Rutan-
Mary Curry of NYC; m Katherine Eiseler (1887-
1969) he died at Roosevelt, Nassau Co. NY;
NYDC

William Myers Rutan - b 1846 p/Isaac M. Rutan-
Elizabeth Aggear of NYC; NYBC

William N. Rutan - (1836-1909) p/Peter C. Rutan-
Rebecca J. Hough of Sussex Co.; he died at
Port Jervis, Orange Co. NY; NYDC

William Norman Rutan - (1865-1936) p/John A.
Rutan-Eunice Carman m Julia Ross (1864-1926)
in 1889 at the Third Presbyt Ch in Wantage
Twp; living in Newton, Sussex Co. in 1920;
Note: Julia was a half-sister of Maggie Poul-
ison wife of Frank Emmet Rutan; 1920C; PPDLN;
EG

William Richard Rutan - (1919-1966) p/Arnold R.
Rutan-Rose E. Mulligan; he was born in NYC
and died at Beach Haven NJ; MRUT

William Richmond Rutan - (1911-1960) p/Edward N.
Rutan-Louise Humes of Newark; m Marie Wilcox;
he died at Buffalo NY and is bur at Elmlawn
Cem (Norman Rutan) NYDC

William Rose Rutan - p/Moses D. Rutan-Ida M.
Rose of Port Jervis, Orange Co. NY; SXHS

William S. Reton - (1829-1878) CW soldier, Cpl
170th N.Y. Infantry; bur at Hampton National
Cem, Hampton VA (Civil War Research Database)

William S. Rutan - bc 1877 p/Melville Rutan-Jennie _____; 1880C

William Service Ruttan - (1876-1950) p/Peter M.
Ruttan-Mary Long m Marietta Adams (1870-1944)
at Oswego NY in 1906; he was born at Green
Point, Ontario and died at Oswego; NYMC;
NYDC; RUTT

William Vermilye Ruton - (1843-1924) p/Benjamin
B. Ruton-Joanna M. Vermilye m Laura Louisa
Hazard (1848-1908) at Central Presbyterian
Church, Orange, Essex Co. NJ in 1875; he may

have served as an Officer in the Civil War
with the 78th U.S.C.T. (or this may to refer
to his son William in the SpAMWar) he was a
bookkeeper and they were living in East
Orange at the turn of the century; they are
bur at Rosedale Cemetery, Orange (Pam Walling) WHIT; 1880C; CDIR
William V. Ruton, Jr. - (1876-1946) p/William V.
Ruton-Laura L. Hazard m Laura Elmer Ware in
1912; he was a corporate officer, Wallace-
Mullin & Co., NYC in 1917; they lived in East
Orange and he died in Toronto (Pam Walling)
1880C; CDIR
William W. Rutan - living in NYC in 1925; he is
related to Joseph V. Rutan; CDIR
Wilson Rutan - bc 1825; he moved to Mills Co. IA
1880C

A L A B A M A

Aaron Rutan - (1850-1876) p/Samuel Rutan-Eliza
Williams m Melinda Carolyn Alberson in 1870;
after his death she married Joseph Brantley
Peacock b 1849 in 1879 ("Holland Family History") GDAW; 1860C

Albert Wilson Rutan - p/John A. Rutan-Beulah
Jones; GDAW

Bonnie Grace Rutan - (1908-1986) p/John A.
Rutan-Ila Bracklin m William Holland; they
lived in Jacksonville FL; GDAW; SSA

Charles Hartley Rutan - (1852-1927) p/Samuel
Rutan-Eliza Williams (see FL listing)
1860C

Collie Mae Rutan - p/John A. Rutan-Beulah Jones
m (1) Roy Jones (2) Charles Wright; GDAW

Elizabeth Rutan - (1848-1926) p/Samuel Rutan-
Eliza Williams (see FL listing)

Hattie Rutan - d 1910 in Jefferson Co. (AL
Death Index)

John Albert Rutan - (c1876-1927) p/Aaron Rutan-
Melinda C. Alberson m (1) Beulah Jones (2)
Ila Bracklin d 1968 at Daleville, Dale Co. in
1911; they were living in Dothan in 1922 (AL
Death Index) she died at Santa Rosa FL; FLDI;
GDAW; MEACH

Myrtie Rutan - p/John A. Rutan-Beulah Jones m
(1) Ben F. Cox (2) _____ Melvin; GDAW

Samuel Rutan - (1819-1910) p/John Rutan-Catherine Coon of Paterson NJ; m Eliza Williams b
1817 from GA; living in Newton, Dale Co. in
1860; later lived in Walton Co. FL; (see FL
listing) 1850C; PCHSP; LDS; 1860C

Virginia Rutan - p/Aaron Rutan-Melinda C. Alberson m John Adkinson at Coffee in 1898; MEACH;
GDAW

William Reton - resident of Baldwin Co.; 1850C

A L A S K A

Charles Hart Ruttan - (1910-1994) p/Arthur C.
Ruttan-Beatrice W. Robertson of Winnipeg m
Evelyn Wilson Meyer b 1912 of Nome; he served
with the RCNVR in WWII; SSA; RUTT

A R I Z O N A

Daniel Ruton - resident of Grant Twp, Johnson
Co.; 1870C

Donald J. Rutan - (1923-1996) Lt. Col., USAF,
bur at Maricopa National Cemetery, Maricopa
(cemetery records)

Gordon James Rutan - b 1891 of Miami, Gila Co. m
Genevieve Lita Wilson b 1895 (see IN listing)
LDS

Harry Rheutan - (1904-1970) of Phoenix; he had
lived in NE; SSA

Helen Rheutan - (1909-1986) of Phoenix; she had
lived in TN; SSA

John R. Ruton - resident of Prairie Twp, Newton
Co.; 1860C

A R K A N S A S

Albert Retan - VP, Bank of Commerce, Little Rock
1893-1898. he may be Albert Hurd Retan of
Steuben Co. NY; CDIR

Andreas Rutan - (1901-1903) bur at Rogers Cem,
Benton Co. (cemetery records)

Ann Rutan - (1824-1900) bur at Rogers Cem, Benton Co. (cemetery records)

Carrie Retan - boarding with Albert Retan in
Little Rock 1895-1896, possibly his daughter;
CDIR

Delta P. Rutan - (1901-1960) she died in San
Fernando, Los Angeles Co. CA; her mother was
an Elliot; CADRI

Zillah E. Retan - (1875-1968) boarding with Albert Retan in Little Rock 1895-1896, possibly
his daughter; she was originally from NY; she
was living in Little Rock in 1935 and died
there; MCRC; SSA; CDIR

C A L I F O R N I A

Adam Poe Rutan - (1840-1926) p/Samuel Rutan-
Sarah Cracraft of OH and San Joaquin Co.; m
Henrietta L. Herbaugh b 1838 in PA at Alameda
in 1872; they were living in Santa Barbara in
1900 and in Los Angeles in 1920; he is bur in
Santa Barbara; no children; GAR; 1860C; LDS;
1920C

Alexander Rutan - b 1889; living in San Francisco; 1920C

Alexander Wallace Rutan - (1880-19<u>72</u>) p/Samuel
M. Rutan-Margaret J. Cantwell of Carroll Co.
OH; m Mabel C. Bradshaw (1883-1941) he was
an attorney in Santa Ana, Orange Co.; she was
from TX; CoBR; SSA; CADRI; JAS

Alexandra Rutan - (1920-1986) p/Alexander W.
Rutan-Mabel C. Bradshaw of Orange Co.; she
died in Santa Barbara; JAS

Alfred Rutan - (1895-1973) of Pico Rivera, Los
Angeles Co.; SSA

Alice Prairs Rutan - she was granted a POA in
the estate of Julia A. Travis (San Francisco
Probate Index)

Alvin Ruttan - (1916-1973) of MO; he died in Los
Angeles; CADRI

Arlie Rutan - (1900-1980) of Costa Mesa, Orange
Co.; SSA

Arthur Retan - b 1855 in PA; m Emma R. _____
b 1855 in PA; 1920C

Arthur Rutan - (1880-1885) p/Samuel Rutan-Semiramis Benson of Los Angeles (George A. Rutan)

Burt Rutan - b 1871 p/Peter Rutan-Mary E. Share
of NJ, IL, IN, MI and NV; he was a merchant
in Monterey; GKB

Byron Volaski Rutan - (1870-1957) he died in San
Joaquin Co.; his mother was a Quiggle; CADRI

C. Retan - sailed to CA from NY in 1855 aboard
the S.S. George Law (Norman Rutan)

C.W. Rutan - (1859-1884) *San Francisco Call
Index*)

Catherine Rutan - (1836-1868) p/Samuel Rutan-
Sarah Cracraft m Denver Samuel Church (George
A. Rutan)

Catherine Rutan - b 1891 in IL; she was born an
Erickson; she was living in San Francisco in
1920; 1920C

Charles Rutan - m Gertrude May Tompkins; he is
probably the son of George A. Rutan-Rhoda A.
Stearns; JAS

Charles Rutan - b 1864 in NY; he was a patient

at Riverside in 1920; 1920C

Charles Rutan - b 1886 in MA; m Elizabeth _____
b 1886 in OH; they were living in Los Angeles
in 1920; 1920C

Charles Rutan - (1891-1968) resident of Hollywood; SSA

Charles A. Rutan - b 1879 p/Samuel Rutan-Semiramis Benson of San Joaquin Co.; 1880C

Charles Delbert Ruttan - (1885-1924) p/Peter
Ruttan-Sarah E. See m (1) Belle Roushon b
1884 at Watertown NY in 1904 (2) Rose Sinai
(1895-1970) in 1913; they were living in Oakland in 1910 and Sacramento in 1920; he was a
naval aviator in WWI and after the war a
painter/photographer; he died in Oakland;
RUTT; 1910C; 1920C

Charles Edwin Ruttan - (1884-1934) p/Charles D.
Ruttan-Martha Duetta m Della Alvira Brown
(1885-1978) at Rochester NY in 1903; they
lived in Hollywood and died in Los Angeles;
RUTT; CADRI

Charles F. Rutan - court reporter in Los Angeles
1888-1890; CDIR

Charles F. Rutan - president of the L.A. Driving
Park Assn in Los Angeles in 1890; CDIR

Charles Frederic Rutan - (1923-1978) he was born
in Reedly, Fresno Co. and died in Los Angeles
LDS; CADRI

Charles H. Rutan - (1892-1968) he died in Los
Angeles; he is probably the adopted son of
Peter C. Rutan of Port Jervis NY; CADRI

Charles William Rutan - (1843-c1923) p/Samuel
Rutan-Sarah Cracraft of OH and San Joaquin
Co.; he was a farmer in KS (see KS listing)
and he died in Fresno (George A. Rutan) 1860C

Charles Longwell Rutan - b 1839 p/Peter Rutan-
Hettie Longwell of NJ; m Paralee Peter in
1876 (*San Francisco Call Index*) divorced in
1883; the CA Genealogy Index calls her Parler
in 1889 he was living in Russian River Twp,
Sonoma Co. (voter records)

Charles Richard Ruttan - (1912-1982) p/Charles
E. Ruttan-Della A. Brown m (1) Virginia Petty
d 1950 in 1938 (2) Frances Adelaide Clark b
1929 in 1951; he was born in NYC and died in
Los Angeles; RUTT; CADRI

Clara E. Rutan - (1876-1885) p/Samuel Rutan-
Semiramis Benson of San Joaquin Co. (see
Edna Rutan, below) 1880C

Clarence E. Rutan - engineer in Los Angeles in 1888; he may be the son of William H. Rutan-Julia Dunning of Port Jervis NY; CDIR

Cornelius William Rutan - (1859-1884) p/Peter Rutan-Mary E. Share of NJ; Note: he is sometimes referred to as **William C.** Rutan; GKB

David F. Rutan - b 1886 p/David F. Rutan-Mary E. Westervelt of NJ; m Etta M. _____ b 1889 of NJ; they were living in Los Angeles in 1920; 1920C

David Melvin Rutan - (1893-1958) of KS; he died in Butte Co.; CADRI

Daniel Morris Rutan - (1897-1927) p/George E. Rutan-Emma J. Crawford m Faye Etta Hoss (1900-1994) at Bartlesville OK in 1919; GKB

Delmer Neil Rutan - (1924-1987) p/Sylvester F. Rutan-Keziah K. Mason of WV; he was born and died at Downey; he is bur at Rose Hill Cem (Randy Hack)

Donald Rutan - b 1923; his mother was a Tubbs; CABRI

Donald Ray Rutan - (1927-2001) from his Obit in the *Orange County Record*, 1 Feb 2001

Edna Rutan - (1876-1885) p/Samuel Rutan-Semiramis Benson of Los Angeles (George A. Rutan)

Elizabeth Rutan - b 1904 p/William L. Rutan-Elizabeth Young; she was living in Sacramento in 1920; 1920C

Ella Rutan - b 1855 in IN; she was living in Long Beach in 1920; 1920C

Emma Rutan - b 1879 p/William M. Rutan-Victoria Emonce of Vallejo; 1880C

Emma Elizabeth Retan - (1907-1994) of Pacific Grove, Monterey Co.; she was born in VT and her mother's surname was Hight (see MI listing) Note: SSA has her Emma E. **Rutan**; CADRI; SSA

Emma J. Rutan - (1875-1969) she died in Santa Clara Co.; her mother was a Ramos; CADRI

Fannie Reton - she was born in CA; LDS

Frances F. Ruttan - (1872-1875) she was born in Canada and died in San Diego; CADRI

Frances D. Reton - (1873-1971) she was born in MO and died in Los Angeles; CADRI

Francis Ruttan - (1898-1995) of Campbell, Santa Clara Co.; he is probably **Francis Erwin Ruttan** (see KS listing) SSA

Francis Milton Ruttan - (1902-1984) p/William Stewart Ruttan-Frances Harper of Victoria BC

and CA; m Henrietta Grace Woodward (1911-
1944) of Berkeley; he was a Major in the USAF
during WWII and after the War an investigator
with the California Highway Patrol; he is bur
at Vacaville-Elmira Cem; she died in Alameda
(cemetery records) RUTT; SSA; CADRI

Frank Ruttan - b 1857 in IA; he m Carrie _____ b
1865 in MO; they were living in Martinez,
Contra Costa Co. in 1910; 1910C

Fred Rutan - (1882-1883) p/Samuel Rutan-Semiramis Benson of Los Angeles (George A. Rutan)

Fred A. Rutan - b 1901 p/Ulysses S. Rutan-Nillah
I. Ford of Siskiyou Co.; 1910C

George Rutan - b 1896 m Marie _____ b 1895; they
were living in Vallejo in 1920; 1920C

George Rutan - (1898-1969) he lived in Chico;
SSA

George A. Rutan - b 1916 p/George A. Rutan-
Rhoda A. Stearns m Irene Goforth (1916-2000)
of Palmdale; her Obit appeared in the *Los
Angeles Daily News*, 29 Sep 2000

George Albert Rutan - (1874-1943) p/Samuel Rutan
-Semiramis Benson of San Joaquin Co.; m Rhoda
Arvilla Stearns at Lemoore in 1912; in 1910
he was living in Fresno and he died in Orange
Co. (Deanna Warren) 1880C; 1910C; CADRI

George Chase Rutan - (1898-1969) p/Ulysses S.
Rutan-Nillah I. Ford of Siskiyou Co.; he died
in Butte Co. and is bur at Oak Hill Cem, San
Jose (cemetery records) 1910C; CADRI

George E. Rutan - (1864-1916) p/Peter Rutan-Mary
E. Share of NJ, IN, IL and NV; m Emma Jane
Crawford (1875-1969) GKB

George E. Rutan - (1916-1963) p/William H. Rutan
-Annie F. Keegan of Boston MA; CADRI; LDS

George E. Rutan, Jr. - (1896-1957) p/George E.
Rutan-Emma J. Crawford m Isabel Mae Spencer
(1895-1981) he died in Santa Clara and she
died in Alameda Co.; CADRI

George Edward Rutan - (1888-1952) p/John Henry
Roughtean-Mary Ellen Cullen of Boston MA; he
died in Los Angeles; CADRI; LDS

George M. Retan - (1889-1970) he was born in NY
and died in Orange Co.; CADRI

George Washington Rutan - (1844-1874) p/Samuel
Rutan-Sarah Cracraft of San Joaquin Co. m
Mary _____ (George A. Rutan) 1860C

Harold L. Retan - (1905-1964) he was born in VT
and died in Ventura Co.; CADRI

Harriet C. Rutan - (1912-1995) p/Alexander W. Rutan-Mabel Bradshaw of Orange Co.; m _____ Westlake (Jonathan A. Smith) SSA; CABRI

Harry Ruttan - b 1902 in TX; he was a "hired man" in Saugus, Los Angeles Co.; 1920C

Harry D. Rutan - (1878-1923) p/David F. Rutan-Mary E. Westervelt of NJ; m Clara D. _____ b 1878; they were living in Pasadena in 1920; he died in a boating accident at Newport as reported in the *Yorba Linda Star* 2 Jan 1923; 1910C; 1920C

Harvey Rutan - (1889-1974) he lived in Granada Hills; SSA

Hazel Rutan - (1896-1982) she was born in CA and died in Spokane WA; SSA

Hazel Ruttan - (1889-1979) she was born in Canada and died in Los Angeles; CADRI

Hazel M. Rutan - b 1891; she was living in San Francisco in 1920; 1920C

Helen Rutan - b 1913 p/David F. Rutan-Etta M. _____ of Los Angeles; 1920C

Helen Rutan - (1893-1988) she lived in Los Nietos, Santa Fe Springs and Whittier; SSA

Helena Jennie Retan - (1875-1955) she was born in Canada and died in Los Angeles; CADRI

Henrietta Lenora Rutan - b 1870 p/William M. Rutan-Victoria L. Emonce of Vallejo; m Frank Likens in 1888 (*San Francisco Call*) LDS

Hiram S. Rattan - b 1852 in WI; he was living in Sacramento in 1880 and Sonoma in 1920; 1880C; 1920C

Homer C. Rutan - "Doc" (1908-1998) of Hemet, Riverside Co; he was born in Stafford KS (his Obit appeared in the *Hemet News*, 10 Jan 1998) SSA

Hugh Rutan - (1897-1980) of Friendly Valley; SSA

Irene Rutan - b 1891; she was living with her mother Mary A. Rutan in San Francisco in 1920; 1920C

Isaac Miers Rutan - b 1815 p/Samuel S. Rutan-Hannah Garrabrant of Belleville NJ; he was a ship's carpenter in Vallejo 1860-1884; Note: the 1860C says he was born in Canada (see Northeast listing) 1860C; CDIR

J.M. Rutan - resident of Vallejo, Solano Co. in 1870; this is probably Isaac (prior entry) 1870C

Jack Dale Ruttan - (1915-1944) p/Charles D. Ruttan-Rose Sinai; he died in Butte Co.;

CADRI
James Rutan - carpenter in West Los Angeles in 1888; CDIR
John Rutan - living at 224 Temple St., Los Angeles in 1888; CDIR
John Rutan - "canvasser" in Los Angeles in 1882; CDIR
John Rutan - farmer living at 833 Temple St., Los Angeles in 1890; CDIR
John Rutan - (1838-c1913) p/Samuel Rutan-Sarah Cracraft of OH; m Betsey Beckwith at San Joaquin in 1865; LDS
John Rutan - p/Alexander W. Rutan-Mabel Bradshaw of Orange Co. (Jonathan A. Smith)
John Forrest Rutan - (1924-1995) m Elsie _____ of Newport Beach; he is bur at Harbor Lawn Memorial Park, Costa Mesa (from his Obit in the *Orange County Register*, 15 April 1995)
John S. Rutan - b 1863 in OH; he m Mary B. _____ b 1861; they were living in San Diego in 1920; 1920C
John W. Rutan - (1918-1946) he was born in IA and died in Riverside; his mother's surname was Williams; CADRI
Joseph Milburn Rutan - (1861-1946) p/James Ruttan-Phily Ann Cadman of Ontario and Sanilac Co. MI; m Marietta A. _____ b 1862; they were living in San Luis Obispo in 1910 and Fresno in 1920; Note: 1920C names him **Joseph R. Rutan**, a laborer; she was living in Kings Co. in 1920; he died in Ventura Co.; RUTT; 1910C; CADRI; 1920C
Joyce Minnie Rutan - b 1904 p/Ulysses S. Rutan-Nillah I. Ford of Siskiyou and Stanislaus Cos.; 1910C; 1920C; CoBR
Julia R. Rutan - (1911-1967) she died in San Mateo; CADRI
Kellogg Rutan - p/Llewellyn A. Rutan-Mary Campbell; he was a Lieutenant, USN in WWI (county history)
L.D. Rutan - rancher in Pomona 1896, 1897; CDIR
Lawrence R. Rutan - (1913-1990) he died in San Bernardino; CADRI
Leonora Clark Rutan - (c1850-1912) she was born in Chicago and she died and was bur in Vallejo (M. Ellsworth)
Leroy J. Rutan - (1887-1967) his mother's surname was Nanny; he died in Placer Co.; CADRI
Leroy R. Rutan - (1887-1965) p/Luther M. Rutan-

Virginia Beard of Elmira NY; he was a hairdresser who lived in Los Angeles; he is bur
at Live Oak Memorial Park, Monrovia; CADRI;
SSA; ROOTSW

Llewellyn A. Rutan - b 1871 p/Peter Rutan-Mary
Share of NJ, NY, IL, and NV; m Mary Campbell
of Santa Cruz in 1899; he was a hotel-keeper
in Salinas; living in Monterey in 1920
("History of Monterey and Santa Cruz Counties") 1920C

Lydia May Rutan - (1872-1967) her mother's sur-
name was Wyatt (she may be the sister of
Wright Samuel Rutan of MO) she died in Los
Angeles; CADRI

M. Rutan - resident of Vallejo, Solano Co. in
1870; 1870C

Madeline Adel Rutan - (1901-1971) p/George E.
Rutan-Emma J. Crawford m Clarence Eugene
Pearce (1886-1950) in 1920 in San Jose where
she lived; GKB; 1920C

Margaret A. Rutan - b 1858 in IA; she was liv-
in Riverside in 1910; Note: the 1910C has her
born in 1851; 1910C; 1920C

Mary Rutan - she was living in Oakland in 1910;
1910C

Mary A. Rutan - b 1873; she was living in San
Francisco in 1920; 1920C

Mary Ann Rutan - p/George E. Rutan-Emma J. Crawford of San Jose; she died young; GKB

Mary N. Rutan - p/Samuel Rutan-Semiramis Benson
(see Nellie Mary Rutan, below)

May L. Rutan - (1872-1967) (see Lydia M. Rutan,
above)

Maurice Rutan - Morris W. (1906-1970) p/Ulysses
S. Rutan-Nillah I. Ford of Stanislaus Co.; he
died there; 1910C; CADRI; 1920C

Melba Eleanor Rutan - (1923-1992) p/Sylvester F.
Rutan-Keziah K. Mason of WV; m John Ivan Stafford b 1916; she died at Whittier and is bur
at Rose Hill Cem (Randy Hack)

Merry C. Rutan - (1915-1975) she was from CO and
died in Los Angeles; another record has her
Merry R. Rutan; CADRI

Morris Rutan - b 1898 m Faye _____ b 1902; they
were living in San Jose in 1920: 1920C

Nellie Mary Rutan - (1877-1971) p/Samuel Rutan-
Semiramis Benson of Los Angeles; m William
Applegate (1876-1941) at Manila, P.I. in 1914
they were divorced in 1939; she died in Carm-

el (George A. Rutan)

Paul Perry Rutan - (1910-1993) m Evangeline ____
(1916-1999) he was born in IA and was an
accountant in San Clemente per his Obit in
the *Orange County Register*; he may be the son
of Bert Rutan (see IA listing) SSA; CADRI

Pauline Rutan - p/William M. Rutan-Victoria
Emonce of Vallejo; 1880C

Peter Rutan - resident of Santa Cruz in 1870; he
may be the son of Peter Rutan-Mary E. Share;
1870C

R.T. Reuton - resident of Brighton Twp, Sacramento Co.; 1860C

Rena M. Rutan - (1866-1943) p/Peter Rutan-Mary
E. Share of NY, NJ, IN, IL and NV; m Ernest
Joseph Dutech (1859-1941) about 1883; Rena
was born in MI; both are bur at Oak Hill Cem,
San Jose; GKB

Robert Ruton - b 1883 in KY; m Annie _____ b
1876 in CO; they were living in Pomona in
1920; 1920C

Robert Wilton Rutan - (1920-1992) p/Wilton L.
Rutan-Josephine Tubbs; he died in San Diego
(Kelly Enokian) CADRI

Roy Rutan - (1887-1967) he lived in Auburn,
Placer Co.; SSA

Ruth A. Rutan - (1908-1969) her mother's surname was Gray; Ruth died in Stanislaus Co.;
CADRI

Samuel Rutan - (1809-1885) p/John Rutan-Nancy
Rusk of Westmoreland Co. PA; m Sarah Cracraft
(1809-1875) of PA in 1832; they were living
in Will Co. IL in 1850 and Elk Horn Twp, San
Joaquin Co. in 1860; they both died in San
Luis Obispo (Kim Vierra) 1850C; 1860C; 1870C

Samuel Rutan - (1851-1883) p/Samuel Rutan-Sarah
Cracraft of San Joaquin Co.; m Semiramis Benson b 1854 in 1875; Samuel was born in IL and
they were living in Union Twp, San Joaquin
Co. in 1870; he died in Los Angeles and she
was a widow at Wesley Ave., West Los Angeles,
in 1890 (George A. Rutan) 1860C; 1870C; CDIR;
1880C

Thomas Ruton - d 1851 (CA Genealogy Index)

Ulysses Schuyler Rutan - (1869-1944) p/Joseph C.
Rutan-Deborah R. Croscroft m Nillah Idell
Ford (1878-1959) of TX at Siskiyou Co. in
1897; they were living there in 1910 and at
Wood, Stanislaus Co. in 1920; Note: the 1910C

has her born in 1879 and the 1920C says 1876
(see OR listing) 1910C; CADRI; 1920C

Verna Margaret Retan - (1901-1995) she was born
in Canada and died in Alameda Co.; CADRI

Vernon Ross Ruttan - (1901-1945) he was born in
Canada and died in San Joaquin Co.; CADRI

Victoria Rutan - p/William M. Rutan-Victoria
Emonce of Vallejo; 1880C

Viola Rutan - b 1910 p/Catherine Rutan; they
were living in San Francisco in 1920; 1920C

Viona Rutan - p/Llewellyn A. Rutan-Mary Campbell
of Monterey; 1920C

Wallace Hatton Rutan - (1908-1955) he was born
in WA and died in Los Angeles; CADRI

Wesley J. Ruttan - b 1860 in Canada; he was living in Miramonte in 1920; 1920C

Wesley Michael Ruttan - (1894-1943) p/Simon G.
Ruttan-Mary A. Kelly m Ina Brunskill b 1894
in 1920; he was born in IA and died in CA;
RUTT

Wheeler Rutan - p/Llewellyn A. Rutan-Mary Campbell; he was a railway postal worker (Santa
Cruz County History)

William Rutan - b 1845 in NYC; probably the son
of Isaac Rutan (see above); living in Vallejo
Solano Co.; 1860C

William Retan - resident of San Francisco; 1870C

William C. Rutan - b 1843 in OH; he was living
in Los Angeles in 1920; 1920C

William Consider Ruttan - (1824-1909) p/Daniel
Ruttan-Rhoda B. Haight m Hannah Gillam (1821-
c1890) in 1846; reported to have left his
wife in Canada and travelled to California
having adopted the name **"Lucky Baldwin**; he
became a prosperous land-developer and died
from a pistol shot perpetrated by a person
(or persons) unknown (Gregory N. Barr) RUTT

William Joseph Ruttan - (1891-1962) p/Simon G.
Ruttan-Mary A. Kelly m Grace V. Gallagher
(1891-1982) he was born in IA and died in San
Diego; she died in FL; Note: RUTT has him
(1890-1960) RUTT; SSA; CADRI

William Lincoln Rutan - (1865-1915) building
inspector; died in Sacramento (See Northeast
Listing); BPL

William Meyers Rutan - b 1845 p/Isaac Miers
Rutan-Eliza Aggear of NYC m Victoria L.
Emonce in Vallejo in 1869; he appears in the
city directory in 1884 in Vallejo living

alone; Note: the 1880C has him born in 1848;
CDIR; 1880C; LDS

William Stewart Ruttan - (1868-1952) p/William
Sherer Ruttan-Sarah Melissa Cadman m Frances
Harper (1872-1975) of York Co. NB; he was a
construction engineer who emigrated to the
U.S. in 1919; he was born in Kaladar, Ontario
and died in San Diego; both are bur at the
Vacaville-Elmira Cem; CADRI; RUTT

Wilton Lynn Rutan - (1895-1982) p/Andreas M.
Rutan of MN; m Josephine Tubbs (1897-1974)
of TX; they lived in Phoenix AZ (Kelly
Enokian) 1920C

C A N A D A

Aaron P. Ruttan - b 1827 p/Abraham Ruttan-
Catherine Dingman m Mary McGuire b 1824; RUTT
PPDLN

Abraham Ruttan - (1815-c1865) p/Michael Ruttan
of Loughborough m Mary Ann See b 1815; Note:
RUTT says some records identify her as Mary
Ann Knight; she was a widow in Lyme Town,
Jefferson Co. NY; RUTT; LDS

Abraham Ruttan - (1831-1897) p/Abraham Ruttan-
Catherine Dingman m Elvira Eloise Gordon
(1841-1906) in 1861; RUTT

Abraham W. Ruttan - b 1798 p/William Ruttan-
Margaret Steel m Catherine Dingman; Note:
RUTT identifies her as **Mary Dingman** and says
they were wed at St. John's Ch, Bath, Ontario
in 1821; PPDLN; LINT; RUTT

Ada May Ruttan - b 1902 at Ryde, Lewisham, Ontario; LDS

Agnes Maria Cowin Ruttan - b 1850 p/Christopher
Ruttan-Phoebe Ann Doars m James Scully and
moved to the U.S.; LDS; RUTT

Aletha Lorinda Ruttan - b 1878 p/William Maitland Ruttan-Rosetta Van Sicle; she was born
at Peel, Toronto Twp; LDS

Alfred Farley Rutan - (1874-1951) p/William
Ruttan-Mary J. Farley m (1) Rebecca Parks
(1864-1936) at Akron Village in 1900 (2)
Hazel Baker d 1979 in Los Angeles; he served
as a Private in the 10th Infantry during the
SpAmWar; he is bur at Mickle Memorial Cem,
Gravenhurst, Ontario; RUTT; LDS

Alice Maud Mary Ruttan - (1868-1945) p/Michael
Ruttan-Rachel Smith m (1) Charles A. West (2)

James Byron Lowe; she was born in Ontario and
died in Auburn, King Co. WA (Obituary Daily
Times) RUTT

Allan Ruttan - (1826-1898) p/Peter W. Ruttan-
Fanny Roblin of Adolphustown; m Caroline
Smith (1832-1905) at Montreal in 1854; he was
a physician; they both died at Napanee; RUTT;
LDS

Alma Ruttan - b 1896 p/Samuel N. Ruttan-Agnes
_____ of Mariposa, Victoria Co., Ontario;
1901C

Alonzo Ruttan - (1846-1927) p/David W. Ruttan-
Nancy Doars of Adolphustown; m Eliza Jane
Rankin (1847-1910) RUTT

Alvie Edison Ruttan - (1878-1951) p/Peter M.
Ruttan-Mary Long (see Northeast listing) RUTT

Amanda Ruttan - p/Jacob Ruttan-_____ Livingston
m Willis S. Warner; they lived in MI; LDS

Anne Ruttan - bc 1806 p/Peter Ruttan-Jemima
Sloot; LDS

Anne Ruttan - b 1868 p/Christopher W. Ruttan-
Mary J. Farley; LDS

Anthony Ruttan - (1844-1931) p/John Ruttan-Mary
Stinson (see IA listing) RUTT; LDS

Bathsheba Ruttan - b 1827 p/Joseph B. Ruttan-
Alley Caniff m Levi Caniff; Note: LDS has her
born in 1825; RUTT; LDS

Charles Ruttan - b 1824 p/Joseph B. Ruttan-Alley
Caniff; RUTT

Charles E. Ruttan - b 1845 p/Michael Ruttan of
Loughborough; Note: LDS has him born as early
as 1831; RUTT; LDS

Charles Gilbert Ruttan - (1845-1932) p/William
Ruttan-Julia Ann Pake m Mary Elizabeth Jane
Abbot (1854-1920) in 1878; they are bur at
the Stockdale Cem, Wooler; LDS; RUTT

Charles Millidge Ruttan - (1883-1970) p/Henry N.
Ruttan-Andrina Barberie of Winnipeg; m Frances Jane Mary Wood (1887-1958) at Winnipeg in
1910; he served as an Officer in both World
Wars, awarded a CBE and was a company official; they are bur at Mt. Pleasant Cem, Toronto; CWW; RUTT

Charles Stuart Rutan - (1808-1894) p/William
Ruttan-Margaret Steel m Mary Brown Rowe
(1816-1886) at Coburg, Hamilton Twp, Ontario;
he died at Fontanella IA; LINT; RUTT

Charles William Ruttan - (1891-1944) p/Charles
G. Ruttan-Mary Abbot of Wooler, Ontario; m

Lucille Metcalf (1891-1966) of Ann Arbor MI
at Detroit in 1912; they are bur at St. Cath-
erines, Ontario; LDS; RUTT
Christopher Ruttan - (1818-1903) p/Michael Ruttan of Loughborough m (1) Phoebe Ann Doars
(1820-1873) in 1838 (2) Sarah Malcolm b 1831
in 1869; LDS; RUTT
Christopher W. Ruttan - (1838-1917) p/Christoph-
er Ruttan-Phoebe A. Doars of Sydenham; m Mary
Jane Farley (1846-1916) at Loughborough Twp
in 1862; Note: LDS has him born in 1840 and
the marriage at Frontenac; LDS; RUTT
Cyrus Franklin Ruttan - (1884-1966) p/John A.
Ruttan-Edith E. Switzer of Harrowsmith; m
Emma Pauline Burley (1896-1938) of Sydenham
in 1912; they died in Oneida Co. NY (see
Northeast listing) RUTT
Daniel Ruttan - (1790-1846) p/William Ruttan-
Margaret Steel m Rhoda Bathsheba Haight d
1868 at Fredericksburg Twp in 1812; they were
born in Adolphustown and lived in Kingston
until their deaths; they are bur at St.
Paul's Chyd, Adolphustown; LINT; LDS; RUTT
Daniel Haight Ruttan - (1818-1897) p/Daniel
Ruttan-Rhoda B. Haight m Melissa Arthur
(1815-1880) (see Northeast listing) RUTT
David Ruttan - (1789-1867) p/Peter Rutan-Jannet-
je Ackerman of Adolphustown; m Elizabeth _____
(1804-1879) RUTT; LDS
David Ruttan - b 1820 p/Joseph B. Ruttan-Alley
Caniff m Elizabeth Content Griffis b 1819;
both were alive in 1865; LDS; RUTT
David Ruttan - b 1845 p/Christopher Ruttan-Phoe-
be A. Doars m Hilda J. Brown b 1849 at Peter-
borough, Havelock Twp, Ontario in 1864; RUTT;
LDS
David A. Ruttan - (1827-1898) p/Michael Ruttan m
Martha Shurley b 1830 in 1851; she was born
in Brockville, Ontario; RUTT; LDS
David John Ruttan - (1860-1928) p/David A. Rutt-
an-Martha Shurley m Ida _____; they lived at
Peterborough; RUTT
David William Ruttan - (1817-1907) p/Peter W.
Ruttan-Fanny Roblin m (1) Nancy Davis (1822-
1894) in 1844 at Prince Edward, Ontario (2)
Louisa (Southard) Vincent d 1910; he and
Nancy are bur at Glenwood Cem, Picton; RUTT;
LDS
Edith Ruttan - (1861-1923) p/Walter Ruttan-Marie

Antoinette Saunders m James A. DeMille b 1869
in 1887; LDS; RUTT

Edna Elitha Ruttan - b 1889 p/John C. Rettan-
Maria Slack of Kingston; m Ernest Mastin;
Note: RUTT calls her **Edna Eletta** Ruttan; LDS;
RUTT

Eleanor Ruttan - bc 1818 p/Peter Ruttan-Jemima
Sloot of Loughborough; m Lorenzo Switzer;
LDS; RUTT

Elgan Victoria Ruttan - (1910-1998) m _____ All-
mark; she died at Kingston (Obituary Daily
Times)

Elisa Adeline Ruttan - b 1817 p/Joseph B. Ruttan
-Alley Caniff of Adolphustown; Note: LDS has
her born in 1824 which is the year of her
baptism; RUTT; LDS

Elisha Ruttan - (1824-1916) p/John Ruttan-Mary
Steel m Susanna Outwater (1835-1893) in 1856;
they both died in Adolphustown and are bur at
the United Church Cem; VWR; RUTT

Eliza Jane Ruttan - (1863-1944) p/Christopher
Ruttan-Phoebe A. Doars m (1) William Malcolm
(1858-1891) (2) William Hendron; LDS; RUTT

Elizabeth Ruttan - m Peter Switzer at Marysburg,
Prince Edward Co., Ontario in 1812 (see Rachel Ruttan, below) RUTT

Elizabeth Ruttan - b 1800 p/William Ruttan-Margaret Steel m (1) Hugh C. Thomson (1791-1834)
in 1816 (2) Rev Dr. Adam Townley; LINT; RUTT

Elizabeth Ruttan - b 1813 p/Joseph B. Ruttan-
Alley Caniff; she died young; RUTT

Elizabeth Ruttan - (1823-1896) p/Peter W. Ruttan
-Fanny Roblin of Northport, Prince Edward Co.
m Samuel Osborne b 1812 in 1843; she died in
Sophiasburg and they are bur there at the
Foster Burying Ground; LDS; RUTT

Elizabeth A. Ruttan - b 1856 p/Abraham Ruttan-
Mary Ann See m Isaac Sharp; they probably
lived in Jefferson Co. NY; RUTT

Enoch George Ruttan - (1850-1924) p/Richard N.
Ruttan-Elizabeth M. Griffis m (1) Caroline
Martha Richardson (1853-1895) at Napanee in
1872 (2) Elizabeth Love (1860-1947) he was a
carpenter in Toronto; RUTT

Ernest Ruttan - b 1890 p/Stewart Ruttan-Fanny
_____ of Victoria; 1901C

Ethel Rutan - of Picton, Ontario m Frank R.
Gardner b 1868; they were living in Picton in
1900 ("Ancestors of Samuel Converse, Jr.")

Ethel Jennie Ruttan - b 1893 (see **Jennie** Ruttan, below)

Fannie Ruttan - b 1871 p/John A. Ruttan-Margaret Bauter; they lived in Jefferson Co. NY (see Northeast listing) RUTT

Frances Ruttan - b 1816 p/John Ruttan-Mary Steel m Peter Outwater b 1807 at Adolphustown in 1831; VWR; RUTT

Frances Pearl Ruttan - b 1903 p/Thomas A. Ruttan -Ethel E. Taggart m Donald Needham (1901-1955) in Shanghai, China; she was a prisoner of the Japanese in Hong Kong, 1941-1943; RUTT

Frank Elgin Ruttan - (1864-1928) p/David W. Ruttan-Nancy Davis m Christiana Carman (1863-1946) at Green Point in 1882; he was born and died at Picton; she died at Winnipeg; he is bur at Glenwood Cem; VWR; RUTT

Frederick R. Ruttan - **Robert F.** (b 1890 p/Isaac Ruttan-Annie H. Gardner of Norwood; m Eliza J. Gallagher about 1925; LDS; RUTT

George Henry Ruttan - (1816-1907) p/John Ruttan-Mary Steel m Matilda Palmer in 1842; he was born in Morris Twp, Huron Co., Ontario; she was born in Victoria District; VWR; RUTT

George R. Ruttan - (1880-1939) he was a grain-broker in Winnipeg; NYTO

George Sidmer Ruttan - (1865-1928) p/Samuel S. Ruttan-Orphey Rozell m (1) Etta Tenant (1874-1900) (2) Ida Stephen (1877-1943) in 1901; RUTT

Gertrude Ruttan - b 1858 p/Walter Ruttan-Maria A. Saunders m Robert Clapp b 1854 in 1875; LDS; RUTT

Henry Ruttan - (1792-1871) p/William Ruttan-Margaret Steel of Adolphustown; m Mary Jones (1799-1873) he was a W1812 soldier, author, inventor, Sheriff of Newcastle and Speaker of the House of Assembly; they are bur at St. Peter's Church Cem; RUTT

Henry Andrew Ruttan - (1881-1958) p/Henry N. Ruttan-Andrina Barberie of Iron Mountain MI m Frances Josephine Flaherty b 1889 at Port Arthur in 1913; Note: RUTT says he was born in Winnipeg and lived in Canada his entire life; she was born in Iron Mountain; RUTT; LDS

Henry Carman Ruttan - (1898-1973) p/Frank E. Ruttan-Christiana Carman m (1) Alberta Eliza-beth Roberts (1898-1963) of Grenville, Sask-

atchewan in 1922; she died in Calgary (2)
Anne Dorothy (1902-1973) she died in Winnipeg
he was a pharmacist and is bur at St. James
Cem, Winnipeg; LDS; RUTT
Henry Jones Ruttan - (1819-1879) p/Henry Ruttan-
Mary Jones m Margaret Pringle (1824-1907) at
Cornwall in 1847; he died at Coburg and is
bur at St. Peter's Church Cem; LDS; RUTT
Henry Norlande Ruttan - (1848-1925) p/Henry J.
Ruttan-Margaret Pringle m Andrina Barberie b
1847 in 1871; he was an Army Officer and eng-
ineer who died in Winnipeg; CWW; RUTT
Henry Peter Ruttan - (1813-1893) p/Peter W. Rut-
tan-Fanny Roblin m (1) Elmida Margaret Lloyd
(2) Mary Ann Taylor b 1817 of Tyendinaga
about 1843; he died in Chatham Twp, Kent Co.,
Ontario; LINT; LDS; RUTT
Henry Peter Ruttan - bc 1810 p/Peter Ruttan-Jem-
ima Sloot; LDS
Henry Phylander Ruttan - (1892-1977) p/Phylander
Ruttan-Sarah A. Roushorne of Houseys Rapids,
Ontario; m Dency Hull Newton b 1894 of James-
town NY at Orilla in 1919; he died in Toronto
LDS; RUTT
Henry T. Ruttan - (1821-1883) p/Daniel Ruttan-
Rhoda B. Haight m Jane Kirkpatrick (1810-
1866) he died in Leavenworth KS (see KS
listing) LDS; RUTT
Irene Mercedes Ruttan - b 1899 p/John H. Ruttan-
Jessie Bruce; RUTT
Isaac Ruttan - b 1844 p/Abraham Ruttan-Mary Ann
See m (2) Sylvia S. Sammons in 1885; RUTT
Isaac Wellington Ruttan - (1848-1902) p/Christo-
pher Ruttan-Phoebe A. Doars of Leeds Twp,
m Annie H. Gardner (1857-1939) of Dummer Twp;
they are bur at Norwood Cem; LDS; RUTT
Jacob Ruttan - (1806-1867) p/William Ruttan-
Margaret Steel m (1) Margaret Clapp (1815-
1846) in 1841 (2) Mary Ann McConkey (1832-
1910) at Fredericksburg in 1855; he died
there and she died at Morven; PPDLN; RUTT
Jacob Ruttan - (1808-1880) p/William Ruttan-
Rebecca Ellis Angel m Annie G. Carnahan Walt-
ers (1804-1882) MEACH; RUTT
Jacob Ruttan - b 1829 p/John Ruttan-Maria _____
of Prince Edward, Picton; LDS; RUTT
Jacob Ruttan - (1833-1871) p/Daniel Ruttan-Rhoda
B. Haight of Adolphustown; m Mrs. Henry Livingston; Note: LDS has him born in 1821; LDS;

RUTT

James Daniel Ruttan - b 1867 p/Christopher W.
Ruttan-Mary J. Farley; Note: RUTT identifies
him as **James Diercks** Ruttan (see Northeast
listing) LDS; RUTT

James Doors Ruttan - (1852-1921) p/Christopher
Ruttan-Phoebe A. Doars m Cynthia Victoria
Lowe at Peterborough in 1874; he died in
Flint MI; LDS; RUTT

James Miles Ruttan - (1851-1909) p/Lorenzo Ruttan-Margaret Harpel of Loughborough; m Alice
Almira Peters (1859-1932) he died at Wagar-
ville, Ontario; RUTT

Jane Ruttan - (1794-1888) p/Peter Ruttan-Jemima
Sloot m John Freeman (1790-1869) in 1812;
PPDLN; LDS; RUTT

Jane Ruttan - (1811-1841) p/Joseph B. Ruttan-
Alley Caniff; RUTT

Jennie Ruttan - **Ethel Jennie** (1893-1980) p/Isaac
Ruttan-Annie H. Gardner of Peterborough; m
William Arthur Murphy (1888-1963) of Dummer,
Ontario; he died at Peterborough and she at
Norwood; LDS; RUTT

Jesse B. Ruttan - (1840-1878) p/Christopher Ruttan-Phoebe A. Doars m Emily Corneal/Cameal b
1841 at Northumberland in 1864; he was born
at Orilla, Ontario; RUTT; LDS

John Ruttan - (1786-1851) p/Peter Ruttan-Jannetje Ackerman m Mary Steel b 1788 in 1807; VWR;
LINT; LDS; RUTT

John Ruttan - (1810-1893) p/William Ruttan-Reb-
ecca Ellis Angel m Maria _____; he died at
Hinchinbrooke Twp; MEACH

John Ruttan - (1816-1898) p/Peter Ruttan-Jemima
Sloot m Mary Ann Stinson (1820-1898) both are
bur at Sydenham; LDS; RUTT

John Ruttan - b 1870 p/Christopher Ruttan-Sarah
Malcolm; RUTT; LDS

John Allen Ruttan - (1862-1956) p/Lorenzo Ruttan
-Levina A. Mintz of Moskow, Lennox & Adding-
ton Co.; m (1) Edith Elizabeth Switzer (1861-
1934) (2) Edith Hunt d 1953; RUTT

John C. Rettan - (1854-1922) p/John Ruttan-Mary
A. Stinson m Mary Eliza Slack d 1906; he
preferred spelling the surname Rettan; LDS;
RUTT

John Caniff Ruttan - (1815-1899) p/Joseph B.
Ruttan-Alley Caniff m Sarah M. Baillie b 1816
RUTT

John Graham Ruttan - (1913-1996) p/Arthur C. Ruttan-Beatrice W. Robinson of Winnipeg; m Mary Louise Harrison b 1915 in 1946; he was and Officer in the Canadian Navy in WWII and after the War served as a judge on the supreme court of British Columbia; he died at Victoria; RUTT; ODI

John H. Ruttan - dc 1913 p/Jacob Ruttan-Margaret Clapp; RUTT

John Henry Ruttan - (1873-1953) p/Jesse B. Ruttan-Emily Cameal of Orillia; m Annie May Cryderman (1882-1952) at Huntsville, her home town; they moved to the U.S. in 1900; he died in Lansing MI and they are bur at Chapel Hill Cem; RUTT;

John Levi Ructan - b 1863 p/Christopher Ruttan-Mary J. Farley m (1) Matilda Jane Miller (1864-1918) at Simcoe in 1883 (2) Minnie Miller (Matilda's brother's widow) he was a lumberman and prospector born in Sydenham; John and Matilda died at Vanderhoff, British Columbia and he is bur at the Masonic Cem, South Burnaby, BC; RUTT; LDS

John S. Ruttan - b 1857 p/Michael Ruttan-Mary Ann Mountainee; LDS

Joseph Ruttan - (1820-1906) p/John Ruttan-Mary Steel m (1) Susan Laid b 1821 (2) Elizabeth Walker before 1864; he was born in Adolphustown and later lived in Huron Co., Ontario; in 1869 he moved to Sanilac Co. MI; from 1881 to 1883 he lived in the Dakota Territory, Mecosta Co. MI and Kalkaska Co. MI; he died at Traverse City and is bur at Clearwater Cem Kalkaska; RUTT; VWR; LDS

Joseph Brant Ruttan - (1783-1832) p/Peter Ruttan-Jannetje Ackerman of Adolphustown; m Alley Caniff (1785-1851) in 1805; he was born at Sorel, Richelieu, Quebec; LDS

Levi Ruttan - b 1840 p/Abraham Ruttan-Mary A. See; RUTT

Lila May Ruttan - b 1896 p/Oliver F. Ruttan-Mary A. Young; RUTT

Lorenzo Ruttan - (1813-1865) p/Peter Ruttan-Jemima Sloot m (1) Margaret Harpel (1814-1853) (2) Levina Ann Mintz (1832-1918) LINT; LDS; RUTT

Lydia Ruttan - b 1827 in Adolphustown; LDS

Mabel Ruttan - b 1892 p/Stewart Ruttan-Fanny _____ of Victoria, BC; 1901C

Mabel Lillian Ruttan - **Lilly** (1884-1983) p/John
Levi Ruttan-Matilda J. Miller m Roy Edwin
Wheeler (1881-1974) at Kamloops BC in 1920;
she was born in Harrowsmith, Ontario and he
at Sarnia, Ontario; they both died at Abbots-
ford, BC; RUTT; LDS

Margaret Ruttan - b 1829 in Adolphustown; LDS

Mary Ruttan - (1772-1859) p/Peter Ruttan-Jannetje Ackerman m Thomas Elmes Matthews ; their
son Peter was hanged for treason for his
involvement in the Mackenzie Uprising in 1838
Mary died at Brougham, Ontario; LINT; RUTT

Mary Ruttan - **Polly** b 1808 p/Peter W. Ruttan-
Fannie Roblin m Elias Clapp Brown d 1853 in
1825; RUTT; LDS

Mary Ruttan - b 1809 p/Joseph B. Ruttan-Alley
Caniff m Isaiah Thompson; RUTT

Mary Ruttan - b 1815 at Adolphustown; LDS

Mary Ruttan - (1826-1883) p/Henry Ruttan-Mary
Jones m Robert Mant Boucher at Nothumberland
in 1845; RUTT; LDS

Mary Elizabeth Ruttan - m Owen Roblin at Adolphustown in 1793; LDS

Mary Elizabeth Ruttan - b 1874 p/Christopher W.
Ruttan-Mary J. Farley; Note: there is another
LDS record that calls her **Mary Ethel** Ruttan;
LDS

Mary Ethel Ruttan - b 1888 p/John L. Ruttan-
Matilda J. Miller; she was born in Muskoka
District; LDS

Mathew Ruttan - b 1802 p/William Ruttan-Margaret
Steel of Haldemand; LINT; PPDLN

Matthew Steel Ruttan - (1810-1905) p/John Ruttan
-Mary Steel of Adolphustown; m Mary Ann
Shearer b 1812 at Tyendinaga, Hastings Co.,
Ontario in 1838; he died at Kaladan; VWR

Mercy Ann Ruttan - b 1853 p/Michael Ruttan of
Frontenac; LDS

Michael Ruttan - (1798-1861) p/Peter Ruttan-Jemima Sloot m (2) Mary Ann Mountainee b 1827 in
1858; LDS; RUTT

Michael Ruttan - (1842-1914) p/Christopher Ruttan-Phoebe A. Doars m (1) Rachel Smith b 1845
in 1863 at Gananoque (2) Louisa Stone (1848-
1941) he was born at Loughborough and died at
Moose Jaw, Saskatchewan; RUTT; LDS

Mildred Estelle Ruttan - (1890-1973) p/John L.
Ruttan-Matilda J. Miller m Robert Murray
(1883-1966) of Hawick, Scotland at Vancouver

in 1919; she was born in Ryde Twp, Ontario
and died at Vancouver; LDS; RUTT

Mildred Keith Ruttan - b 1905 p/Oliver F. Ruttan
-Mary A. Young; RUTT

Miles Ruttan - b 1846 p/William Ruttan-Eliza
Vanluven of Simco, Midland District; m (1)
Mary Jane Davis b 1846 (2) Sarah Elizabeth
Bard Marks (1850-1938) RUTT; LDS

Minnie Antoinette Ruttan - (1885-1959) p/William
P. Ruttan-Margaret Ann Moxom m Francis Jeff-
rey Burch at Belleville, Ontario where she
was born; she died at Thunder Bay, Ontario;
RUTT; LDS

Nancy Matilda Ruttan - (1809-1890) p/Peter W.
Ruttan-Fanny Roblin m Matthew R. Benson at
Prince Edward in 1834; RUTT; LDS

Oliver Franklin Ruttan - (1871-1938) p/Miles
Ruttan-Mary J. Davis m Mary A. Young b 1876
in 1894; RUTT

Oliver James Ruttan - (1895-1958) p/John L. Ruttan-Matilda J. Miller m Gladys V. McPherson
b 1897; he was born at Muskoka District,
Bracebridge and died at Sproat Lake, British
Columbia (BC Death Index) LDS

Percy Grant Ruttan - (1893-1952) p/John L. Ruttan-Matilda J. Miller m Mabel Victoria Mizon b
1903 at Salmon Arm, BC; he was born at Bracebridge, Ontario and died at Kamloops, BC; she
was born at West Thurrock, England; LDS; RUTT

Peter Ruttan - (1742-1829) a Loyalist from Berg-
en Co. NJ (see Northeast listing)

Peter Ruttan - (1771-1838) p/Peter Ruttan-Janne-
tje Ackerman m Jemima Sloot (1776-1861) at
Cranestown Twp in 1790; Jemima was the daugh-
ter of Michael Sloot, a Lieutenant in the
Loyalist forces from Mt. Sinai, Suffolk Co.
NY; PPDLN; RUTT

Peter Ruttan - (1807-1879) p/Joseph B. Ruttan-
Alley Caniff m Barbara Ellen Howe (1816-1854)
in 1832; he was born at Adolphustown and died
at Odessa; RUTT

Peter Ruttan - bc 1808 p/Peter Ruttan-Jemima
Sloot; LDS; RUTT

Peter Matthew Ruttan - (1839-1886) p/Henry P.
Ruttan-Elmida M. Lloyd m Mary Long b 1842;
RUTT

Peter William Ruttan - (1787-1861) p/William
Ruttan-Margaret Steel m Fannie Roblin (1787-
1841) in 1807; LINT; PPDLN; LDS

Phoebe Ruttan - b 1806 p/Joseph B. Ruttan-Alley
Caniff m John Binninger at St. Thomas Ch,
Hastings in 1825; RUTT; LDS

Phoebe Ruttan - b 1811 p/Peter W. Ruttan-Fanny
Roblin; LDS; RUTT

Phoebe Ann Ruttan - (1858-1924) p/Christopher
Ruttan-Phoebe A. Doars; LDS; RUTT

Phoebe Jane Ruttan - (1865-1952) p/Christopher
Ruttan-Mary J. Farley m Alexander Hubert
Rogers at Tamworth in 1883; RUTT

Philip Ruttan - (1820-1900) p/Peter W. Ruttan-
Fanny Roblin m Abigail Jane Reid (1825-1903)
in 1841; he was born at Adolphustown; RUTT;
LDS

Phylander Ruttan - (1857-1947) p/Wesley J. Ruttan-Hannah E. Doars m Sarah Ann Roushorne
(1866-1931) he was born at Gravenhurst, Ontario and died at Parry Sound; she died at
Bracebridge, Ontario; RUTT

Rachel Ruttan - m Peter Switzer at Marysburg,
Prince Edward Co., Ontario in 1809 (see
Elizabeth Ruttan, above) RUTT

Rachel Ruttan - b 1796 p/Peter Ruttan-Jemima
Sloot m William Vermilyea; LDS; PPDLN; RUTT

Rachel S. Ruttan - (1822-1895) p/John Ruttan-
Mary Steel m Daniel Outwater (1817-1902) VWR

Rebeccah Ruttan - m Robert Grimmon at Fredericksburg Twp in 1814; LDS

Reginald Jesse Ruttan - (1898-1969) p/John L.
Ruttan-Matilda J. Miller m (1) Beatrice J.
Perras (2) Martha A. Ryder; he lived in Mani-
toba and died at Kelowna, BC (BC Death Index)
RUTT

Richard Nugent Ruttan - b 1822 p/Joseph B. Ruttan-Alley Caniff m Elizabeth Maria Griffis b
1822; RUTT

Robert Anderson Ruttan - (1855-1912) p/Henry J.
Ruttan-Margaret Pringle m Nenon Margaretta
Louisa Armstrong (1863-1944) at St. John's
Ch, Toronto in 1882; he was in the real-est-
ate/insurance business and died at Port
Arthur (Thunder Bay) Ontario; RUTT

Robert Frederick Ruttan - (see Frederick Ruttan,
above)

Robert Fulford Ruttan - (1856-1930) p/Allan Rut-
tan-Caroline Smith; he was Dean at McGill
University and a member of the Royal Society
of Canada; he was born at Newburg, Ontario
and died at Montreal; CWW; RUTT

Robert James Ruttan - (1877-1953) p/John C. Rettan-Mary E. Slack; RUTT

Ross Earl Ruttan - (1886-1907) p/John L. Ruttan-Matilda J. Miller of Frontenac; he died at Fernie, BC (BC Death Index) LDS

Roy A. Ruttan - b 1884 p/Samuel N. Ruttan-Agnes _____ of Mariposa, Victoria Co., Ontario; 1901C

Ruth Ruttan - (1815-1899) p/Peter W. Ruttan-Fanny Roblin m John Benson at Hastings in 1836; LDS

Samuel N. Ruttan - (1862-c1924) m Agnes _____ b 1863; they were living at Mariposa, Victoria Co., Ontario in 1901; 1901C

Samuel S. Ruttan - b 1838 p/George H. Ruttan-Matilda Palmer m Orphy Rozell (1844-1908) at Elma, Ontario in 1866; RUTT

Sarah Ruttan - (1803-1886) p/Peter Ruttan-Jemima Sloot m John Switzer (1798-1879) LDS; RUTT; PPDLN

Sarah Elizabeth Ruttan - (1844-1918) p/Jacob Ruttan-Margaret Clapp m Charles Edgar Smith (1841-1935) at Niagara Falls in 1866 (see IA listing) RUTT

Sidney A. Ruttan - b 1853 p/Walter Ruttan-Maria A. Saunders m Mary Ellen Dainard b 1859 in 1879; Note: RUTT has him born in 1857; LDS; RUTT

Sinthy E. Ruttan - b 1850 p/Michael Ruttan; she was born at Frontenac; RUTT; LDS

Stella E. Ruttan - **Estella** b 1888 p/Sidney A. Ruttan-Mary E. Dainard; LDS; RUTT

Stewart Ruttan - b 1867 m Fanny _____ b 1872 in NB; they were living in Victoria BC in 1901; 1901C

Stewart Nelson Ruttan - b 1872/5 p/Andrew A. Ruttan-Alice Gallagher m Mary Esther (Jessie) Grant b 1883 at St. Ola, Hastings Co. in 1900 RUTT

Stewart Wilson Ruttan - (1831-1901) p/John Ruttan-Mary Steel m (1) Nancy Reddick (1822-1853) (2) Mary Bower (1833-1865) VWR

Valet Ruttan - b 1891 p/Samuel N. Ruttan-Agnes _____ of Mariposa, Victoria Co., Ontario; 1901C

Walter Ruttan - (1828-1892) p/Peter W. Ruttan-Fanny Roblin m Maria Antoinette Saunders (1837-1895) RUTT; LDS

Walter Ruttan - b 1894 p/Samuel N. Ruttan-Agnes

_____ of Mariposa, Victoria Co., Ontario;
1901C

Wealthy Ann Ruttan - b 1855/6 p/Christopher Ruttan-Phoebe A. Doars m Peter Ferguson; RUTT; LDS

Wesley John Ruttan - (1830-1908) p/Michael Ruttan m Hannah Emily Doars (1827-1902) LDS; RUTT

Willard Ruttan - b 1907 p/George S. Ruttan-Ida Stephens m Verna McCoy; RUTT

William Ruttan - (1817-1903) p/Joseph B. Ruttan-Alley Caniff m Mary Ann Pake (1822-1909) he was born in Adolphustown and died at Wooler, Ontario; both are bur at Stockdale Cem; RUTT

William Ruttan - (1821-1905) p/Peter Ruttan-Jemima Sloot m Eliza Vanluven (1820-1903) in 1838; he was born and died in Sydenham, Ontario; RUTT

William Arthur Ruttan - (1909-1997) of Provost, Alberta (Obituary Daily Times)

William Consider Ruttan - b 1819 p/Daniel Ruttan-Rhoda B. Haight of Adolphustown (see CA listing)

William David Ruttan - b 1849 p/David W. Ruttan-Nancy Davis m Phoebe Emma Norman (1851-1953) in 1873; she died in Winnipeg; LDS; RUTT

William James Ruttan - (1870-1940) p/Michael Ruttan-Rachel Smith m Hannah Bertha Brooks (1880/1-1937) at Orillia Twp, Simcoe Co. in 1898; they lived in Clyde, Lewisham; LDS; RUTT

William Martin Ruttan - (1841-1927) p/William Ruttan-Julia A. Pake m Amanda Maybee (1847-1925) in 1865; he was a veterinarian and a village constable in the Wooler area; Note: LDS says they were wed in 1863 at Northumberland; RUTT; LDS

William Maitland Ruttan - m Rosetta Van Sicle; LDS

William Sherer Ruttan - (1839-1912) p/Matthew S. Ruttan-Mary Ann See of Adolphustown; m Sarah Melissa Cadman (1843-1931) he died at Hatzic, BC; RUTT

William Winfield Ruttan - b 1865 he was a resident of MO who moved to Melfort, Sasketchewan in 1901; hardware/lumber merchant and MP (Melfort webpage) CWW

Wilmot Smith Ruttan - b 1844 p/Philip Ruttan-Abigail J. Reid m Amanda Adelaid White in 1869 at Hastings; LDS

C O L O R A D O

Clarence E. Rutan - (1917-2001) of Fort Collins, he lived in Colorado Springs and he is bur there at Evergreen Cem (Obit in *The Gazette*, 13 May 2001

Elizabeth Rutan - b 1882 in NJ; she was living in Denver in 1920; 1920C

Fred H. Rutan - (1889-1954) m Feryl E. _____ (1901-1987) both are bur at Mt. Pisquah Cem, Cripple Creek, Teller Co. (cemetery records)

Henry P. Ruton - b 1860 in WI; m Agnes _____ b 1874 in WV; they were living in Cripple Creek in 1920; 1920C

Henry S. Rutan - b 1850 in OH; he was a miner in Ouray Co. in 1880; 1880C

J.H. Retan - living at Silver Creek, Custer Co. in 1880; 1880C

Jessie Rutan - (1895-1987) of Wheat Ridge, Jefferson Co.; SSA

Lydia Rutan - m John Curtis Borton (1854-1932) at Kit Carson Co. after 1915, his second wife she was Lydia Windsor the widow of Henry T. Rutan of NE (see NE listing) (Lois Borton Werline)

Venetia Rutan - b 1886 in IA; she was living in Denver in 1920; 1920C

William Ruton - b 1908 p/Henry P. Ruton-Agnes _____ of Cripple Creek; 1920C

D E L A W A R E

Beatrice J. Rutan - (1896-1991) p/Fred W. Rutan-Ida M. Boone m Albert Stetser (1886-1968) in 1918; they lived in Wilmington; 1900C; 1920C; SSA; MCRC

Boyd H. Rutan - b 1904 p/Fred W. Rutan-Ida M. Boone of New Castle; 1920C

Clara Mae Rutan - b 1917 p/Dana F. Rutan-Mildred Fowler; MCRC

Dana Frederick Rutan - (1890-1920) p/Fred W. Rutan-Ida M. Boone of Elmira NY; m Mildred Fowler at Philadelphia in 1915; they were living in New Castle in 1920; Note: Mildred Fowler Rutan m Raymond G. Wildrick (see PA listing) 1920C; MCRC

Dorcas Amelia Rutan - b 1918 p/Frederick W. Rutan-Edna W. Armstrong m William Martin; ROOTSW; MCRC

Edwin E. Rutan - (1868-1924) p/James C. Rutan-Amelia C. Breese of Waterford MN, Philadelphia and Chemung Co. NY; m (1) Elsie M. Palmer (1873-1907) in 1894 (2) Margaret Riley b 1881 at Philadelphia in 1908; he was born in Dakota Territory or MN and served as a Captain in the 1st Delaware Infantry in the SpAm War; he was living in Wilmington in 1900; 1900C; MCRC; USARCH

Edwin Palmer Rutan - **Palmer** b 1896 p/Edwin E. Rutan-Elsie M. Palmer of Wilmington; m Georgiana Simpson in 1920; he saw service in WWI; 1900C; MCRC; VA

Eleanor L. Rutan - (1906-1926) p/Edwin E. Rutan Elsie M. Palmer m William Todd in 1926; Note: MCRC has her born in 1905; USARCH; 1920C; MCRC

Elsie May Rutan - b 1893 p/Fred W. Rutan-Ida M. Boone m Carl Zoch (1892-1973) at Wilmington in 1912; SSA; 1900C; MCRC

Frederick Wolcott Rutan - (1864-1940) p/James C. Rutan-Amelia C. Breese of Horseheads, Chemung Co. NY m (1) Ida May Boone b 1868 in NY (2) Edna W. Armstrong in 1907; Ida was living in New Castle in 1920; Fred was a carpenter and a Pullman Co. agent; he died in Elmira NY; 1900C; MCRC; 1920C; NYDC; USARCH

Harry Ruton - b 1887 in Philadelphia; he registered for the WWI draft in Wilmington (draft records)

Helen Betty Rutan - (1919-1920) p/Dana F. Rutan-Mildred Fowler; MCRC

Janet Rutan - b 1908 p/Fred W. Rutan-Edna W. Armstrong m (1) Dean Alderman (1915-1987) in Grey Eagle MN (2) Delwin Clabaugh at Swanville MN in 1966; MCRC; ROOTSW; SSA

Lidia Celia Rutan - b 1888 p/Fred W. Rutan-Ida M. Boone m Ralph Dinsmore at Wilmington in 1912; she was born in NY; 1900C; MCRC

Mildred E. Rutan - b 1899 p/Fred W. Rutan-Ida M. Boone m Harry Lodge in NY in 1928; 1900C; MCRC

Paul Jesse Rutan - (1891-1969) p/Fred W. Rutan-Ida M. Boone m Margaret Walls b 1894 at the Asbury Methodist Ch in Smyrna in 1919; he was

born in Wilmington and served in WWI; 1900C;
MCRC; SSA; 1920C

FLORIDA

A. Rutan - living in St. Augustine, St. John's
Co. in 1825; 1825C
Aaron Rutan - b 1850 p/Samuel Rutan-Eliza Will-
iams (see AL listing) 1860C
Adelaide M. Rutan -b 1839 p/Samuel Rutan-Eliza
Williams; living in Newton, Dale Co. AL in
1860; Note: Adelaide was actually Eliza's
daughter by her first husband, James Mallette
MEACH
Albert W. Rutan - (1916-1995) he died in Duval
Co.; FLDI
Allan A. Retan - **Allen** (1908-1996) of NY; he is
bur at Edgewater Cem, Edgewater, Volusia Co.
(see Frances O. Retan, below) ROOTSW; SSA;
FLDI
Alvin Lester Rutan - d in 1942 in Pinellas Co.;
FLDI
Annie Rutan - (1872-1946) p/Charles Hartley Rut-
an-Nancy Dykes of Walton Co.; m (1) Labon
Scott Flournoy (1867-1900) in 1889 (2) _____
Fry; she was living in Alvin TX in 1927 per
her father's Obit; Note: one record has her
death in 1947; 1880C; GDAW; 1885C; OKAFL
Charles Hartley Rutan - (1852-1927) p/Samuel
Rutan-Eliza Williams of AL; m Nancy
"Nannie") Dykes (1854-1917) in 1870; he was a
grocer in Walton Co. who died at Defuniak
Springs; she lived in Freeport and is bur at
the Hatcher Cem (from her Obit in the *Holmes
County Advertiser*) 1880C; MEACH
Charles Hartley Rutan - (1914-1990) p/Hartley E.
Rutan-Ettie L. Strickland of Walton Co.; he
died in Hillsborough Co.; GDAW; FLDI
Charlotte Louise Rutan - b 1920 p/Hartley E.
Rutan-Ettie L. Strickland m C.F. Padgett;
GDAW
Coralee Rutan - (1887-1913) p/Charles H. Rutan-
Nancy Dykes m Willie Lee George at Walton Co.
in 1906; GDAW; CoMR
Cornelius Rutan - d 1839; Musician, 1st Regiment
of Infantry during the Seminole Wars; died at
St. Augustine of a concussion resulting from

137

a fall off a horse (see Northeast listing)
(Florida War Death List, 1836-1842)

Daisy R. Rutan - (1884-1975) p/Samuel Rutan-Mary
E. Taunton m Charles Wilbur Wahl (1877-1915)
in 1911; Note: one record says he died in
1917; they are bur at the Hatcher Ch of God
Cem, Freeport (cemetery records) 1885C; CoMR;
MEACH

Dale Andrew Ruttan - (1922-1941) p/James Gordon
Ruttan-Olive Z. Davis; EM3, U.S. Navy, crew
member aboard the U.S.S. Arizona at Pearl
Harbor, MIA; USARCH; MEACH; OKAFL

Dell Rutan - (1917-1997) p/Emmet Rutan-Eva Withers m Barbara Arlene McLaughlin in 1951; he
died in Manatee Co.; GDAW; FLDI

Dell D. Rutan - b 1878 p/Emmet Rutan-Eva L. _____
of Bay Co.; (see prior entry; there is a
problem here) 1880C

Dorcas Rutan - b 1879 p/Frederick W. Rutan-Edna
A. _____ of Duval Co.; 1880C

Doyle Rutan - p/Emmet Rutan-Eva L. Withers m
Xeripha Johnette Peel in 1951 (see Dell Rutan
above) GDAW

Earl Proctor Rutan - (1907-1990) he died in
Orange Co.; FLDI

Edna Jane Rutan - b 1869 p/Frederick W. Rutan-
Edna A. _____ of Duval Co.; 1880C

Edward J. Rutan - **Joseph Edward** (1884-1961)
p/Charles Hartley Rutan-Nancy Dykes of Walton
Co.; m (1) Eva McLeod in 1910 (2) Jeanette
Colvin in 1918; they were living in Luffkin
TX in 1917 (from his mother's Obit) 1885C;
GDAW

Eleanora E. Rutan - (1929-1998) she died in Lee
Co.; FLDI

Elizabeth Rutan - (1847-1926) p/Samuel Rutan-
Eliza Williams m (1) James Quigley (2) James
McGowan; she died in Pensacola; GDAW; MEACH

Emmet Rutan - b 1843; living in Millville, Bay
Co. in 1885; 1880C; 1885C

Emmet Rutan - (1882-1957) p/Samuel Rutan-Mary E.
Taunton m Eva L. Withers; he lived in Bay Co.
(from his WWI draft registration) and he died
in St. Petersburg; GDAW; FLDI

Ernest Rutan - (1876-1880) p/Samuel Rutan-Mary
E. Taunton; he is bur at the Hatcher Ch of
God Cem, Freeport; MEACH

Eugene Rutan - living in Walton Co. in 1885;
this may be **Hartley E.** Rutan; 1885C

Euphrosine Rutan - m Peter Porter at St. John's
  Co. in 1823; Note: FL marriage records have
  him Peter Parier; LDS
Frances Rutan - (1915-1993) she died in Hernando
  Co.; FLDI
Frances O. Retan - (1909-1990) bur at Edgewater
  Cem, Volusia Co. (see Allan A. Retan, above)
  (cemetery records) FLDI
Francis M. Rutan - b 1841 p/Samuel Rutan-Eliza
  Williams; living in Newton, Dale Co. AL in
  1860; actually Francis is the son of Eliza
  and her first husband, James Mallette; 1860C;
  MEACH
Franklin George Rutan - d 1952 in Tampa; FLDI
Frederick W. Rutan - b 1825 in NY m Edna A. _____
  b 1843 in PA; they were living in Duval Co.
  (see DE listing) 1880; 1880C
George Austin Retan - d 1969 in Broward Co.;
  he was probably born in 1886 and an author-
  ity on school management; ROOTSW; FLDI
George William Rutan - (1915-1966) he died in
  Manatee Co.; FLDI
Guilford C. Rutan - (1908-1998) he died in High-
  lands Co.; FLDI
Harry E. Rutan - d 1967 in Dade Co.; FLDI
Hartley Eugene Rutan - (1878-1956) p/Charles H.
  Rutan-Nancy Dykes of Walton Co.; m Ettie
  Louise Strickland in 1910; he was a soldier
  in the SpAmWar, 7th Co., U.S. Coast Artillery
  Note: the 1880C calls him **Hartley C.** and his
  military records call him **Hartley E. Ruton**;
  he was living in Tampa in 1927 (per his fath-
  er's Obit) 1880C; 1885C; GDAW
Helen Victorine Rutan - (1921-1992) she died in
  Flagler Co.; FLDI
Henry Newton Rutan - d 1968 in Sarasota; FLDI
James Rutan - (1885-1885) p/Charles H. Rutan-
  Nancy Dykes; he is bur at the Hatcher Ch of
  God Cem, Freeport; MEACH; GDAW
James Gordon Ruttan - (1889-1978) p/Andrew Pre-
  andal Ruttan-Ardelia Fordham m Olive Z. Davis
  (1893-1941) he was born in Paris, Ontario and
  died in St. Petersburg; RUTT
James L. Rutan - (1903-1977) he died in Seminole
  Co. (see Lindsay Rutan in WV listing) FLDI
John Rutan - p/Samuel Rutan-Eliza Williams; liv-
  ing in Newton, Dale Co. AL in 1860; 1860C;
  MEACH
John Rutan - d 1967 in Walton Co.; FLDI (see

John E. Rutan, below)

John Albert Rutan - d 1955 in Jacksonville; FLDI

John C. Rutan - (1921-1994) he died in Polk Co.;
FLDI

John E. Rutan - (1894-1967) p/Charles H. Rutan-
Nancy Dykes m Della Moore (1898-1966) in 1917
from the 1917 Obit of his sister-in-law,
Ethel L. Sharpless; he was a WWI soldier who
lived in Bonifay (from his mother's Obit) and
later at Defuniak Springs, Walton Co.; ROOTSW
GDAW; SSA

John Oliver Rutan - (1919-1985) p/John Rutan-
Della Moore (County Obituary Index) GDAW

Joseph Edward Rutan - (see Edward J. Rutan,
above)

Joseph Edward Rutan - m Elsie Sapp (1923-1981)
she was born in Jacksonville and died in Ft.
Lauderdale; Note: this is probably not the
Joseph of the prior entry; ROOTSW

Juell Rutan - p/Emmet Rutan-Eva L. Withers m
Lucille Mears; GDAW

Lena Rutan - (1877-1920) p/Samuel Rutan-Mary E.
Taunton of Walton Co.; unm, she is bur at the
Hatcher Ch of God Cem, Freeport; 1885C; MEACH

Lillie Rutan - (1876-1888) p/Charles H. Rutan-
Nancy Dykes of Walton Co.; she is bur at the
Hatcher Ch of God Cem, Freeport; 1880C; MEACH
1885C

Linza A. Rutan - (1903-1996) she died in Lee
Co.; FLDI

Lorena J. Rutan - (1905-1996) she died in Manatee Co.; FLDI

Louise Addie Ruttan - b 1881 p/Andrew P. Ruttan-
Ardelia Fordham; unmarried she died at St.
Petersburg; RUTT

Lulu E. Ruttan - (1915-1977) she died in Highlands Co.; FLDI

Mabel Rutan - Maybelle (1882-1968) p/Charles H.
Rutan-Nancy Dykes m William Michael King
(1877-1959) at Walton Co. in 1902; he was
born in Walton Co.; they were living in New
Port Richey in 1927 (from her father's Obit)
she died in Levy; FLDI; GDAW

Mabel Annette Rutan - b 1912 p/Hartley E. Rutan-
Ettie L. Strickland; GDAW

Margaret Rutan - d 1947 m _____ Hale; she died
in Highlands Co.; FLDI

Marion V. Rutan - (1914-1995) died in Pinellas
Co.; FLDI

Marjorie Eunice Rutan - b 1918 p/John Rutan-
Della Moore m Louper Houston; GDAW
Mary Rutan - (1900-1990) m _____ Mooney; she
died in Pinellas Co.; FLDI
Mary Jane Rutan - (1880-1958) p/Samuel Rutan-
Mary E. Taunton of Walton Co.; unm, she is
bur at the Hatcher Ch of God Cem, Freeport;
her Obit appeared in the *Pensacola News-
Journal*, 20 April 1958; 1885C; MEACH; FLDI
Mary Jane Rutan - b 1869 p/Emmet Rutan-Eva L.
_____ of Walton Co.; m George Traffer at Bay
Co. in 1885; 1880C; GDAW
Melvin J. Rutan - (1900-1984) p/Joseph Volney
Rutan of NY; he lived in St. Petersburg (Russ
Hauver) SSA
Nancy Rutan - m John W. McNeel at Walton Co. in
1909; Note: records have her Rowtan and
Reutan; CoMR; OKAFL
Ralph Eugene Rutan - (1916-1934) p/Hartley E.
Rutan-Ettie Strickland; GDAW
Robert Daniel Reton - (1929-1995) he died in
Broward Co.; FLDI
Robert Glen Rutan - d 1951 in Dade Co.; FLDI
Ronald C. Rutan - (1921-1996) he died in Orange
Co.; FLDI
Ronald E. Rutan - (1919-1990) he died in Pin-
ellas Co.; FLDI
Samuel Rutan - (1819-1910) p/John Rutan-Cather-
ine Coon of Paterson NJ m (1) Eliza Williams
(1814/7-1873) widow of James Mallette, the
business partner of Samuel in 1845; she was
from GA; they lived in Dale Co. AL some time
between 1839 and 1865 (2) Mary Elizabeth
Taunton (1841-1918) a school-teacher from
Elba, Coffee Co. AL in 1873; he was a sheriff
and grocer in Walton Co. and is bur at the
Hatcher Ch of God Cem, Freeport; GDAW; 1860C;
LDS
Samuel Rutan - (1874-1894) p/Charles H. Rutan-
Nancy Dykes of Walton Co.; he is bur at the
Hatcher Ch of God Cem, Freeport; 1880C; 1885C
MEACH
Warren Daniel Rutan - (1921-1988) m Frances _____
(1915-1933); he served in the USCG and is bur
at the Florida National Cemetery, Sumter Co.
(cemetery records)
William H. Rutan - (1907-1980) he is bur at Ser-
enity Gardens Memorial Park, Largo, Pinellas
Co.; ROOTSW

William Henry Ruttan - d 1968 in Lake Co.; FLDI
William Teddy Rutan - (1880-1942) p/Charles H.
 Rutan-Nancy Dykes of Walton Co.; he served
 with the U.S. Marine Corps in the SpAmWar;
 Nancy's 1917 Obit mentions a son, William T.
 Rutan of Wilmington DE; he was living in Los
 Angeles in 1927 (his father's Obit) where he
 died; 1885C; CADRI

G E O R G I A

Helen L. Rutan - (1912-1988) of Cherokee Co.
 (State Death Index)
John Retan - a W1812 soldier who served with the
 1st Regiment (Johnston's) Georgia Militia
 (War of 1812 database)
John F. Ruton - b 1841 a farm laborer in Morgan,
 Calhoun Co.; he was born in GA; 1860C
Joseph Rutan - (1910-1986) of Atlanta; he also
 lived in MT; SSA
Lizzie Ruton - m J.M. Bolden at Forsythe Co. in
 1902; CoMR

H A W A I I

Henry Ruttan - (1919-1942) he is bur at the
 National Memorial Cemetery of the Pacific,
 Oahu

I D A H O

Curtis Wallace Rutan - resident of Shoshone Co.;
 1910C
Emma May Retan - m Benjamin Henry Hyde at Oreana
 Owyhee Co. in 1891 (see MI listing) CoMR
Fred Reton - b 1875 m Mabel _____ b 1890; living
 in Ada Co. in 1910; he was born in NE and she
 in IA; 1910C
Herbert Rutan - (1891-1987) of Meridien, Ida Co.
 SSA
J.W. Rutan - m Charlotte White at Coeur D'Alene
 15 Nov 1910 (Idaho marriage records)
Nancy E. Rutan - (1924-1999) she died at Merid-
 ien per her Obit in the *Idaho Statesman*, 2
 Feb 1999

A.R. Rutan - m Anna Kenyon in Livingston Co. in 1886; IMI

Abraham Rutan - b 1851 p/Lawrence D. Rutan-Jane _____ of Grundy; he was born in NJ; 1880C

Abraham Rutan - m Mary Ball in Kendall Co. in 1875; he is probably the son of Daniel Rutan-Maria Ackerman of NJ b 1846; CoMR

Abram Rutan - m Sarah Jane Banks at Livingston Co. in 1865; IMI

Adam Poe Rutan - b 1841 p/Samuel Rutan-Sarah Cracraft of Will Co.; he was born in OH (see CA listing) 1850C

Allen Rutan - (1891-1978) p/John H. Rutan-Cora I. Lee of Homer, Champaign Co.; SSA; 1900C

Allen M. Retan - b 1859 p/Ebenezer Retan-Phoebe Clark of Steuben Co. NY; m Amanda Seapy b 1853 in 1882 at Elgin Twp, Kane Co.; they were living there in 1910; CoMR; 1910C

Alvah L. Rutan - (1868-1947) m Amanda J. Fury (1872-1952) in 1892; both are bur at Janesville (New Gordon) Cem, Pleasant Grove Twp, Coles Co. (cemetery records) 1900C; IMI

Amanda Rutan - m Arthur Judson Durand in 1861 at Plato, Kane Co. (Durand Genealogy)

Anna Rutan - m Willis E. Finch at Cook Co. in 1891; she may have been a widow; IMI

Arlene Rutan - m Harold Turner and they lived in Danville (from her daughter Evelyn Ann's Obit in the *Springfield Journal-Register*, 1995) Evelyn was born in 1931

Audria Rutan - (1800/03-1865) p/Daniel Rutan-Mary Hazel of MD and OH; m Jonathan Ogden (1801-1876) in 1821 or 1824 and they lived in Gridley Twp, McLean Co.; he was a farmer born in Pickaway Co. OH; he is bur at Pennell Cem, Towanda, McLean Co. (Kutsbach Family Tree) Note: LDS has her **Nadria** Rutan; LDS

Betty Jean Johnson Rutan - she is bur at Gundy Cem, Newell Twp, Vermilion Co. (cemetery records)

Carl Rutan - (1895-1975) p/John H. Rutan-Cora I. Lee of Fithian, Vermilion Co.; m Murza _____ ; 1900C; SSA; CRC

Carrie Adelia Rutan - p/Henry T. Rutan-Mary Fouser m John P. Shearer at Will Co. in 1885; (Pat Brand) IMI

Catherine Rutan – bc 1830 p/Layton Rutan-Dorothy
Hull m Peter Shafer; IMI
Catherine Rutan - bc 1836 p/Samuel Rutan-Sarah
Cracraft; she was born in OH (see CA listing)
1850C
Catherine N. Rutan - b 1857 p/Peter Rutan-Mary
E. Share of NJ; GKB
Charles W. Rutan – bc 1842 p/Samuel Rutan-Sarah
Cracraft; he was born in OH (see CA listing)
1850C
Clifford Rutan - (1905-1970) of Charleston,
Coles Co.; SSA
Clifford H. Rutan - m Olive L. Bryant at Coles
Co. in 1926 (see prior entry) CoMR
D.V. Retan - m Alice Power at Cook Co. in 1876;
IMI
Daniel Ratan - resident of Plainfield, Will Co.;
1860C
Daniel D. Rutan - (1829-1889) of NJ; m Keziah
Eve Zabriskie (1832-1902) they moved to NE
and died there (Pat Brand)
David Henry Rutan - (1838-1903) p/Layton Rutan-
Dorothy Hull m (1) Emily Comer d 1861 at
Coles Co. in 1858 (2) Sarah Bain at Coles Co.
in 1865 (3) Mary Virginia (Molly) Soey (1847-
1920) a widow (Mary Elder?) at Coles Co. in
1878; Emily is bur at the Old Gordon (Shiloh)
Cem; David and Mary are bur at Pleasant
Prairie Cem, in Pleasant Grove Twp, Coles Co.
(cemetery records) David was a CW soldier
serving in the 66th Illinois and 14th Miss-
ouri Infantry (see MO listing) USARCH; CoMR
Donna Ruth Rutan - (1913-1951) she was born in
IL and died in Los Angeles; her mother was a
Clarke; CADRI
Dorothy Rutan - m Paul Shannon at Coles Co. in
1918; CoMR
Dorothy E. Ruttan - (1908-1969) she lived in IL
and died in Los Angeles; CADRI
Dortha Rutan - **Dollie** (1869-1910) m George Man-
ual Caylor bc 1864 at Coles Co. in 1888; LDS;
CoMR
Ebenezer Retan - (1825-1904) p/Barnet Retan-Sar-
ah Drew of Sussex Co. NJ and Steuben Co. NY;
m Phoebe Clark b 1827; they lived in Elgin
Twp, Kane Co. and owned property in Thayer
Co. NE (Thayer Co. Atlas, 1900) MEACH; 1900C
Edith Rutan - (1906-1930) p/Alva Rutan-Amanda
Fury of Coles Co. m Robert Earl Best b 1902

in 1925; she was born in Lerna; CoMR; ROOTSW;
1910C

Edna Pearl Rutan - m Victor McMorris at Coles ·
Co. in 1914; CoMR

Edwin J. Reton - CW soldier, musician (Civil
War Research database)

Elias Howard Rutan - (1868-1870) (see Howard
Rutan, below)

Ella C. Rutan - b 1881/2 p/Samuel T. Rutan-Mah-
ala Marrs m Raymond H. Snider at Edgar Co. in
1900; IMI; 1900C; ROOTSW

Elmer Ruttan - d 1982; he is bur at Rock Island
National Cemetery (cemetery records)

Elmira Ruttan - m Francis M. Harris at Iroquois
Co. in 1879; IMI

Emily Clarke Rutan - (1889-1956) she lived in IL
and died in Los Angeles (see Donna Ruth Rutan
above) CADRI

Emily Jane Rutan - b 1887 p/Francis Rutan-Mary
E. _____; 1900C

Emma Ruttan - m George R. Nash at Kane Co. in
1865; IMI

Erma Pauline Rutan - m Grant P. Mullenax at
Coles Co. in 1928; CoMR

Everett B. Rutan - m Clara A. Gilbert b 1876 at
Grand Rapids, LaSalle Co. in 1894; LDS

Frances Rutan - b 1901 p/Matthias Rutan-Anna
Sharpe of LaSalle Co. (Farmers Directory,
1917) 1910C

Frank Rutan - b 1860 m Ida _____ b 1857; he was
born in OH; they were living in Orange Twp,
LaSalle Co. in 1900; 1900C

Frank Rutan - b 1875 m Carrie M. Reynolds b 1877
at Charleston, Coles Co. in 1895; she was
born in KY; CoMR; 1900C

Frank Chase Rutan - (1862-1922) m Anna Chambers
(1863-1941) they were both born in OH and
lived in Chicago; he was a civil engineer who
died in NYC and she died in Los Angeles (see
Northeast listing) 1900C; NYTO; CADRI

Frank H. Rutan - b 1858 m Anne _____ b 1868;
Frank was born in OH; living in Chicago in
1910; Note: this may be Frank Chase Rutan;
(see prior entry) 1910C

Fred Rutan - b 1889 p/John H. Rutan-Cora I. Lee
of Vermilion Co.; 1900C

George W. Rutan - bc 1844 p/Samuel Rutan-Sarah
Cracraft of OH; living in Will Co. in 1850;

Harry Rutan - (1902-1978) of Chicgo; SSA

Harry F. Rutan - m Pauline May Jackson at Coles
Co. in 1922; CoMR

Hattie Rutan - m Claudie Grove at Coles Co. in
1911 (see Myrtle Rutan, below) CoMR

Helen Rutan - (1917-1999) m _____ Thomas of
Urbana (Obituary Daily Times)

Helene Rutan - b 1851 p/Peter Rutan-Mary E.
Share of NJ; GKB

Henry Rutan - resident of Pleasant Grove Twp,
Coles Co.; 1860C

Henry Rutan - d 1905 m Mary Virginia Elder in
1878; he died at Neoga, Columbia Co. (see
David Henry Rutan, above) IMI

Henry Terhune Rutan - (1841-1919) of NJ (m) 1
Mary Fouser at Will Co. in 1861 (Pat Brand)
IMI

Howard Rutan - (1906-1964) p/John H. Rutan-Cora
I. Lee of Vermilion Co.; 1910C; SSA

Howard Elias Rutan - (1868-1870) p/Daniel D.
Rutan-Keziah E. Zabriskie of Will Co. (Pat
Brand) YRR; CoBR

Ira Rutan - nephew of William Rutan;1900C

Isaac Rutan - purchased land in 1818 (state land
records)

Ivy I. Rutan - **Iva** b 1893 p/Alvah L. Rutan-Amanda J. Fury m Chauncey D. Whicker in 1913;
1900C; CoMR

J.W. Rutan - elected "Thistle Commissioner" in
Chicago in 1882 ("History of Early Chicago
and Its Settlements") (see Joel W. Rutan,
below)

Jack E. Rutan - (1923-1999) m Catherine Davenport in 1948; he was an electrical engineer
born in Danville; he lived in Denver and died
in TX (from his Obit in *The Rocky Mountain
News*, 19 Sep 1999)

James Ruton - resident of Greenville P.O., Bond
Co.; 1860C

James Rutan - m Zella Blanche Mills b 1886 at
Stewardson; he was a Methodist minister and
they later lived in OK ("Randall Lewis Family
of Hopkinton RI and Delaware Co. NE")

Jennie Rutan - (1876-1942) p/Joel W. Rutan-Viol-
etta Young of Scranton PA; m William C.
Wascher (1874-1963) at LaGrange Co. in 1900;
he was a farmer and road commissioner in Saginaw MI where they died; he is bur at the
Blumfield Twp Cem (from his Obit in the *Saginaw News* (Jody Zorsch) 1900C

Jennie Rutan - b 1897 p/John H. Rutan-Cora I.
Lee of Vermilion Co.; 1900C

Jessie Rutan - (1883-1884) p/David H. Rutan-Mary
V. Soey; she is bur at Pleasant Prairie Cem,
Pleasant Grove Twp, Coles Co. (cemetery rec-
ords)

Joel W. Rutan - b 1846 p/Peter Rutan-Maria Compton of Bradford Co. PA; m Violetta Young b
1847; they moved to IL about 1880 and lived
LaGrange, Cook Co.; 1860C; 1900C

John Rutan - b 1828 p/John Rutan-Jane Davis of
Washington Co. PA; m Nancy Thompson b 1829;
they lived in Homer and in 1860 in Vance Twp,
Vermilion Co.; they were both born in PA;
GSNJ; CRC; 1860C

John Rutan - m Martha Hiatt at Fulton Co. in
1868; IMI

John Rutan - bc 1838 p/Samuel Rutan-Sarah Cracraft; he was born in OH (see CA listing)
1850C

John D. Rutan - resident of Gallatin Co. in 1818
and Jackson Co. in 1820 (state land records)
1818C; 1820C

John J. Rutan - he was living in Saline Precinct
Brownsville, Jackson Co. (Lisa Lockett) Note:
he may be the W1812 soldier who acquired a
land patent in Jackson Co. as well as the son
of John Rutan-Jannitje Brower of NJ who m
Sally Ann Webb (see Northeastern listing)
1820C

John Henry Rutan - b 1860 m Cora I. Lee (1870-
1950) he lived in Homer and later they resided in Vance Twp, Vermilion Co.; CRC; 1900C

Joseph Ruton - m Silence _____ (1804-1849)
ROOTSW

Joseph Rutan - d 1886; he was a resident of Meredosia Twp, Morgan Co. and is bur at Oakland
Cem (cemetery records)

Joseph Retton - resident of Joliet in 1892; CDIR

Joseph Rutan - bc 1834 p/Samuel Rutan-Sarah Cracraft (see OR listing) 1850C

Joseph Rutan - b 1904 p/John H. Rutan-Cora I.
Lee of Vermilion Co.; 1910C

Josiah Rutan - b 1848 p/Daniel Rutan-Maria Ackerman m Sarah J. Taylor in 1869; they were
living in Blackstone, Livingston Co. in 1872
(Randy Lucke) CoMR; IMI

Kenneth L. Rutan - (1893-1966) p/John H. Rutan-
Cora I. Lee m Lula F. Steffy (1894-1961) he

was a farmer in Bismarck, Vermilion Co. in
1920; they are bur at Oakwood Cem, Vermilion
Co. (cemetery records) SSA; 1920C; ROOTSW

Kittie Rutan - (see Sarah Kathryn Rutan, below)

Lauros P. Rutan - (1904-1948) p/William Rutan-
Bertha Fretz m Freda Melvina Harshman (1903-
1998) at Mulberry IN in 1926 (from Freda's
Obit) 1920C

Lawrence D. Rutan - (1827-1898) p/Daniel Rutan-
Maria Ackerman of NJ; m Jane _____ b 1830 in
NJ; they were living in Grundy in 1880 (see
CA listing) 1880C

Layton C. Rutan - (1884-1953) p/Samuel T. Rutan-
Mahala Marrs m Catherine (Kate) Beavers
(1885-1960) in 1903 at Coles Co.; they were
living there in 1910; she was born at Hutton
Twp, Coles Co.; they are bur in that county
at Mound Cem (Les Hickenbottom) (Beavers Family website) 1900C; 1910C; CoMR; ROOTSW

Leah Jane Rutan - b 1837 p/Daniel Rutan-Maria
Ackerman of NJ; m Lucius Case Tuttle at Will
Co. in 1860; IMI; LDS

Lee Allen Rutan - bur at Grundy Cem, Newell Twp.
Vermilion Co.(cemetery records)

Leona Rutan - b 1894 p/Matthias Rutan-Anna
Sharpe of LaSalle Co.; Note: she may be a
daughter by the first wife; 1910C

Lettie Rutan - (1900-1900) bur at Pleasant Prairie Cem, Pleasant Grove Twp, Coles Co. (see
Nettie Rutan, below) (cemetery records)

Lillie F. Rutan - b 1884 p/Francis Rutan-Mary E.
_____; 1900C

Lois Rutan - d 1992 m _____ Poole; her Obit was
in the **Elmhurst Press**

Lottie Rutan - b 1889 p/Matthias Rutan-Anna
Sharpe; Note: she may be a daughter by the
first wife; 1900C

Lucy B. Ruttan - m William F. Brown at LaSalle
Co. in 1866; she is Lucy Buckley Rowe Ruttan
the daughter of Charles Stuart Ruttan (see IA
listing)

Mabel Rutan - p/John H. Rutan-Cora I. Lee; CRC

Mae Rutan - b 1899 p/John H. Rutan-Cora I. Lee;
Note: in all likelihood these two entries
represent the same person; 1900C

Margaret Rutan - m Levi Barr at Coles Co. in
1885; LDS

Margaret Rutan - p/Henry Rutan-Mary Virginia
Elder m George Washington Reed b 1870 of

Neoga, Cumberland Co.; LDS; ROOTSW

Maria Ratan - resident of Plainfield, Will Co.; 1860C

Marie Elizabeth Rutan - b 1852 p/Daniel D. Rutan -Keziah E. Zabriskie m Charles Dey (Pat Brand)

Martha Rutan - m Frank Richardson at Champaign Co. in 1891; IMI

Mary Rutan - (1849-1850) p/Samuel Rutan-Sarah Cracraft; the 1850C says she was born in IL but another record says OH (George A. Rutan)

Mary Rutan - m S.B. Moore at Coles Co. in 1892; CoMR

Mary E. Rutan - b 1858/9 p/John Rutan-Nancy Thompson of Vermilion Co.; she appears to be living there in 1900 with her brother William 1860C; 1900C

Mary Jane Rutan - (1819/20-1876) of Brownsville, Jackson Co.; m Naaman/Newman Burgess bc 1802 from Boston at the First Congregational Ch of New Orleans in 1837; she died there and is bur at the Girod St. Cem (Lisa Lockett) she may be the daughter of John D. Rutan-Sally Ann Webb of NJ and Brownsville

Matthias Rutan - b 1852 p/Samuel Rutan-Anna Elliot of Washington Co. PA; m (1) Emma Taylor in LaSalle Co. in 1875 (2) Priscilla Ann Sharpe b 1872 in 1898; Priscilla was born in PA; he moved to Homer and was living in Farm Ridge Twp, LaSalle Co. in 1900; Note: the IMI has him wed to Mrs. Anna Redmen (1917 County Farmers Directory) IMI; LDS

Mildred Rutan - p/Matthias Rutan-Priscilla Ann Sharpe of LaSalle Co. (1917 Farmers Directory

Myrtle Rutan - m Claudie Groves in 1903 at Coles Co.; he m Hattie Rutan in 1911; CoMR

Myrtle M. Rutan - m Russell J. Jenkins at Coles Co. in 1926; CoMR

Nancy Rutan - bc 1829; she was living in Hardin Co. in 1856; 1856C

Nathan Rutan - b 1868 p/John Rutan- Nancy Thompson of Washington Co. PA; m Elsie _____ b 1888; living in Vermilion Co. in 1910; GSNJ; 1900C; 1910C

Nellie Rutan - b 1886 p/Matthias Rutan-Priscilla A. Sharpe; Nellie is probably the daughter of his first wife; 1900C

Nettie Rutan - (1900-1900) she is bur at Pleas-

ant Prairie Cem, Pleasant Grove Twp, Coles
Co. (cemetery records) (see Lettie Rutan,
above)

Olive Lucille Rutan - (1908-1985) m Axton Collum
(1919-1961) at Humrick in 1957; he died in
Charleston, Coles Co.; CoMR; CoDR; ROOTSW

Rachel Ratan - resident of Plainfield, Will Co.
in 1860 (see Daniel Ratan, above) 1860C

Rachel J. Rutan - b 1856 p/John Rutan-Nancy
Thompson of Vermilion Co.; 1860C

Rachel M. Rutan - m William M. Wilcox at Will
Co. in 1862; IMI

Rhoda B. Rheutan - m William W. Foster at Cook
Co. in 1874; IMI

Roscoe Rutan - b 1892 p/Frank C. Rutan-Anna
Chambers; 1900C

Roscoe D. Rutan - b 1894 p/Alvah L. Rutan-Amanda
J. Fury m Mabel Morgan at Coles Co. in 1919;
CoMR

Russell Rutan - (1908-1987) p/Nathan Rutan-Elsie
_____ of Vermilion Co.; he lived in Sandoval,
Marion Co.; 1910C; SSA

Russell Layton Rutan - (1905-1996) p/Layton
Rutan-Kate Beavers of Charleston, Coles Co.;
m Dorothea P. Lippincott (1909-1986) in 1927
at Charleston, Coles Co.; 1910C; CoMR; SSA

S. Estella Rutan - m Daniel Harry Day at Will
Co. in 1886; IMI

Sado Rutan - m George Fury at Coles Co. in 1892;
Note: CoMR calls her **Sada** and him George
Funay; CoMR; IMI

Samuel Rutan - b 1809 p/John Rutan-Nancy Rusk m
Sarah Cracraft bc 1809 of Mansfield OH; he
was a farmer in Wilmington, Will Co. in 1850;
migrated to CA (George A. Rutan) 1850C

Samuel Rutan - p/John Rutan-Nancy Thompson of
Washington Co. PA; GSNJ

Samuel Rutan - m Martha Rickey at Champaign Co.
in 1887; IMI

Samuel Rutan - (1905-1995) p/Nathan Rutan-Elsie
_____ of Vermilion Co.; he lived in Fairmount
1910C; SSA

Samuel B. Rutan - b 1880; a resident of Farm
Ridge Twp, LaSalle Co; 1900C

Samuel T. Rutan - (1839-1915) p/Layton Rutan-
Dorothy Hull of Charleston Twp, Coles Co.; m
Mahala Marrs (1849-1915) at Coles Co. in 1865
Note: the Beavers Family website identifies
her as **Mahala Meyers** and the IMI calls her

Mahala Morris; he is bur at Mound Cem, Charleston (Shirley Nees) LDS; IMI; CoMR; 1900C

Sarah Charlotte Rutan - m Andrew Jackson Redman, Jr. (1876-1939) in 1908 at LaSalle Co.; he was born at Farm Ridge and is bur at Grand Ridge Cem; ROOTSW

Sarah E. Rutan - b 1839 p/Layton Rutan-Dorothy Hull (Shirley Nees)

Sarah Kathryn Rutan - "Kittie" (1877-1961) m George Vernon Pearcy (1873-1946) at Charleston, Coles Co. in 1896; she was born at Union Twp, Cumberland Co. and died in Charleston; he is bur at Roselawn Cem in that city; ROOTSW

Silence Ruton - (1804-1849) m J. Joseph; they lived in Meredosia Twp, Morgan Co.; ROOTSW

Silvia A. Rutan - b 1886 p/Francis Rutan-Mary E. _____; 1900C

Stella Rutan - p/Henry T. Rutan-Mary Fouser (Pat Brand)

Theodore Rutan - (1907-1982) SSA

Tillie May Rutan - b 1872 p/Josiah Rutan-Sarah J. Taylor of Blackstone, Livingston Co. Randy Lucke) (see IA listing)

Vern E. Rutan - bur at Grundy Cem, Newell Twp, Vermilion Co. (cemetery records)

William Ruton - resident of Hamilton Co.; 1850C

William Rutan - b 1837 in OH; he was a resident of St. Clair Co. in 1860; 1860C

William Rutan - bc 1835; resident of Greene Co.; LDS

William Rutan - p/John Rutan-Nancy Thompson of Washington Co. PA; he was living in Vermilion Co. in 1860; GSNJ; 1860C

William Rutan - b 1853; a resident of Vance Twp, Vermilion Co. (see prior entry) 1900C

William Rutan - b 1898 p/Frederick H. Rutan-Anna _____ of Adams Co.; 1910C

William Rutan - b 1907 p/George H. Rutan-Emma Topper of Cook Co.; 1910C

William Rutan - (1907-1980) (see prior entry) SSA

William H. Rutan - b 1889 p/Francis Rutan-Mary E. _____; 1900C

I N D I A N A

Abraham Rutan - (1825-1917) p/Abraham Rutan-
Olive Burt of Washington Co. PA; m Elizabeth
Scales (1840-1898) in 1856; they moved to
Jackson Co. about 1865; they are bur at
Sutherland Cem, Jackson Twp, Bartholomew Co.;
Note: his gravestone says he was born in 1830
CoMR; MAR; 1870C
Abraham Rutan - (1872-1955) p/Abraham Rutan-
Elizabeth Scales of Freetown, Jackson Co.; he
died in Bartholomew Co.; CRC; 1920C; MAR
Abraham Rutan - d 1920 at Salt Creek Twp, Jack-
son Co.; CoDR
Alice Rutan - p/Calvin Rutan-Sarah Combs (Patty
Smith)
Allie Rutan - m Harry A. McDole in Tippecanoe
Co. in 1895; CoMR
Alta May Rutan - d 1904 in Salt Creek Twp, Jack-
son Co,; CoDR
Alta May Rutan - d 1926 in Salt Lake Twp, Jack-
son Co,; ROOTSW
Andrew Jackson Rutan - (1863-1931) p/Abraham
Rutan-Elizabeth Scales of Bellefontaine,
Logan Co. OH; m Delilah Margaret Harvey
(1866/8-1943) in 1891; they were living in
Bartholomew Co. in 1920; he died at Columbus
and is bur at Garland Brook Cem, Columbus,
Bartholomew Co.; CRC; MAR; CoMR; 1920C
Anna Bell Rutan - (1901-1992) p/Andrew J. Rutan-
Delilah M. Harvey of Bartholomew Co.; m Clay-
ton Tilton Smith in 1922; 1920C; MAR
Anna May Rutan - b 1894 p/Sherman L. Rutan-Josie
Shane m Ora Ayers; they were living in Morgan
Co. in 1916 and later in Los Angeles; CoMR;
IBRI
Archibald Rutan - (1835-1903) m Eliza Stephens
(1836-1917); both from OH; farmer living in
Walnut Twp, Montgomery Co. in 1900; he died
in Linnsburg, Montgomery Co.; she died in
Walnut Twp (see OH listing) CoDR; CoMR; 1900C
Archie Rutan - (1907-1979) p/James Rutan-Emma
Phegley of Jackson Co.; he lived in Seymour;
1920C; SSA
Archie Rutan - (1908-1973) p/Walter A. Rutan-
Mary E. Roberts; he lived in Seymour, Jackson
Co.; 1920C; SSA
Austin Rutan - p/Hiram G. Rutan-Estella McKinley
of Morgan Co.; MCOPL
B. Rutan - m Orville Lafara; they were living in
Henry Co. in 1917; IBRI

Barbara E. Rutan - (1865-1879) p/Abraham Rutan-
Elizabeth Scales of Logan Co. OH; she is bur
at Sutherland Cem, Bartholomew Co.; CRC; MAR;
CoDR

Benjamin R. Rutan - m Sarah E. Scott at Greene
Co. in 1870; CoMR

Bernice Rutan - b 1917 p/Walter A. Rutan-Mary E.
Roberts; 1920C

Bert E. Rutan - b 1860 (see Elias B. Rutan,
below)

Bertha E. Rutan - (1893-1971) p/Bert E. Rutan-
Mary L. Weekly m Ora Hall b 1893 in Bartholomew Co. in 1914; Note: there is another CoMR
that says she wed Robert D. Hall in 1917;
1900C; SSA; CoMR

Bessie F. Rutan - b 1885 m Edgar Brown at Montgomery Co. in 1911; CoMR

Calvin H. Rutan - b 1848 in OH m Sarah Combs b
1849 in OH in Clinton Co. in 1871; they were
living in Lafayette, Tippecanoe Co. 1885-91;
and Clinton Co. in 1920; 1900C; CDIR; CoMR;
1920C

Catherine Rutan - b 1882 p/Calvin H. Rutan-Sarah
Combs (Patty Smith)

Catherine Rutan - m Howard Whisman at Bartholomew Co. in 1917; CoMR

Catherine Rutan - m Joseph Johnson at Clinton
Co. in 1907; CoMR

Charles Calvin Rutan - (1901-1973) p/William
Rutan-Bertha Fretz m Ethel M. Jenkins at
Clinton Co. in 1920; SSA; LDS; CoMR

Charles Edgar Rutan - (1893-1971) p/Andrew J.
Rutan-Delilah M. Harvey of Bartholomew Co.;
m Minnie Chandler (1896-1977) in 1953; he
died in Columbus, Bartholomew Co. and is bur
at Garland Brook Cem, Columbus (cemetery records) 1920C; MAR; SSA

Charles F. Rutan - m Lizzie Winters in Allen Co.
in 1876; he was a machinist in Ft. Wayne in
1878; CDIR; CoMR

Chester Rutan - (1907-1910) he is bur at Sutherland Cem, Jackson Twp, Bartholomew Co. (cemetery records) CoDR

Christina Rutan - "Chrissie" (1859-1941) p/Isaac
Rutan-Christiana Stone m Curtis Teague; Note:
according to the 1880C she was born in 1857;
MCOPL; 1880C

Christena Rutan - m Noah A. Lemen at Owen Co. in
1884; CoMR

Clarence Rutan - p/Lester Rutan; CRC

Claudine P. Rutan - (1889-1971) m Willard L.
Stephenson (1885-1968) at South Bend in 1909
she died in Elkhart Co.; Note: she is shown
as Ruton in the CoMR; CoMR; CoDR; ROOTSW

Clemina M. Rutan - **Clemma Mae** m Raleigh B. Waggoner at Clinton Co. in 1897; CoMR

Cornelius William Rutan - b 1859 p/Peter Rutan-
Mary E. Share of LaPorte (see CA listing)
1860C; GKB

Cyrus Ray Rutan - (1897-1966) p/Andrew J. Rutan-
Delilah M. Harvey of Jackson Co.; m Bertha
Mae Golden b 1859 in 1919; he died in Columbus, Bartholomew Co.; Note: CoMR says they wed
in 1920; MAR; CoMR

Saniel Rutan - (1867-1899) m Sarah Bixler b 1868
of Darke Co. OH at LaGrange Co. in 1892; he
is bur at English Prairie Cem, LaGrange Co.;
CoMR; ROOTSW

David Rutan - b 1844 p/Jesse Rutan-Susanna _____
of Steuben Co.; he was born in OH; 1860C

David Rutan - m Nila Mae Napier in 1947 at Indianapolis; CoMR

David H. Rutan - (1886-1949) p/Calvin H. Rutan-
Sarah Combs m (1) Ruth E. Miller in 1914 (2)
Ellen (Luella) D. Halliman b 1885 in NJ at
Frankfort in 1918; both marriages were in
Clinton Co.; he and Luella lived in Bloom-
field. Essex Co. NJ and later in Westchester
Co. NY (Patty Smith) 1900C; CoMR; PCHSQ;
1920C

David W. Rutan - (1862-1937) p/Abraham Rutan-
Elizabeth Scales m Ellen Brock b 1868; Note:
CRC has his wife as Emma E. born in 1857;
they were living in Van Buren Twp, Brown Co.
in 1900; MAR; 1900C; CRC; 1920C

Donald R. Rutan - (1921-1998) he lived in IN and
died in Hildago Co. TX; (Indiana Biographical
Index) TXDR

Earl V. Rutan - (1900-1969) p/Layton T. Rutan-
Cora P. Curtis m Martha K. Burns at Morgan
Co. in 1921; they lived in Martinsville; CoMR
1900C; SSA

Eben Benjamin Rutan - (1899-1903) p/Andrew J.
Rutan-Delilah M. Harvey; he died in Jackson
Co.; CoDR

Eleanor V. Rutan - p/John W. Rutan-Reefa Chadwick of Walnut Twp, Montgomery Co. (Farmers
Directory, 1920)

Elias B. Rutan - (1845-1864) p/Abraham Rutan-
Mary Logston, CW soldier who died at Ander-
sonville Prison (see OH listing) MAR
Elias Bert Rutan - b 1860 p/Abraham Rutan-Eliza-
beth Scales m Mary Lavina Weekly at Jackson
Co. in 1888; he was a laborer in Columbus in
1919; CRC; MAR; CDIR
Eliza Rutan - (1836-1917) she died at Walnut
Twp, Marion Co.; CoDR
Elizabeth Rutan - bc 1835 m Aaron Hurtt at Miami
Co. in 1856 (Kathy Rust)
Elizabeth Rutan - m John W. Hughes; they lived
in Tippecanoe; their child wed in 1883; CoMR
Elsie Ethel Rutan - (1907-1994) p/Andrew J.
Rutan-Delilah M. Harvey of Bartholomew Co.; m
George Spencer in 1929; MAR; 1920C
Emma Rutan - b 1880; she was living in Martins-
ville, Morgan Co. in 1900; 1900C
Emma Rutan - (1879-1940) m William Thomas Rumph
(1860-1931) in 1914 in Jackson Co.; ROOTSW
Emma Rutan - m Sylvanus Lewis at Morgan Co. in
1913; CoMR
Ernest Rutan - b 1918 p/James Rutan-Emma Phegley
1920C
Ervin Rutan - (1908-1973) of Lowell, Lake Co.;
SSA
Erwin Rutan - (1905-1976) of Indianapolis; SSA
Eva Rutan - b 1911 p/Hiram G. Rutan-Esta McKin-
ley of Morgan Co.; IBRI
Evelyn L. Rutan - m Earl Hatfield II (1925-1986)
he was born and died in Bartholomew Co.;
ROOTSW
F.W. Rutan - d 1920 in Columbus, Bartholomew Co.
CoDR
Flossie Mae Rutan - (1892-1977) p/Andrew J.
Rutan-Delilah M. Harvey m Henry Wagner b 1891
she was born in Seymour and is bur at Riverview Cem, Seymour, Jackson Co.; Note: Henry
is also called Henry Waggoner; MAR; CoDR;
CoMR; ROOTSW
Frank C. Rutan - b 1886 m Bessie Sering/Sebring
b 1887 at Montgomery Co. in 1905; they were
living in Ft. Wayne in 1920; Note: the 1920C
calls her Lizzie; CoMR; 1920C
George Rutan - (1871-1944) p/Abraham Rutan-Elizabeth Scales of Salt Creek Twp, Jackson Co.;
m Caroline Wilcox b 1875 in 1893; they were
living in Bartholomew Co. in 1920; MAR; CRC;
1900C; CoMR; 1920C

George Rutan - (1906-1983) of Gary; SSA
Goldie Frances Rutan - (1897-1964) p/Edward
    Rutan-Inola Woods of Martinsville, Morgan
    Co.; m Benjamin G. Ratts (1896-1971) in 1914;
    she died in Paragon, Morgan Co. (John Oker-
    son) (Wokal Ancestors) CoMR; SSA; LDS; ROOTSW
Gordon James Rutan - b 1887 p/Sherman Rutan-All-
    etta B. Whysong; Note: LDS has him born in
    Kingsley KS but he is in Elkhart Co. birth
    records; 1900C; LDS; CoBR
Grant Rutan - (See Hiram Grant Rutan)
Harlin H. Rutan - b 1891 p/Elias B. Rutan-Mary
    L. Weekly; 1900C
Hazel Rutan - b 1885; living with her uncle,
    Perry Vanalstrom in Wayne Twp, Allen Co. in
    1900; 1900C
Helen Rutan - bc 1851 p/Peter Rutan-Mary E.
    Share   of LaPorte Co.; she was born in PA;
    1860C
Howard H. Rutan - b 1891 m Leila Whisman b 1895
    at Bartholomew Co. in 1914; they were living
    in Columbus in 1920; Note: one record has him
    born in 1890; she is called **Lula Inkerman
    Whisman** in Indiana marriage records; CoMR;
    1920C
Hiram Grant Rutan - (1866-1937) p/Isaac Rutan-
    Minerva Sloan m Estella (Esta) McKinley in
    1893; farmer in Jefferson Twp, Morgan Co.
    1900-1920; CoMR; 1900C; 1920C
Hiram W. RuTon - b 1855 m Louise Perry b 1856;
    both from NY; living in Goshen, Elkhart Co.
    in 1920; CoMR; 1920C
Isaac Rutan - m Ruth Roger at Decatur Co. in
    1835; CoMR
Isaac Rutan - (1832-1916) p/Layton Rutan-Dorothy
    Hull of NJ and IL; m (1) Christiana Stone d
    1860 in 1856 (2) Minerva Sloan Dailey in 1861
    the 1870C shows him b 1837 in NJ and living
    in Jefferson Co.; the 1880C shows no wife; he
    was living with his son Hiram Grant Rutan in
    1900; CoMR; 1870C; 1880C; 1900C
James Rutan - m Julia Ann Cook at Elkhart Co. in
    1845; CoMR
James Rutan - (1872-1930) p/Stephen Rutan-Susan-
    na Stuart of Charleston, Coles Co.; he was a
    soldier in the SpAmWar, serving with the
    158th Indiana Volunteer Infantry; unm, he was
    a farmer who lived in Martinsville, Morgan
    Co. (from his military pension file) 1900C;

USARCH; CoBR; 1920C

James B. Rutan - (1877-1955) p/Abraham Rutan-
Elizabeth Scales of OH and Jackson Co.; m
m Emma Phegley b 1868 in 1903; they were
living in Bartholomew Co. in 1920; MAR; CRC;
CoMR; 1920C

James D. Rutan - m Lydia B. Coulter b 1873 at
Delaware Co. in 1893; CoMR

James Eli Rutan - b 1866 p/Archibald Rutan-Eliza
Stephens m Fairy W. Miller at Montgomery Co.
in 1895; (from his father's CW pension file)
they were living in Montgomery Co. in 1888;
CoMR; USARCH; CDIR; ACPL

James H. RuTon - b 1906 p/Hiram W. RuTon-Louise
Perry of Elkhart Co.; 1920C

Jasper M. Rutan - (1872-1895) he died in Marion
Co.; CoDR

Jennie Rutan - b 1858 in OH; m _____ Myans; she
was living in Dekalb Co. in 1900 (see Milton
Rutan, below and the next entry) CoMR

Jennie Rutan - m Amzi Myers in Steuben Co. in
1886; CoMR

Jennie B. Rutan - b 1880 m Martin W. Pinrod at
Clinton Co. in 1903; CoMR

Jesse Rutan - bc 1799 in MD m Susannah _____ bc
1791 in VA; they were living in Salem Twp,
Steuben Co. in 1860; 1860C

Joel A. Rutan - (1820-1903) p/Lewis Rutan-Cath-
erine E. _____ of Fayette Co. PA; m Mary E.
_____ bc 1841; living in Salem Twp, Steuben
Co. in 1900; he was a justice of the peace
and lived at one time in Smithfield Twp,
Dekalb Co. where he died; he is bur at County
Line Cem; Note: one record has him **Joel A.**
Rutan; 1900C

John Andrew Rutan (1928-1987) p/Cyrus R. Rutan-
Bertha M. Golden m Martha Alta Colsher at
Decatur in 1946; he was born in Bartholomew
Co. and died in Vermilion Co.; MAR

John Wiley Rutan - b 1893 p/James E. Rutan-Fairy
Miller m Reefa Chadwick b 1897 of Mace in
1917; they were living in Montgomery Co. in
1920; John was a farm-hand (Farmers Directory
1920; Reefa is identified in "Some Descendants of John Endicott, Governor of Massachusetts Bay Colony"; 1920C

John William Rutan - (1857-1913) p/Abraham Rutan
-Elizabeth Scales m (1) Louisa Pernetta Hupp
(1859-1897) in 1878 at Jackson Co. where she

died (2) Emma Retta Coffman b 1874 in 1907; as a widow Emma remarried in 1914; CRC; LDS; ACPL; 1900C; CoMR

Josephus Rutan - (1869-1870) p/Abraham Rutan-Elizabeth Scales; he is bur at Sutherland Cem Bartholomew Co.; Note: he has been misident-ified as **Josephine** Rutan; CoDR; MAR

Juanita R. Rutan - m Perry Hibschman at St. Joseph Co. in 1946; CoMR

Julia Rutan - b 1856 m Charles T. Clark at Allen Co. in 1913; Note: another record has her born in 1844; CoMR

Julia Rutan - b 1902 m Paul Collier in Morgan Co. in 1928; ACPL

Julia Ann Rutan - m Peter Eisenbice at Elkhart Co. in 1848; Note: she may be Julia Ann Cook married to James Rutan in 1845 (see above) CoMR

Katherine Rutan - m Jack Edward Watson (1923-1981) he was born at Greensburg, Decatur Co. and died at Indianapolis; ROOTSW

Lauros Rutan - (1903-1948) p/William Rutan-Bertha Fretz m Freda Melvina Harshman at Mulberry in 1926; were living in Tippecanoe Co. in 1919 (Farmers Directory) he is bur at Fairhaven Cem, Mulberry; ROOTSW

Lawrence Paul Rutan - (1919-1974) he was born in Columbus, Bartholomew Co. and died in Louisville, KY (Kentucky death records)

Leroy Rutan - b 1822 in OH m _____ _____ b 1833; they were living in Washington Twp, Clinton Co. in 1860 (see next entry) 1860C

Leroy Rutan - m Phebe Pegg (1837-1917) in Clinton Co. in 1867; Phebe lived with her brother Clark Pegg in Washington Twp, Clinton Co. in 1900; Note: the 1900C has her born in 1832; she died in Center Twp, Clinton Co.; CoMR; 1900C; CoDR

Lester Rutan - m Iona Edell Stoughton b 1900 in 1920; ROOTSW

Lester S. Rutan - (1896-1980) p/George Rutan-Caroline Wilcox; he lived in Edinburgh IN; SSA; 1900C; CRC

Levi Rutan - b 1840 p/Jesse Rutan-Susanna _____ of Steuben Co.; he was born in OH; 1860C

Levi Rutan - CW soldier, 19th Indiana Volunteer Infantry; he was from Dekalb Co. (Regimental muster roll) in 1885 he was a member of the Dekalb County Guard, part of the 30th Regi-

ment stationed at Camp Allen, Ft. Wayne
(county history)

Loasie Rutan - b 1894 p/Edward Rutan-Inola Woods
(see **Susie J.** Rutan, below)

Loren C. Rutan - (1921-1944) p/Layton T. Rutan-
Cora P. Curtis m Marie Payne in 1942; he was
a WWII soldier, Pfc, 320th Infantry, 35th
Divison, KIA; he is bur at the Lorraine Amer-
ican Cemetery, St. Avold, France; USARCH;
CoMR

Louis B. Rutan - b 1889 p/Elias B. Rutan-Mary L.
Weekly m Katherine L. Bonham b 1890 in 1916
at Bartholomew Co.; Note: he is listed as
Louis Routan in the marriage index; 1900C;
CoMR

Louisa Molan Rutan - (1817-1862) m George Gordon
(1804-1889) of York Co. PA; both died in
Augusta IL; ROOTSW

Lyda Rutan - b 1872 she was a resident of Washington Twp, Morgan Co. in 1900; 1900C

Lydia Rutan - m James D. Coulter; they lived in
Tippecanoe Co; had a child in 1893; CoBR

Lydia A. Rutan - m Peter Anthony in Dekalb Co.
in 1855 by Joel A. Rutan, J.P. (her father?)
CoMR

Margaret Ruton - resident of White River Twp,
Hamilton Co.; 1850C

Marion S. Rutan - (1867-1867) p/Abraham Rutan-
Ekizabeth Scales of Logan Co. OH; she was the
twin of Mary A. Rutan; she is bur at Sutherland Cem, Bartholomew Co.; MAR; CoDR; CRC

Marion Virgil Rutan - b 1895 p/George Rutan-
Caroline Wilcox m Eva M. Snepp b 1896 at
Bartholomew Co. in 1918; CoMR; 1900C

Martha J. Rutan - m George Andrew Rowinsky
(1831-1897) of Lancaster Co. PA in 1856; he
died at Mechanicsburg OH; CoDR; ROOTSW

Mary Rutan - b 1879 resident of Martinsville,
Morgan Co.; 1900C

Mary Rutan - m William Jason Fruits (1873-1954)
he was born near Alamo IN and died in Tangier
he m (2) Lola Hall and is bur at the Wayne-
Masonic Cem, Montgomery Co.; ROOTSW

Mary Ann Rutan - (1876-1954) p/Abraham Rutan-
Elizabeth Scales; she was living in Freetown,
Jackson Co. in 1920; she died in Bartholomew
Co. and is bur at Sutherland Cem; CRC; MAR;
1920C

Mary C. Rutan - m Joseph H. Johnson at Tippe-

canoe Co. in 1903; CoMR
Mary E. Rutan - m William C. Yount at Tippecanoe
Co. in 1877; CoMR
Mary E. Rutan - b 1885 m Cyrus J. Attkinson b
1883 in Knox Co. in 1908; CoMR
Mary E. Rutan - b 1885 p/David W. Rutan-Ellen
Brock of Brown Co.; 1900C; 1900C; CoMR
Mary Edith Pauline Rutan - (1904-2001) p/Andrew
J. Rutan-Delilah M. Harvey m Charles Golden
in 1924; Note: her death notice in the
Seymour Tribune says her married name was
Hoag (Obituary Daily Times) MAR
Mary Ellen Rutan - b 1875 p/Archibald Rutan-
Eliza Stephens of Montgomery Co.; m Francis
Logan there in 1896 (some info from her fath-
er's CW pension file); Note: one county rec-
ord identifies her husband as Francis Miller;
USARCH; CoMR
Mary H. Rutan - b 1905 p/Layton T. Rutan-Cora P.
Curtis of Morgan Co.; m Ollie G. Carter at
Morgan Co. in 1923; Note: a county record
says she was born in 1901; CoMR; 1920C
Mary K. Ruton - m Wilber L. Johnson in Clinton
Co.; CoMR
May Rutan - m Charles O. Bailor, a school-teach-
er; ROOTSW
Milton Rutan - b 1871 in OH; he was living with
his sister, Jennie Myan in Fairfield Twp,
Dekalb Co. in 1900; 1900C
Minerva Penrod Rutan - b 1847 p/John P. Rutan-
Nancy Thompson m George W. Allison (1846-
1912) at Clinton Co. in 1886; CoMR
Minnie Rutan - b 1895 m Walter Ward in Morgan
Co. in 1914; CoMR
Nella E. Rutan - m Joseph A. Wood at Bartholomew
Co. in 1919 (Indiana marriage records) (see
Zelma E. Rutan, below
Nellie Rutan - b 1887 m Charles Lewis at Mont-
gomery Co. in 1906; CoMR
Nellie B. Rutan - (1880-1882) she died in Tippe-
canoe Co.; CoDR
Nellie Marie Rutan - (1911-1991) p/Andrew J.
Rutan-Delilah M. Harvey m Harry Kershaw in
1947; she died in Indianapolis; 1900C; MAR
Nora Rutan - b 1890/91 m Elbert Cogle at Mont-
gomery Co. in 1912; they were living in Boone
Co. 1917-1919; Note: state birth records have
him as Egbert Cogle; CoMR; IBRI
Oscar Rutan - (1897-1979) he lived in IN and

died in Sun Valley CA; SSA

Oscar L. Rutan - d 1903 in Salt Creek Twp, Jackson Co.; CoDR

Peter Rutan - resident of Sheffield Twp, Tippecanoe Co. in 1860; 1860C

Peter Rutan - bc 1828 p/Cornelius Rutan-Caty Van Alen of NJ; m Mary E. Shares bc 1830; he was a blind music teacher and composer in LaPorte Co.; they later lived in CA (see CA listing) 1860C

Phoebe Jane Rutan - (1859-1880) p/Abraham Rutan-Elizabeth Scales m William Henry Ault at Jackson Co.in 1880 (Walters-Howton Genealogy) CRC; MAR

Raymond Rutan - b 1903 m Barbara Lucilla Culley (1909-1995) of Clinton Co.; ROOTSW

Robert Rutan - m Arthena Shepherd (1922-2000) they lived in Brownstown and she is bur at Acme Cem, Seymour IN (from her Obit in the *Louisville Courier-Journal*, 10 June 2000)

Robert A. Rutan - b 1869 p/Archibald Rutan-Eliza Stephens; he was a farmer in Walnut Twp, Montgomery Co.in 1920 (Farmers Directory) 1920C

Robert A. Rutan - m Marie Emma Goad (location uncertain) KKI

Robert W. Rheutan - he was a boiler-maker living with his sister Rosina in Michigan City IN 1893-1894; CDIR

Rose A. Rutan - m William H. Bright in Morgan Co. in 1883; they moved to OK (Roberta Hammer) (see next entry)

Roseanna Rutan - b 1862; she was living with Isaac Rutan in Morgan Co. in 1880; 1880C

Rosina B. Rheutan - living with her brother Robert in Michigan City 1893-1894 and alone in 1896; CDIR

Roy Rutan - (1902-1991) he lived in IN and died in Orlando FL; SSA

Roy Rutan - (1906-1986) of Lebanon, Boone Co.; he lived in AZ; SSA

Ruth E. Rutan - d 1994; m Eugene Kenneth Druart (1915-1995) at Columbus, Bartholomew Co. in 1937; he was born in Indianapolis; they both died in Ft. Wayne; CoMR: ACPL

Samuel J. Rutan - b 1892 p/Daniel Rutan-Sarah Bixler of LaGrange Co.; m Celia Jackson b 1896; they were members of the West Creighton Christian Ch, Ft. Wayne (church records) LDS

Sarah Rutan - (1874-1954) p/Abraham Rutan-Elizabeth Scales of Freetown, Jackson Co.; unm, she died in Bartholomew Co.; CRC; MAR

Sarah Rutan - b 1857; she was living with Isaac Rutan in Morgan Co. in 1880 (relationship uncertain) 1880C

Sarah Rutan - m John W. Schworm at LaGrange Co. in 1900; CoMR

Sarah Rutan - bc 1850 p/Abraham Rutan-Mary Logston of OH (see next entry) MAR

Sarah C. Rutan - (1850-1920) died in Mulberry, Clinton Co.; CoDR

Sarah Jane Rutan - (1843-1921) p/Layton Rutan-Dorothy Hull m Andrew Jackson Carr (1834-1914) at Morgan Co. in 1860; CoMR; LDS

Sherman Rutan - b 1865 p/Squire Rutan-Hannah _____ of Van Wert Co. OH and Goshen, Elkhart Co.; m Alletta Bell Whysong b 1864 at Steuben Co. in 1885; she was a widow in Elkhart in 1922; CoMR; 1900C; CDIR

Sherman L. Rutan - (1866-1944) p/Isaac Rutan-Minerva S. Dailey m Josie Shane (1873-1912) at Morgan Co. in 1891; they are both bur at Schultz Cem, Martinsville, Morgan Co.; CoMR; CoDR

Squire Rutan - b 1853 m Susan R. Combs b 1861; they were both from OH; he is listed as a farmer/brick-maker born in Dayton OH in the city directory of Sheffield Twp, Tippecanoe Co., 1878-1891; in 1900 they lived in Madison Twp, Clinton Co.; 1900C; CDIR

Susan May Rutan - b 1895 p/Daniel Rutan-Sarah Bixler of LaGrange Co.; m Frank E. Summers b 1891; LDS

Susie J. Rutan - b 1894 p/Edward Rutan-Inola Woods m Grover C. Shuler at Morgan Co. in 1912; 1900C; CoMR

Thurman Rutan - b 1915 m Eunice Brazelton b 1915 at Fountain Co. in 1936; CoMR

Vanderveer Rutan - **Van** b 1844 p/Peter Rutan-Mary Watson m Mary _____ b 1844; both from OH; they were living in Dayton IN in 1891 and in Clinton Co. in 1900; 1850C; 1900C; CDIR

Velma Rutan - bc 1905 m Freeman G. Waddle (1905-1980) in 1929 ("Henry Waddle and His Descendants")

Velma Rutan - b 1913 p/James Rutan-Emma Phegley; 1920C

Verna Rutan - b 1914 p/Walter A. Rutan-Mary E.

Roberts; 1920C

Virgil S. Rutan - Vergil (1889-1962) p/Sherman
Rutan-Alletta B. Whysong m Maude M. Miller
(1890-1969) at Elkhart Co. in 1910; both died
in Gary; 1900C; CoMR

Virginia Rutan - b 1859 p/Leroy Rutan-Phoebe
Pegg of Clinton Co.; 1860C

Wallace Rutan - (1895-1970) of Barnard, Putnam
Co.; SSA

Walter A. Rutan - (1881-1947) p/John Rutan-Pern-
etta Hupp m Mary Elizabeth (Molly) Roberts
(1880-1960) at Jackson Co. in 1902; they were
living in Freetown, Jackson Co. in 1920; both
were born in Hamilton Twp, Jackson Co. and he
is bur at White's Chapel, Hamilton Twp (cemetery records) LDS; 1900C; 1920C

Wiley Rutan- b 1893 (see John Wiley Rutan,
above)

William Rutan - b 1875 m Stella Stagner in 1920
at Marion Co.; CoMR

William B. Rutan - (1852-1884) he died in Colfax
Clinton Co.; CoDR

William Edgar Rutan - d 1907 at Salt Creek Twp,
Jackson Co.; CoDR

Zelma E. Rutan - b 1900 p/Lester Rutan, a grand
daughter of Abraham Rutan of OH; m Joseph A.
Wood b 1885 at Bartholomew Co. in 1919 (see
Nella E. Rutan, above) CoMR

I O W A

A. Ruton - bc 1846 m Sabrina _____ b 1852 of OH;
they were living in Glenwood Twp, Mills Co.
in 1880; 1880C

Abraham P. Rutan - (1818-1899) m Mary Ann Phelps
(1832-1909) he was born in NJ and she in IA;
in 1860 they were living in Marietta Twp,
Marshall Co.; he died in St. Clair Co. MO; he
may be related to John Rutan of MI ("History
of Marshall Co.") (Marc Wheat) 1870C; 1880C;
CoDR

Abram Rutan - bc 1844 p/Daniel D. Rutan-Maria
Ackerman of NJ; m Mary R. _____ bc 1851 of
NY; they were living in Armstrong Grove,
Emmet Co. in 1880 and later he lived in CA
and "in the Dakotas"; 1880C; YRR

Anna L. Rutan - b 1910 p/Charles W. Rutan-Anna

Feloy of Greene Co.; 1920C

Anson Clark Rutan - (1872-1902) p/John C. Rutan-
Mary Emma Hart of Iowa City; he moved with
his family to KS about 1875; his death was
reported in the Wichita Death Index; 1900C;
LDS

Anthony Ruttan - (1844-1931) p/John Ruttan-Mary
Ann Stinson of Kingston, Ontario m Mary
Matilda Heavlin (1843-1904) of Mills OH in
1868; he was a stationary engineer and farmer
who emigrated to the U.S. in 1868; he died in
DesMoines; both are bur at Oakview Cem, Albia
Troy Twp, Monroe Co.; LDS; RUTT

Archibald Rutan - m Nancy Geer at Hardin Co. in
1856; CoMR

Bert Ruton - b 1876 m Eva _____ b 1887; he was
born in MN and she in IL; they were living in
Clear Lake, Cerro Gordo Co. in 1920; 1920C

Catherine Rutan - (1813-1881) p/John Rutan-Catherine Coon of Paterson NJ; m Ellis Edward
Collins d 1876 in 1835; they moved to Belvidere IL about 1845 and Janesville IA about
1854; both are bur at the Presbyt Ch Cem (see
Northeast listing) (Collins Bible: ACPL)

Catherine Frances Rutan - (1911-1998) m _____
Chappe; she was born in Jersey City, Hudson
Co. NJ and died in DesMoines (Obituary Daily
Times)

Charles A. Ruton - bc 1872 p/A. Ruton-Sabrina
_____ ; he was born in NJ; 1880C

Charles Alva Ruttan - b 1893 p/Charles S.M. Ruttan-Matilda A. Meyers m Josie B. Brown (1895-
1979) in 1917; 1900C; RUTT

Charles Dwayne Ruttan - b 1923 p/Grover C. Ruttan-Sarah E. Cooper m (1) Ida Cloe Jolley b
1925 at Salt Lake City in 1945 (2) Iona _____
(3) Ruth Imogene Hall (1929-1978) (4) Sharon
Montez Stivers at Orange Co. CA in 1961; Note
RUTT has him born in 1924 (Sandi White) RUTT

Charles H. Rutan - b 1897 p/Henry B. Rutan-
Eliza E. Ruble of Marion Co.; m Rena _____
b 1902; they lived in Marion Co. in 1920;
1920C

Charles Otis Rutan - (1883-1943) p/William H.
Rutan-Cervilla M. Wiley m Lieucetta F. Miller
(1895-1980) at Carstairs, Alberta in 1913; he
was born in Miles City MT and died at Forest
Grove OR; she was born at Orillia IA and died
at Hillsboro OR (Kim Vierra) 1920C

Charles Stuart Ruttan - (1808-1894) p/William
Ruttan-Margaret Steel m Mary Brown Rowe
1816-1886) of Berkshire MA in 1832; he was
born in Canada, emigrated to the U.S. in 1864
and died in Fontanella; RUTT
Charles W. Rutan - bc 1875 p/Enos K. Rutan-Harriet Miller m Anna Feloy (1875-1935) they were
living in Scranton, Greene Co. in 1920; they
died there and are bur at Scranton Cem (cemetery records) TDR; 1880C; 1920C
Claire A. Rutan - b 1905 p/Sydney P. Rutan-Lulu
B. _____ ; 1920C
Clarence Hamlet Ruttan - (1915-1959) p/Grover C.
Ruttan-Sarah E. Cooper m Edith Newel; he was
born at Cuba, Mantua Twp, Monroe Co.; he is
bur at the Keokuk National Cemetery, Lee Co.
cemetery records say he was born in 1914;
RUTT
Curtis William Rutan - (1875-1961) p/William H.
Rutan-Cervilla M. Wiley m (1) Beth _____ (2)
Ruby _____ ; he was born in Iowa City and died
in CA (Kim Vierra)
Dale Ruttan - b 1902 p/Francis C. Ruttan-Grace
Belzer; 1920C
Daniel D. Rutan - (1819-1888) of Washington Co.
PA; m Delilah _____ ; they are bur at Dunreath
Cem, Marion Co. (cemetery records)
Darlene May Ruttan - b 1922 p/Grover C. Ruttan-
Sarah E. Cooper m John Howard Walsh about
1940; she was born in Hamilton, Marion Co.;
Note: RUTT has her wed to Aaron Harper in
1940 (Sandi White) RUTT
Delilah Rutan - b 1893 p/Henry B. Rutan-Eliza E.
Ruble of Marion Co.; Delilah was born in OH;
1900C
Delta Glende Ruttan - b 1907 p/Grover C. Rutan-
Sarah E. Cooper m Harry Fane in 1926; she was
born at Hynes, Mantua Twp, Monroe Co.; 1920C;
RUTT
Dorothy Rutan - (1908-1989) SSA
E.R. Rutan - a blacksmith in Shellsburg, Carbon
Twp, Benton Co. in 1878 (County Biographies)
Edith Rose Ruttan - (1884-1943) p/Henry C. Rutt-
an-Mary A. Carnefix m Frank Clay Ward in 1908
Edith was born at Fontanella and died in Kan-
sas City; RUTT
Edward Rutan - bc 1871 p/Levi Rutan-Mattie Cran-
dle; 1880C
Elizabeth Rutan - b 1831 p/James Rutan-Mary _____

of NJ; she was living in Clayton Co. in 1850;
1850C

Elizabeth Rutan - (c1828-1908) m George Wattson
(1819-1879) at Delhi IA in 1860; Elizabeth
was born in NJ and George was from Philadelphia and Jefferson Co. NY (from her Obit in
the *Manchester Press*, 22 Oct 1908); she is
probably the daughter of John Rutan-Catherine
Coon of Paterson NJ; she is bur at Evergreen
Cem, Delhi; (Ruth Wattson) EVG

Ella Rutan - b 1895 p/Henry B. Rutan-Eliza E.
Ruble; 1920C

Elsie Ruttan - b 1912 p/Francis C. Ruttan-Grace
Belzer; 1920C

Enos K. Rutan - bc 1845 p/Abner H. Rutan-Arena
Littel of Champaign Co. OH m Harriet Miller
bc 1849; living in Canton Twp in 1880 and
Shellsburg, both Benton Co. in 1900; Enos was
born in OH and Harriet in PA (see E.R. Rutan,
above) Enos was living with his son Wiley in
Green Co. in 1920; 1880C; WSIM; 1900C; 1920C

Estella Jane Ruttan - b 1909 p/Francis C. Ruttan
-Grace Belzer of Troy Twp, Monroe Co. m Jacob
Howard Robinson (1905-1967) he was born in
Urbanna Twp, Monroe Co. and died at Mills Co.
RUTT; CoMR

Francis Ruttan (1902-1983) of Eddyville, Wapello
Co.; SSA

Francis Clyde Ruttan - (1871-1955) p/Anthony
Ruttan-Mary M. Heavlin of Marion Co.; m Grace
Belzer b 1876 in 1901; they were living in
Wapello Co. in 1920; he died at Albion, Mar-
ion Co. and is bur at Highland Cem, Eddyville
(Jackie Nielson) RUTT; 1920C

Frank Rutan - bc 1867 p/Abram Rutan-Mary R. _____
of IL; 1880C

Frank Leslie Ruttan - (1895-1981) p/Charles S.M.
Ruttan-Matilda A. Meyers m Anna Verna Crawford b 1904 in 1922 at Kansas City; RUTT;
1900C; SSA

Franklin W. Rutan - (1873-1878) p/William H.
Rutan-Cervilla M. Wiley (Kim Vierra)

Fred Reton - b 1875 he was a resident of Maple
Grove, Ada Co.; Fred was born in NE (see
Mabel Reton, below) 1910C

Fred Rutan - m Roxie Goldie Elder b 1892 in 1911
ROOTSW

Frederick A. Rutan - bc 1878 p/Josiah D. Rutan-
Sarah J. Taylor of Emmet Co.; 1880C

George F. Ruton - resident of Elk Twp, Clayton
Co.; 1860C

George W. Rutan - (1893-1972) p/George Archibald
Rutan-Laura C. ____; they were living in
Cedar Rapids in 1920; he died in Ft. Myers
FL; 1900C; 1920C; SSA

Gladys Edna Ruttan - (1912-1966) p/Grover C.
Ruttan-Sarah E. Cooper m James Lang; she was
born at Frakers, Mantua Twp, Monroe Co. and
is bur at Oakview Cem; RUTT

Gladys Idella Ruttan - (1891-1912) p/Charles
S.M. Ruttan-Matilda A. Myers of Grove Twp;
m Cornelius Morford Wright, Jr.; 1900C; RUTT

Grace Beatrice Ruttan - (1907-1997) p/Francis C.
Ruttan-Grace Belzer of Mantua Twp, Monroe Co.
she was born in Givin IA; 1920C; CoBR; RUTT

Grace Lenoir Rutan - (see Lenoir Rutan, below)

Grover Cleveland Ruttan - (1885-1945) p/Anthony
Ruttan-Mary M. Heavlin of Pella Lake Prairie
Twp; m Sarah Edna Cooper (1889-1967) at Mant-
ua Twp, Avery Co. in 1907; they were living
in Wapello Co. in 1920; he died in Cathedral
City, Riverside Co. CA; both are bur at Oak-
view Cem, Albia, Monroe Co. (Jackie Neilson)
RUTT; 1920C; LDS

Hannah Ruton - bc 1879 p/A. Ruton-Sabrina ____;
1880C

Henry B. Rutan - b 1861 m Eliza Ellen Ruble b
1863; both from PA; living in Red Rock Twp,
Marion Co.; Eliza was a widow in 1920; 1900C;
1920C

Iantha Hannah Rutan - (1848-1935) p/William
Rutan-Hannah J. Clark of OH; m Orlando Chester Donaldson (1852-1934) in 1877; she was a
school-teacher in Iowa City in 1870; Note:
she is listed as **Janetha** in the 1870C; she
was born in Lexington Twp OH, wed in Iowa
City and died in Palo Alto CA; he died in
Fresno (Kim Vierra) LDS; 1870C

Imogene Rutan - b 1906 p/Sydney P. Rutan-Lulu B.
____; 1920C

Imogene I. Rutan - (1865-1933) she is bur at
Cedar Memorial Cem, Cedar Rapids (cemetery
records)

Irene Rowe Ruttan - (1899-1977) p/Charles S.W.
Ruttan-Matilda A. Meyers of Grove Twp; m
Charles Kenyon; 1900C; RUTT

Jacob Ruttan - bc 1808 m Ann ____ bc 1806;
carpenter in Cedar Twp, Lucas Co. in 1870;

Jacob was born in Canada; 1870C

James Rutan - b 1799 m Mary _____ b 1794; he
was a farmer born in NJ living in Garnavillo
Twp, Clayton Co. in 1850; Mary was born in
PA where he had lived; 1850C

James Rutan - bc 1871 p/Abram Rutan-Mary R. _____
he was born in IL; 1880C

James L. Rutan - b 1862/64 p/Abraham P. Rutan-
Mary A. Phelps; James was born in MN ("History of Marshall Co., Iowa") 1880C

James William Ruttan - (1879-1943) p/Anthony
Ruttan-Mary M. Heavlin n Naomi Belle Peart
(1886-1968) in 1903; they were living in
Knoxville, Marion Co. in 1920; he was a coal
miner who was killed in a truck accident; he
is bur at Graceland Cem, Knoxville; Note: the
1920C lists him as William; Naomi was born in
OH and died in Los Angeles CA (Jackie Neilson) RUTT; 1920C; CADRI

Jennie Isabel Rutan - (1888-1974) SSA

Jennie May Rutan - (1868-1948) p/Levi Rutan-
Mattie Crandle m William Casper Coffman
(1860-1909) of Bristol IL in Marshalltown;
Note: as with her parents her surname is
sometimes spelled Ruttan; 1880C; LDS

Jessie Rutan - bc 1876 p/Levi Rutan-Mattie
Crandle; 1880C

John Rutan - (1839-1864) p/David Rutan-Eleanor
Lyons Durbin of Carroll Co. OH; he was a CW
soldier, 11th Iowa Volunteer Infantry, wounded Shiloh and KIA near Atlanta in August 1864
he is bur the Marietta GA National Cemetery;
he enlisted from Hardin Co. ("Iowa Soldiers
in the War of the Rebellion") 1860C; USARCH

John Ruton - b 1918 p/Bert Ruton-Eva _____ of
Clear Lake; 1920C

John Clark Rutan - (1839/41-1904) p/William
Rutan-Hannah J. Clark of OH; m Emma M. (Mary
Emma) Hart (1848-1918) in Iowa City in 1867;
CW soldier, 2 Lt., 41st Iowa Volunteer Infan-
try, Captain, 7th Iowa Cavalry; lumberman and
real estate investor; moved to Wichita KS
about 1875; in 1909 Emma was living in Yakima
WA and died in Seattle as did he (Kim Vierra)
("Iowa Soldiers in the War of the Rebellion")
Note: Rutan Avenue in Wichita is named after
him; 1870C; USARCH; 1900C; OAR

John Wesley Rutan - (1881-1941) p/William H.
Rutan-Cervilla M. Wiley m (1) May _____ (2)

Anna ____; he was born in SD and died in
Tacoma WA (Kim Vierra)
Josiah D. Rutan - (1849-1894) p/Daniel D. Rutan-
Maria Ackerman of NJ and Emmet Co.; m Sarah
Josephine Taylor (1850-1910) in IL where she
was born (see IL listing) they are bur at Oak
Hill Cem, Estherville, Emmet Co. (cemetery
records) CRC; 1880C
Katie Ruton - bc 1876 p/A. Ruton-Sabrina ____;
she was born in NJ; 1880C
Kenneth Eugene Ruttan - p/Grover C. Ruttan-Sarah
Edna Cooper m Alberta Davis; he was born at
Bidwell, Wapello Co.; RUTT
Laura Rutan - b 1869 in PA; she was living in
Cedar Rapids in 1920; 1920C
Lavina Jane Ruttan - (1910-1945) p/Grover C.
Ruttan-Sarah E. Cooper m Elmer Ragen; she was
born at Hynes, Mantua Twp, Monroe Co; 1920C;
RUTT
Lenoir Rutan - **Grace Lenoir** (1905-1998) p/Char-
les W. Rutan-Anna Feloy of Greene Co.; she
died in Calhoun Co.; 1920C; CoDR
Leroy A. Ruttan - (1904-1974) p/Charles S.W.
Ruttan-Matilda A. Meyers of Grove Twp; the
family moved to KS; RUTT; 1900C
Levi Rutan - bc 1841 in Canada; m Mattie Crandle
bc 1844 in NY; they were living in Marshall
Co. 1889-1890; he is possibly the son of
Abraham Ruttan-Mary Ann See of Lyme Town,
Jefferson Co. NY; Levi sometimes identfied as
Levi Ruttan; 1880C; 1900C
Lida Ruttan - b 1914 p/Francis C. Ruttan-Grace
Belzer; 1920C
Lida E. Rutan - b 1885 p/Enos K. Rutan-Harriet
Miller of Champaign Co. OH m Herbert Dickin-
son; 1900C; TDR
Lillian Rutan - b 1902 in ND; she was the step-
daughter of Crist Danielson; 1920C
Lloyd Earl Ruttan - (1902-1980) p/Charles S.W.
Ruttan-Matilda A. Meyers of Grove Twp; the
family moved to KS (see KS listing) RUTT;
1920C
Lewis Andrew Ruton - (1921-1966) m Valda Thorsen
he is bur at Unionville Cem, Appanoose Co.;
he was born at Davis (cemetery records)
Mabel Reton - b 1890 she was a resident of Maple
Grove, Ada Co. (see Fred Reton, above) 1910C
Margaret Rutan - **"Maggie"** b 1873 p/Abraham P.
Rutan-Mary Ann Phelps ("History of Marshall

County, Iowa") 1880C

Margaret A. Ruttan - **Margaretta** b 1874 p/Anth-
ony Ruttan-Mary M. Heavlin of Marion Co.; m
John Gore at Mahaska, Oskaloosa Co. in 1893;
she was living in DesMoines in 1931 (Jackie
Neilson) LDS; RUTT

Marti Rutan - m Harry C. Tillingast (1865-1956)
of Sioux City; he m (2) Louisa M. Cavanaugh;
he died in Los Angeles; ROOTSW

Mary A. Rutan - bc 1875 p/Abram Rutan-Mary R.
_____; she was born in IL; 1880C

Mary Ann Ruttan - (1876-1931) p/Anthony Ruttan-
Mary A. Heavlin of Marion Co. m James Beer-
Smith (1872-1955) at Pekay, Mahaska Co.; she
died at Bear River, Routt Co. CO (from her
father's Obit) Note: the Beer Family changed
their surname to Smith (Luann Kline; Jackie
Neilson) RUTT; LDS

Mary Emma Rutan - (1879-1965) p/John C. Rutan-
Emma M. Hart of Iowa City; she moved with her
family to KS about 1875; m John Kelly (1831-
1912) and moved to WA; she died in Seattle
(Kim Vierra) 1870C; MCRC; USARCH; 1900C

Maude M. Rutan - bc 1877 p/Abram Rutan-Mary R.
_____; she was born in IL; 1880C

Melvin Ruttan - (1907-1972) p/James W. Ruttan-
Naomi B. Peart; he died in Sonoma CA; 1920C;
CADRI

Morton Leigh Rutan - (1878-1952) (see KS listing)

Nancy Rutan - b 1829 in IL; she was a resident
of Hardin Co. in 1856; she may have been the
widow of Archibald Rutan (see above) 1856C

Nancy Rutan - m Samuel Becker at Hardin Co. in
1863 (see prior entry) CoMR

Naomi Ruth Ruttan - (1918-1991) p/James W.
Rutan-Naomi B. Peart; she died in Orange Co.
CA; CADRI

Olive Bell Rutan - d 1964 m Oscar Buss; her Obit
appeared in the *Waterloo Press* 6 Dec 1964

Orpha Rutan - bc 1871 p/Josiah D. Rutan-Sarah
J. Taylor of Emmet Co.; 1880C

Paul Ruton - b 1910 p/Bert Ruton-Eva _____ of
Clear Lake; 1920C

Peter Rutan - resident of Jackson Co.; 1860C

Preston Rutan - b 1908 p/Sydney P. Rutan-Lulu B.
_____; Note: Preston may be incorrect; the
microfilm was difficult to read; 1920C

Raymond Albert Ruttan - (1918-1937) p/Grover C.

Ruttan-Sarah E. Cooper; he was born in Bidwell, Wapello Co. and is bur at Oakview Cem;
RUTT

Robert Ruttan - (1920-1973) he lived in IA and
died in Sonoma Co. CA; CADRI

Samuel Ruton - resident of Elk Twp, Clayton Co.
(see George F. Ruton, above) 1860C

Samuel Rutan - b 1833 p/James Rutan-Mary _____
of NJ; he was born in PA and was living in
Clayton Co. in 1850; 1850C

Samuel Rutan - b 1871 p/Abraham P. Rutan-Mary A.
Phelps ("History of Marshall County, Iowa")

Simon Gillam Ruttan - (1857-1907) p/William Consider Ruttan-Hannah Gillam m (1) Mary _____
(2) Mary Agnes Kelly (1854-1923) from Ireland
at Great Barrington MA in 1887; they were
living at Logan Twp in 1900; Simon died at
Hawarden and both are bur there at St. Mary's
Cem although another record says Calvary Cem
(cemetery records) RUTT; 1900C

Stella Ruton - b 1908 p/Bert Ruton-Eva _____ of
Clear Lake; 1920C

Stella Rutan - (1908-2001) m _____ Belding (from
Mason City newspaper 8 July 2001)

Stella Ruttan - b 1913 p/Francis C. Ruttan-Grace
Belzer; 1920C

Sydney P. Rutan - b 1878 m Lulu B. _____ b 1877;
he was born in IN and she in IA; they were
living in Cedar Rapids in 1920; 1920C

Terry Edna Ruttan - (1882-1955) p/Anthony Ruttan
-Mary M. Heavlin of Otley, Summit Twp, Marion
Co.; m (1) Charles Benton Crews at Mahaska
Co. in 1899 (2) Henry Wiley at Monroe Co. in
1904; she is bur at Oakview Cem, Albia, Mon-
roe co. (Jackie Neilson) LDS; RUTT

Tilley May Rutan - b 1872 p/Josiah D. Rutan-
Sarah J. Taylor; she was born in IL; 1880C

Waley Rutan - b 1871 (see **Wiley David** Rutan,
below)

Wesley Redhead Rutan - (1857-1934) p/William
Rutan-Hannah J. Clark of Iowa City; he died
in Mountain View CA (Kim Vierra) 1870C

Wiley David Rutan - (1871-1935) p/Enos K. Rutan-
Harriet Miller of Champaign Co. OH m (1)
Florence _____ (2) Irene Gertrude _____
(1883-1936) he was living in Cedar Rapids in
1900 and Scranton, Greene Co. in 1920; Wiley
and Irene are bur at Scranton Cem (cemetery
records) TDR; 1900C; 1920C

William Rutan - (1807-1880) p/John Rutan-Nancy
   Rusk of OH; m Hannah Jane Clark (1815-1895)
   he was a "farm Hand" in Iowa City in 1870;
   they are bur at Oakland Cem, Iowa City (see
   OH listing) (Kim Vierra) 1870C
William A. Rutan - bc 1879 p/Abram Rutan-Mary R.
   _____; he was born in IL; 1880C
William D. Rutan - bc 1872 p/Enos K. Rutan-
   Harriet Miller; 1880C
William Edward Ruttan - (1904-1984) p/James W.
   Ruttan-Naomi B. Peart; 1920C
William Henry Harrison Rutan - (1842-1918) p/
   William Rutan-Hannah J. Clark of OH and Iowa
   City; m Cervilla Medora Wiley (1852-1931) at
   Omaha NE in 1872; he died in Spokane WA; she
   was born at Noble Co. OH and died at Wapato
   WA (Kim Vierra)
Wilson Ruton - bc 1825 in NJ; in 1880 he was
   living with his son A. Ruton; 1880C

K A N S A S

Arthur Retan - b 1854 m Emma R. Hadlock; they
   were living in Trego Co. in 1900; her name
   is from their son David's CA death record; he
   was born in NY and she in MA; 1900C
Arthur Rutan - (1885-1972) he lived in KS and
   died in Grand Mesa CO; SSA
Bessie B. Retan - b 1889 p/Arthur Retan-Emma R.
   Hadlock of Trego Co.; 1900C
Charles Edward Rutan - (1871-1930) m Cora Viola
   Cash b 1874 in 1897; he was born in OH and
   she in KS; he was a painter/paper-hanger;
   they lived in MO and in Detroit MI; she was a
   widow in Detroit in 1931 (Donna Hitz) VIRUT;
   1910C; CDIR; 1920C
Charles Stuart William Rutan - (1851-1933) p/
   Charles Stuart Rutan-Mary B. Rowe of IA; m
   (1) Ida Millar (1855-1882) in IL in 18_76_ (2)
   Matilda Anetta Meyers (1861-1928) in 1888 at
   Adair Co.; there were no children from the
   first marriage; they were living in Grove Twp
   IA in 1900; RUTT; 1900C
Charles William Rutan - (1842-1925) p/Samuel
   Rutan-Sarah Cracraft m Ida _____ (1865-1907)
   they were living in Capioma Twp, Nemaha Co.
   in 1870; lived in CA for a time and are bur

at Sabetha Cem, Nemaha Co. (cemetery records)
1870C

Clara Rutan - (1894-1973) of Medicine Lodge,
Barber Co.; SSA

David Melvin Retan - (1893-1958) p/Arthur Retan-
Emma R. Hadlock of Trego Co.; he died in
Butte Co. CA; 1900C; CADRI

Edwin R. Ruttan - b 1851 p/Henry T. Ruttan-Jane
Kirkpatrick m Sarah Jane Mansfield; they
lived in Topeka KS (see MO listing) RUTT

Emily J. Rutan - b 1820 p/John Rutan-Nancy Rusk
m (1) Thomas Edmonson at Richland Co. OH (2)
Lyman Sweetland; she died at Valley Center KS
ROOTSW

Emma E. Ruttan - m John Lewis Ochs; they were
living in Leavenworth in 1895-1896; CoMR;
CDIR

Frances Mae Ruttan - (1875-1969) p/Henry K. Ruttan-Gertrude V. Wiggins m Harmon Wynn Sandusky in 1903; RUTT; 1900C

Francis Ervin Ruttan - (1898-1985) p/William H.
Ruttan-Mabel F. Fenton m Anna Louise Conrow
(1901-1955) in 1920 at Brookville, Saline Co.
they both died in Santa Clara CA; RUTT; SSA;
CADRI

Frank Leslie Ruttan - (1895-1981) of Kansas City
(see IA listing) SSA

Grace L. Ruttan - b 1878 p/Henry K. Ruttan-Gertrude V. Wiggins m Oscar Schrey; she is listed
alone in the Leavenworth Co. Farmers Directory in 1921; RUTT; 1900C

Granville Adolphus Ruttan - (1877-1935) p/David
Ruttan-Irene _____ m (2) Betty Helvy (1882-
1969) of Baxter Co. AR; he died in Joplin MO;
she died in Quartzville AZ; RUTT

Gertrude Winona Ruttan - (1904-2001) p/William
H. Ruttan-Ida May Sacks; (Obituary Daily
Times) RUTT

Henry Kirkpatrick Ruttan - (1849-1887) p/Henry
T. Ruttan-Jane Kirkpatrick m Gertrude Valeria
Wiggins (1855-1925) in Owego, Tioga Co. NY in
1872; he died in Leavenworth and she at St.
Joseph MO; he is bur at Mount Muncie Cem
(cemetery records) RUTT; 1900C

Henry Thorp Ruttan - (1820-1883) p/Daniel Ruttan
-Rhoda B. Haight of Ontario; m Jane Watson
Kirkpatrick (1810-1886) at Ithaca, Tompkins
Co. NY in 1842; she was born in NC; they
lived in Elmira NY; he died in Leavenworth;

RUTT
Irene Rowe Ruttan - (1899-1977) p/Charles S.M.
Ruttan-Matilda A. Meyers m Charles Kenyon;
RUTT
James L. Rutan - b 1863 m Carrie P. _____ b 1864
living in Dighton Twp in 1900; 1900C
James L. Rutan - pastor of the M.E. Church of
Dighton (from one of the marriage certificat-
es he signed as presiding clergyman) (see
prior entry)
Jay Bartlet Rutan - (1895-1966) p/Oliver Rutan-
Tempa Mason; he was born in Carroll Co. MO;
SSA; LDS
John H. Retan - b 1888 p/Arthur Retan-Emma R.
Hadlock of Trego Co.; 1900C
Leroy A. Ruttan - (1904-1974) p/Charles S. W.
Ruttan-Matilda A. Meyers m Clarabelle Fox
(1907-1991) in 1929; they lived in Kansas
City for over 50 years; she died in Leaven-
worth and is bur at Highland Park Cem (from
her Obit in the *Kansas City Star*)
Lloyd Earl Rutan - (1902-1980) p/Charles S.W.
Rutan-Matilda A. Meyers m Letha Hill (1902-
1967) in Kansas City; RUTT; SSA
Luverne A. Rutan - (1907-1960) p/Morton L. Rutan
-Louise H. Stratton; she died in San Diego CA
(Kim Vierra) CADRI
Marion B. Rutan - (1850-1911) p/Henry T. Ruttan
-Jane W. Kirkpatrick m Joseph A. Fuller; she
was born in Ithaca NY; RUTT
Mary E. Rutan - (1871-1965) p/John C. Rutan-Mary
E. Hart (see IA listing)
Michael A. Ruttan - d 1981 his Obit appeared in
the *Leavenworth Times*, 9 July 1981
Miles Henry Ruttan - (1909-1941) p/William H.
Ruttan-Ida M. Sacks m Agnes Martin d 1956 at
Kansas City in 1933; he was an osteopathic
physician; they both died in Kansas City;
RUTT
Morton Leigh Rutan - (1878-1952) p/John C. Rutan
-Mary E. Hart of Wichita; m Louise H. "LuLu"
Holmes; he died in San Diego CA; USARCH;
1900C; CADRI
Olive Ahretta Rutan - b 1889 p/Oliver Rutan-
Tempa Mason of Osceola, St. Clair Co. MO; m
Schell Hensley at Bucklin Co. in 1908; LDS
Oliver Rutan - b 1862 p/John Rutan-Sarah _____
of Prosperity PA; m Tempa Almeda Mason at
Safford in 1886;

Ollie Rutan - a cook at the Thomas Sanitarium in
Wichita in 1910; CDIR
Russell Lee Ruttan - (1905-1937) p/William H.
Ruttan-Ida M. Sacks of Oak Mills; he was an
osteopathic physician; he died in Neosho MO;
RUTT
Sherman Rutan - (1917-1989) p/Charles E. Rutan-
Cora V. Cash of Horton m (2) Rosaleta Sherley
in 1954; he died in Batesville AR and both
are bur there at Oakland Cem (cemetery rec-
ords) (David Simrak)
Wallace H. Rutan - (1908-1955) p/Morton L. Rutan
-Louise Holmes (Kim Vierra)
William Charles Rutan - b 1842 (see **Charles
William** Rutan, above)
William Henry Ruttan - (1873-1940) p/Henry K.
Ruttan-Gertrude V. Wiggins m (1) Mabel Flor-
ence Fenton (1879-1970) in 1896; they divorc-
ed about 1902 (2) Ida May Sacks (1884-1969)
in 1903 at Atchison Co.; he was born in Cres-
co IA; was a driver in Leavenworth in 1890
and he died in Ellis; Ida died in Lawrence
and her Obit appeared in the *Leavenworth
Times*, 8 June 1969; RUTT; 1900C; CDIR
William Merle Ruttan - (1897-1947) p/William H.
Ruttan-Mabel F. Fenton of Leavenworth; m
Vera May Highley b 1902 of Grainfield at Hays
in 1920; he died in Bakersfield, Kern Co. CA;
RUTT
Wilma Ruttan - (1909-1952) p/William H. Ruttan-
Ida M. Sacks; she was born in Wallace and
died at Hays; her Obit appeared in the *Leav-
enworth Times*; RUTT

K E N T U C K Y

Abraham Rutan - resident of Marysville, Mason
Co.; 1860C
Abraham Rutan - CW soldier, 19th Kentucky Caval-
ry (Civil War Muster Rolls) Note: another
record has him a member of the 10th Kentucky
Cavalry (U.S.)
Alfred Ruton - resident of Bath Co.; 1850C
Phillip Rutan - m Ruby Anna Lee Trimble b 1926
at Johnson Co.; ROOTSW

L O U I S I A N A

John D. Rutan - resident of Ascension Parish in
1830 and Orleans Parish in 1860 (see IL listing) 1830C; 1860C

Margaret Reuton - resident of New Orleans; 1870C

M A R Y L A N D

Anna Rutan - (1785-1787) p/John Rutan-Catherine
Jones of Morris Co. NJ; Note: HOYE has her as
Anne (1783-1787); GSNJ; HOYE

Audria Rutan - b 1779 p/John Rutan-Catherine
Jones of Morris Co. NJ; she was born in Miff-
lin Co. PA; GSNJ

Catherine Rutan - b 1794 p/John Rutan-Catherine
Jones of Morris Co. NJ; GSNJ; HOYE

Charles Retan - resident of Baltimore, 1850-1870
1850C; 1870C

Daniel Milton Rutan - (1779-1851) p/John Rutan-
Catherine Jones of Morris Co. NJ m (1) Mary
Hazel (1776-1808) (2) Mary Riddle in 1810;
they moved to Champaign Co. OH in 1818 (see
OH listing) GSNJ; MEACH; ACPL; TDR

David Rutan - (1782-1841) p/John Rutan-Catherine
Jones of Morris Co. NJ; m Esther ____; they
lived in MD until 1845; MEACH; HOYE

Deborah Rutan - m Thomas Jefferson Duval (1807-
1871) of Prince Georges Co.; ROOTSW

Elizabeth Rutan - p/David Rutan-Esther ____;
MEACH

Hannah A. Rutan - p/David Rutan-Esther ____;
she was living in Logan Co. OH in 1865; MEACH

Howard Rutan - (1892-1981) he lived in MD and
died in St. Petersburg FL; SSA

Isaac Rutan - b 1788 p/John Rutan-Catherine
Jones of Morris Co. NJ; m Hannah Pearson in
1809 at Allegany Co.; he had died by 1837;
GSNJ; LDS

Isaac Rutan - bc 1810 p/Isaac Rutan-Hannah Pearson; MEACH; GSNJ

Jesse Rutan - bc 1799 m Susanna ____ b 1791/98
in VA; they were living in OH in 1850 and IN
in 1860; 1850C; 1860C

Mary Rutan - (1792-1842) p/John Rutan-Catherine
Jones of Morris Co. NJ; m William Waller Hoye
in 1814; his first wife was Eleanor Slicer

who he married in 1796 in Allegany Co.; CoMR;
LDS; HOYE; GSNJ

Permilia Retan - resident of Baltimore (see
Charles Retan, above) 1860C

Peter Rutan - (1776-1858) p/John Rutan-Catherine
Jones of Morris Co. NJ; m (1) Elizabeth
McIlrath (1771-1845) (2) Mary Webb (1788-
1855) in 1846; he was living in Sandy Creek,
Allegany Co. in 1800 and moved to Markleys-
burg, Fayette Co. PA in 1812; they later
in Carroll Co. OH; GSNJ; LDS; MEACH

Phoebe Rutan - b 1814 m (1) Tobias Hoff b 1807
in 1830 (2) Reuben Shahan (Judy Peace) ROOTSW

Samuel P. Rutan - m Emily E.A. Fowler in Baltimore in 1833; LDS

Sarah Rutan - b 1775 p/John Rutan-Catherine
Jones of Morris Co. NJ; m Joseph Moore (1770-
1838) they moved to Fayette Co. PA (Moore
Family webpage) LDS; GSNJ

Sarah Rutan - bc 1810 p/Isaac Rutan-Hannah Pearson; MEACH; GSNJ

Squire Rutan - b 1818 p/David Rutan-Esther _____
of Garret Co.; m Sarah Moore; they were living Selbyport in 1840 and Fayette Co. PA in
1850; 1840C; MEACH

Stephen P. Rutan - (1811-1864) p/David Rutan-
Esther _____ of Garret Co.; m Rebecca Welch
French (1820-1894) at Fayette Co. PA in 1835;
they moved to MI and he served as a CW soldier with the 27th Michigan Volunteer Infantry
he died of disease at Washington DC and is
bur at Arlington National Cemetery; Note: his
CW pension file says he was born in 1822;
apparently he lied about his age when he enlisted; 1890C; MEACH; CoMR; USARCH

William M. Rutan - (1846-1909) p/Stephen P.
Rutan-Rebecca W. French of Allegany Co. MD;
m Clarinda Taylor in 1874 (See MI listing);
CRC; DARLDC

M I C H I G A N

A. Retan - m Harriet P. Brown, a widow in Hudson
Lenawee Co. in 1863; CoMR; 1870C; LDS

A.D. Retan - m Melinda Doyle in Hudson, Lenawee
Co. in 1859; he owned a tannery there in 1863
CoMR; CDIR

Abraham Rutan - acquired land in Ionia Co. in

1837 (Michigan land records) Note: he may be
the son of Judge James Rutan and the Abraham
P. Rutan who appears later in MI

Abram S. Retan - (1827-1864) p/John Retan-Margaret Smith m (1) Caroline McCrary (c1831-
c1858) at Oakland Co. about 1849 (2) Hester
Lawrence b 1829/32 at Owosso, Shiawassee Co.
in 1859; he was a drayman (Barbara Bombassei)
1860C; CoMR

Abram S. Retan, Jr. - b 1862 p/Abram S. Retan-
Hester Lawrence (Barbara Bombassei)

Adam Retan - m Esther Robinson (Terri Bartley)

Adam Poe Rutan - b 1841 p/Samuel Rutan-Sarah
Cracraft of OH; he was in CA in 1860 (see CA
listing) 1850C

Adda Retan - (1853-1853) p/Benjamin S. Retan-
Lucy A. Pennel; she is bur at Commerce Cem,
Oakland Co. (Barbara Bombassei)

Adelbert Rutan - (see John Adelbert Rutan,
below)

Aden Retan - b 1863 p/Adam Retan-Esther Robinson
m Fidelia Jacobs b 1866 in WI; he was a farmer in Greendale Twp, Midland Co. (Terri Bartley) CoMR

Adelaide E. Retan - **Adie** (1854-1936) p/Henry K.
Retan-Katherine Voorheis m Frank A. Scofield
(1855-1929) of Newark NJ at Ovid in 1879; he
owned a buggy company; she was born in Ovid
and died in Detroit; both are bur at Elsie MI
(Harold Retan) (Barbara Bombassei) LDS

Agnes Ruttan - p/David Ruttan-Irene _____ of
Attica Twp, Lapeer Co.; RUTT

Albert Retan - m Melissa Chubb of Hammondsport
NY at Grand Rapids in 1875 (see AR listing)
CoMR

Albert Retan - m Eliza Jane Hazelton in 1903;
ROOTSW

Albert P. Retan - (1842-1928) p/John H. Retan-
Henrietta Huff of Seneca Co. NY m (1) Elizabeth Fox d 1883 in 1867 (2) Elizabeth Bennington (1858-1902) from PA at Fairfield, Lenawee Co. in 1884 (3) Magdeline Burt b 1854 in
1916; he was a CW soldier, 18th Michigan Volunteer Infantry; he lived in Woodland, Barry
Co., Manchester, Washtenaw Co., Odessa, Ionia
Co. and Bronson, Branch Co.; he is bur at
Lakeside Cem, Lake Odessa Twp, Ionia Co.
(cemetery records) 1870C; USARCH; 1900C

Alta Retan - (1873-1917) bur at Weston Village

Cem, Fairfield Twp, Lenawee Co. (cemetery records)

Alta Rutan - (1888-1971) of Jackson, Jackson Co.; SSA

Amanda Rutan - (1859-1887) p/Peter C. Rutan-Jane Sherman of Sullivan Co. NY; m Luther F. Warner in Midland in 1878; MCRC; LDS

Amos Elwood Rutan - (1891-1891) p/James D. Ruttan-Cynthia V. Lowe of Lapeer Co.; he died in Mayfield; RUTT

Amos Giles Ruttan - (1850-1874) p/Joseph Ruttan-Susan Laid of Sanilac Co.; RUTT

Amy Retan - b 1850 p/Benjamin S. Retan-Lucy Pennel of Shiawassee Co.; 1860C

Andrew Austin Ruttan - (1905-1988) p/Enoch G. Ruttan-Elizabeth Love of Toronto; m Carolyn Elizabeth Marshall b 1911 at Buffalo NY in 1933; they lived in South Lyon, Oakland Co.; RUTT; MDI

Andrew E. Retan - (1847-1925) p/John R. Retan-Catherine Emmons of Kent Co.; m Helen Louisa Day (1850-1911) in Grandville in 1875; CW soldier, 1st Michigan Light Artillery; he was a farmer in Byron Center, Wyoming Twp, Kent Co. in 1890 and a contractor in Grand Rapids 1900-1912; Note: he is shown as Andrew P. Retan in the 1900C; 1850C; CoMR; USARCH; 1900C; CDIR; KCH

Andrew Preandal Ruttan - (1853-1925) p/David Ruttan-Elizabeth C. Griffiths m Ardelia Fordham (1854-1933); he was born at Napanee, Ontario and died at Highland Park (see FL listing) RUTT

 Ann Retan - bc 1848 p/James Retan-Urania Conover of Seneca Co. NY and Lenawee Co. m (1) Daniel S. Richardson; they were living in Isabella Co. in 1890 (2) _____ Duffy and they lived in St. Louis, Gratiot Co. (Jonathan O. Gushen)

Ann C. Retan - b 1853 p/Benjamin S. Retan-Lucy A. Pennel of Shiawassee Co.; 1860C

Archie Rutan - (1881-1973) p/William M. Rutan-Clarinda P. Taylor m (1) Mabel Maud Lombard (2) Imo Nummo (1880-1967) he was born in Hillsdale Co. and died in Jackson; he and Mabel are bur at Aldrich Cem and Imo is bur at East Liberty Cem (Pat Jenkins) CoBR; SSA; 1900C

Archie Rutan - m Mabel _____; he was a farmer

and fruit-grower in Hillsdale Co., 1919-1924;
(Farmers Directory) (see prior entry)

Arlie Rutan - (1877-1961) p/William M. Rutan-
Clarinda P. Taylor m George Jay Pullen in
1899; she was born in Hillsdale Co. (Pat Jenkins)

Armina Retan - b 1854 p/Benjamin S. Retan-Lucy
A. Pennel m Augustus Ables (1851-1915) at
Owosso in 1875 (Barbara Bombassei)

Arthur F. Retan - a clerk with the Jackson Fire
Clay Co. Jackson in 1887; CDIR

Augustus Rutan - b 1880 p/John W. Rutan-Flora
Townsend m Elizabeth Dyer b 1885 of Saginaw
(Terri Bartley)

Augustus Rutan, Jr. - (1906-1906) p/Augustus
Rutan-Elizabeth Dyer; his Obit appeared in
the *Saginaw Evening News*, 3 April 1906)
(Jody Zorsch)

Aville Rutan - (1875-1957) p/William M. Rutan-
Clarinda P. Taylor m George Otto Baker in
1903; she was born in Hillsdale Co. and died
in Jackson (Pat Jenkins)

Beatrice Maude Ruttan - (1888-1888) p/James D.
Ruttan-Cynthia V. Lowe; she died in Holly MI;
RUTT

Benjamin Smith Retan - (1825-1902) p/John Retan-
Margaret Smith of NJ; m (1) Lucy A. Pennel
(1827-1859) at West Bloomfield, Oakland Co.
in 1850 (2) Emma E. Hill (1841/6-c1901) of
Sciota at Owosso in 1860; they divorced; (3)
Ann Preston Lapp (1852-c1913) born in Canada
at Owosso; he was a city marshal in Owosso
in 1863; Lucy is bur at Commerce Cem, Oakland
Co. (Barbara Bombassei) (Harold Retan) CDIR;
1870C; MMI; 1900C; VA

Bertha Retan - (1874-1889) p/Harrison L. Retan-
Cecelia A. Estes; she is bur at Maple Grove
Cem, Ovid, Clinton Co.; Note: one record has
her year of death as 1879 (Barbara Bombassei)
(Harold Retan)

Betty Rutan - p/Earl L. Rutan-Bessie _____ (Daniel Rutan)

Blanche Rutan - she was a waitress in Detroit in
1927; married to a Rutan; CDIR

Carl M. Rutan - (1893-1987) p/David M. Rutan-
Olive A. Stone; he died in Jackson; 1900C;
SSA

Caroline Retan - "Carrie" b 1858 p/Abram S.
Retan-Hester Lawrence of Shiawassee Co.; m

(1) William Emery Knowles at Ingham Co. in 1875 (2) Lyman Irland in 1887 (Barbara Bombassei) LDS

Catherine Rutan - bc 1836 p/Samuel Rutan-Sarah Cracraft; she later lived in IL and CA (George A. Rutan) 1850C

Cecelia Marie Retan - (1851-1934) p/John Retan-Sarah J. Ireland of Shiawassee Co.; m William Henry Johnson b 1848 in 1873; she was born in Henderson and died in Detroit; Note: LDS has her born in 1857; he was born William Henry Juno (Barbara Bombassei) LDS

Cecil Rutan - p/Earl L. Rutan-Bessie _____ (Daniel Rutan)

Charles Retan - (1879-1895) p/Henry B. Retan-Zoe _____; he died at Owosso (Barbara Bombassei)

Charles Ruttan - (1905-1952) p/George S. Ruttan-Ida Stephen m (1) Estelle Nelson; he died in Miami FL; RUTT

Charles B. Ruttan - (1903-1977) of Ferndale, Oakland Co.; MDI

Charles R. Rutan - (1909-1982) he lived in PA and Detroit and died in Macomb Co.; SSA; MDI

Charles W. Rutan - bc 1842 p/Samuel Rutan-Sarah Cracraft; he later lived in IL and CA (George A. Rutan 1850C

Clara Rutan - bc 1848 in MA; she was living in L'Anse Twp, Baraga Co. in 1880; she may be Clara Cowles the wife of George W. Rutan; 1880C

Clare Rutan - p/Rantie Rutan-Grace Adams (Pat Jenkins)

Clare A. Retan - (1889-1931) p/Frank A. Retan-Florence _____; he was the State Attorney General in 1926; he is bur at Calvary Cem, Hillsdale Co. (cemetery records) 1900C; NYTO

Cleon W. Rutan - (1911-1989) p/Rantie Rutan-Grace Adams (Pat Jenkins)

Clizzie L. Retan - (1898-1987) Note: she is listed as Rutan in the 1900C; MDI; 1900C

Clyde Rutan - b 1883 p/William Rutan-Alice Stradworthy m Ika Moselle Collacott (1885-1973; he was a bookkeeper in Saginaw in 1919; she died in Saginaw and is bur at the Vanderbilt Cem (from her Obit in the *Saginaw News*) 1900C; CDIR

Cyril Retan - (1886-1888) p/Frank A. Retan-Florence _____; he is bur at Calvary Cem, Hillsdale Co. (cemetery records)

D.M. Rutan - m Laura _____; he was a farmer in
Jerome, Hillsdale Co., 1919-1924 (Farmers
Directory)

Daniel Ruttan - m Susie _____; he was a machinist in Flint in 1919 living at the same address as Edward Ruttan; CDIR

David Mark Rutan - (1874-1945) p/Stephen Rutan-
Nancy McLain of Somerset Twp, Hillsdale Co.;
m Olive A. Stone b 1874; he is bur at Somerset Center Cem, Hillsdale Co.; Note: he is in
the 1900C as **Mark D.** Rutan; Olive's surname
from her son Theron's death certificate (cemetery records) 1880C; 1900C

Deloss Retan - b 1851 p/Abram S. Retan-Hester
Lawrence of Shiawassee Co. (Barbara Bombassei) (see OR listing) 1860C

Dolores Maxine Ruttan - b 1918 p/Isaac E. Ruttan
-Lydia C. White; RUTT

Donald S. Rutan - (1894-1929) p/William M. Rutan
-Clarinda P. Taylor m Mabel King; he was a
WWI soldier who was killed in a construction
accident after the War; he is bur at Aldrich
Cem, Hillsdale Co.(cemetery records) (Pat
Jenkins) 1900C; CRC

Dora Retan - b 1858 p/James Retan-Urania Conover
of Lenawee Co. (Jonathan O. Gushen) LDS

Doris M. Rutan - (1919-1983) probably the wife
of Harold Rutan; she is bur at Fairview Cem,
Mantion, Wexford Co. (cemetery records)

Dorothea Louise Ruttan - (1911-1996) p/Christo-
pher Ruttan-Mary J. Dundas of Alden; she died
in Traverse City; Note: the Obituary Daily
Times has her born in 1912; VWR

Earl Retan - (1914-1977) of Adrian, Lenawee Co;
he lived in CA; SSA

Earl Arthur Ruttan - (1900-1988) p/Elisha Ruttan
-Clare Morley of Pontiac; m Mary Agness Will-
hauck b 1903 at Monroe in 1923; they lived in
Medina, Lenawee Co.; VWR; RUTT; MDI; SSA

Earl Lee Rutan - (1879-1932) p/Stephen Rutan-
Nancy McLain m (1) Florence M. _____ (1882-
1902) (2) Bessie _____ (1887-1963) he was a
farmer in Jerome, 1919-1924 (Farmers Directory) all bur at Somerset Center Cem, Hillsdale Co. (cemetery records) CRC; 1880C; 1900C

Edgar H. Retan - m Lena Myers at Lincoln Twp,
Isabella Co. in 1884; LDS

Edith Rutan - d 1971 m William Olen Cornell
(1898-1986) he was born at White Lake Twp and

died at Rochester; she died at Holly; ROOTSW

Edith Blanch Ruttan - (1894-1959) p/Christopher Ruttan-Mary J. Dundas of Clearwater Twp; she died at Saginaw and is bur at Clearwater Twp Cem (from her Obit in the *Saginaw News*) VWR; 1900C; RUTT

Edith M. Retan - b 1891 p/James H. Retan-Rebecca A. Stringer of Shiawassee Co.; ROOTSW

Edward Ruttan - m Lydia ____; he was a machinist in Flint in 1919 living at the same address as Daniel Ruttan; CDIR

Elinor C. Retan - b 1898 p/Frank A. Retan-Florence ____; 1900C

Elisha Ruttan - (1871-1935) p/Joseph Ruttan-Elizabeth Walker m Clarabelle (Clare) Morley (1887-1952) from DE in 1897; he died at Mount Clemens, Macomb Co. and she at Muskegon; VWR; RUTT

Elizabeth Rutan - bc 1810 she was the sister of Stephen P. Rutan m John Leach; they lived in Hillsdale Co. (from Stephen's CW pension file) USARCH

Elizabeth Retan - (1860-1902) of Woodland; she is bur at Lakeside Cem, Lake Odessa Twp, Ionia Co. (cemetery records)

Elizabeth A. Retan - "Lib" (1858-1938) p/John M. Retan-Sarah J. Ireland of Shiawassee Co.; m Menville Almarion Bacon (1855-1938) in 1875; she died in Rush Twp, Shiawassee Co. 1860C; ROOTSW

Elizabeth Jane Ruttan - (1893-1981) p/Christopher Ruttan-Mary J. Dundas m Vernon G. Grove (1884-1959) at Traverse City in 1919; RUTT; VWR; 1900C

Ellen Retan - b 1853 p/Abram S. Retan-Hester Lawrence of Shiawassee Co.; 1860C; 1870C

Elmer Retan - b 1855/57 p/Abram S. Retan-Hester Lawrence of Shiawassee Co.; m (1) Elsie ____ (1861-1880) (2) Eva A. Niver (1867-1905) at Hazelton in 1881; he was a blacksmith living in Owosso in 1900; Elsie is bur at Unadilla Village Cem and Eva is bur at Oak Hill Cem, Owosso; Note: he is listed as **Elmore** in the 1860C (Shiawassee District Library surname files) (Barbara Bombassei) 1860C; 1870C; 1900C

Elmer Rutan - (1907-1967) of Royal Oak; SSA

Elwood Retan - (see Henry Elwood Retan, below)

Emma Retan - b 1867 p/Abram S. Retan-Hester

Lawrence (Barbara Bombassei)

Emma E. Ratan - b 1846; lived in Owosso; 1900C

Emma Elizabeth Retan - (1907-1994) p/Fred S.
Retan-Iretta M. Hight; she was born in Burl-
ington VT and died in Monterey CA; unm (Terry
Campbell) CADRI

Emma May Retan - she was a school-teacher in MI
who moved to Oreana ID in 1889; m Benjamin
Henry Hyde (see ID listing) PERSI

Emma R. Ruttan - b 1874 p/David Ruttan-Irene
_____ m Arthur Stinnett; she was born in KS;
RUTT

Emmerson James Ruttan - (1903-1968) p/Christo-
pher Ruttan-Mary J. Dundas of Kalkaska Co.;
m Jean Adeline Needham b 1907 at Howell in
1931; he was an electrician and was sometimes
known as **J. Emmerson** Ruttan; RUTT; SSA

Emma E. Ratan - b 1846; living in Owosso, Shiawassee Co. in 1900; 1900C

Esther Retan - d 1888 p/Melvin Retan-Jane Laurence; she is bur at Sherman City Cem, Isabella Co. (cemetery records)

Esther Ann Rutan - m Samuel W. Dake at Hillsdale
Co. in 1859; MMR; CoMR

Ethel May Retan - (1885-1895) p/Albert Retan-
Elizabeth Bennington; she is bur at Lakeside
Cem, Lake Odessa Twp, Ionia Co. (cemetery
records) (information from her father's CW
pension file) 1894C

Florence L. Retan - b 1908; she lived in Hillsdale Co. (see Herbert W. Retan, below)

Frank Arthur Retan - (1864-1917) m Florence _____
(1864-1919) they were living in Hudson Twp,
Lenawee Co. in 1900; both are bur at Calvary
Cem. Hillsdale Co. (cemetery records) 1900C

Frank E. Retan - (1860-1860) p/Henry K. Retan-
Katherine M. Voorheis; he was born and died
in Oakland Co. (Barbara Bombassei)

Fred Smith Retan - b 1862 p/Benjamin S. Retan-
Emma E. Hill of Owosso m Iretta May Hight b
1861 in Niles MI in 1892; he was a minister
at the First Baptist Ch in Niles; he left the
ministry and was engaged in business in Boston, at various times they lived in Detroit,
Albany NY, Parkersburg WV and Burlington VT;
Iretta was a school teacher in Hawaii, 1888-
1892 (Barbara Bombassei)(Terry Campbell)

Frederick Ruttan - (1876-1968) of Algonec, St.
Clair Co.; he died in Macomb Co.; MDI; SSA

Frederick Retan - b 1899 p/Harrison L. Retan-
Cora B. Riker; 1900C

George Christopher Ruttan - (1901-1974) p/Chris-
topher Ruttan-Mary J. Dundas m Janet Wager-
shutz (1911-1975) they lived in Williamston,
Ingham Co. VWR; SSA; MDI

George D. Retan - (1845-1860) p/Henry Retan-
Katherine Voorheis; she was born and died in
Oakland Co.; he is bur in Commerce Village
Cem (Barbara Bombassei) (Harold E. Retan)

George W. Rutan - bc 1844 p/Samuel Rutan-Sarah
Cracraft; he later lived in IL and CA (George
A. Rutan) 1850C

George W. Retan - bc 1843 p/William Retan-Tryphena Mead (Barbara Bombassei)

Geraldine Retan - b 1890 p/Frank A. Retan-Florence _____ of Lenawee Co.; 1900C

Geraldine Retan - m Raymond B. Page; ROOTSW

Gertrude Rutan - (1887-1969) p/John W. Rutan-
Flora Townsend m Fred Lasell/Loiselle (1885-
1956) he was born in Saginaw; they are bur at
Lakeside Cem, Holly, Oakland Co. (Terri Bartley) 1900C

Glenn W. Rutan - (1900-1970) p/Earl L. Rutan-
Florence M. _____ of Jerome, Hillsdale Co.; m
Lucy _____ (1902-1986) in 1930; they are bur
at Somerset Center Cem (cemetery records)
(Daniel Rutan) CRC; 1900C; SSA

Gordon V. Ruttan - (1903-1984) of Detroit; SSA

Grace L. Rutan - b 1898 p/David M. Rutan-Olive
A. Stone; 1900C

Guerd H. Retan - (1881-1945) p/Jay V. Retan-
Alice Powers; he was a banker who was born
and died in Ovid (Barbara Bombassei)

Gwendolyn Rutan - p/Rantie Rutan-Grace Adams
(Pat Jenkins)

Hannah Rutan - b 1855 p/Stephen P. Rutan-Rebecca
W. French of Hudson, Lenawee Co. (from her
father's CW pension file) USARCH

Hannah Rutan - (1855-1904) m Alna Weaver in 1883
he was from NY (see prior entry) ROOTSW

Harold Retan - (1908-1970) of Jasper; SSA

Harold Rutan - (1908-1985) he is probably the
son of Milton Rutan-Jennie _____; he lived in
Mantion, Wexford Co. and is bur there at
Fairview Cem (cemetery records) (see Doris M.
Rutan, above) SSA; MDI

Harold Edward Ruttan - (1920-1981) p/Isaac E.
Ruttan-Lydia C. White m Lucille M. Smith in

1968; he served in the U.S. Navy and died in Lebanon PA; RUTT

Harold J. Ruttan - (1911-1996) p/John N. Ruttan-Grace Harriet Martin of Belleville, Ontario; m (1) **Edna Rose Gaulin** b 1914 (2) **Verna Adella Teeter** b 1921 in 1949; he lived in Roseville, Macomb Co.; MDI; RUTT

Harold Lee Retan - (1905-1964) p/Lee H. Retan-Helena J. Fox of Owosso; m June Claire Davenport b 1907; he was born in VT, lived in No. Hollywood CA in 1955 and died in Orange Co.; Note: info on June from "Descendants of Samuel Ranson"; SSA; VA; CADRI

Harrison L. Retan - (1843-1920) p/Henry K. Retan-Katherine Voorheis m (1) Cecelia A. Estes (1850-1874) at Ovid in 1869 (2) Sarah Jane Reynolds (1859-1938) at Clinton Co. in 1882; they were living in Owosso, Shiawassee Co. in 1900; Cecelia is bur at Maple Grove Cem, Ovid Clinton Co.; Sarah died in Lansing (cemetery records) Note: at least one record calls him Harrison D. Rutan; (Harold Retan; Barbara Bombassei) 1850C; LDS; 1900C

Harrison L. Retan - b 1858 m (1) Cornelia A. Bell in Clinton Co. in 1876 (2) Cora B. Riker b 1864 in Lincoln Twp, Isabella Co. in 1883; he was born in OH; 1870C; 1900C; LDS

Harriet B. Retan - (1896-1896) p/Frank A. Retan-Florence A. _____; she is bur at Calvary Cem, Hillsdale Co. (cemetery records)

Harriet E. Retan - (1848-1913) p/Henry K. Retan-Katherine Voorheis m Dennis T. Covert in 1873 she is bur at Maple Grove Cem, Ovid (cemetery records) (Harold Retan; Barbara Bombassei)

Harriet P. Rutan - m James Mitchell at Washtenaw Co. in 1859; LDS

Harry Retan - (1888-1888) p/Harrison D. Retan-Sarah J. Reynolds; he is bur at Maple Grove Cem, Ovid, Clinton Co. (cemetery records)

Harvey D. Ruttan - d 1920 p/James Ruttan-Phily Ann Cadman; RUTT

Henry Retan - a laborer in Saginaw in 1919; CDIR

Henry B. Retan - b 1853 p/William Retan-Sarah Van Kuren m (1) Zoe _____ (2) Cora Varney Soules a widow, at Saginaw in 1890; they were living in Genesee in 1900 (Barbara Bombassei) (see Marcus Retan, below) 1900C

Henry C. Retan - (1843-1916) p/James Retan-Urania Conover of Seneca Co. NY m (1) Catherine

B. Partridge (1848-1877) in 1870 (2) Elizabeth Hill Hinkle (1841-1918) a widow, at
Fulton OH; he was a CW soldier serving in the
33rd Michigan Volunteer Infantry; he lost his
right arm at battle of Gaines Mill VA; he
died at Fairfield; all three are bur at Weston Village Cem, Fairfield Twp, Lenawee Co.;
Note: Catherine's headstone reads (1853-1887)
(cemetery records) (some info from his CW
pension file) (Jonathan O. Gushen) USARCH;
CoMR

Henry C. Retan - (1888-1888) see Harry Retan,
above)

Henry Elwood Retan - (1874-1917) p/Henry C.
Retan-Catherine B. Partridge; he was a physician living in Charlotte in 1900; he is bur
at Weston Village Cem, Lenawee Co. (cemetery
records) (see OH listing) 1900C

Henry G. Retan - CW soldier, Co. G, 16th Michigan Volunteer Infantry; this may be Henry C.
Retan (Regimental muster roll)

Henry F. Ruttan - d 1942, WWII soldier, Pvt.,
104th Field Artillery Battalion, 27th Infantry; his name appears on the War Memorial at
Honolulu, HI; USARCH

Henry K. Retan - (1817-1906) p/John Retan-Margaret Smith of NJ; m Katherine M. Voorheis
(1820-1900) at Commerce Twp, Clinton Co. in
1850; they were living in Ovid in 1870, with
their daughter Adelaide Scofield at Gratiot
Co. in 1880 and with son Harrison in 1900;
he was a grocer in 1863 and a hotel-keeper
(from his death certificate) Katherine was
born in Peapack, Somerset Co. NJ; they are
bur at Maple Grove Cem, Ovid (Barbara Bombassei) (Harold Retan) 1850C; 1870C; CDIR; 1880C
1900C

Herbert Rutan - (1909-1979) of Jackson Co.; MDI;
SSA

Herbert W. Retan - b 1909 in Hillsdale Co.; CoBR

Ina Rutan - (1879-1963) p/William M. Rutan-Clarinda P. Taylor m (1) Leon A. Mercer in 1903
(2) Samuel Calhaun; she was born in Hillsdale
Co.; Note: CoMR has her first marriage to
Leon A. Wallace (Pat Jenkins) 1900C; CoMR

Irena Retan - b 1868 p/James H. Retan-Loretta
_____ of Ottawa Co.; LDS

Irma M. Retan - m Daniel Haines in 1865 at
Clinton Co.; LDS; CoMR

Irvin W. Ruttan - (1905-1979) p/Christopher Ruttan-Mary J. Dundas m Marguerita A. Warner b 1909 at Northville in 1934; they lived in Detroit; VWR; RUTT; SSA; MDI

Isaac Edward Ruttan - (1893-1973) p/James D. Ruttan-Cynthia V. Lowe m Lydia Catherine White b 1900 at Sterling, Arenac Co. in 1917; RUTT; SSA; MDI

Isabel Rutan - b 1853 p/Stephen P. Rutan-Rebecca W. French of Cuyahoga Co. and later Hillsdale Co. (from her father's CW pension file) USARCH

J. Emerson Ruttan - (See Emmerson James Ruttan, above)

James Rutan - b in NJ; he was a judge living in Shiawassee Co.; earlier he lived in Wood Co. OH and later in MN and IA (Barbara Bombassei)

James Rutan - acquired land in Wayne Co. in 1835 (Michigan land records)

James Rutan - a watchman in Detroit in 1927; CDIR

James Retan - (1825-1896) p/Peter Retan-Polly Hatt of Seneca Co. NY m Urania Conover (1822-1915) of NJ; they moved from Seneca Co. in 1858; both are bur at Fairfield Village Cem; Note: LDS calls her **War-Ann**; her gravestone has **Ura A.** (1822-1913) (Jonathan O. Gushen) LDS; 1870C

James Ruttan - (1841-1910) p/Joseph Ruttan-Susan Laid m (1) Phily Ann Cadman at Kingston in 1860 (2) Martha Jane Sample (1848-1880) of NY in 1872 at Croswell, Sanilac Co. (3) Margaret N. _____ ; he died at Custer Twp, Sanilac Co.; RUTT

James B. Retan - married in Iosco Co. in 1889; the bride not specified; CoMR

James Boyd Ruttan - (1922-1925) p/Isaac E. Ruttan-Lydia C. White; he died in Gladwin; RUTT

James Doars Ruttan - (1853-1921) p/Christopher Ruttan-Phoebe Ann Doars m Cynthia Victoria Lowe (1855-1923) at Parry, Peterborough Co., Ontario in 1874; they were living in Clayton Twp in 1900; he was born in Loughborough, Ontario and died in Flint; she died in Genesee (Lowe Family homepage) 1900C; RUTT

James H. Retan - (1844-1912) p/John Retan-Sarah J. Ireland of Shiawassee Co.; m Rebecca Ann Stringer Marlatt (1850-1925) in 1881; she was born in Elgin Co., Ontario and died in Wex-

ford Co.; he is bur at Riverside Cem, Henderson, Shiawassee Co.; she is bur at Cornell
Cem, Mesick (cemetery records) (Barbara Bombassei) 1860C; LDS; 1870C

Jane A. Retan - d 1900 p/Melvin R. Retan-Jane A.
Laurence of Isabella Co.; she is bur at Sherman City Cem, Isabella Co. (cemetery records)

Jay V. Retan - (1851-1899) p/Henry K. Retan-
Katherine Voorheis m Alice Powers (1858-1901)
in 1876; he was living in Commerce Twp, Oakland Co. in 1860 and he died in Ovid; after
his death she remarried (Barbara Bombassei)
1860C

Jesse M. Rutan - d 1910 p/Milton Rutan-Jennie
_____; he is bur at Fairview Cem, Mantion,
Wexford Co. (cemetery records)

Jessie Rutan - m John H. Timms (1899-1981) of
Fife Lake at Petosky; he was a mail-carrier
who died at Lake Worth FL; he is bur at Fife
Lake Cem (from his Obit in the *Kalkaskian*,
13 Aug 1981)

John Retan - (1787-1846) m Margaret Smith
1793/3-1864; they were both born in NJ; he
died in Oakland Co. and she in Owosso; both
are bur at Four Towns Cem, Waterford; Note:
according to Barbara Bombassei John may have
been born in Nova Scotia and thus may be related to David Ruttan the Loyalist (see Northeast listing) (Harold Retan)

John Rutan - (1839-1862) a CW soldier, Co. A,
1st Michigan Cavalry; he was from Allegan,
he is bur at Alexandria VA National Cemetery
(Civil War muster rolls) CoDR

John Rutan - bc 1823 p/James Rutan of NJ; m
Harriet Smedley bc 1826 of PA at Owosso in
in 1841 and later lived in Shelby Twp, Macomb
Co.; CoMR; 1850C

John Rutan - bc 1838 p/Samuel Rutan-Sarah Cracraft; 1850C

John Ruttan - (1873-1874) p/Joseph Ruttan-Susan
Laid of Sanilac Co.; RUTT

John Adelbert Retan - b 1868 p/Albert Retan-
Elizabeth Fox m Emma _____ b 1872; they were
living in Fairfield, Lenawee Co. in 1900
(from his father's CW pension file) 1900C

John C. Retan - b 1817 in NY; he was living with
his son-in-law John Partridge in Lenawee Co.
in 1900; 1900C

John C. Retan - b 1857 p/William Retan-Sarah Van

Kuren m Lariza Thayer Dodge in 1900 (Barbara
Bombassei) 1900C
John F. Ruttan - (1910-1983) of St. Clair; MDI
John Frederick Rutan - (1918-1993) he lived in
MI and died in Dallas TX; TXDR
John H. Retan - b 1817 m Caroline _____ b 1827;
they are bur at Canandaigua Cem, Madison Twp,
Lenawee Co. (cemetery records without death
years)
John Henry Ruttan - (1873-1953) p/Jesse B. Rutt-
an-Emily Cameal m Annie M. Cryderman (1882-
1952) he was born in Canada and died in Lansing; both are bur at Chapel Hill Cem; RUTT
John Melvin Retan - (1820-1866) p/John Retan-
Margaret Smith m (1) Sarah Jane Ireland
(1827-1908 at New Haven, Shiawassee Co. in
1843; he was born in NJ and she in NY; they
were living in Owosso in 1850 and she died at
Rush Twp, Shiawassee Co.; Note: CLA has her
born in 1824 and another record has him as
John Nelson Retan, that she was born in 1826
and she m (2) Seth Porter in 1877; she is bur
at West Haven Cem (Barbara Bombassei) CLA;
1850C; CoMR
John R. Retan - (1807-1881) m Catherine Emmons
(1819-1895) in NY in 1843; he was a farmer,
born in NJ who moved to Kent Co. in 1843;
they were living in Wyoming Twp, Kent Co. in
1870; Note: the Michigan Death Index has a
John R. Retan (1809-1882) born in NJ the son
of Peter Retan and ?Clannsa _____; 1850C;
MDI; 1870C; KCH
John W. Rutan - b 1855 in NY; m (1) Flora Townsend (1863-1940) at Midland in 1879; apparently divorced; she m (2) Charles Newton Hilborn
in 1907; she is bur at Lakeside Cem, Holly,
Oakland Co. (Terri Bartley) 1900C; LDS
Joseph Rutan - bc 1834 p/Samuel Rutan-Sarah Cra-
craft; he later lived in OR; 1850C
Joseph Ruttan - (1864-1921) p/Joseph Ruttan-
Elizabeth Walker (1842-1880) m Hattie Vander-
voort (1860-1945) in Susquehanna PA; he was
born in Lindsay, Ontario and died in Elgin OR
VWR; RUTT
Julia D. Retan - (1865-1937) p/William Retan-
Sarah Van Kuren m _____ Marble; she is bur at
Oak Hill Cem (Shiawassee Co. District Library
surname file)
Kate Rutan - living with Andrew E. Rutan in

Grand Rapids in 1908; CDIR

Lee Rutan - (1883-1927) p/Stephen P. Rutan-Nancy
McLain m Zula Avadelle Patch (1888-1957) in
1906; both are bur at Somerset Center Cem,
Hillsdale Co.; "Descendants of William Patch"
1900C; CoDR; CRC

Lee Hill Retan - (1872-1930) p/Benjamin S. Retan
-Emma E. Hill of Owosso; m Helena Jennie Fox
(1876-1955) at Christ Episcopal Ch, Owosso in
1900; he served in the SpAmWar as a Lieutenant, 33rd Michigan Infantry; he worked for
Fred S. Retan in Albany NY and Burlington VT,
1904-1906; he was an electrician, city police
man and bookkeeper (from his pension file) as
well as a railway foreman in Owosso in 1919;
he died in Grand Rapids and Helena died in
Glendale CA; they are bur at Oak Hill Cem;
her gravestone says she was born in 1874
(Shiawassee Co. District Library surname
file) (Barbara Bombassei) VA; CoMR; CDIR;
1900C

Lemuel Benedict Retan - (1858-1938) p/Peter Ret-
an-Thankful Skinner m (1) Eliza Jane Jay d
1904 (2) Alta Mae Terpening (1873-1917) about
1908; he is bur at Weston Village Cem, Fairfield Twp, Lenawee Co. (cemetery records)
RRET

Leo W. Rutan - b 1890 p/John W. Rutan-Flora
Townsend m Anna _____; he was born in Elmira
NY and was a taxi driver in Detroit in 1927;
NYBC; 1900C; CDIR

Leona Rutan - d 1916 p/Milton Rutan-Jennie _____
m Willis Anway (1886-1914) both are bur at
Fairview Cem, Mantion, Wexford Co. (cemetery
records)

Levi C. Retan - (1885-1931) p/Lewis E. Retan-
Betsey H. _____; m Lila G. _____; he is bur
at Fairfield Village Cem, Lenawee Co. (cemetery records) 1900C

Lewis E. Retan - (1849-1926) p/James Retan-Urania Conover of Seneca Co. NY and Lenawee Co.;
m Betsey H. _____ (1846-1929) they were both
born in NY; they were living in Lenawee Co.
in 1900; both are bur at Fairfield Village
Cem where she is listed as **Helen** Retan (cemetery records) Note: In NY in the 1850C he
is enumerated as **Louis W.** Retan (Jonathan O.
Gushen) 1850C; 1900C

Lila G. Retan - b 1885; she is bur at Fairfield

Village Cem, Lenawee Co. (cemetery records)
she is likely the wife of Levi C. Retan,
above

Lillian B. Retan - (1863-1895) p/William Retan-
Sarah Van Kuren m James L. Marble (1856-1939)
about 1879; he was born at Aurelius, Ingham
Co.; she was born at Livingston Co. (Marble
Genealogy) CoBR

Lillie Rutan - b 1861 p/Stephen P. Rutan-Rebecca
W. French of Hillsdale Co. (from her father's
CW pension file) USARCH

Lillie May Retan - **Lily Mary** (1864-1871) p/Henry
K. Retan-Katherine Voorheis; she was born in
Owosso and died in Ovid; she is bur at Maple
Grove Cem, Ovid, Clinton Co. (Harold Retan)
CoDR; MDI

Louis W. Retan - (see Lewis E. Retan, above)

Luanna Retan - m Samuel J. Hinkley in Lenawee
Co. in 1856; Note: she may be **Lewanny** Retan
in the 1850C as the daughter of John Rutan;
LDS

Lucela Ruttan - **Lucille** b 1898 p/Elisha Ruttan-
Clare Morley of Kalkaska Co.; m Elwood Richardson; VWR; RUTT

Lucille Lowe Retan - b 1899 p/Fred S. Retan-
Iretta M. Hight; she was born in Parkersburg
WV (Terry Campbell)

Lucy Ruttan - (1869-1943) p/Joseph Ruttan-Elizabeth Walker m George Morris at Pontiac; RUTT

Lucy A. Retan - p/Benjamin S. Retan-Lucy A. Pennel m Charles M. Miller at Atrium Twp in 1869
(Barbara Bombassei)

Lyle Rutan - (1907-1992) p/Rantie Rutan-Grace
Adams; he lived in Jackson Co. (Pat Jenkins)
MDI; SSA

Maybelle M. Retan - (1884-1948) probably the
wife of Archie Rutan (1881-1973) she is bur
at Aldrich Cem. Hillsdale Co. (cemetery records)

Manning Rutan - from NJ; proprietor of Rutan &
Vanloo General Store in 1863 at Greenville,
Montcalm Co.; he also owned a sawmill; CDIR

Marcus Retan - (1892-1931) p/Henry Retan-Cora
Soules; he was born in Chesaning MI; was liv-
ing in Genesee Co. in 1900 and died in Marion
IN; he is bur in Saginaw; Note: his Obit in
the *Saginaw News* identified his mother as
Mrs. Guy Haven; 1900C

Marcus H. Retan - m Zoa Barberry in Genesee Co.

192

in 1876; Note: Henry B. Retan, see above, m
Zoe _____; LDS

Margaret Retan - m Dean C. Wright in 1846; LDS

Margaret A. Retan - (1849-1869) p/Henry K. Retan
-Katherine Voorheis; she was a milliner and
is bur at Maple Grove Cem, Ovid, Clinton Co.
(cemetery records) (Harold Retan) MDI

Maria Retan - Ann Mariah (1838-1941) p/William
Retan-Tryphena Mead m John S. Teeples (1833-
1913) at Commerce, Oakland Co. in 1855; she
was born in Pontiac and died in Highland,
Oakland Co.; they are bur at Oak Grove Cem,
Milford; he was a hotel-keeper in Milford;
(Barbara Bombassei)("Descendants of Jacob
Teeples") ROOTSW

Marie Retan - b 1894 p/Harrison L. Retan-Cora
B. Riker; 1900C

Marion Retan - m Roseida Allen in Isabella Co.
in 1881; LDS

Marium Townsend Retan - Marian (1846-1931) p/
John H. Retan-Henrietta Huff of Ovid, Seneca
Co. NY; m John Willet Partridge (1844-1918)
in 1866 at Morencia, Lenawee Co.; she was
born in Seneca Co. NY and died at Weston
(Partridge database) WWW; LDS; 1870C

Mark David Rutan - b 1874 (See David Mark Rutan)

Martha Rutan - b 1882 p/John W. Rutan-Flora
Townsend; 1900C

Martha Grant Rutan - m Joseph Alexander Freiber-
ger (1904-1954) at Sanilac Co. about 1926; he
previously wed Geraldine Flannery about 1924
("Descendants of Alexander Hall")

Martha L. Retan - b 1849 p/William Retan-Sarah
Van Kuren m Charles S. Harris bc 1840 in 1879
at West Haven, Shiawassee Co.; she was born
in Oakland Co. (Barbara Bombassei)

Martin S. Retan - b 1851 p/William Retan-Sarah
Van Kuren; living with his mother in Rush Twp
in 1900 he is called Martin **Reton** in the census (Barbara Bombassei) 1900C

Mary Rutan - (1849-1850) p/Samuel Rutan-Sarah
Cracraft; Mary was born in IL; 1850C

Mary Retan - b 1854 p/John M. Retan-Sarah J.
Ireland of Shiawassee Co.; 1860C

Mary A. Rutan - (c1842-1902) p/John Rutan-Harriet Smedley m Peter Napoleon Cook b 1840 in
1869 at Washtenaw; she was a "granddaughter
of Judge Rutan"; he was born at Antrim, Shiawassee Co. and served in the CW as a Major

in the 10th Michigan Cavalry; he later was an attorney and a member of the Board of Regents at the University of Michigan ("Midwest Pioneers: Michigan Biographies") 1850C; LDS

Mary Ann Retan - b 1859 p/William Retan-Sarah Van Kuren m Jacob R. Good (1844-1918) at Rush in 1877; he was born in Germany and died at Caldonia, Shiawassee Co.; Note: another record says she was born about 1847 (Barbara Bombassei) ROOTSW

Mary Catherine Retan - b 1879 p/Andrew E. Retan-Helen L. Day of Kent Co.; USARCH

Mary E. Retan - (1861-1880) she was married to a Retan and the daughter of Gilbert and Alvina May; she died in Unadilla, Livingston Co.; MDI

Mary Henrietta Retan - (1853-1867) p/John M. Retan-Sarah J. Ireland; she died at Rush Twp, Shiawassee Co.; Note: CoDR has 1854 as her birth year; LDS; MDI

Mary Jemima Ruttan - (1878-1942) p/James D. Ruttan-Cynthia V. Lowe m George Daniel Costello at Goodrich in 1896; RUTT

Mary S. Retan - **Mary E.** b 1843 p/John R. Retan-Catherine Emmons of Kent Co. m Abram/Abraham Jones b 1835 of Madison NE in 1865; she was born in NJ or NY and he in Cumberland Co. NJ; he was a millwright who served in the Civil War; 1850C; KCH; CoMR; MMI

Matilda Retan - bc 1845 p/James Retan-Urania Conover of Seneca Co. NY and Lenawee Co.; m George A. Potes at Lenawee in 1862 (Jonathan O. Gushen) LDS

Matilda Rutton - d 1871 at Lenawee Co. (see prior entry) MDI

Mattie S. Rutan - bc 1870, she was the daughter of Huldah Kosier of Isabella Co.; 1880C

Mattie S. Retan - m William B. Lamkin at Mt. Pleasant, Isabella Co. in 1887; LDS

Maurice Elgin Retan - (1911-1996) p/Lemuel B. Retan-Alta M. Terpening m Marie Elizabeth Goudy (1919-1961) RRET

Mehitabel Rutan - b 1831 m Ira Stone b 1799 at Owosso, Shiawassee Co. in 1859 (Judy Breedlove

Melissa Retan - she was living in Ionia Co. in 1898 (Rutan v Anna E. Sherwood, et al; Ionia Circuit Court)

Melvin Robert Retan - (1849-1917) p/John M.

Retan-Sarah J. Ireland m Jane Ann Laurence d
1900; they were living in Coldwater Twp, Isabella Co. in 1900; he is bur at Riverside Cem
Shiawassee Co. and she at Sherman City Cem,
Isabella Co. (cemetery records); Note: LDS
has him born in 1860; he is sometimes shown
as **Robert Melvin** Retan; CoDR; 1850C; LDS;
1900C

Mildred Rutan - (1899-1987) p/Adelbert Rutan-
Emma _____; she is listed as Retan in the
MDI; 1900C; MDI

Mildred Rutan - Betty (1916-1996) m _____ West-
fall; she lived in Kalamazoo (Obituary Daily
Times)

Mildred Geneva Rutan - b 1905 p/William H. Rutan
-Elsie Stevenson (Terry Campbell) 1920C

Milton Rutan - (1869-1951) m Jennie _____ (1862-
1942) they are both bur at Fairview Cem, Mantion, Wexford Co. (cemetery records)

Milton Wheeler Rutan - (1901-1950) p/Earl L.
Rutan-Florence M. _____; he is bur at Somerset Center Cem, Hillsdale Co. (cemetery
records) Note: per Daniel Rutan his dates are
(1902-1950)

Minnie Retan - b 1872 p/Henry C. Retan-Catherine
B. Partridge; she was born in Fulton Co. OH
(see OH listing) ROOTSW

Minnie Rutan - p/Stephen Rutan-Nancy McLain; she
died young (Pat Jenkins)

Neva Belle Rutan - p/Archie Rutan-Mabel M. Lombard m Samuel Finch (Pat Jenkins)

Nina Retan - d 1906 p/Elmer Retan-Eva A. Niver;
she died in infancy and is bur at Oak Hill
Cem (Shiawassee Co. District Library surname
files)

Olive J. Retan - (1856-1918) p/John M. Retan-
Sarah J. Ireland of Shiawassee Co.; m Rice
Martin after 1879; Note: LDS has misidentif-
ied as **Oliver J.** Retan; 1860C; LDS

Ora Rutan - owned a restaurant in Hillsdale Co.
1919-1924 (Farmers Directory)

Orpha Rutan - (1873-1948) p/William W. M. Rutan-
Clarinda Taylor m Orin A. Parish in 1893; she
was born in Hillsdale Co. (Pat Jenkins)

Paul Rutan - b 1927 p/Milton W. Rutan-Greeta
_____ (1904-1994) (Daniel Rutan)

Peter Retan - b 1776 he was from Seneca Co. NY
m (2) Polly Hatt (1793-1871) of Seneca Co.;
she is bur at Canandaigua Cem, Madison Twp,

Lenawee Co. (see Northeast listing) RRET;
1870C
Peter Retan - (1826-1894) p/Peter Retan-Polly
Hatt of Seneca Co. NY; m Thankful Skinner
(1831-1891) both are bur at Old Lowe Cem,
Fairfield Twp. Lenawee Co. (cemetery records)
RRET
Phoebe Jane Ruttan - b 1875 p/James D. Ruttan-
Cynthia V. Lowe m Clarence H. Roberts at May-
field, Lapeer Co. in 1893; RUTT
Rantie Rutan - (1883-1961) p/William M. Rutan-
Clarinda P. Taylor m Grace Adams (1883-1945)
he was a farmer in Jerome, 1919-1924, (Farm-
ers Directory) both are bur at Aldrich Cem,
Hillsdale Co. (cemetery records) LDS; 1900C
Ray Retan - d 1961; his Obit appeared in the
Grand Rapids Press
Ray R. Retan - he was a reporter for the Daily
News, Grand Rapids in 1908; (see Roy R.
Rutan, below)
Raymond Arthur Retan - (1893-1941) p/Harrison D.
Retan-Sarah J. Reynolds; he was born in Ovid
and died in Lansing ; he is bur at Mt. Hope
Cem (Harold Retan)(Barbara Bombassei) ROOTSW;
SSA
Rhoda Rebacon Ruttan - (1886-1886) p/James D.
Ruttan-Cynthia V. Lowe of Lapeer Co.; RUTT
Robert Melvin Retan - (1849-1917) (see Melvin R.
Rutan, above)
Roy Rutan - (1894-1966) SSA
Roy Retan - b 1897 p/Harrison L. Retan-Cora B.
Riker; 1900C
Roy Retan - (1913-1986) of Romulus, Wayne Co.;
SSA
Roy R. Retan - **Ray** b 1877 p/Benjamin S. Retan-
Emma E. Hill m Eva V. Powers b 1879 in 1900;
he was a newspaper editor and later lived in
Omaha NE; Note: he is listed as Roy R. Rutan
in the 1900C (Barbara Bombassei) 1900C
Royce Blake Rutan - (1894-1966) p/John W. Rutan-
Flora Townsend m Edith A. Stygall (1895-1971)
of England; he served with the Canadian
forces in WWI; he was a driver in Detroit in
1927 (Bob Young) 1900C; CDIR
Ruth Retan - (1903-1940) p/Benjamin S. Retan-
Emma E. Hill; she is bur at Oak Hill Cem
(Barbara Bombassei)
Ruth Leone Retan - (1903-1942) p/Lee H. Retan-
Helena J. Fox of Owosso, Shiawassee Co.; she

is bur at Oak Hill Cem, Owosso (from her father's SpAmWar pension file) (Retan website)

Ruth M. Retan - (1920-2001) m _____ Grieder; she lived in Morenci (Obituary Daily Times)

Samantha A. Retan - b 1857 p/James Retan-Urania Conover of Lenawee Co.; m Nelson A. Kennedy (1852-1913) in 1874 at the Baptist Ch, Fairfield, Lenawee Co.; he died in Toledo OH (Jonathan O. Gushen) CoMR; ROOTSW

Samuel Rutan - bc 1810 in PA; m Sarah Cracraft bc 1809 in PA; 1850C

Samuel Ruttan - (1893-1970) probably the son of George Sidmer Ruttan-Etta Tenant; m Ethel Rozell; he died in Detroit; SSA; RUTT

Samuel S. Ruttan - b 1838 p/George H. Ruttan-Matilda Palmer m Orphy Rozell (1844-1908) RUTT

Sarah Retan - p/John R. Retan-Catherine Emmons of Kent Co.; m James Morrison; KCH

Sarah Retan - (1859-1938) m _____ Karr; she is bur at Mt. Hope Cem, Lansing, Ingham Co. (cemetery records)

Sarah Etta Rutan - b 1856/58 p/Stephen P. Rutan-Rebecca W. French of Hillsale Co. (from her father's CW pension file) USARCH

Sarah Jane Retan - b 1838/39 p/William Retan-Tryphena Mead m Albert Franklin Dodge b 1832 at Oakland Co. in 1856; he was from Wilson Twp, Niagara Co. NY (Barbara Bombassei) LDS

Sarah Jane Rettan - (1841-1929) m James Dowker bc 1836 about 1867; they were born in Canada; she died in Akron, Tuscola Co.; ROOTSW

Simeon Bishop Rutan - b 1867 p/Hudson Rutan-Mary J. Bell of Sussex Co. NJ; he was a foreman in Pontiac in 1920; CDIR

Stephen Rutan - (1850-1927) p/Stephen P. Rutan-Rebecca W. French m Nancy McLain (1846-1931) at Woodstock MI in 1871; he was born in Fayette Co. PA and she in Clinton, Lenawee Co.; they were living in Somerset Twp, Hillsdale Co. in 1900 he is bur at Somerset Center Cem (cemetery records) (Pat Jenkins) VWR; USARCH; 1880C; 1900C

Stephen Rutan, Jr. - (1877-1902) p/Stephen Rutan -Nancy McLain; he is bur at Somerset Center Cem, Hillsdale Co. (cemetery records) 1880C; 1900C

Stephen P. Rutan - (1811-1864) m Rebecca W.

French bc 1816 (see MD listing)

Ted L. Retan - (1899-1978) of Grand Rapids; SSA; MDI

Theora Retan - d 1962; her Obit appeared in the *Grand Rapids Press*; Note: she is likely to be Theora V. Allen (1902-1962) the wife of Ted L. Retan whom she married in 1921 at Kalamazoo; she was born in Watervliet; ROOTSW

Theron Augustus Rutan - (1899-1984) p/David M. Rutan-Olive A. Stone; he died in Stanislaus Co. CA; 1900C; CADRI

Thomas Retan - (1906-1977) he died at Brownsville, Cameron Co. TX; SSA

Uriah Retan - b 1872 p/Henry C. Retan-Elizabeth L. Hinkle Hill; he was born in NY and may be a son by her first marriage (from information in Henry's CW pension file) 1900C; USARCH

Vera May Retan - b 1893 p/Fred S. Retan-Iretta M. Hight m V.R. Bartevian (Terry Campbell)

Vernon Edward Retan - (1890-1977) p/Harrison D. Retan-Sarah J. Reynolds m Lovina E. Gill (1892-1963) of Canada in 1912; he was born in Ovid, Clinton Co.; he married and died in Lansing and they are bur at Mt. Hope Cem (Barbara Bombassei) (Harold Retan) ROOTSW; SSA

Willard Ruttan - (1907-1986) p/George S. Ruttan-Ida Stephen m Verna McCoy; he lived in FL; RUTT; SSA

Willard M. Retan - (1846-1861) p/John M. Retan-Sarah J. Ireland of Shiawassee Co.; Note: he is enumerated as **William** in the 1850C; 1860C; LDS

William Retan - shoe/boot store owner in Clayton in 1863; CDIR

William Retan - (1815-1895) p/John Retan-Margaret Smith of NJ m (1) Tryphena Mead d 1845 in 1838 (2) Sarah Van Kuren (1821-1904) at Waterford in 1846; Sarah was born in NY; they died in Shiawassee Co. (Barbara Bombassei)

William Rutan - he acquired land in Grayling in 1889 (Michigan land records)

William H. Rutan - purchased land in Oscoda Co. in 1865 and 1869; BLM

William H. Ruttan - (1902-1985) of Clay, St. Clair Co.; MDI

William Hudson Rutan - b 1855 p/Hudson Rutan-Mary J. Bell of Sussex Co. NJ m Alice Stradwothy b 1857; they were both born in NJ; they were living in Corwith Twp in 1900 and Vanderbilt in 1902, both Otsego Co. (some information from his father's CW pension file) he was a hotel-keeper in Corwith (Terry Campbell) USARCH; 1900C

William Hudson Rutan, Jr. - b 1878 p/William H. Rutan-Alice Stradworthy m Elsie Stevenson b 1882; he was born in VT; KKI; 1900C

William J. Rutan - bc 1845 p/John Rutan-Harriet Smedley; 1850C

William Wiley McLain Rutan - (1846-1909) p/Stephen P. Rutan-Rebecca W. French m Clarinda Phoebe Taylor (1855-1921) at Moscow MI in 1874; he was a CW soldier serving with his father in the 27th Michigan Volunteer Infantry; both are bur at Aldrich Cem, Hillsdale Co,; one record has their wedding at Somerset; 1850C; 1890C; 1900C; CRC; CoMR

Zella Lina Rutan - (1887-1974) p/William M. Rutan-Clarinda P. Taylor m (1) Arthur J. Pond (2) Milton Morehouse (3) Howard Kerr; she died in Jackson (Pat Jenkins) 1900C

M I N N E S O T A

Abel Rutan - resident of Olmsted Co.; 1860C

Abram Rutan - b 1846 p/Daniel D. Rutan-Maria Ackerman of Passaic Co. NJ; m Mary R. _____; Abram was living in Emmet Co. IA in 1880; and in Hoff Twp, Pope Co. MN in 1900; 1880C; 1900C

Albert Retan - d 1909 in Hennepin Co.; MNDCI

Andreas Manicunas Rutan - p/Andrew J. Rutan-Anne J. Faddis of LeSueur; 1870C

Andrew Jackson Rutan - (1827-1869) p/Samuel B. Rutan-Nancy Ann Jackson of Harrison Co. OH; m Anne J. Faddis b 1830; Andrew was a physician and a member of the first state Legislature; he died in LeSueur; 1860C; JN; 1857C; 1865C

Anton Rutan - of Dawson MN; he was one of a group who left Dawson for the Klondike gold fields in March 1897 (from an article in the *Dawson Sentinel*)

Archibald Rutan - d 1909 in Steele Co.; MNDCI

Charles Rutan - b 1859 p/Andrew J. Rutan-Anne J. Faddis of LeSueur; Note: the 1860C index has a Charles Ruton of LeSueur; 1860C; 1865C

Charles F. Rutan - b 1854 in MA; m Lizzie _____
b 1855 in OH; he was a machinist at the Nov-
elty Iron & Brass Works, Minneapolis, 1890-
1900; Charles may have lived in NJ in 1870
and Spokane WA in 1900; CDIR; 1900C
1900C

Clara Rutan - b 1886; she was a cook at the
Lutheran Ladies Seminary, Redwing, Goodhue
Co.; 1920C

E.F. Rutan - m Georgia Anna Estella _____
(1852-1887) she is bur at Mound Cem, Ottawa
Twp, LeSueur Co. (see next entry)(Minnesota
Cemetery Transcription Index)

E. Perry Rutan - m F. Estelle Putnam in LeSueur
Co. in 1872; (See Perry E. Rutan, below); LDS

Edna Armstrong Rutan - d 1940 in Todd Co.; Note:
she may be the widow of F.W. Rutan of DE;
MNDCI

Emily Rutan - d 1931 in Norman Co.; the widow of
a Rutan; MNDCI

George Ruttan - d 1925 in Hennepin Co.; MNDCI

George F. Rutan - (1883-1900) he is bur at Maple
Lawn Cem, Wells Twp, Rice Co. (Minnesota Cemetery Transcription Index) CoDR

George M. Rutan - he was a CW soldier; was living in Albert Lea, Freeborn Co. in 1890;
1890C

Gladys Rutan - p/Andreas M. Rutan; ROOTSW

Hattie Rutan - b 1900 in WI; she was living in
Duluth in 1920; 1920C

Henry Rheutan - living in Minneapolis in 1870;
1870C

Henry Rheutan - bc 1854; store clerk in Winona
Co. in 1870; he was born in NY and is probably a brother of Leonard L. Rheutan (see below) 1870C

Henry G. Rheutan - (1876-1904) p/Leonard L.
Rheutan-Tina H. _____ of Winona; he was a Pvt
12th Regimental Band, SpAmWar; he is bur at
Woodlawn Cem, Winona (cemetery records)
("Minnesota Volunteers in the Spanish-Americ-
an War and the Philippine Insurrection")
1900C

James Rutan - d 1866; Olmsted county commissioner in 1855; he was born in NY and lived in OH
moved to IA after 1860 and lived in MO where
he died "in a runaway" ("Olmsted County History"; "Centennial of Rochester, Minnesota")
1860C

James Rutan - resident of Winona in 1884 (County name index)

James P. Rutan - b 1870 m Edna E. _____ b 1874; they were both born in IL and were living in Sauk Center Twp, Stevens Co. (see OR listing) 1900C

John Rutan - (1900-1979) p/Andreas M. Rutan (Kelly Enokian)

Leonard L. Rheutan - (1846-1902) m Tina H. _____ he was born in NY and she in Norway; he was an engineer; he is bur at Woodlawn Cem, Winona; she was living alone there in 1920 (cemetery records) 1870C; 1880C; 1900C; 1920C

Levi Ruttan - b 1840 m Mattie Crandle at Oneida NY in 1867; he was born in Canada and died in Alkin MN; she died in Marshalltown IA; ROOTSW

Mary Rutan - d 1872; she is bur at Marion Cem, Marion Twp, Olmsted Co. (Minnesota Cemetery Transcription Index)

Mary J. Rheutan - (1872-1892) p/Leonard L. Rheutan-Tina H. _____ of Winona Co.; she is bur at Woodlawn Cem, Winona; Note: her dates are from the cemetery records and show her as Mary Leroy Clark, daughter of L.L. Rheutan; 1900C

Perry Escalpious Rutan - (1850-1920) p/Andrew J. Rutan-Anne J. Faddis m Mabel _____ b 1861/63 they were living in Blue Earth, Mankato Co. 1908-1929; Note: the city directory for 1908 has him **E. Percival** Rutan; he appears to had a first wife, Georgia A. E. Putnam; he died in Nicollet Co.; MNDCI; 1857C; 1865C; 1900C; 1920C; CDIR

Robert Rutan - (1907-1975) p/Andreas M. Rutan (Kelly Enokian)

Roy Rheutan - d 1948; he lived in St. Louis Co.; CoDR

Samuel I. Rutan - d 1855 he is bur at Marion Cem, Marion Twp, Olmsted Co. (Minnesota Cemetery Transcription Index)

W.S. Ruttan b 1844 in Canada; living in Deer River Twp in 1900; this may be Wilmot Smith Ruttan son of Philip Ruttan-Abigail Reid; 1900C

William Rutan - b 1879 p/Abram Rutan-Mary R. _____ of Pope Co.; he was born in IL; 1900C

William W. Rutan - b 1865 p/Andrew J. Rutan-Anne J. Faddis (this may be William Winfield Rutan of MO) LDS

Wilton Lynn Rutan - (1865-1982) p/Andreas M.
Rutan; he lived in CA and died in AZ (Kelly
Enokian)

MISSISSIPPI

Lucille E. Rutan - (1918-1974) she was born in
MS and died in CA; CADRI
Mollie Jane Ruton - (1862-1940) m Atlas Frank
Poole (1852-1935) she died in Dekalb, Kemper
Co.; ROOTSW

MISSOURI

Abraham P. Rutan - he died at Lafayette, St.
Clair Co.; he may be the son of Daniel Rutan-
Maria Ackerman of NJ and IL; CoDR
Alfred Rutan - p/Charles E. Rutan-Cora V. Cash;
VIRUT
Arthur Edward Reton - m Frances Dewey (from DAR
appl# 59336) he was a bookkeeper at J.T.
Reton & Son in Kansas City, 1889-1891; CDIR
Celia Reton - m George F. Coomber in Jackson in
1881; LDS
Charles Ruttan - (1893-1975) of Columbia, Boone
Co.; he is probably Charles Alva Ruttan (see
IA listing) SSA
Charles E. Rutan - b 1910 p/Charles E. Rutan-
Cora V. Cash of Brown Co. KS; living at St.
Joseph MO in 1920 and Detroit MI in 1931; he
was a roofer; 1910C; 1920C; CDIR
Donald Harold Ruttan - (1917-1986) he was born
in MO and died in Alameda CA; his mother was
a Williams; CADRI
Dorothy J. Rutan - b 1913 p/Charles E. Rutan-
Cora V. Cash of St. Joseph, Buchanan Co.; m
_____ Rowader; VIRUT; 1920C
Edna May Rutan - n 1904 p/Wright S. Rutan-Martha
E. Cosby of Kansas City; m Charles Edward
Buchner at Kansas City in 1925; LDS
Edwin Ruttan - he was a carpenter living in St.
Joseph in 1890 (see KS listing) CDIR
Elizabeth Ruton - resident of Ozark Co.; 1850C
Elmer R. Rutan - b 1907 p/Charles E. Rutan-Cora
V. Cash; he was born in KS and died in CA;
VIRUT; 1910C

Harry Joseph Rutan - b 1914 p/Charles E. Rutan-
   Cora V. Cash of St. Joseph; he later lived in
   Detroit MI; VIRUT; 1920C; CDIR
Harry Max Rutan - (1924-1993) he was born in MO
   and died in San Patricio TX; TXDR
James Cosby Rutan - b 1908 p/Wright S. Rutan-
   Martha E. Cosby of St. Louis; LDS
John Rutan b 1879 p/John O. Rutan-Martha Wyatt;
   1880C
John Ruton, Sr. - resident of Cooper Co.; 1830C
John B. Reton - employee of J.T. Reton & Son,
   Type Foundry in Kansas City, 1889-1891; CDIR
John T. Reton - principal, J.T. Reton & Son,
   Kansas City, 1889-1891; CDIR
John Cecil Rutan - (1889-1970) p/Charles Edward
   Rutan-Cora Viola Cash of KS; m Lovinya K.
   Boor; he died in AZ; VIRUT; SSA
John O. Rutan - b 1838 m Martha Wyatt b 1844; he
   was born in OH and she in IA; they were liv-
   ing in Smithfield, Cass Twp, Fulton Co. IL in
   1870 and in Hiawatha, Brown Co. KS in 1880
   (David Smirak) (Donna Hitz) LDS
Joseph Paul Rutan - d 1943 (*St. Louis Post-Dis-
   patch Index*)
Kesia Rutan - resident of Liberty Twp, Schuyler
   Co.; 1870C
Letitia Rutan - m L.D. Wiggins in 1875; LDS
Letty Ruton - b 1875 in Dent; LDS
Margaret M. Rutan - resident of St. Ferdinand
   Twp, St. Louis Co.; 1860C
Marion Rutan - m Catherine Potter at Boone Co.
   in 1872; CoMR
Martha Helen Rutan - b 1908 p/Charles E. Rutan-
   Cora V. Cash m _____ Olson; Note: 1910C has
   her **Martha E.** Rutan; VIRUT; 1910C
Mary Belle Rutan - b 1868/70 p/John O. Rutan-
   Martha Wyatt; she was born in IL; 1880C
May Rutan - b 1873 p/John O. Rutan-Martha Wyatt
   of Hiawatha, Brown Co. KS; 1880C
Myrtle F. Ruton - (1910-1998) of Springfield;
   Note: another record has this person **Myrle**
   (Obituary Daily Times)
Nancy H. Ratan - m Sidney S. Johnson at Platte
   Co. in 1848; LDS
Nancy Murnett Rutan - b 1902 p/Charles E. Rutan-
   Cora V. Cash m Homer Benjamin Catron of Fair-
   play; she was born in KS; VIRUT; LDS
Sarah Jane Rutan - m Edward George Gallagher at
   Bolivar in 1904; LDS

Sherman M. Rutan - b 1918 p/Charles E. Rutan-
Cora V. Cash of St. Joseph, Buchanan Co.;
VIRUT; 1920C
William A. Reton - employe of J.T. Reton & Son,
Kansas City, 1889-1891; CDIR
William Winfield Rutan - resident of MO; he
moved to Melfort, Sasketchewan in 1901; he
was a hardware/lumber dealer (see MI listing)
(Melfort webpage)
Wright Samuel Rutan - b 1876 p/John O. Rutan-
Martha Wyatt of Kansas City; m Martha Evelyn
Cosby b 1885 in K.C. in 1903; she m (2) _____
Pickart; Note: another record has Wright born
in St. Louis in 1881 as well as Martha; LDS

M O N T A N A

William Rutan - postmaster and hotel keeper in
Jefferson City in 1867 (Pacific Coast Direct-
ory)
William Rutan - (1879-1962) SSA
William A. Rutan - purchased federal land in
Cascade Co. in 1919; BLM
William A. Rutan - (1904-1962) he died in Yell-
owstone Co. (state death index)

N E B R A S K A

Anna Mae Rutan - b 1924 p/Arthur H. Rutan-Anna
E. Rosenbrock m _____ Johnson, divorced (Pat
Brand)
Archibald Rutan - m Nancy Geer at Hardin Co. in
1856; CoMR
Arthur H. Rutan - (1885-1972) p/Henry T. Rutan-
Lydia W. Lockhardt m Anna E. Rosenbrock
(1884-1967) he was born in Seward and they
lived in Beaver City, KS and CO; they both
are bur at Stamford Cem (Pat Brand) 1900C
Arthur H. Rutan, Jr. - (1914-1918) p/Arthur H.
Rutan-Anna E. Rosenbrock; he is bur at Stam-
ford Cem (Pat Brand)
Benjamin Ruttan - a farmer in Keith Co. in 1890
(county farmers directory)
Bruce Rutan - p/Arthur H. Rutan-Anna E. Rosen-

brock (Pat Brand)

C.B. Ruttan - p/J.B. Ruttan-Ellen J. _____ of Dawson Co., a female; 1900C

Charles Ackerman Rutan - (1885-1971) p/Lawrence A. Rutan-Harriet M. Canham of Staplehurst; m Beulah Mae Matthews (1893-1984) at Oxford in 1910; she died and is bur at Bayard (Pat Brand) 1900C; SSA

Clarence Rutan - (1918-2001) p/Arthur H. Rutan-Anna E. Rosenbrock m Tina Tilley d 1987 of Ft. Collins CO; (Pat Brand)

Ella Rutan - (1865-1933) m Ira S. Horner in Wenona, LaSalle Co. IL she died in Dorchester and is bur at Dorchester Cem (Terri Taylor)

Floyd H. Rutan - b 1910 p/Arthur H. Rutan-Anna E. Rosenbrock m Sylvia _____ (Pat Brand)

Frances Nolan Rutan - (1920-1935) p/Herbert D. Rutan-Nettie Faubion (Pat Brand) YRR

Frank I. Rutan - (1860-1950) he is bur at Dorchester Cem, Saline Co. (cemetery records)

Gene Bernard Rutan - b 1921 p/Herbert D. Rutan-Nettie Faubion (Pat Brand) YRR

George J. Rutan - (1900-1977) of Sicily; he is bur at Dorchester Cem, Saline Co. (cemetery records)

Gertrude Rutan - (1904-1986) she is bur at Dorchester Cem, Saline Co. (cemetery records)

Grace Rutan - b 1920 p/Arthur H. Rutan-Anna E. Rosenbrock m Myron Johnson (Pat Brand)

Harriet Eve Rutan - (1898-1990) p/Lawrence A. Rutan-Harriet M. Canham m William Jennings Bryan Cuckler (1896-1983) in 1915 (Pat Brand) 1900C

Helen Estella Rutan - (1903-1989) p/Lawrence A. Rutan-Harriet M. Canham m Roy E. Lowe (1893-1976) in 1923 (Pat Brand) CoMR

Henry Terhune Rutan - (1841-1919) p/Daniel D. Rutan-Maria Ackerman of Paterson, Passaic Co. NJ and Will Co. IL; m (1) Mary Fouser (2) Lydia Windsor Lockhardt, b 1855, a widow born in IA, in 1883; he lived in Stamford NE and is bur at Stamford Cem (see IL listing) Note: after he died Lydia wed J.C. Borton (see CO listing) (Pat Brand) 1900C; YRR; ROOTSW

Herbert Dewitt Rutan - (1891-1987) p/Lawrence A. Rutan-Harriet M. Canham m Nettie Faubion (1897-1983) in 1917 at Alma, Harlan Co.; (Pat Brand) YRR; 1900C; ROOTSW

Herbert Dewitt Rutan - b 1900; he was from Wilsonville, Furnas Co.; LDS

Howard Rutan - graduate of Rockhigh H.S., Rock
Co. (school records)

Howard Rutan - b 1921 p/Arthur H. Rutan-Anna E.
Rosenbrock m Jene _____ he lived in Palm
Desert CA (Pat Brand)

Ida F. Rutan - (1857-1945) landowner in Saline
Co. in 1930; according to cemetery records
she was Ida F. Horner, bur at Dorchester Cem,
Saline Co. (she was probably the wife of
Frank I. Rutan, see above)

John B. Ruttan - b 1856; he was probably the son
of Henry Peter Ruttan-Mary Ann Taylor m Ellen
or Eleanor J. Smith b 1854 in Dawson Co.;
they were living in Ringgold, Dawson Co. in
1920; he was born in Canada and she in PA;
RUTT; CoMR; 1900C

John B. Ruttan - m Rosella Gunn in Dawson Co.;
CoMR

Kenneth Edward Rutan - (1916-2001) p/Charles A.
Rutan-Beulah M. Matthews; he died at Oxford
(Pat Brand) (his Obit appeared in the *Kearney
Hub*, 2 Feb 2001)

Lara Rutan - b 1839 in IL; she was living alone
in Staplehurst, Seward Co.; 1900C

Lavinia Ann Rutan - (1884-1964) p/Lawrence A.
Rutan-Harriet M. Canham m William Mulford Dey
(1861-1942) in 1902; she died Lavinia Ann
Brown (Metz Mortuary database) (Pat Brand)

Lawrence Ackerman Rutan - (1859-1951) p/Daniel
D. Rutan-Keziah Zabriskie of NJ and Will Co.
IL; m Harriet M. ("Hattie") Canham (1864-
1952) of IL in 1883 at Livingston Co. IL;
they moved to Seward Co. in 1884; he was born
in Broughton IL; she died at Huntley NE; both
are bur at Furnas Co. Cem, Oxford (cemetery
records) (Pat Brand) CoMR; 1900C

Lawrence Burnette Rutan - (1915-1970) p/Charles
A. Rutan-Beulah M. Matthews; he died in San
Mateo CA (Pat Brand) CADRI

Leonard Kyle Rutan - b 1918 p/Herbert D. Rutan-
Nettie Faubion (Pat Brand)

Lillie Bell Nancy Rutan - (1894-1981) p/Lawrence
A. Rutan-Harriet M. Canham m Roy Irvin d 1962
in 1922; Note: she is listed as **Lillian** Rutan
in the 1900C (Pat Brand) 1900C

Lloyd Alford Rutan - p/Charles A. Rutan-Beulah
M. Matthews (Pat Brand)

Lovina Rutan - b 1884 p/Lawrence A. Rutan-Harriet M. Canham (see Lavinia Rutan, above)

Mabel Edith Rutan - (1900-1970) p/Lawrence A.
Rutan-Harriet M. Canham m Frank Medinger
(1899-1970) in 1921; they lived in Huntley
(see IL listing) (Pat Brand) CoBR; CRC

Maria Elizabeth Rutan - (1852-1931) p/Daniel D.
Rutan-Keziah E. Zabriskie m Charles W. Dey in
1887; she was born in Bergen Co. NJ and died
in Staplehurst (Pat Brand)

Mary Jane Retan - (1842-1911) m William Novell d
1906 at Watertown NY in 1859; she was born in
Canada; he died at Columbus NE and is bur at
the Columbus Cem (from his Obit in the *Columbus Telegram*)

Melvin E. Rutan - (1918-1984) Staff Sergeant,
U.S. Army; he is bur at Ft. McPherson National Cemetery, Lincoln Co. (cemetery records)
(see next entry)

Melvin Elwood Rutan -p/Charles A. Rutan-Beulah
M. Matthews (Pat Brand)

Mildred Leah Rutan - (1896-1986) p/Lawrence A.
Rutan-Harriet M. Canham m Marshal Harvey
Richman (1888-1977) in 1920; they both died
at the Methodist Home at Holdrege NE and are
bur at Bainbridge Cem, near Huntley (Pat
Brand) 1900C

Myrtle Jane Rutan - (1889-1926) p/Lawrence A.
Rutan-Harriet M. Canham of Staplehurst,
Seward Co.; m Raymond Alfred Matthews d 1950
in 1910 at Staplehurst; she died in Omaha and
is bur at Furnas County Cemetery, Oxford
(cemetery records) (Pat Brand) LDS; 1900C;
CoMR

Nancy Rutan - m Samuel Becker in Hardin Co. in
1863 (see Archibald Rutan, above) CoMR

Ollie May Rutan - **Olla** (1887-1967) p/Lawrence A.
Rutan-Harriet M. Canham of Seward Co.; m Harlan Campbell (1892-1954) in 1911 (Pat Brand)
1900C

Pearl Leona Rutan - b 1904 p/Lawrence A. Rutan-
Harriet M. Canham m (1) Hiram E. Runcie
(1899-1964) in 1922 (2) Lester Woods d 1990
in 1977; she was alive in 2000 (Pat Brand)

R.E. Rutan - living in Staplehurst in 1890
(county farmers directory)

Robert Devern Rutan - p/Charles A. Rutan-Beulah
M. Matthews (Pat Brand)

Rosetta Rutan - m Edward Day Horner (1870-1927)
(see IL listing)

Russell Kendal Rutan - b 1926 p/Herbert D. Rutan
-Nettie Faubion (Pat Brand) YRR
Ruth Rutan - b 1911 p/Arthur H. Rutan-Anna E.
Rosenbrock m Forest E. Willour (Pat Brand)
Ruth Gertrude Rutan - (1907-1907) p/Lawrence A.
Rutan-Harriet M. Canham she is bur at Furnas
County Cem (cemetery records) (Pat Brand)
Velma Mae Rutan - p/Charles A. Rutan-Beulah M.
Matthews (Pat Brand)

N E V A D A

G.W. Rutan - attended local political meetings
in Winnemucca as reported in the *Humboldt
Register* 1863
Nellie Rutan - p/Charles L. Rutan-Margery Dod-
ril of Vinton WV; m James Rodick of Las Vegas
(from her father's Obit)
P. Rutan - witness to the marriage of M.K. Vasey
to Mrs. L. Fisher at Reno, 12 Dec 1877; CoMR
Peter Rutan - m Anna Brain at Elko in 1878
(Idaho marriage records)
Peter Rutan - music teacher in Boise ID, Winnemucca and Battle Mountain NV from several
articles in the Humboldt Co. *Silver State* and
the *Peoples' Advocate* (mostly 1879) his wife
is described as Mrs. B. Rutan

N E W   M E X I C O

Fred M. Rutan - m Norma V. _____ (1926-1971)
(from her Obit in the *Albuquerque Journal*
Louisa A. Rutan - she married a Rutan; her maid-
en name was Niccols (from her brother George's Obit in the *Worcester Telegram & Gazette*
19 Feb 1997

N O R T H   C A R O L I N A

Albert Rutan - (1889-1974) m Fannie _____ (1891-
1971) they lived in Greensboro; she died in
Winston-Salem; NCDI; SSA
Edna Alberta Rutan - (1897-1989) she married a
Rutan; her maiden name was Gill; she was, at

her death, a widow in Henderson; NCDI
George W. Rutan - CW soldier, regiment unavailable (see MN listing) ACPL
Homer Leo Rutan - (1910-1979) he was born in VA and lived in Greensboro; NCDI; SSA
Lamont Rutan - (1906-1975) SSA
Myrtle Rutan - (1910-1995) of Greensboro (from her Obit in the *Greensboro News & Record*)

N O R T H   D A K O T A

James P. Rutan - landowner, Morton Co. in 1913; BLM
John Rutan - bc 1859 in OH; he was a farmer in Bismarck, Dakota Territory in 1885; 1885C

O H I O

Abraham Rutan - (1825-1917) p/Abraham Rutan-Olive Burt m Elizabeth Scales (1840-1898) in 1856; he was born "near Wheeling"; she was from Belmont Co.; she died in Jackson Co. IN; Note: one record has her dying in 1917; MAR; LDS; CoBR
Abraham Rutan - (1791-1852) p/Samuel Rutan-Elinor Bedell of Washington Co. PA; m (2) Mary Logston b 1806 at Morgan Co. in 1845; Mary m (3) Simon Fisher d 1858 at Belmont Co. in 1855 and lived in Tippecanoe, Miami and Monroe Cos. IN (from son Elias' CW pension file); LDS; USARCH
Abraham George Rutan - d 1873 m Harriet Hicks d 1881 of Ludlow MA; he was a CW soldier in the 175th Ohio Volunteer Infantry; he lived in Russellville and Ripley, Brown Co. (from his CW pension file) (see Northeast listing) ACPL; USARCH
Abraham R. Rutan - (1854/56-1928) m Anna McMore; he died in Houston TX; LDS
Ada Kathryn Rutan - (1904-1990) unm; ODI; LDS
Adelaide Rutan - b 1840 in MA; living in Cleveland in 1900; she may be Adelaide Griggs the first wife of Rynier Rutan of NY; 1900C
Adaline Rutan - (1836-1922) she died at Beulah Park, Cuyahoga Co. at the home of her daughter, Mrs. James Hussey; Note it is also spelled **Adeline** (Cleveland Public Library Necrology

File) ODI

Adelbert Rutan - Del (1881-1949) p/Arnoldus L. Rutan-Mila Ferguson (see Del Rutan, below)

Albert T. Routan - d 1958 at Lakewood, Cuyahoga Co.; ODI

Alexander Wallace Rutan - (1880-19<u>72</u>) p/Samuel M. Rutan-Margaret J. Cantwell; attorney in Santa Ana CA; JN; CRC; CAROHS

Alfred Monroe Rutan - (1884-1966) p/John Rutan-Sarah J. Lee m Lottie C. Miller b 1880 in 1908; they were living in Preble Co. in 1920; he died in New Paris, Preble Co. however ODI says he died in Dayton; SSA; CoMR; 1920C; ODI

Alice Lucille Rutan - b 1904 p/Hiram E. Rutan-Mary Emily Farnsworth of Xenia; m J. Harold White/Whitt (1899-1956) at Newport KY in 1922 she was born in Spring Valley, he died in Gary; WSIM; 1920C; ROOTSW

Alice R. Rutan - d 1921 in Champaign Co.; ODI

Allensworth Rutan - b 1822 in Harrison Co.; CoBR

Amanda Rutan - (1853-1917) p/Abraham Rutan-Susan Springer of Westmoreland Co. PA; m Frank D. Mentzer b 1849 in 1880 at Richland Co.; she is probably Abraham's daughter by his first wife; LDS; CoMR

Andrew J. Ruton - resident of Pulaski Twp, Williams Co. (see next entry) 1850C

Andrew Jackson Rutan - (1827-1869) p/Samuel B. Rutan-Nancy Ann Jackson; m Anne Jane Faddis b 1830; physician in Ruggles Center, Ashland Co.; they were living in Williams Co. in 1850 Anne was born in PA; they moved to MN (see MN listing); ACOHS; JN

Ann Rutan - resident of Zanesville, Logan Co.; 1860C

Ann Eliza Reuton - m John Fogelsong at Greene Co. in 1836; LDS

Ann J. Rutan - d 1923 in Van Wert Co.; ODI

Anna Rutan - b 1814 p/John Rutan-Nancy Rusk m Abner Cracraft (1811-1841) in 1833; he was born in Washington Co. PA and died in Richland Co.; MEACH; ROOTSW

Anna Elizabeth Rutan - b 1870 p/Abraham Rutan-Susan Springer m Adolph Kramer in 1893; LDS; 1880C

Anna H. Rutan - (1851-1912) p/Samuel B. Rutan-Nancy Ann Jackson m (1) Lewis H. Allensworth in 1870, divorced in 1877 (2) Horace Hatton in 1877; both marriages occurred in Harrison

Co.; Anna died in Columbiana Co.; she is bur
at the Cadiz Union Cem, Harrison Co. (Doris
C. West) JN; LDS

Anna L. Rutan - (1847-1847) p/William Rutan-Hannah J. Clark; she was born and died in Lexington Twp (Kim Vierra)

Anna Maria Rutan - b 1869 p/Peter Rutan-Elizabeth S. Markley; ROOTSW

Arlington R. Rutan - b 1901 in WV; living with
William C. Rutan in Akron in 1920; (see WV
listing)

Arnoldus Leander Rutan - (1852-1925) p/Abner H.
Rutan-Emily Gray m Mila Ferguson (1848-1893)
at Union Twp in 1878; he was living in Bellefontaine, Logan Co. in 1920; he died in Mechanicsburg and is bur at Maple Grove Cem;
Note: RUDR has Mila born in 1844 and the
marriage in 1877 (cemetery records) 1900C;
WSIM; 1920C; CoMR; LDS; RUDR

Athaliah Rutan - b 1818 p/Nicholas Rutan-Mary
_____ m Hugh Burns b 1810 in Ashland Co. in
1839; MHAWS; CoMR

Athalia Rutan - **Althea** (1854-193<u>6</u>) p/John Rutan-
Susanna Egner of Ashland Co; m George W.
Kreider (1849-1931); she is bur at Cumberland
Cem, Evans Twp, Marshall Co. IA; CoBR; MHAWS

Audria Rutan - (1803-1852) p/Daniel Rutan-Mary
Hazel of MD; m Jonathan Ogden b 1801 at Gosh-
en Twp, Champaign Co. in 1824; they moved to
McLean Co. IL; ACPL; LDS; CoMR

Avis Louise Ruton - (1916-1916) p/Edgar S. Ruton
-Eva B. Harris of Licking Co.; WHIT

Bell E. Rutan - she was a seamstress in Mansfield in 1883; CDIR

Benjamin B. Rutan - (1920-1975) he died in
Marysville, Union Co.; ODI

Bertha Viola Rutan - (1874-1942) p/John Rutan-
Susanna Egner of Ashland Co.; m Wilfred Geary
(1867-1950) in 1895; they were living in Mar-
athon IA in 1898; Note: LDS has her mother as
Suzanne Ellis, says Bertha was born in Noble
Co. and that she wed Wilfred in 1897; still
another record says she was born in LaSalle
Co. IL; MHAWS; LDS

Bessie L. Rutan - d 1967 in Dayton; ODI

Calvin J. Rutan - (1849-1907) p/Peter Rutan-Mary
Watson of Butler Co.; he is bur at the Presbyterian Ch Cem, Champion Twp, Trumbull Co.;
1850C; TCCI

Catherine Rutan - **Katherine** (1807-1891) p/William Rutan-Hannah Lane m Solon Gilson b 1800 of Barnet VT at Trumbull Co. in 1835; CoMR

Catherine Rutan - (1808-1831) p/Daniel Rutan-Mary Hazel of MD; m John Walker in 1829; TDR; ACPL

Catherine Rutan - (1813-1837) p/John Rutan-Nancy Rusk m Robert Dicksen in 1837 at Richland Co. Note: his surname spelled **Dickson/Dixon**

Catherine Rutan - (1836-1868) p/Samuel Rutan-Sarah Cracraft; she was living in Will Co. IL in 1850 and San Joaquin CA in 1860; MEACH; 1850C; LDS; 1860C

Catherine Rutan - bc 1837 p/Jesse Rutan-Susanna _____; 1850C

Catherine Rutan - p/Squire Rutan m Benjamin Albert Bollinger in Van Wert Co. in 1870 (Tina Pratt)

Catherine Rutan - m John Barnheisel at Darke Co. in 1873; ROOTSW

Catherine Rutan - b 1905 p/Glen Rutan-Hazel D. McAdams of Champaign Co. m Sam Cunningham; WSIM; TDR; 1920C

Charles Rutan - p/Enos K. Rutan-Hattie Miller; TDR

Charles E. Retan - (1886-1918) son of Lena Retan of Fostoria; he was born at Mt. Pleasant MI; WWI soldier who enlisted at Bowling Green 1 April 1918 and died in camp of pneumonia 15 April 1918; he was assigned to the 158th Depot Brigade ("Ohio Military Men, 1917-18")

Charles Leroy Rutan - (1900-1991) p/James D. Rutan-Tressa Steyer of Gallia Co.; m Margery Dodrill (1903-1991) in 1921; he was born in Putnam Co. WV and she at Vinton; he worked for Wheeling Steel Co. in Steubenville OH; they both died in Boulder City NV and are bur at Vinton Cem (from his Obit in the *Putnam Democrat*) (see NV listing)

Charles Owen Rutan - (1905-1979) p/Zelora E. Rutan-Alice Robinson of Champaign Co.; m (1) Laura Marie Hill b 1907; he may have had a second wife Jessie _____; Note: 1920C has him born in 1906; he died in Champaign Co.; CoMR; ODI; 1920C

Charles William Rutan - (1897-1980) p/Warren Rutan-Clara Gove of Champaign Co.; m Hazel Tiley; he was a WWI soldier enlisting at Columbus Barracks in July, 1918; he was a

resident of So. Charleston OH at the time;
he lived in Old Lyme CT and died at Norwich
CT (see Northeast listing) ("Ohio Military
Men, 1917-1918") CoMR; RUDR; 1900C; WSIM; TDR
Clarissa Marie Rutan - p/Ira A. Rutan-Mary T.
Kramer of Preble Co.; m Christie Worth Carl-
isle b 1915 in Ledford IL; ROOTSW
Clay Rutan - m Ethel May McCumber (1892-1952) in
Vinton Co. where she was born; she m (1)
Schuyler S. Webb b 1872 (3) Clarence Dilley;
ROOTSW
Clay Rutan - b 1884 p/Arnoldus L. Rutan-Mila
Ferguson of Logan Co.; m Effie Robinson
(1886-1949) they were living in Forest, Hard-
in Co. 1920-1939; CoMR; 1900C; 1920C; TDR
Clyde Henry Rutan - (1907-1966) p/James D. Rutan
-Tressa Steyer of Gallia Co.; m Mabel Mae
Balch (1909-1975) he was born in Confidence,
Putnam Co. WV; she in Ripley, Jackson Co. WV;
Note: the 1920C has him **Henry C.** Rutan; he
died in Jefferson Co.; TDR; RUDR; ROOTSW; ODI
Clyde Henry Rutan, Jr. - p/Clyde H. Rutan-Mabel
M. Balch m Joanne Gunderman at Springfield,
Clark Co. in 1946; ROOTSW
Columbus Oregon Rutan - (1845-1846) p/Samuel
Rutan-Sarah Cracraft (George A. Rutan)
D.B. Rutan - b 1884 m Myrtle _____ b 1887;
living in Springfield, Clark Co. in 1920;
he was an auctioneer there in 1921; 1920C;
CDIR
Dale Rutan - m _____ Robinson; they lived in
Newark, Licking Co. (from her mother's 1929
Obit)
Damanthus Rutan - b 1819 p/Daniel M. Rutan-Mary
Riddle of Champaign Co., unm; TDR
Daniel Rutan - (1798-1891) p/Peter Rutan-Charity
Corselius of Sussex Co. NJ; m Mary A. Mattox
(1798-1884) they were both born in NJ and in
1821 he is found as a farmer in Butler Twp,
Darke Co.; they were there through 1880; he
died in Madison Twp; MEACH; 1850C; 1880C
Daniel Rutan - b 1867 m Sarah Bixler b 1868;
they relocated to IN (see IN listing) LDS
Daniel Milton Rutan - (1779-1851) p/John Rutan-
Catherine Jones of NJ/MD; m (1) Mary Hazel
(1776-1908/09) (2) Mary Riddle b 1781 at
Champaign Co in 1819; he was living with his
son, Abner Harvey Rutan in 1850; he is bur at
Maple Grove Cem, Goshen Twp (cemetery rec-

ords) (see MD listing); LDS; GSNJ; 1850C;
CoMR

Daniel Milton Rutan - (1811-1842) p/Daniel M.
Rutan Mary Riddle m Hannah Colwell (1812-
1886) at Champaign Co.; WSIM; CoMR; TDR

Daniel William Rutan - (1839/40-1913) p/Daniel
M. Rutan-Hannah Colwell m Angeline Lucy Kimball (1846-1925) at Milford Center, Union Co.
in 1864; he was a CW soldier, 13th Ohio Volunteer Infantry who received a battlefield
commission after the Battle of Chickamauga;
he was a teacher before the War and a stock-
dealer afterward; both are bur at Maple Grove
Cem, Champaign Co.; Note: some records refer
to her as **Lucy Angeline**; OAR; CoMR; LDS; CRC

David Rutan - (1808-1841) p/Peter Rutan-Elizabeth McIlrath of Fayette Co. PA and Carroll
Co. OH; m Eleanor Lyons in Montgomery Co. in
1832; as a widow she wed George Durbin about
1843 and they lived in Trumbull Co. IA and IN
(some information from her sons' CW pension
files) CAROHS; USARCH

David Oliver Rutan - (1843-1926) p/Alexander A.
Rutan-Sarah Workman m Anna Hewitt Ebersole
(1844-193_2_ in 1870 at Center Twp, Carroll
Co.; CW soldier, 186th OVI; he was a "wool-
buyer" and politician, AKA **"Deacon"** (Harrison: 282) they were living in St. Petersburg
FL in 1920; CRC; JN; LDS; CAROHS; 1900C; CDIR

David William Rutan - b 1875 p/Daniel W. Rutan-
Lucy A. Kimball m Georgia (Georgianna) Griffin (1885-1960) they were living in Marysville
Villa, Union Co. in 1910; he was a carpenter
in Dayton in 1919; TDR; CDIR

Del Rutan - **Adelbert** (1881-1949) p/Arnoldus Rutan-Mila Ferguson m Ona Mabel Hinton (1892-
1955) they are both bur at Treacles Creek
Cem, Goshen Twp. Champaign Co. (cemetery records)

Delilah Rutan - (1810-1851) p/Daniel Rutan-Mary
Riddle of Champaign Co.; m Ira Freeman in
1847; MEACH; WSIM; TDR; CoMR

Delmer Neil Rutan - (1924-1987) his mother was
named Mason; he died in Los Angeles; he is
probably the son of Frank S. Rutan-Keziah
Mason of OH; CADRI

Delota A. Rutan - (1879-1958) of Preble Co.; ODI

Dewitt Rutan - (190_7_-1982) p/Glen Rutan-Hazel D.
McAdams of Champaign Co.; m (1) Margaret Bum-

gardner (1909-1945) (2) Venus Maxwell; he was
a school teacher in Springfield OH in 1939
and there he died; ROOTSW; CoMR; TDR; SSA

Dianthus Rutan - b 1819 (see Damanthus Rutan,
above) LDS

Dwight D. Rutan - (1905-1967) p/David W. Rutan-
Georgia Griffin; he died in Dayton; TDR; SSA

Earl Rutan - (1900-1990) SSA

Edgar Harold Ruton - (1902-1958) p/Edgar S. Ruton-Eva B. Harris of Licking Co.; m (3) Mildred K. Marsh; he is bur at Newark Memorial
Gardens; WHIT; ODI

Edgar Justus Rutan - (1898-1972) p/Howard F.
Rutan-Amy Sands m Emma Elizabeth _____ (1903-
1980) he was born at Sparta TN and lived in
Van Wert Co. before and after WWI; he served
in WWI with the 145th Infantry and he was
severely wounded in Sep 1918; he died in Toledo; they are bur at the I.O.O.F. Cem, Tully
Twp, Van Wert Co. (cemetery records) (some
information from his father's Obit) (Maggie
Zimmerman); CoDR; SSA; RUDR; 1920C

Edward Rutan - a student in Columbus, 1891-1892;
CDIR

Edward Cecil Rutan - b 1883 p/Abraham R. Rutan-
Anna McMore of Mansfield; m Elizabeth Huyck b
1885; he died in Houston TX; LDS

Effy Rutan - **Effie** bc 1802 p/Peter Rutan-Charity Corselius of Sussex Co. NJ m David Mattox
at Preble Co. in 1821; CoMR; MEACH

Elias Reton - resident of Springfield, Clark Co.
1840C

Elias B. Rutan - d 1864 p/Abraham Rutan-Mary
Logston; he was a CW soldier, 44th OVI;
captured at the Battle of Brice's Crossroads
MS; he died at Camp Sumter, Andersonville GA;
VA; USARCH

Elias Edgar Ruton - (1830-190_9_) p/Alexander B.
Ruton-Sarah Sayre of NYC; m Frances Ann Force
(Fannie) Carpenter (c1835-1903) at Jersey
City NJ in 1855; jeweler in NYC living in
Caldwell, Essex Co. NJ until about 1870;
moved to Jersey Twp, Licking Co.; bur at the
Presbyt Chyd; Note: one record has 1904 as
his year of death; WHIT; FH; SFH; 1880C

Eliza Jane Rutan - (1828-1888) p/Daniel Rutan-
Margaret Carr m Rev. Sheridan Baker (1824-
1890) at Carroll Co. in 1849; they lived in
Beaver Co. PA; she died in Newburg OH; ROOTSW

LDS; CoMR

Elizabeth Rutan - d 1819 in Stark Co.; CoDR

Elizabeth Rutan - b 1806 p/Peter Rutan-Charity
Corselius of Sussex Co. NJ; BOGGS

Elizabeth Rutan - d 1922 in Erie Co.; ODI

Elizabeth Rutan - d 1921 in Morrow Co.; ODI

Elizabeth Pearl Rutan - b 1912 p/James D. Rutan-
Tressa Steyer of Gallia Co.; m Irvin L. Wood-
rum (1906-1964) in 1928 at Gallia Co.; he was
born at Lesage, Cabell Co. WV and died in
Oberlin, Lorain Co.; Note: RUDR has him born
in 1906; ROOTSW; 1920C; RUDR

Ella Jane Rutan - (1866-1937) p/Abraham Rutan-
Susan Springer of Richland Co.; m Frank Conrad Vogenberger (1860-1918) in 1897; they
died in Langhorne, Berks Co. PA; RER; LDS;
1880C

Ella May Rutan - b 1868 p/Peter Rutan-Elizabeth
S. Markley; ROOTSW

Elmer Rutan - (1891-1928) p/Silas Rutan-Flora S.
_____; he was a resident of Darke Co. in
1920; he is bur at Beamsville Cem, Richland
Twp, Darke Co.; 1900C; 1920C; CoBR

Elwood Retan - b 1874 p/Henry C. Retan-Catherine
B. Partridge; lived in MI; named as H. Elwood
Rutan (from his father's CW pension file);
LDS identifies him as **Henry Elwood** Retan (see
MI listing) USARCH; LDS

Emery B. Rutan - (1906-1974) he lived in Newton
Falls, Trumbull Co.; ODI; SSA

Emily Jane Rutan - (1839-1899) p/Samuel B. Rutan
-Nancy Ann Jackson m John Dennis in 1865 at
Cadiz Twp, Harrison Co.; she died in Jeffer-
son Co; 1850C; LDS

Emma Elizabeth Rutan - (1903-1980) bur at the
I.O.O.F. Cem, Tully Twp, Van Wert Co.
(Maggie Zimmerman E-Mail)

Emma K. Rutan - bc 1845 p/Abner Harvey Rutan-
Arrency Littel of Goshen, Champaign Co.;
1850C

Enos Kingsley Rutan - bc 1841 p/Abner Harvey
Rutan-Arrency Littel of Champaign Co.; m Hattie Miller; WSIM; TDR

Eshmael D. Rutan - (1910-1972) he died at Warren
Trumbull Co.; ODI

Esther Rutan - p/Clay Rutan-Effie Robinson; TDR

Florence Rutan - p/Clay Rutan-Effie Robinson;
TDR

Frank S. Rutan - (1899-1926) p/James D. Rutan-

Tressa Steyer of Gallia Co. m Keziah Mason
(1900-1973); 1920C; RUDR; TDR

Frederick Charleston Rutan - (1909-1916) p/Glen
Rutan-Hazel D. McAdams of Champaign Co.; he
is bur at Treacles Creek Cem (cemetery records) LDS; TDR; WSIM

George D. Rutan - b 1907 p/Hiram E. Rutan-Mary
E. Farnsworth of Xenia; 1920C

George Owen Retan - b 1882 p/Samuel B. Retan-
Eliza Jane Jay of Fulton Co.; LDS

Gertrude Angeline Rutan - (1890-1962) p/Glen
Rutan-Nettie Doak of Champaign Co.; LDS; TDR;
WSIM

Gilbert Norman Ruton - (1906-1996) p/Edgar S.
Ruton-Eva B. Harris m Margaret Varner (1907-
1991) he is bur at Newark Mem Park, Licking
Co.; Note: SSA has him born in 1904; 1920C;
WHIT; SSA

Glen Ames Rutan - (1897-1971) p/Benjamin Milton
Rutan-Jennie Owen of Champaign Co.; m Ethel-
lyn Burnham; they lived in Maryville, Union
Co.; WSIM; SSA

Goldie Rutan - b 1901 p/Silas Rutan-Flora S.
?Martin; 1910C

Goldie Rutan - d 1941 m Charles B. Shode (1898-
1960) of Darke Co. ("The Posterity of John
Adam Stager") (see prior entry) ODI

Hallie Arela Rutan - (1902-1997) p/James D.
Rutan-Tressa Steyer of Gallia Co.; m Anthony
Murray (1893-1978) in 1921; she is bur at
Vinton Memorial Park, Vinton WV (from her
Obit in the *Putnam Democrat*) 1920C; RUDR; TDR

Hannah Rutan - (1765-1825) of Warren, Trumbull
Co.; NYEP

Hannah Rutan - (1840-1901) p/Henry Lane Rutan-
Mary Guy m John C. Crawford (1839-1876) she
living with her brother Martin in 1900; she
is bur at Oakwood Cem, Warren Twp, Trumbull
Co. (cemetery records) 1850C; 1900C

Hannah Rutan - m Orlando Donaldson (1852-1934)
in 1877; he died in Fresno CA (Donaldson webpage)

Hannah Rutan - (1832-1902) p/Daniel Rutan-Margaret Carr m George Thompson b 1833 at Carroll
Co. in 1856; 1850C; JN; LDS; ROOTSW

Hannah Rutan - bc 1848 p/William Rutan-Hannah
Clark of Richland Co. (see **Iantha** Rutan,
below) 1850C

Hannah A. Rutan - resident of Logan Co.; she was

an affiant in the CW pension file of Stephen
P. Rutan of MD and MI in 1864; USARCH

Hannah Caroline Rutan - b 1910 p/James D. Rutan-
Tressa Steyer of Gallia Co.; m Mickey McBride
b 1904 in 1927; 1920C; RUDR

Hannah Darlington Rutan - (1838-1927) p/David R.
Rutan-Magdeline Baldinger m Alpheus Hugh
Underwood (1836-1890) in 1864 at Mechanicsburg, Champaign Co.; Note: one record has his
middle name as Harrison ("Biographical Ency-
lopedia of Ohio") LDS; CoMR

Harriet Rutan - bc 1818 in MA; a widow living
with her daughter Mary Sertel of Brown Co. in
1883 (she is the widow of Abraham George
Rutan) 1870C; USARCH

Harry Virgil Ruton - (1891-1962) p/Edgar S.
Ruton-Eva B. Harris m (2) Ethel Loretta
Headley (1896-1943); he was living in Newark
when he enlisted as a WWI soldier in July
1918; he served in the 158th Depot Brigade,
the Military Police and the 87th Engineers;
he was living in Newark in 1920 and he is bur
at Cedar Hill Cem; ("Ohio Military Men, 1917-
1918") (cemetery records) WHIT; ODI

Hattie Rutan - d 1935 in Carroll Co.; ODI

Henry C. Retan - (1844-1916) p/James Retan-Urey
Conover of Seneca Co. NY; m (1) Catherine B.
Partridge (1848-1877) in 1870; (2) Elizabeth
Hill Hinkle, a widow d 1918; living in Royal-
ton Twp, Fulton Co. in 1880; also lived in MI
(see MI listing); USARCH; 1880C

Henry C. Rutan - b 1907 p/James D. Rutan-Tressa
Steyer of Gallia Co. (see **Clyde Henry** Rutan,
above) 1920C

Henry Elwood Retan - (See Elwood Retan, above)

Henry Hazel Rutan - (1801-1820) p/Daniel Rutan-
Mary Hazel of MD, unm; CoBR; TDR

Herman C. Rutan - (1917-1986) he died in Union
Co.; ODI

Hiram Edgar Rutan - bc 1869 p/Daniel W. Rutan-
Lucy A. Kimball of Champaign Co.; m Mary
Emily Farnsworth (1877-1960); living in Xenia
Green Co. in 1920; Note: 1920C records his
wife as Emma b 1899; 1880C; DARLDC; 1920C;
CRC; WSIM

Homer Rutan - (1878-1963) p/James Rutan-Elizabeth Crego m Nanny _____ b 1883; residents of
Springfield, Clark Co.; 1910C

Hope Rutan - (1872-1872) p/Samuel M. Rutan-Jos-

ephine M. Cantwell; she is bur at Grandview
Cem, Carrollton (cemetery records)

Howard Hazel Rutan - b 1892 p/Warren Rutan-Clara
Gove of Champaign Co.; m Mary Lee Chapman
(1894-1924) he was living in Washington DC
in 1939; 1900C; CoMR; WSIM; TDR

Hugh Elwood Rutan - b 1915 p/William C. Rutan-
Frances P. Bonar of Akron; LDS

Ichabod Clark Rutan - (1838-1839) p/William Rutan-Hannah J. Clark (Kim Vierra)

Iantha Hannah Rutan - (1848-1935) (see IA listing)

Ira Albert Rutan - (1884-1937) p/Silas Rutan-
Flora S. _____ m Mary Thanks Kramer b 1884;
they were living in Preble Co. in 1920; 1900C
1920C

Irwin Rutan - p/Clyde H. Rutan-Mabel M. Balch m
(1) Margaret Nelson (2) Elaine Peters;
ROOTSW

Isaac Rutan - bc 1832 p/John Rutan-Hannah Shriver; 1850C

Isabel Rutan - m Arnold Barker b 1810 at Harris-
on Co. in 1831; he was a physician; he m (2)
Sarah Ellmaker in Van Buren Co. IA in 1844;
ROOTSW

Isabell Ann Rutan - (1833-1926) p/William Rutan-
Hannah J. Clark m William W. Kirkwood (1835-
1915) (Kim Vierra)

Isabella E. Rutan - **Isabel** b 1830 p/Daniel Rutan
-Margaret Carr of Carroll Co.; 1850C

Isabella E. Rutan - (1832-c1892) of Kilgore,
Carroll Co.; m Joseph L. Scott at Carroll Co.
in 1854; she was a teacher; he was from Mt.
Pleasant Twp, Washington Co.; they lived in
Venice of that county; LDS; ROOTSW

Jacob Rutan - (1908-1909) p/James D. Rutan-Tressa Steyer of Gallia Co.; he is bur at Wade
Chapel Cem, Wade, Putnam Co. WV (cemetery
records) RUDR

Jacob Ruttan - m Burrit Strong Bedortha b 1846
of Sheffield, Lorain Co.; ROOTSW

James Dudley Rutan - (1870-1952) p/John H. Rutan
-Caroline Minor of WV; m Tressa Arela Steyer
(1874-1951) in 1895; they were both born in
VA; they were living in Gallia Co. in 1920;
he died in Gallipolis; they are bur at Wade
Chapel Cem, Wade, Putnam Co. WV; 1920C; RUDR;
LDS

James L. Rutan - b 1892 p/Silas Rutan-Flora S.

?Martin; he is listed as **James Luther Martin**,
a step-son in the 1910C; 1900C; 1910C

James Lesley Rutan - (1903-1997) p/James D. Rut-
an-Tressa A. Steyer of Gallia Co.; m Inez
Reynolds Morehouse b 1899; he was born in
Putnam Co. WV and died at Maitland, Orange
Co. FL; he is bur in Vinton Co.; Note: the
Railroad Retirement Board has him born in
1904; 1920C; RUDR; TDR; ROOTSW

James Samuel Rutan - (1874-1888) p/Samuel M.
Rutan-Josephine Margaret Cantwell of Carroll
Co.; he is bur at Grandview Cem (cemetery
records) Note: LDS shows him as **James Williams Rutan**; 1880C; LDS; CAROHS

James T. Rutan - (1846-1921) m Elizabeth Crego b
1846; they both born in PA; they were living
in Canaan Twp, Madison Co. in 1900 and in
Springfield, Clark Co. in 1920; 1900C; 1910C;
LDS; 1920C; ODI

James Williams Rutan - b 1873 (see James Samuel
Rutan, above) LDS

Jesse Rutan - living in New Jefferson, Harrison
Co.; 1830C

Joanna Isabelle Rutan - b 1849 p/Justus Rutan-
Hannah A. _____ (see **Anna Belle** Rutan, above)

John Rutan - (1744-1833) p/John Rutan-Sarah Manning of Morris Co. NJ; RW soldier and front-
tier scout; he moved from NJ to VA and settled on land in Hampshire Co. left to him by
his father; later in life he lived in Westmoreland Co. PA; he is bur at the Pioneer
Cemetery, Warren Twp, Trumbull Co. (cemetery
records) CCPL; MRCL; SXHS; WCHS; TCCI

John Rutan - (1774-1835) he is bur at Mahoning
Ave. Cem; Warren Twp, Trumbull Co. (cemetery
records)

John Rutan - (1778-1821) p/John Rutan-Hannah
Frazer of Westmoreland Co. PA m Nancy Rusk
(1784-1853) of PA in 1804; he is bur at the
Strausberg Baptist Cem, Washington Twp, Richland Co.; as a widow Nancy m Samuel McClure
b 1765 in VA at Richland Co. in 1822; she was
Nancy Moffit in the 1850C (see Nancy Rutan,
below) Note: another record has him born in
1763 so he may be a son by John's first wife,
Catherine; CoMR; LDS; ROOTSW; MEACH

John Rutan - he was a Private in Capt. Alvatt's
Co., W1812 (Ohio Military Records)

John Rutan - he was a W1812 soldier serving in

the 2nd Regiment (Cosgreave's) Ohio Militia
(Ohio Military Records)

John Rutan - he was a schoolteacher in Crawford
Co. in 1843; PERSI

John Rutan - b 1808 p/Peter C. Rutan-Charity
Corselius of Sussex Co. NJ and Preble Co.;
BOGGS

John Rutan - (1826-1898) p/Nicholas Rutan-Mary
_____ m Susanna Egner (c1835-1904) in Ashland
Co. in 1852; living in Marshall Co. IL in
1870; he died at Dorchester NE; bur at Mag-
nolia Cem, Putnam Co. IL; she died at Tonica,
LaSalle Co. IL; ACPL; LDS; 1870C; MEACH;
MHAWS

John Rutan - (1839-1864) p/David Rutan-Eleanor
Durbin of Springboro, Warren Co.; CW soldier,
11th Iowa Infantry; killed at the siege of
Atlanta; LWEB; USARCH

John Rutan - (1827-c1869) he was probably the
son of Daniel Rutan-Mary A. Mattox m Eve Ann
Spencer bc 1853; they lived in Butler Twp,
Darke Co. in 1850; he was a farmer; 1850C

John Rutan - (1820-1843) p/John Rutan-Nancy Rusk
of Richland Co.; m Susan Seltzer in 1843;
CoMR; MEACH

John Rutan - d 1915 in Preble Co.; ODI

John Rutan - d 1927 m Anna Foster (1880-1929)
she m (2) James Roof of Tabor in 1928; she
was born in Moundsville WV and died in Akron
(from her Obit in the *Free Press Standard* of
Carrollton)

John Rutan - b 1906 p/Clay Rutan-Effie Robinson;
1910C; TDR

John B. Rutan - (1799-1868) p/Peter Rutan-Elizabeth McIlrath of Fayette Co. PA m Hannah Shi-
vers b 1801 of MD in Harrison Co. in 1830;
he was a farmer in Liberty Twp, Crawford Co.
in 1850; CoMR; 1850C; JN

John Clark Rutan - (1839-1904) p/William Rutan-
Hannah J. Clark (see IA listing) (Kim Vierra)
1850C; LDS

John L. Rutan - (1886-1970) of Harrison Co.; ODI

John L. Rutan - (1907-1962) of Sandusky Co. m
Lydia Fehlhaber; he died in Fremont OH (Hayes
Center Obituary Index)

John M. Reton - b 1820; LDS

John M. Rutan - (1909-1962) he died in Union Co.
ODI

John Milton Rutan - b 1907 p/Benjamin M. Rutan-

Jennie Owen m J. Bernice Price b 1914 in 1940
WSIM

Joseph C. Rutan - (c1834-1909) p/Samuel Rutan-
Sarah Cracraft of OH, Will Co. IL and San
Joaquin CA; m Deborah R. Croscroft in 1857 at
Fairview, Richland Co.; divorced in 1890;
(from his CW pension file); (See OR listing)
(George A. Rutan) 1860C; ROOTSW; LDS

Joseph Paul Rutan - (1921-1921) p/Zelora E.
Rutan-Alice Robinson of Champaign Co.; CoDR;
USARCH

Joseph W. Rutan - (1846-1864) p/Squire Rutan-
Sarah _____ of Van Wert Co.; he was a CW
soldier, 52nd Ohio Volunteer Infantry who
died of wounds sustained in the siege of Atlanta; he is bur at the Chattanooga National
Cemetery (cemetery records) CoBR

Lawrence Leonard Rutan - (1907-1973) p/David W.
Rutan-Georgiana Griffin; he lived in New Lebanon and died in Dayton; 1910C; SSA; ODI; TDR

Lemuel B. Rutan - 1880C

Lester Rutan - m Iona Edell Stoughton b 1900 in
1920; ROOTSW

Levi Rutan - bc 1840 p/Jesse Rutan-Susanna _____
he was living in Salem Twp, Steuben Co. IN in
1860; 1850C; 1860C

Lewis Rutan - p/Clay Rutan-Effie Robinson (see
Louis Rutan, below) TDR

Louie May S. Rutan - (1860-1899) m Charles E.
Preble at Cuyahoga Co. in 1884; she died in
Cleveland and is bur at Lake View Cem
(Cleveland Public Library Necrology File)
LDS

Louis Rutan - m Faye Gobrecht about 1928; they
divorced; ROOTSW

Louis C. Rutan - (1908-1977) p/Clay Rutan-Effie
Robinson m Delores Rahn (1898-1981) he died
in Columbus and she in Oakland IL (Rutherford
B. Hayes Presidential Center Obituary Index)
1910C; SSA

Lovina Rutan - **Lavina/Levina** (1815/16-1843) p/
Daniel Rutan-Mary Riddle m Curtis Moore Bay
(1814-1846) in Champaign Co. in 1842; Note:
some records have him **Curtis Bay Moore**; CoMR;
LDS; WSIM

Loyd Albert Rutan - (1901-1979) p/Samuel Leroy
Rutan-Rosa Derrer of Mansfield; he was born
in Mansfield and died in El Monte CA; RER;
CADRI; SSA

Lucille Marie Ruton - (1907-1981) p/Edgar S.
  Ruton-Eva B. Harris of Licking Co.; m (1)
  Charles Williams Andrews (2) Ray Yates; she
  is bur at Wilson Cem (cemetery records) WHIT
Lucinda J. Rutan - (1825-1913) p/Daniel Rutan-
  Mary Riddle m Peter Edgar Colwell bc 1824 in
  1843; CoMR; 1850C
Lucy L. Rutan - (1882-1965) she died at Fremont,
  Sandusky Co.; ODI
Lucy W. Rutan - b 1897 p/Glen Rutan-Hazel D.
  McAdams m Wingate Tullus; 1900C; TDR
Lucy Winnifred Rutan - b 1898 p/Benjamin M.
  Rutan-Jennie Owen m Leo Colman; LDS; WSIM;
  1900C
Lydia Rutan - (1822-1885) p/Daniel Rutan-Mary
  _____ m George A. Tedford (1823-1900) of
  Harrison Twp, Darke Co.; he is bur at St.
  John's Cem, Darke Co; Note: there is another
  record that says she was born in 1828; ROOTSW
Lydia Rutan - b 1818 p/Peter C. Rutan-Charity
  Corselius of Sussex Co. NJ; m Thomas Squire/
  Squier at Butler Co. in 1839; EG; LDS
Margaret Rutan - (1825-1893) m George Nupp at
  Harrison Co. in 1849; Note: another LDS rec-
  ord has her born in 1828; LDS
Margaret Rutan - (1885-1978) m Harvey Clement
  Petry (1883-1973) of Preble Co.; ROOTSW
Margaret Ruttan - m Thomas Huggins (1788-1862)
  of Charleston SC in 1817; he died in Meigs
  Co. (Barbara Ivey)
Margaret Evelyn Rutan - b 1903 p/Warren Rutan-
  Clara Gove of Champaign Co.; m Elmer A. Stew-
  art in 1925; 1920C; CoMR; WSIM
Margery Rutan - b 1910 p/David W. Rutan-Georgia
  Griffin; 1910C; TDR
Maria Rutan - b 1810 p/Peter C. Rutan-Charity
  Corselius of Sussex Co. NJ; m John Murphy at
  Butler Co. in 1834; Note: one record has him
  John Murphey; EG; LDS
Martha J. Rutan - resident of Perry Twp; 1850C
Martha J. Rutan - p/Daniel Rutan-Hannah Colwell
  m George Andrew Rowinsky in 1858; LDS
Martha Leora Rutan - Mattie (1874-1950) p/Abra-
  ham Rutan-Susan Springer of Richland Co.; m
  John Peter Groff (1871-1964) in 1898; they
  lived in Pavonia, Richland Co.; 1880C; RER;
  LDS
Marvin Rutan - (1903-1972) p/David W. Rutan-
  Georgia Griffin; he lived in Oakland, Mont-

gomery Co. and died in Dayton; 1910C; ODI;
TDR

Mary Rutan - (1849-1850) p/Samuel Rutan-Sarah
Cracraft (George A. Rutan)

Mary Rutan - she was a milliner in Cincinnati
in 1861; CDIR

Mary Rutan - d 1916 in Trumbull Co.; ODI

Mary A. Rutan - m William H. Pitman at Darke Co.
in 1875; LDS

Mary Ann Rutan - (1817-1892) p/Samuel Rutan-
Olive Burt of Washington Co. PA; m Samuel
Marquis (1817-1902) of Belmont Co. in 1839;
they both died at Sharon, Noble Co. and are
bur at the Sharon Cem (cemetery records)
1850C; ROOTSW

Mary Ann Rutan - (c1841-1925) p/Samuel Rutan-
Nancy Ann Jackson m (1) Isaac Shamp (1841-
1918) in 1871, they divorced, (2) Gotlieb
Smith (1843-1925) in 1885; both marriages
were in Harrison Co.; she died in Bowerstown,
Harrison Co.; she and Gotlieb are bur at
Leesville Cem, Orange Twp, Carroll Co.; Isaac
in East Liverpool, Columbiana Co.; Note: LDS
has her (1841-1926) and one record calls her
Mary B. Rutan (Doris C. West) 1850C; LDS; JN

Mary Ann Rutan - b 1859 m William H. Pittman b
1853 at Darke Co. in 1875; ROOTSW

Mary Annette Rutan - b 1900 p/Warren Rutan-Clara
Gove of Champaign Co.; m Joseph J. Mooney;
they were living in Columbus in 1939; 1920C;
WSIM; CoMR; TDR

Mary Jones Rutan - (1818-1901) m Jacob Hazel in
1848; Note: CCMR has her Mary M. Rutan and he
Jacob Heazle; WSIM; CoMR; TDR

Mary Melissa Rutan - (1864-1924) p/Abraham Rutan
-Susan Springer of Westmoreland Co. PA; m
John Franklin Bruckhart b 1864 in 1891; 1880C
RER; LDS

Merrill E. Rutan - b 1904 p/Homer Rutan-Nannie
_____ m Martha Lee Coburn b 1908 at Mechanicsburg, Champaign Co.; 1910C; ROOTSW

Mila Rutan - p/Clay Rutan-Effie Robinson; TDR

Milton Rutan - d 1922 in Champaign Co.; ODI

Milton Harrison Rutan - bc 1843 p/Abner H. Rutan
-Arrency Littel m Anna Brockman; no children;
1850C; WSIM; RUDR

Minnie M. Rutan - (1909-1958) she died in Union
Co.; ODI

Monroe Rutan - (1884-1966) (See Alfred Monroe

Rutan)

Nancy Jane Rutan - p/David Rutan-Eleanor Lyons
m Samuel Nichols; USARCH

Nelle R. Rheutan - (1874-1966) widow of Lucas
Co.; she died in Toledo; CoDR; ODI

Nellie Rutan - b 1880 p/Daniel W. Rutan-Angeline
L. Kimball of Champaign Co.; m Dr. Harry Os-
born Whitaker b 1875 in 1901; they lived in
Dublin OH; CoMR; TDR; WSIM; CRC

Newell Reton - resident of Chagrin Falls, Cuyahoga Co.; 1850C

Nicholas H. Rutan - (1786-1860) p/John Rutan-
Catherine _____ of NJ; m Mary _____ (1789-
1869; both died in Milton Twp, Ashland Co.
and are bur at Sultzer Cem; Note: other records say that his mother was Hannah Frazer
and that Mary (1786-1863) was bur at Imhoff
Cem, Paradise Hill, Ashland Co.; Nicholas was
a W1812 soldier (George A. Rutan) 1850C; RER;
MEACH; USARCH

Nixon Rutan - b 1827 p/Daniel Rutan-Mary Mattox
m Mary A. _____ bc 1852; they lived in Madison Twp, Butler Co. and Butler Twp, Darke Co.;
1850C; ROOTSW; 1880C

Oliver Rutan - (See David Oliver Rutan)

P.E. Rutan - m Lucinda Caldwell; they adopted
Mary Jane Freeman, daughter of Delilah Rutan;
TDR

Patty Rutan - bc 1800 p/Peter C. Rutan-Charity
Corselius of Sussex Co. NJ; m Robert Gilmore
in Preble Co. in 1818; Note: according to
family bible records she was born **Susan Rutan**
BOGGS

Peter Rutan - resident of Gratis Twp, Union Co.;
1820C

Peter Rutan, Jr. - (1813-1886) p/Peter C. Rutan-
Charity Corselius of Sussex Co. NJ; m Mary
Watson (1815-1891) in 1837; he was a brick-
maker in Madison Twp, Butler Co.; both are
bur at the McDole (Lauramie Missionary Baptist) Cem, Sheffield Twp, Tippecanoe Co. IN;
BOGGS; 1850C; LDS; 1860C

Peter Rutan - (1825-1903) probably the son of
John B. Rutan-Hannah Shriver m (1) Catherine
Margaret Warren (1826-1863) in Crawford Co.
in 1848; (2) Elizabeth Stough Markley (1828-
1921) in 1865; farmer in Holmes Twp, Crawford
Co. in 1850; CW soldier, 102nd OVI; carpenter
in Annapolis, Holmes Twp in 1880 and living

in Orange Twp, Ashland Co. in 1899; (some of
this from his CW pension file) Elizabeth was
born in Franklin Twp, Crawford Co. (Joyce
Wilson) 1850C; LDS; 1880C; USARCH; 1900C;
Phana Rutan - **Fanny** b 1826 p/Abraham Rutan-Olive
Burt of Washington Co. PA; m Jacob Scott at
Delaware Co. in 1850; RICR; LDS
Philip Rutan - m Evelyn _____ (1914-1982) she
died in Fremont; Note: this same source shows
that Philip had a wife Lucy who died at Fre-
mont, Sandusky Co. in 1965 (Rutherford B.
Hayes Presidential Center Obituary Index)
Raymond B. Rutan - (1821-1988) of Martins Ferry,
Belmont Co.; ODI
Rebecca Rutan - (1815-1876) p/Abraham Rutan-
Olive Burt of Washington Co. PA; m Thomas
Hill at Morgan Co. in 1836; she died in Aug-
laize Co. and is bur at Buckland OH; ROOTSW;
RICR; LDS
Rebecca Rutan - (1816-1881) p/Peter C. Rutan-
Charity Corselius of Sussex Co. NJ; m Samuel
Eberhart (1807-1887) at Butler Co. in 1836;
they moved to Tippecanoe Co. IN before 1850;
both are bur at the McDole Cem, Tippecanoe
Co.; BOGGS; LDS
Rebecca J. Rutan - m William H. McVay at Trum-
bull Co. in 1866 (see SD listing) LDS
Rebecca R. Rutan - (1848-1916) p/William Rutan-
Mary A. Magruder of Bellefontaine, Logan Co.;
m John Beatty Williams (1837-1908) in 1865;
1850C; CoMR; LDS
Richard Leander Rutan - (1912-1986) p/Zelora E.
Rutan-Alice Robinson of Champaign Co.; he
died in London, Madison Co.; USARCH; ODI
Robert Rheutan - (1902-1997) m Mary _____ (1913-
1996) they lived in Damascus, Mahoning Co.
and Salem, Columbiana Co.; SSA; 1920C
Robert Bruce Rutan - (1907-1975) p/Zelora E.
Rutan-Alice Robinson of Champaign Co.; they
lived in Lewisburg; 1920C; SSA; USARCH
Rolland Frank Rutan - (1900-1989) p/Glen Rutan-
Hazel D. McAdams of Champaign Co.; m Phyllis
Ernestine Perry (1900-1965); she died at
Springfield, Clark Co.; ODI; SSA; 1920C; TDR
Romaine Beatrice Rutan - b 1917 p/William C.
Rutan-Frances P. Bonar of Akron; LDS
Rosa A. Rutan - (1877-1967) a widow, she died in
Guernsey Co.; ODI
Rose Ella Rutan - (1870-1927) p/John Rutan-Sus-

anna Egner of Ashland Co.; m Edward Day Horner; one record calls her **Rosetta** Rutan (Terri Taylor) ROOTSW

Roy Rutan - p/James D. Rutan-Tressa Steyer of Gallia Co. (he is mentioned in his brother James' 1997 Obit)

Russell T. Rutan - (1914-1999) p/Ira Rutan-Mary T. Kramer of IN; m Mary Wright in 1937; he was a farmer who is bur at Mound Hill Union Cem, Eaton (from his Obit in the *Register-Herald* of Eaton)

Ruth Rutan - b 1918 p/Zelora Rutan-Alice Robinson of Champaign Co.; USARCH

Ruth Ann Rutan - (1834-1836) p/Samuel Rutan-Sarah Cracraft; she is bur at Webster Cem, Springfield Twp, Richland Co. (cemetery records)

Sally Rutan - resident of Goshen Twp, Champaign Co.; 1860C

Samuel Rutan - (1809-1885) p/John Rutan-Nancy Rusk of PA; m Sarah Cracraft b 1809 in 1832; they were living in Will Co. IL in 1850; they died in CA; (George A. Rutan) 1850C; ROOTSW

Samuel Rutan - (1832-1856) p/John Rutan-Hannah Shriver; he is bur at Nankin-Orange Cem, Ashland Co. (cemetery records) Note: the 1850C has him born in 1829; 1850C

Samuel Rutan - d 1914 in Mahoning Co.; ODI

Samuel B. Retan - m Eliza Jane Jay; they lived in Fulton Co.; LDS

Samuel B. Rutan - (1801-1874) p/Peter Rutan-Elizabeth McIlrath of MD and Fayette Co. PA; m Nancy Ann Jackson (1810-1892) at Harrison Co. in 1826; he was an inn-keeper at Montgomery Twp, Ashland Co. in 1850; CoMR; 1850C; JN LDS; 1880C

Samuel Martin Rutan - (1840-1892) p/Alexander A. Rutan-Sarah Workman of Carroll Co.; m Josephine Margaret Cantwell (1846-1887) in Davenport IA in 1869; he was a CW soldier serving as a Sergeant in the 98th Ohio Volunteer Infantry; in civilian life he was a merchant in Carrolton; both are bur at the Grandview Cem, Carrollton (Cantwell Bible: DAR) Note: LDS has him born in 1841; she is sometimes called Margaret Josephine; CoMR; LDS; 1850C; USARCH; 1880C

Samuel Milton Rutan - (1910-1922) p/Zelora E. Rutan-Alice Robinson; Note: county records

show the death of **Samuel S.** Rutan, with these
dates, as "kin of Z.E. Rutan"; USARCH

Sarah Rutan - b 1804 p/Peter C. Rutan-Charity
Corselius of Sussex Co. NJ; m Nathan B. Williams b 1796 of Campbell Co. KY at Butler Co.
in 1827; they later lived in Tippecanoe Co.
IN (Carol Black-Rossow) EG; BOGGS; LDS

Sarah A. Rutan - (1848-1860) p/David R. Rutan-
Magdelina Baldinger; 1850C; TDR; CoBR

Sarah Alice Rutan - (1836-1918) p/Daniel Rutan-
Margaret Carr m David Patton b 1823 about
1855 at New Rumley, Carroll Co.; she was born
in Louden, Carroll Co. and died in Rumley,
Harrison Co.; ROOTSW; 1850C; LDS

Sarah Ann Rutan - b 1827 p/Lewis Rutan-Catherine
_____ of Carroll Co. m John Doty (1809-1885)
at Ashland Co. in 1852; they moved to Shelby
Co. in 1867 and also lived in Crawford and
Richland Cos.; she was alive in 1901 ("Doty
Family in America") 1850C; LDS; CoMR

Sarah J. Rutan - (1831/32-1897) p/Daniel Rutan-
Margaret Carr; she died in Butler Co.;
ROOTSW

Sarah Jane Rutan - b 1836 p/William Rutan-Hannah J. Clark m William Phillips, a judge in
Ohio (Kim Vierra) 1850C

Sarah Oliver Rutan - (1887-1972) p/David O.
Rutan-Anna H. Ebersole of Carroll Co.; unm;
Note: one record calls her Sarah D. Rutan;
"Ebersole Families" calls her Sarah Olive
CoBR; 1920C; CDIR

Sherman M. Rutan - (1896-1965) p/James D. Rutan-
Tressa Steyer of Gallia Co.; m Alice Hatfield
b 1910 in 1931; he died at Bidwell, Gallipolis Co.; RUDR; ODI; TDR

Silas Rutan - m (1) M.A. Bennhusel at Darke Co.
in 1878 (2) Lovinia S. Martin in 1897; Note:
another record calls her Flora S. Martin b
1865; LDS; 1910C; 1920C

Silas Ruton - m Rachel DeCamp at Darke Co. in
1883; LDS

Susan Rutan - (see Patty Rutan, above)

Sylvester Franklin Rutan - (see Frank S. Rutan,
above)

Treva Rutan - m Leroy Button b 1905 in 1944;
they lived in Arcanum ("Button Families of
America")

Ursula Rutan - m James Manly at Mercer Co. in
1850; Note: as **Arsala** Rutan she is listed in

the 1846 Mercer County Index to Guardianships
and is mentioned in the probate papers of
Rebecca Rutan Williams of Champaign Co., 1916
she has also been identified as **Catherine
Ursula** Rutan; CoMR; 1870C; LDS; ROOTSW
Vashti Britten Rutan - (1827-1910) m Ransom
Patrick (1826-1904) in 1849; he was born in
Union Twp, and died at Mechanicsburg both in
Champaign Co.; she is called **Vesta** in county
marriage records) WSIM; CoMR
Virginia Rutan - p/David W. Rutan-Georgia Griff-
in; TDR
Virginia Pearl Rutan - p/Sherman M. Rutan-Alice
Hatfield m Edward Lee Kirby b 1936 in 1857;
he died in Gallipolis; ROOTSW
Wallace Rutan - (See Alexander Wallace Rutan)
Warren Rutan - (1866/67-1938) p/Daniel W. Rutan-
Clara Maud Gove (1866-1952) in Union Twp,
Champaign Co. in 1891; Clara was born in Lew-
iston ME; CRC; 1900C; CoMR; LDS
Wesley R. Rutan - (1857-1934) p/William Rutan-
Hannah J. Clark (Kim Vierra)
Wiley David Rutan - p/Enos K. Rutan-Harriet Mil-
ler; he lived in Scranton IA (see IA listing)
TDR
William Rutan - (1744-1833) p/John Rutan-Sarah
Manning of Morris Co. NJ; he was a RW soldier
serving in the Pennsylvania Militia; he is
bur at the Old Cemetery, Warren Twp, Trumbull
Co. (cemetery records) MEACH
William Rutan - (1807-1880) p/John Rutan-Nancy
Rusk m Hannah Jane Clark (1814-1890) in 1832;
he was a merchant in Troy Twp, Richland Co.
in 1850; they moved to IA; she was born in
Washington Co. PA; they both died in Iowa
City, Johnson Co. IA (George A. Rutan; Kim
Vierra) MEACH; 1850C
William Rutan - (1814-1878) p/Daniel Rutan-Mary
Riddle m Mary Ann Magruder (1813-1900) at
Logan Co. in 1835; he was a saddler in Lake
Twp in 1850; they lived in Bellefontaine; TDR
WSIM; CoMR; LDS; 1850C
William Rutan - (1835-1835) p/Alexander A. Rutan
Sarah Workman of Carroll Co.; CoBR; JN
William Rutan - (1822-1900) p/John B. Rutan-
Hannah Shriver m Robinia Patterson (1829-
1901) at Carroll Co. in 1850; he was a farmer
in Liberty Twp, Crawford Co. in 1850; Robinia
was living in Orange Twp, Ashland Co. in

1900; they are bur at Nankin-Orange Cem, Ashland Co. (cemetery records) Note: one record calls her **Robenia Wood** (Janice McMurry) 1850C LDS; 1900C; JN

William Rutan - bc 1839; he was living with Peter Colwell-Lucinda Rutan; 1850C

William Rutan - m Mary Griffith at Morgan Co. in 1861; LDS

William Rutan - b 1912 p/Glen Rutan-Hazel D. McAdams of Champaign Co. m Margaret A. Saleture of MN; one record has him **Daniel William** WSIM; TDR; 1920C

William Rutan - (1891-1966) of Akron; SSA

William Andrew Rutan - (1867-1957) p/John Rutan-Susanna Egner of Ashland Co.; he died in Mitchell, Davison Co. SD; he is bur at White Lake SD; MHAWS; LDS

William Henry Harrison Rutan - (1842-1918) p/ William Rutan-Hannah J. Clark (see IA listing) 1850C

William Willis Rutan - (1914-1985) p/Zelora Rutan-Alice Robinson of Champaign Co.; m Edith Gwendolyn Dyer b 1917 in 1936; he died in Springfield, Clark Co.; RUDR; ODI; USARCH; 1920C

Willis Omar Rutan - b 1902 p/Glen Rutan-Hazel D. McAdams m Ida Shy (1903-1933); LDS; SSA; TDR; 1920C

Wilton Rutan - (1895-1982) he lived in OH and died in Phoenix AZ (see MN, CA listings) SSA

Winifred Rutan - p/Glen Rutan-Hazel D. McAdams; WSIM

Zelora Estel Rutan - (1877-1962) p/Arnoldus Rutan-Mila Ferguson of Union Twp, Champaign Co.; m (1) Charry Alice Robinson (1878-1921) in 1903 (2) Minnie Gertrude Spigelmoyer (1890-1951) at Piqua OH in 1924; he served in the SpAmWar, Private, 3rd Ohio Volunteer Infantry; he was farmer and a farm implement salesman; he lived in Springfield, Urbana and Mechanicsburg; he died in Dayton and is bur at Maple Grove Cem, Mechanicsburg (cemetery records) 1880C; 1900C; USARCH; 1900C; SSA; RUDR; 1920C; CoMR

Zelora Estel Rutan - (1852-1897) p/Abner H. Rutan-Emily Gray m Laura A. Cheever bc 1852 in Logan Co. in 1877; school teacher in Wayne Co.; no children; he died in Toledo, Lucas Co.; WSIM; LDS; 1870C; ROOTSW

Abraham Dwight Rutan - (1909-1992) m Herma _____
he died in Lane Co.; ORDI
Albert Rutan - (1905-1987) he lived in CA and in
Gold Hill OR; SSA
Albert E. Rutan - (1905-1987) m Antoinette _____
he served as a Major in the USAF, died in
Jackson Co. and is bur at Eagle Point Nation-
al Cemetery, Jackson Co. (cemetery records)
ORDI
Anna Rutan - d 1908 in Baker Co.; ORDI
Beth Una Rutan - (1914-1978) she died in Multno-
mah Co.; ORDI
C. Rutan - resident of Yoncalla Precinct, Doug-
las Co.; 1870C
Charles F. Rutan - resident of Portland in 1909;
CDIR
Charles Otis Rutan - d 1943 in Washington Co.
(see IA listing) ORDI
Clifford Oren Rutan - (1817-1968) p/Charles O.
Rutan-Lieucetta F. Miller m Evelyn Marie
McConnell b 1918 of Murphy ID in 1944; he was
born in Carstairs, Alberta and died at Port-
land (Kim Vierra)
Deloss J. Rutan - (1897-1973) of Lebanon, Linn
Co.; m Frances Cecile Harvey (1892-1974) she
was from Moscow, Lackawanna Co. PA; she died
in Lebanon; SSA; ORDI; ROOTSW
Dwight Rutan - d 1936 m Orpha Ann _____; he died
in Lane Co.; ORDI
Edgar Lewis Rutan - (1907-1966) p/Everett B.
Rutan-Clara A. Gilbert m Zelma _____; he liv-
ed in Eugene and died in Multnomah Co.; ORDI;
LDS
Elizabeth Rutan - d 1930 in Portland Co.; ORDI
Everett Brinton Rutan - d 1934 m Clara A. Gil-
bert d 1953; he died in Portland and she in
Multnomah Co.; LDS; ORDI
Floyd Joseph Rutan - (1916-1977) of Clatsop Co.;
ORDI
Frederick Ruttan - (1892-1967) of Portland; ORDI
George Wallace Rutan - b 1915 p/Charles O. Rutan
-Lieucetta F. Miller m (1) Beth McConnell in
1940 (2) Mary Ohlmann Green of South Norwalk
CT; he was born in Carstairs, Alberta (Kim

Vierra)

Georgia Rutan - m W.H. Young in 1890 (State marriage records)

Harvey Harry Rutan - (1927-1990) m Lonice _____ ("History of Klamath County") he died in Klamath Co.; ORDI

James Rutan - resident of Yoncalla Precinct, Douglas Co.; 1880C

James P. Rutan - d 1951 m Edna E. _____ d 1954; they died in Lane Co.; ORDI

James Scott Rutan - (1913-1992) m Evelyn _____; he died in Washington Co.; ORDI

Joseph C. Rutan - (c1835-1909) p/Samuel Rutan-Sarah Cracraft of PA, OH, IL, MI and CA; m Deborah R. Croscroft in 1867, they divorced in 1890; he was a CW soldier. 1st Oregon Infantry; he was a farmer in Champoeg, Marion Co.; he lived in San Diego and died in National City CA (information from his CW pension file) Note: according to George A. Rutan Deborah was from the same family as Joseph's mother despite the spelling difference; 1890C USARCH

Joseph C. Rutan - m Murtilla T. Graham in 1894 (see prior entry) LDS

Mary Etta Rutan - (1861-1935) her Obit appeared in the *North Pacific Recorder*, Seventh Day Adventist Obituaries

Oliver Perry Rutan - (1902-1986) m Alma Enolm (1905-1979) they died in Washington Co. (from their Obits in the *North Pacific Recorder*) (see Northeast listing)

Peter V.A. Rutan - resident of Baker Co. in 1880 Note: possibly Peter the blind musician, the son of Cornelius Rutan and Catherine Van Alen of NJ (see Northeast and NV listings) 1880C

Ulysses Schuyler Rutan - (1868-1944) p/Joseph C. Rutan-Deborah R. Croscroft of Marion Co.; m Nillah I. Ford (1878-1959) she was from TX; they were living in Stanislaus Co. CA in 1920 USARCH; 1920C

Wesley John Rutan - (1913-1969) p/Charles O. Rutan-Lieucetta F. Miller m (1) Thelma Swain (2) Hattie Paulsen b 1913 in 1949; he was born in Carstairs, Alberta and died in Forest Grove OR (see IA listing) (Kim Vierra)

Abraham Rutan - (1791-1852) p/Samuel Rutan-Elinor Bedell of Morris Co. NJ m (1) Olive Burt b 1796 (2) Mary Logston of MD in 1845; Abraham and Olive lived in Cameron VA (now WV) after his marriage to Mary they moved to OH and he is bur at Key Cem, Mt. Vernon, Belmont Co. OH (Andi Wilson) MCRC; MAR; RICR; TDR

Abraham Rutan - (1825-1917) p/Abraham Rutan-Olive Burt m Elizabeth Scales (see OH listing) MAR

Adam Weir Rutan - (1849-1941) p/John Rutan-Susannah M. Van Dyke m (1) Annie M. Wright d 1884 (2) (Mary) Elizabeth Sanders Simpson (1852-1945); living in Morris Twp, Washington Co. in 1900; GSNJ; 1850C; CRC; 1900C

Addison Rutan - (See Joseph Addison Rutan)

Addison Morris Rutan - (1900-1979) p/Elmer L. Rutan-Flora R. Crawford of Washington Co.; m Pauline Mankey (Ken Antall) GSNJ

Albert Curtis Rutan - (1900-1975) p/Theodore Rutan-Mary Roupe of Morris Twp; m Mildred Kuhn; they lived in Washington Co.; 1900C; SSA; GSNJ

Aldean Rutan - **Gayle Aldean** (1913-1988) p/John F. Rutan-Greta B. Miller of Washington Co.; m James Edward Sherer (1912-1963) of Carnegie Allegheny Co. in 1934; MCRC; GSNJ; RUDR

Alfred Buchanan Rutan - (1862/65-1942) p/George Rutan-Rachel Ewing; m Johanna Mankey b 1861 in 1890; living in Morris Twp, Greene Co. in 1900; he died in Greene Co.; Note: LDS says his mother was Sallie Winget; GSNJ; CoMR; 1880C; 1900C

Alice M. Rutan - (1874-1936) p/Israel Rutan-Elizabeth McGlumphy of Greene Co.; m (1) Dave Lemons in 1900 (2) D.A. Williams; she died in Pittsburgh and is bur at Hopewell Cem; Note: she sometimes was known as **Minnie A.** Rutan; GSNJ; ROOTSW

Alice Ruth Rutan - (1904-1955) p/Thomas F. Rutan -Ida McCollum of Morris Twp, Greene Co.; m Elmer Grinnage in 1930; she died at Nineveh and is bur at Beulah Cem; Elmer was alive at the time of her death (from her Obit in the *Wayne Republican*)(Donna Mohney) Note: a possible second marriage to Perlie Swiger is not mentioned in the Obit; GSNJ; MEACH

Alonzo Rutan - bc 1869 p/Henry Rutan-Eliza Hackett of Columbia Twp, Bradford Co.; 1880C

Alonzo Rutan - m Helen C. White of Tioga Co. in 1918; he was a farmer in Snedekerville, Bradford Co. in 1907; GSNJ; CDIR; CoMR

Alonzo Rutan - b 1878 m Carrie _____ b 1876; they were living in Bradford Co.; 1910C

Alvah R. Rutan - (1827-1877) m Abigail _____ (1824-1893) of Sussex Co. NJ; they lived in Benton, Columbia Co. and sold land in Fairmount Twp, Luzerne Co. in 1868; MCRC; CIMB

Amanda Retan - (1828-1849) of Tioga Co.; she was probably the wife of one of the sons of Joseph B. Retan; she is bur at Ames Hill Cem, Sullivan Twp, Tioga Co.; Note: her maiden name was Edgeton (cemetery records) WTWP

Amanda Rutan - (1853-1917) p/Abraham Rutan-Susan Springer; she was born in Weston, Westmoreland Co. (see OH listing) ROOTSW

Amantha L. Rutan - (see Mantie Rutan, below)

Angela Retan - (1836-1896) she was born in Dogget Mills and is bur at Millerton Cem, Jackson Twp, Tioga Co. (cemetery records) WTWP

Angeline E. Rutan - **Angie** b 1897 p/Lemuel J. Rutan-Rosa B. Wakefield of Wyoming Co.; 1900C (see Northeast listing)

Angie Rutan - m Denver Franklin Yoho (Yoho Family webpage)

Ann Rettan - resident of West Earl Twp, Lancaster Co.; 1850C

Anna Rutan - (1771-1819) p/"Elder"Abraham Rutan of Morris Co. NJ; m Moses Squier b 1770 in 1790 at Washington Co. (NJ Genealogies:4821-NJHS) Note: LDS names her husband Aaron D. Squier; LITT; LDS; NJHS

Anna Elizabeth Rutan - b 1870 p/Abraham Rutan-Susan Springer of Westmoreland Co. (see OH listing) ROOTSW

Arnold Rutan - (1900-1969) he was born in PA and died in Staten Island, NY; he is probably Arnold Robert Rutan (see Northeast listing) SSA

Arthur Sherman Rutan - (1907-1985) p/John F. Rutan-Gretta B. Miller m Elizabeth J. Krause (1914-1975) in 1935; he lived in Bentleyville Washington Co.; Note: the Rutan file at GSNJ has his year of death as 1935; RUDR; GSNJ; MCRC; SSA

Artie Leota Rutan - b 1887 p/Daniel Rutan-Mary
Adams of Greene Co.; m William Uren; they
lived in Wheeling WV; GSNJ

Augusta Rutan - b 1851 p/Joel Rutan-Katherine
Smith of Pike Co. (see Olive Augusta Rutan,
below) 1860C

Austin Retan - b 1887 p/Edmund A. Retan-Rena
_____ of Tioga Co.; 1910C

Austin Rutan - b 1890 p/Samuel Rutan-Flora _____
he may be the son of Samuel I. Rutan-Florence
Mae Carter; 1900C

Austin R. Rutan - (See Richard Austin Rutan)

Bartley Delbert Rutan - (1901-1954) p/Richard A.
Rutan-Sarah E. Gunn m Rebecca Duncan (1906-
1998) she was born in Cameron WV and died at
Wexford PA; both are bur at Highland Cem,
Cameron, Marshall Co. WV (cemetery records)
GSNJ

Barton Rutan - **Burton** b 1864 m Matilda (Tillie)
Rooney b 1863; they resided in Carbondale,
Lackawanna Co. 1900-1910, she was a widow
there living with her son Gordon in 1920;
Note: the 1910C calls him Burton born in 1867
and says she was born in 1877; 1900C; CDIR;
1910C

Benjamin Rutan - m Eva Hendershot in 1877; Note:
there is a record that they had a son Clyde,
as did the couple in the next entry but their
dates would indicate that they are two different Benjamins; ROOTSW

Benjamin A. Rutan - b 1871 m Mary Eva Pittenger
b 1880; both from Sussex Co. NJ; living in
Pike Twp, Bradford Co. in 1900; 1900C

Betty Rutan - p/Harry M. Rutan-Nellie H. Miller
(from her brother James' Obit)

Byron E. Rutan - (1883-1936) p/J.L. Rutan-Lottie
E. _____ of Bradford Co.; m (1) Josephine E.
Gaylord (1880-1917) in 1903; (2) Ella Trow-
bridge (1896-1985) in 1917; 1900C; 1920C;
CoMR; ROOTSW

Calvin J. Rutan - b 1896 p/Elmer L. Rutan-Flora
R. Crawford of Washington Co.; 1920C

Carl Rutan - p/Harry M. Rutan-Nellie H. Miller
(from his brother James' Obit)

Caroline Rutan - bc 1854 p/John Rutan-Sallie
Winget of Morris Twp, Greene Co.; LDS

Carrie Rutan - b 1874 p/Henry Rutan-Eliza Hackett of Bradford Co.; 1900C

Catherine Rutan - b 1785 p/Samuel Rutan-Elinor

Bedell m Daniel Sanders b 1783 in 1804 at
Morris Twp, Washington Co.; both born in NJ;
("History of Washington County", Beers: 926)
LDS

Catherine Rutan - p/John Rutan-Catherine _____
of Westmoreland Co.; m Asa Lane (George A.
Rutan) MEACH

Catherine Rutan - b 1839 p/Stephen P. Rutan-Rebecca W. French of Fayette Co.; 1850C; MEACH

Cela Rutan - (see Selah Rutan, below)

Charles Ruton - resident of Easton Borough,
Northampton Co.; 1860C

Charles Rutan - b 1867 p/Joseph Rutan-Rachel
_____ of Fulton Co.; 1910C

Charles Frankin Rutan - (1881-1931) p/Daniel
Rutan-Mary D. Adams m Minnie Alberta Chambers
b 1883 in 1901 (PSAR:286) Note: the 1920C has
him **Charles J.** Rutan; CoMR; PSAR; GSNJ

Charles Owen Rutan - (1898-1977) p/Forrest Rutan
-Flora E. McGlumphy of Washington Co. (see
Owen Rutan, below) 1900C

Charlotte Rutan - b 1837 p/Daniel Rutan-Lucy
Compton of NJ; 1850C

Clarence Edward Rutan - (1889-1889) p/Samuel I.
Rutan-Florence M. Carter; GSNJ

Clifford G. Rutan - b 1884 p/Frank M. Rutan-
Ellen V. Carter; he was living in Jeannette
Westmoreland Co. in 1910; 1900C; GSNJ; 1910C

Clyde Rutan - (1899-1983) p/Benjamin A. Rutan-
Mary E. Pittenger of Bradford Co.; he lived
in Scranton; Note: another record shows that
his mother was Eva J. Hendershot; 1900C; SSA

Curtis Rutan - bc 1871 (see Daniel Curtis Rutan,
below)

Daniel Rutan - (1806-1890) m Lucy Compton (1807-
1882) he was a laborer in Texas Twp, Wayne
Co. in 1850; they were living in Prompton in
1880; 1850C; 1880C

Daniel Rutan - (1835-1905) p/Samuel Rutan-Elizabeth Jones m (1) Sarah Wynso (2) Ellen Taylor
b 1855 (3) Mary Dunlap Adams (1831-1900) he
was a farmer, stock-raiser and fur-trader who
lived in Aleppo Twp, Greene Co.; he died in
Cameron WV; 1850C; ROOTSW; GSNJ; LDS; PSAR

Daniel Curtis Rutan - (1871-1926) p/Daniel Rutan
-Ellen Taylor of Greene Co; m Mary Emma Moss
(1871-1925); Note: he is probably the son of
the third wife, Mary D. Adams; according to
Paul R. Rutan he was married to Molly Murray;

MEACH; GSNJ

Daniel D. Rutan - (1819-1888) p/John Rutan-Jane Davis m Martha (Patty) Dille (1812-1855) in 1857 at Morris Twp, Washington Co.; Martha is bur at Upper Ten Mile Cem, Prosperity; Daniel lived in Prosperity until 1864, moved to Homer, Champaign Co. IL and then to Marion Co. IA (from his son William's CW pension file) (cemetery records) CRC; USARCH

Daniel E. Rutan - (1849-1933) p/Daniel Rutan-Lucy Compton of NJ; m Elizabeth Reynolds bc 1857; they were living in Prompton, Wayne Co. in 1880 and in Scranton in 1910; Elizabeth was born in England; 1850C; MCRC; 1880C; 1910C; NYMC

Daniel Moss Rutan - (see Moss Rutan, below)

David Rutan - b 1808 p/Peter Rutan-Elizabeth McIlrath of Fayette Co.; m Elenor Lyons; they moved to Carroll Co. OH (see OH listing) and he died in Marshall Co. IA in the early 1840's; LDS; JN; CoMR

David Retan - b 1849; he was living with his brother Edmund in Tioga Co.; 1910C

David Ruton - resident of Sheshequin, Bradford Co.; 1860C

David C. Rutan - b 1839 p/Peter Rutan-Maria Compton of Bradford Co.; m Harriet P. Perry of Brooklyn, Susquehanna Co. in 1861; he was a CW soldier, Pvt., 26th Pennsylvania Militia they lived in Athens and Wells Twp, Bradford Co.; 1860C; MCRC; CoMR; SQHS; BCPAHS

Davis Rutan - (See James Davis Rutan)

Delbert Bartley Rutan - p/Richard Austin Rutan-Sarah E. Gunn (see Bartley D. Rutan, above)

Dennis S. Rutan - b 1850 p/Adam T. Rutan-Abigail Tinsman of Blairstown, Warren Co. NJ; m Lois Arminda Shay bc 1857 in 1878; they lived in Jessup Twp, Susquehanna Co.; Note: according to the 1910C he was born in 1852 and she in 1860; 1900C; 1910C

Dorothy M. Rutan - **Dollie** b 1889 p/Frank M. Rutan-Ellen V. Carter m (1) Charles B. Boyd (2) Alvin R. Wise; GSNJ; 1900C

Dora Rutan - she was a stenographer in Washington Co. in 1914, living at the same address as Frank M. Rutan (see prior entry) CDIR

Edgar Rutan - m Mary Belle Pryor at Washington Co. in 1923 (Bedillon Marriages)

Edgar A. Retan - b 1862 m ?Evolie _____ b 1862

residents of Mansfield, Tioga Co.; 1920C

Edith Rutan - (1876-1888) p/W.K. Rutan-Ettie
_____; she is bur at Kimble Cem, Lackawaxen
Twp, Pike Co. (cemetery records)

Edmund A. Retan - b 1865 m Rena _____ born in
NY; they were residents of Tioga Co.; (see
Edgar A. Retan, above) 1910C

Edwin Rutan - b 1876 in NY; p/James C. Rutan-
Amelia M. Breese; (see DE listing); Note:
other records have him born in 1868; 1900C

Eleanor Rutan - b 1844 p/Stephen P. Rutan-Rebecca W. French of Fayette Co.; 1850C; MEACH

Elinor Rutan - b 1818 p/Abraham Rutan-Olive Burt
MAR

Eliza Ruton - resident of Franklin Twp, Washington Co.; 1860C

Elizabeth Rutan - (1758-1839) m Andrew Poe
(1742/47-1823 in 1780/90 at Williamsport (now
Monongahela) PA; they later lived in Ravenna
OH; Andrew was a RW soldier in the Washington
Co. Militia; they also lived in Beaver Co.;
Elizabeth was born in Essex Co. NJ (PSAR:275)
and according to Bob Meachem she may be the
daughter of John Rutan-Sarah Manning; Andrew
was born in Frederick MD (DAR appl #11915,
Daisy Poe Pratt) Elizabeth was bur at Mill-
creek Cem; Note: the Baldwin Papers at the
ACPL claim that Andrew was the uncle of **Edgar
Allan Poe**, but another source says Andrew
descended from the Pfau family; PSAR; MEACH;
LDS; CRC; DARLDC; ACPL

Elizabeth Rutan - (1808-1862) she is bur at Mt.
Herman Baptist Cem, Washington Co. (cemetery
records)

Elizabeth Rutan - (1795-1819) p/John Rutan-Catherine _____ m Matthias Shepler (1790-1863) he
was born in Bethleham Twp, Stark Co. OH; ACPL

Elizabeth Rutan - p/Abraham Rutan-Olive Burt of
Washington Co.; m _____ Scaggs; RICR

Elizabeth Rutan - bc 1831 p/Daniel Rutan-Lucy
Compton of NJ; 1850C

Elizabeth Rutan - bc 1906 p/Frank E. Rutan-Martha Fleming m Hubert Royster, M.D. (1905-1995)
at Sewickley in 1936; they lived in ME; NYT;
SSA

Ella Jane Rutan - (1866-1937) p/Abraham Rutan-
Susan Springer of Westmoreland Co.; ROOTSW

Ellsworth Rutan - d 1894 m Drucela _____; he
died in Greene Co.; CoDR

Ellsworth Rutan - p/Harry M. Rutan-Nellie H.
Miller (from his brother James' Obit)

Emma Rutan - (1843-1923) m James Andrew Gault b
1838 in 1862; he was a banker/merchant born
in New Wilmington, Lawrence Co. 1862; they
lived in Kittanning, Allegheny Co. where she
died; he was alive in 1914 (county history)
(see Amy Newton Rutan in the Northeast
listing) ROOTSW

Erwin Jesse Rutan - b 1876 p/James C. Rutan-Amelia Breese of Philadelphia; he is found as
Irwin Rutan, a clerk in Philadelphia in the
city directory for 1900; CDIR; 1900C

Esther Rutan - b 1904 p/Barton Rutan-Matilda
Rooney of Carbondale, Lackawanna Co.; 1910C

Ethel E. Rutan - (1892-1976) p/J. Lewis Rutan-
Lottie E. _____ m Martin M. Sterling of
Auburn in 1914; 1900C; CoMR; SSA

Eva Marie Rutan - (1889-1894) p/Ellsworth Rutan
of Greene Co.; CoDR

Everett Rutan - m Mary Hampton b 1824 in Wash-
inton Co.; ROOTSW

F. Guy Rutan - (1891/92-1968) p/Joel Rutan-Edith
Weed; bur at Dunsmore Cem, Scranton PA; Note:
this is probably Franklin G. Rutan who died
in No. Plainfield NJ (see Northeast listing
and Franklin Rutan, below) SSA; PCHSQ

Fanny Rutan - b 1826 p/Abraham Rutan-Olive Burt
of Washington Co.; MAR

Forest Rutan - bc 1871 p/George Rutan-Rachel
Ewing of Morris Twp, Washington Co.; m Flora
E. McGlumphy b 1874 in 1895; they were living
in Greene Co. in 1920; GSNJ; 1900C; 1920C

Frances Gertrude Rutan - (1912-1977) p/Harry M.
Rutan-Hazel Miller m Clarence Vernon Anderson
d 1958; she was born near Nineveh, Morris Twp
Washington Co.; she is bur at Rosemont Cem,
Rogersville; ROOTSW

Frances Pauline Rutan - (1917-2000) p/Elmer L.
Rutan-Flora R. Crawford m Orlando E. Day d
1980 in 1936; she lived in Washington (her
Obit appeared in the *Pittsburgh Post-Gazette,*
4 Jan 2000) GSNJ

Francis Marion Rutan - b 1848 p/John Rutan of
Buffalo Twp, Washington Co.; m Ellen Virginia Carter b 1855 in So. Strabane Twp; he was
a school janitor in Washington in 1914; CDIR;
GSNJ; 1880C; 1900C

Frank E. Rutan - b 1863 m Martha Fleming b 1865;

he was born in NJ and was living in Sewickley
in 1900 (see Northest listing) FER

Frank E. Rutan, Jr. - b 1899 p/Frank E. Rutan-
Martha Fleming; 1900C

Frank Melvin Rutan - (1871-1954) p/Israel Rutan-
Elizabeth McGlumphy m (1) Rosa A. McClintock
(1876-1967) (2) Mary J. Paul; he was born at
Prosperity and Rosa at Ursina, Somerset Co.
PA; Frank and Rosa lived in Toronto OH and
Rosa died in Cambridge OH; they are bur at
Hopewell Cem, Nineveh, Greene Co.; ROOTSW;
1900C; GSNJ

Franklin G. Rutan - p/Joel Rutan-Edith Weed of
Scranton; he was living in Brooklyn NY in
1942 per his sister Hazel's dc (See F. Guy
Rutan, above); BDC

G. Walter Rutan - (see George Walter Rutan,
below)

Gayle Aldean Rutan - (see Aldean Rutan, above)

George Rutan - (1831-1901 of Greene Co.; CoDR

George A. Retan - b 1887 m Edith Y. _____ b 1900
residents of Galeton, Potter Co.; 1920C

George B. Retan - b 1886; resident of Tioga Co,;
1910C

George Henry Rutan - (1868-1925) p/Israel Rutan-
Elizabeth McGlumphy of Greene Co.; m Belle
Newman (1861-1929) of Harveys PA in 1908;
CoMR; 1900C; 1920C

George Paul Rutan - (1902-1931) p/James S. Rutan
-Fannie Anderson; unm; he is bur at Rosemont
Cem, Rogersville (cemetery records) GSNJ

George Randall Rutan - (1910-1978) p/Theodore
Rutan-Mary Roupe; he lived in Finleyville;
GSNJ; SSA

George Roy Rutan - (1893-1925) p/Samuel I. Rutan
-Flora M. Carter m Goldie Stump (1908-1979)
1900C; SSA; GSNJ

George Walter Rutan - (1882-1955) p/Byron Rutan-
Josephine Gaylord m Joanna M. Sprout in 1905;
the wedding announcement was in the *Montrose
Democrat*, 15 June 1905; he died in Los Angeles; SQHS; CADRI

Glenn Curtis Rutan - b 1919 p/John Franklin
Rutan-Gretta B. Miller m Marybelle Porter-
field b 1921 of Belmont Co. OH; GSNJ; RUDR

Goldie M. Rutan - (1908-1979) she is bur at
Rosemont Cem, Rogersville (cemetery records)
(see Jacob Rutan, below)

Gordon S. Rutan - (1898-1943) p/Barton Rutan-

Tillie Rooney m Elizabeth McGlynn b 1903 in
1923 at St. Rose of Lima Ch, Carbondale; he
was a painter living with his widowed mother,
Matilda Rutan in Carbondale in 1920; Note;
the census has him **Gordon J.**; 1900C; CDIR;
ROOTSW

Hancle Rutan - (1894-1987) p/James S. Rutan-
Fannie Anderson m Gay NcCracken (1913-1960)
they lived in Washington Co.; Note: Marshall
Co, WV records have a record that Hancle
married in 1916; 1900C; SSA

Hannah J. Retan - (1855-1860) p/Levi C. Retan-
Phebe Frost; she is bur at Millerton Cem,
Jackson Twp, Tioga Co. (cemetery records)
WTWP

Hannah Jemima Rutan - (1850-1930) p/Samuel Rutan
m Leonard Dille b 1841 in 1872; ROOTSW

Harland Rutan - b 1893 p/Frank M. Rutan-Ellen V.
Carter; a box-maker, listed as **Harley** in the
Washington city directory for 1914; 1900C;
CDIR

Harley Rutan - b 1896 p/Theodore Rutan-Mary
Roupe; (see Robert Harley Rutan, below)

Harry Rutan - (1878-1963) SSA

Harry E. Rutan - b 1881 p/Daniel E. Rutan-Elizabeth Reynolds of Wayne Co.; m Lavinia L.
(**"Vinnie"**) Williams b 1876 of Uniondale in
1904; he was a salesman; Note: his birthyear
is from his marriage certificate; NYMC; CoMR;
1880C

Harry Melvin Rutan - (1883-1955) m Hazel Nellie
Miller (1894-1968) they are bur at Upper Ten
Mile Cem, Prosperity, Washington Co. (cemet-
ery records) ROOTSW

Harry W. Ruton - b 1887 of Philadelphia; he enlisted at New Castle DE (WWI enrollment records)

Hazel Gelma Rutan - b 1898 p/Theodore Rutan-Mary
Roupe m Clarence Morrison; GSNJ

Henry Rutan - (1829-1911) p/Daniel Rutan-Hannah
Corselius of Sussex Co. NJ; m Eliza Hackett
(1843-1921) he was a CW soldier, 15th New
Jersey Volunteer Infantry; he was a dairy
farmer living in Columbia Twp, Bradford Co.
in 1900; they also lived at Virtus; they are
bur at Baptist Hill Cem, Columbia Twp, Bradford Co. (their dates are from cemetery records) CDIR; 1900C; USARCH

Henry Phylander Ruttan - m Dency Hull Newton

(1894-1981) she was born in Newtontown, Crawford Co. (see Canada listing) ROOTSW

Hershel Rutan - p/Harry M. Rutan-Nellie H. Miller (from his brother James' Obit)

Hester Ann Rutan - b 1836 p/Stephen P. Rutan-
Rebecca W. French of Fayette Co.; MEACH;
1850C

Hezekiah Rutan - (1829-1889) of NJ; m (1) Matilda Ann Hayes (2) Sarah Burn; lived in East
Pittsburgh; he died in Kittanning (see Northeast listing) 1860C; FER

Howard Rutan - p/Hancle Rutan-Gay McCracken
(from the Obit of his brother Robert)

Howard E. Rutan - d 1946 of PA; Seaman 1st Class
U.S. Navy; awarded the Bronze Star; missing
in action; his name is on the WWII memorial
at Honolulu, HI; USARCH

Howard L. Rutan - (1902-1967) p/James N. Rutan-
Maud Logan of Washington Co.; he lived in
Rimersburg, Clarion Co.; SSA; 1910C

Icie Rutan - (1879-1959) p/Daniel Rutan-Mary D.
Adams m (1) J.M. McCormick (2) William Parker
GSNJ

Ida Rutan - b 1865 p/James D. Rutan-Evaline
Sanders m William Clutter; GSNJ; 1880C

Ida C. Rutan - p/J. Lewis Rutan-Lottie E. _____
m Lee Farr of Wilmot in 1911; CoMR

Ida M. Retan - (1855-1910) p/Matthew K. Retan-
Margaret A. Mitchell of Bradford Co.; she is
bur at Millerton Cem, Tioga Co. (cemetery
records) ROOTSW

Irene Rutan - p/Harry M. Rutan-Nellie H. Miller
m Jack Morris (from her brother James' Obit)

Isabelle Rutan - p/Harry M. Rutan-Nellie H.
Miller m James Pettit (from her brother
James' Obit)

Israel Rutan - (1820/30-1906) p/Jacob Rutan-
Elinor Sayres m Elizabeth McGlumphy (1832-
1909) in Richhill Twp, Greene Co. about 1852;
he died at Graysville and is bur at Hopewell
Cem (cemetery records) GSNJ; 1900C; ROOTSW

Jacob Rutan - b 1779 p/Samuel Rutan-Eleanor
Bedell m Elinor Sayres in Aleppo, Greene Co.;
he is bur at Hopewell Cem; Note: there is a
NJ record that says he m Mary Sayres; GSNJ;
MCRC

Jacob Rutan - Ed (1906-1969) of Beaver Co.; he
served in the USAF in WWII; he is bur at
Rosemont Cem, Rogersville (cemetery records)

SSA

Jacob Edward Rutan - probably the son of Joel
Tartus Rutan m Alice Jane Grim (1900-1977)
she was born in Jackson Twp, Greene Co. and
died at Wood Ridge in the same county; ROOTSW

Jacob Lewis Rutan - b 1853 p/Adam T. Rutan-Abigail Tinsman of Warren Co. NJ; m Charlotte
(Lottie) E. _____ b 1851 in 1880; they were
living in Wyalusing Twp, Bradford Co. 1900-
1910; Note: he is generally referred to as
J. Lewis Rutan; 1900C; 1910C

James Rutan - resident of Wells Twp, Bradford
Co.; 1830C

James Rutan - Justice of the Peace in Bradford
Co. in 1831; BCPAHS

James Rutan - b 1811 m Rebecca _____ bc 1815;
he was a farmer in Georges Twp, Fayette Co.;
Note: this is a census error; this is **Stephen
P. Rutan** of MD (see below) 1850C

James Rutan - resident of Harrisburg, 1887-1890;
CDIR

James C. Rutan - (1838-1911) p/Peter Rutan-Jane
Sherman of Elmira NY; m Amelia M. Breese b
1841; living in Philadelphia in 1900; and he
is shown as **James J.** Rutan in the 1900 city
directory; CAREY; 1900C; CDIR

James S. Rutan - (1863-193_7_) p/Selah Rutan-Amy
Ewing m Margaret Frances ("Fannie") Anderson
(1865-1942) they are bur at Rosemont Cemetery
Rogersville (cemetery records) 1900C; GSNJ
1900C; GSNJ

James Smith Rutan - (1838-1892) p/Alexander A.
Rutan-Sarah Workman of Carroll Co. OH; m
Eliza McNeely Cox (1844-1922) in 1865; he was
a CW soldier, 1st Lieutenant, 101st Pennsyl-
vania Infantry; State Senator; named by Pres-
ident Grant to be U.S. Consul at Florence,
Italy, but he declined; U.S. Marshal and
Collector, Port of Pittsburgh; he died at
Allegany City and Eliza was in East Liverpool
Columbiana Co. in 1891-92 and in Beaver Co.
in 1900; she died in Santa Rosa CA; USARCH;
NYT; CoMR; 1910C; JN; CDIR

James W. Rutan - (1913-2000) p/Harry M. Rutan-
Nellie H. Miller; he was born at Nineveh and
worked in a lumberyard; he died at Prosperity
and is bur there at Upper Ten Mile Cem (from
his Obit) ROOTSW

Jane Rutan - b 1826 p/Jacob Rutan-Elinor Sayre

m Samuel Ewart b 1829 in Greene Co. in 1843;
CoMR; GSNJ

Jessie Pearl Rutan - (1885-1944) p/Daniel Rutan-
Mary D. Adams m (1) D. Boyd Emory (2) A.
Marshall Johnson; GSNJ; MEACH

Joel Rutan - (1822-1869) m Katherine _____
(1824-1869; he was born in NJ; Joel was a
carpenter in Lackawaxen Twp, Pike Co. in 1850
they are both bur at Kimble Cem, Pike Co.
(cemetery records) 1850C

Joel F. Rutan - b 1870 m Edith Avalda Weed
(1871-1948) of Dunmore, Lackawanna Co.; her
mother, Ida Adams, was a daughter of President John Quincy Adams; Edith lived in Scranton (from her Obit in the *Hazelton Standard-
Sentinel*) 1910C

Joel Tartus Rutan - **Tartus** bc 1869 p/James D.
Rutan-Evaline Sanders m Ida _____ b 1879;
they were living in Greene Co. in 1910; GSNJ;
1880C; 1900C; 1910C

John Rutan - (1744-1833) p/John Rutan-Sarah
Manning of Morris Co. NJ; m (1) Catherine
_____ (2) Hannah Frazer (probable) he was a
RW soldier serving with the Westmoreland Co.
Militia in 1762 and the Pennsylvania Second
Battalion; in 1789 he was a Lieutenant in the
6th Battalion (see OH listing) PAARCH; MEACH

John Rutan - m Hannah Aller in 1824; LDS

John Rutan - (1778/84-1821) p/John Rutan-Catherine _____ of Westmoreland Co.; m Nancy Rusk
(see OH listing) (George A. Rutan)

John Rutan - (1796-1885) p/Samuel Rutan-Eleanor
Bedell of Washington Co.; m (1) Jane Davis d
1839 (2) Susannah Meek Van Dyke (c1805-1884)
he was a farmer; LITT; GSNJ; CRC; 1850C; RUDR

John Rutan - bc 1820 m Sallie Winget bc 1813 at
Morris Twp, Greene Co.; LDS

John Rutan - b 1828 p/John Rutan-Jane Davis m
Nancy Thompson; farmer in Morris Twp, Washington Co. in 1850; moved to Homer IL (see IL
listing) 1850C; CRC; GSNJ

John Rutan - b 1838 p/Stephen P. Rutan-Rebecca
W. French of Fayette Co.; 1850C

John Rutan - bc 1847 p/Daniel Rutan-Lucy Compton
of NJ; 1850C

John Rutan - p/Harry M. Rutan-Nellie H. Miller
(from his brother James' Obit)

John C. Reton - resident of Carlisle Borough,
Cumberland Co.; 1850C

John Calvin Rutan - (1896-1985) p/Elmer Lorenzo
Rutan-Flora Rebecca Crawford of Washington
Co.; m Marie Thomas and they lived in Greens-
burg, Washington Co.; he died in Jeannette;
SSA; GSNJ; 1900C; CRC

John Forrest Rutan - (1923-1961) he was born in
PA and died in Orange Co. CA; CADRI

John Franklin Rutan - (1879-1961) p/Joseph Addison Rutan-Annie Eliza Day m Gretta Belle
Miller (1885-1970) in 1904; he was a soldier
in the SpAmWar serving with the 84th Coast
Artillery; he was the principal compiler of
the Rutan family of southwestern PA collection held by the GSNJ at the Alexander Library, Rutgers University; he was a clerk in
Washington Co. in 1914; CDIR; 1900C; GSNJ

John Henry Rutan -(1875-1927) p/Daniel Rutan-
Ellen Taylor m Anna L. Foster b 1881 in 1897;
she was from WV; they were living in Washington Co. in 1910; GSNJ; 1880C; 1910C

John M. Rutan - b 1816 p/Abraham Rutan-Olive
Burt; MAR

John P. Rutan - resident of Franklin Twp, Luzerne Co.; 1850C

John W. Ruton - resident of Philadelphia; 1830C

John W. Rutan - employe at the State Arsenal at
Harrisburg, 1887-1890; CDIR

John W. Rutan - b 1859 in OH; living in Philadelphia in 1900; probably John Workman Rutan
the son of Alexander A. Rutan; he owned a
building supply company in Philadelphia in
1900; 1900C; CDIR

Joseph Rutan - b 1837 m Rachel _____ b 1842;
residents of Fulton Co.; 1910C

Joseph Rutan - CW soldier, Pvt. 53rd Pennsylvania Infantry; he enlisted as a substitute,
November 1864; ROOTSW

Joseph Addison Rutan - (1840-1926) p/John Rutan
-Susannah Van Dyke of Morris Twp, Washington
Co.; m (1) Abigail Caroline Elmes (1841-1870)
in 1863 (2) Annie Eliza Day (1847-1928) in
1871; he died in Prosperity; Note: "The History of the Lindley Family in America":39
calls his first wife **Hadassah Elmer** of Van
Buren, Washington Co.; GSNJ; 1850C; 1900C;
MCRC; CRC

Joseph B. Retan - (1801-1870) m Hannah _____
(c1805-1855) he was born in NY; a farmer and
a cooper in Wells Twp, Bradford Co.; he died

in Tioga Co.; Note: cemetery records have him
(1802-1878) 1850C; WTWP

Katherine Rutan - resident of Washington Co. in
1914; CDIR

Kathryn J. Rutan - m Ivan Bambarger b 1905 in
Amity, Washington Co.; ROOTSW

Kenneth Rutan - b 1905 p/Victor Rutan-Abbie A.
Jones of Susquehanna Co.; 1910C

Kenneth Wayne Rutan - (1910-1978) p/John F. Rut-
ab-Gretta B. Miller of Washington Co.; GSNJ;
RUDR

Laura C. Rutan - (1844-1893) of Carmichaels;
CoDR

Laura E. Rutan - b 1870 p/Joseph Rutan-Rachel
_____ of Fulton Co.; 1910C

Leda Retan - b 1893 p/Edgar A. Retan-Evolie ____
of Tioga Co.; 1920C

Lee Rutan - (1886-1899) p/Daniel Rutan-Mary D.
Adams; GSNJ

Lemuel Jefferson Rutan - (1850-1929) m (1) Eliza
Angeline Guile (1852-1879) at Lymanville in
1875 (2) Ella _____ b 1857 (3) Rosa Baker
Wakefield (1861-1941) Eliza was born at Auburn, Susquehanna Co. and is bur at Bunnell
Cem, Auburn; their wedding announcement in
the *Independent Republican* calls him **Lemuel
F.** Rutan; he and Ella were living in Spring-
ville in 1880; in 1900 he and Rosa were liv-
in Washington Twp, Wyoming Co.; she is bur at
Homer, Cortland Co. NY; he was born in Blairstown, Warren Co. NJ; ROOTSW; CoMR; 1880C;
1900C

Leona May Rutan - (1896-1933) p/Forest Rutan-
Flora E. McGlumphy m Roland Parker; she died
in a fire and is bur at Canonsburg; Note: in
the 1920C she is listed as **Leona Farrabee**,
living with her parents; 1900C; GSNJ; 1920C

Leroy Rutan - resident of Clinton Twp, Wayne Co.
1860C

Lester Hartman Rutan - (1908-1988) p/Elmer L.
Rutan-Flora R. Crawford m Mildred Lenora
Lighter (1909-1999) of Deer Lick; they lived
in Washington Co. and she died in Greensburg
(from her Obit in the *Pittsburgh Post-Gazette*
4 Sep 1999) GSNJ; SSA

Levi C. Retan - (1829/30-1894) p/Joseph B. Retan
-Hannah _____ of Southport Town, Chemung Co.
NY m (1) Phebe A. Frost of Rutland in 1854
(2) Adeline Seely (1831-1874) (3) Angeline

Corzette Wilson (1835-1896) he was a farmer
and blacksmith and later a local politician
in Wells Twp, Bradford Co.; he is bur at Mil-
lerton Cem, Jackson Twp, Tioga Co.; 1850C;
WTWP
Lida L. Retan - b 1893 p/Edmund A. Retan-Rena
_____ of Tioga Co.; 1910C
Lindsey Hustler Rutan - b 1868 p/Daniel Rutan-
Ellen Taylor of Greene Co.; m Cordelia Edith
Wright b 1875 in 1897; they were living in
Washington Co. in 1910 and later in Mantua OH
1880C; GSNJ; 1910C
Lon Rutan - Lonnie (1877-1957) p/Henry Rutan-
Eliza Hackett m Carrie Watkins b 1875 at
State Line, Chemung Co. NY; he was a farmer
in Columbia Twp, Bradford Co. in 1900; he is
bur at Baptist Hill Cem, Columbia Twp (cemet-
ery records) NYMC; CDIR; 1900C
Lucy Rutan - b 1841 p/Daniel Rutan-Lucy Compton
of NJ; 1850C
Lucy Rutan - b 1884 p/Henry Rutan-Eliza Hackett
m George Parcell Knapp at Columbia and Wells
Baptist Ch, Coryland in 1906 (from a local
newspaper announcement and her father's CW
pension file) 1900C; USARCH
Luman Rutan - b 1878 p/Lemuel J. Rutan-Eliza A.
Guile m Elizabeth Titman b 1875 in 1902; CoMR
Lydda V. Rutan - b 1858 p/Israel Rutan-Elizabeth
McGlumphy of Greene Co.; ROOTSW
Lydia Rutan - bc 1806 p/Jacob Rutan-Elinor Say-
res m John Phillips (1806-1863) in 1828 at
Washington Co.; she was born in Center Twp,
Greene Co. where they lived; GSNJ; LDS
Mabel Rutan - (1906-1996) of Washington (from
her Obit in the *Pittsburgh Post-Gazette*)
Mabel Blanche Rutan - b 1902 p/Charles F. Rutan-
Minnie Chambers m Jesse Welling (1898-1966)
at Greene Co. in 1920; GSNJ; ROOTSW
Mabel Edith Rutan - b 1905 p/John Franklin Rutan
-Gretta B. Miller m Clarence Shakespeare b
1893 of Wilmington DE; GSNJ; RUDR
Maggie L. Retan - (1874-1878) p/Lemuel J. Rutan-
Ella _____; she died in Tioga Co. and is bur
at Millerton Cem (cemetery records) 1880C;
WTWP
Malinda Rutan - bc 1833 p/Samuel Rutan-Elizabeth
Jones m Selah Clutter b 1827; he was born in
Greene Co.; GSNJ; 1850C; ROOTSW
Malvinia Retan - (1811-1866) m James Howe b

1782; she was born in Steuben Co. NY and he
in VT; she died in Nelson, Tioga Co. (Rick
Losey) (Rich MacAlpine) Note: she is also
identified as **Melvina** Retan; LDS

Mantie Rutan - **Amantha L.** (1879-1959) p/Adam W.
Rutan-Annie M. Wright of Washington Co.; m
Roy G. Bedillion (1878-1962) they both are
bur at Lone Pine Cem, Amwell Twp, Washington
Co. (cemetery records) Note: Roy is descended
from Marie Petilon, the wife of Abraham Rutan
(1658-1713) GSNJ

Margaret Rutan - p/Lemuel J. Rutan-Eliza A.
Guile of Lymanville, Bradford Co.; ROOTSW

Margaret Rutan - (1832-1898) p/John Rutan-Jane
Davis m John A. Black (1826-1880) in 1860;
he was a CW soldier, captured at Gettysburg,
and a carpenter; he was killed from a kick of
a horse ("Washington County History", Beers:
1174) CRC; GSNJ; 1850C

Margaret Rutan - (1919-1982) p/Harry M. Rutan-
Nellie H. Miller m _____ Toland; she lived in
Graysville, Greene Co. (from the Obit of her
sister Frances) SSA

Margaret Irene Rutan - b 1909 p/Thomas F. Rutan-
Ida McCollum m W. Bentley Carpenter (1901-
1978) in 1927; he was born at Graysville,
Greene Co. and is bur at Rosemont Cem, Rogersville (cemetery records) GSNJ; 1920C; ROOTSW

Margaret M. Rutan - (1859-1930) p/James D. Rutan
-Evaline Sanders; she was living with Joel T.
Rutan, her brother, in Greene Co. in 1910;
she is bur at Upper Ten Mile Cem. Prosperity
(cemetery records) 1880C; GSNJ; 1910C

Marian Rutan - b 1918 p/Victor Rutan-Abbie A.
Jones of Susquehanna Co.; 1920C

Mark Retan - (1864-1872) p/Levi C. Retan-Adeline
Seely of Tioga Co.; he is bur at Milleton Cem
Jackson Twp; Note: cemetery records identify
him as **Mack** Retan; WTWP

Martha Rutan - b 1824 p/Abraham Rutan-Olive Burt
of Washington Co.; m Perry Smith; MAR; RICR

Martha Jean Rutan - **Jennie** (1865-1937) p/Israel
Rutan-Elizabeth McGlumphy m Frank McCollum;
both are bur at Hopewell; GSNJ; MEACH

Martin C. Rutan - (1909-1978) p/Victor Rutan-
Abbie A. Jones of Susquehanna Co.; he died in
San Mateo CA; 1910C; CADRI

Mary Rutan - m John Lybarger b 1802 at Bedford
Co.; CoMR

Mary Rutan - b 1832 p/Peter Rutan-Maria Compton of Bradford Co.; m Isaac Decker in Elmira NY; GSNJ; 1860C; MCRC

Mary Ann Rutan - b 1820 p/Abraham Rutan-Olive Burt m Samuel Marquis (see OH listing) LDS

Mary B. Rutan - a domestic in the Crosbie household, Washington Co. in 1914; CDIR

Mary E. Rutan - (18_61_-1942) p/Israel Rutan-Elizabeth McGlumphy; unm, she was living with her sister Jennie McCollum in Morris Twp, Greene Co. in 1900; GSNJ; 1900C

Mary Edna Rutan - (1878-1914) p/Joseph Addison Rutan-Annie Eliza Day m James B. Conley b 1870; Note: MCRC has her (1873-1942) GSNJ; MCRC

Mary Elizabeth Rutan - (1898-1980) p/Elmer L. Rutan-Flora R. Crawford m (1) Harmon Samuel McKee (1895-1939) (2) C.E. Ryan; she was born at Cherry Tree PA (Ken Antall) GSNJ; 1900C

Mary Ella Rutan - (1842-1918) m John N. Dille (1833-1917) they are bur at Upper Ten Mile Cem, Prosperity; ROOTSW

Mary Jane Rutan - b 1841 p/Stephen P. Rutan-Rebecca W. French of Fayette Co.; MEACH; 1850C

Mary Lyda Rutan - b 1922 p/Charles F. Rutan-Minnie Chambers m John M. Allison; Note: Paul R. Rutan says she was the wife of _____ Wright in 1974; MEACH; GSNJ

Mary Rachel Rutan - b 1894 p/Alfred Buchanan Rutan-Johanna Mankey m Robert Lee Clutter in 1915 (see IL listing) GSNJ; CoMR

Matthew K. Retan - (1827-1902) p/Joseph B. Retan -Hannah _____ of Southport Town, Chemung Co. NY; m Margaret A. Mitchell (1831-1904) of Jackson Twp, Tioga Co. in 1851; he lived in Seneca Co. NY and was a farmer in Wells Twp, Bradford Co. and later a local politician; he is bur at Millerton Cem, Tioga Co. (cemetery records) WTWP; 1850C

Maurice Rutan - b 1899 p/Elmer L. Rutan-Flora R. Crawford of Washington Co. (see Morris Rutan, below) 1920C

May Ruton - b 1883; a resident of Carbondale, Lackawanna Co.; 1910C

Melinda Rutan - b 1832 p/Abraham Rutan-Olive Burt of Washington Co.; MAR

Melissa Rutan - b 1838 p/Abraham Rutan-Olive Burt of Washington Co.; MAR

Melissa Rutan - (1844-1894) p/John Rutan-Susanna

Van Dyke; unm; Note: MCRC says she died in
1918; 1850C; MCRC; GSNJ

Melvin Rutan - p/Addison Ellsworth Rutan; he was
living with his mother Anna (Annie E. Day?)
in Greene Co. in 1910; MEACH; 1910C

Melvina Retan - (1811-1866) (see Malvinia Retan,
above)

Mildred Fowler Rutan - m Raymond G. Wildrick,
M.D.; they were living in Germantown in 1933;
("John Wildrick of New Jersey") she appears
to be the widow of Dana F. Rutan (see DE
listing)

Mildred Geneva Rutan - (1905-1986) m Clarence
Hamilton Starnaman (1902-1952) in 1932; she
lived in Philadelphia and died at Ellsworth,
Antrim Co. MI (see MI listing) ROOTSW

Minnie A. Rutan - (see Alice M. Rutan, above)

Morris Rutan - (1900-1979) of Waynesburg, Greene
Co. (see Maurice Rutan, above) SSA

Moss Rutan - **Daniel Moss** (1896-1952) p/Daniel C.
Rutan-Mary E. Moss m Gertrude Davis in 1920;
Note: CoBR has his mother Mollie Murray; and,
there are records of Moss Rutan, a minister;
GSNJ; SSA

Myrtle Rutan - b 1901 p/Samuel I. Rutan-Flora M.
Carter; 1920C

Nancy Rutan - p/David Rutan-Elenor Lyons m Samuel Nichols; JN

Nancy Rutan - b 1826 p/John Rutan-Jane Davis m
John Clutter and moved to Homer IL (see IL
listing) CRC; GSNJ

Nicholas H. Rutan - (1786-1860) p/John Rutan-
Catherine _____ of NJ; W1812 soldier, a Corp-
oral in Capt. Daniel McKown's Regiment, Pennsylvania Militia May 1813 and in Hill's Regiment; m Mary _____ (1798-1869) they lived in
Milton Twp, Ashland Co. OH (see OH listing)
LDS; MEACH; PAARCH; USARCH

Nina Rutan - (1889/90-1972) p/James S. Rutan-
Fannie Anderson m Stewart Edward Frye in 1911
she died in CA; 1900C; CoMR; GSNJ

Norval Austin Rutan - b 1893 p/Samuel I. Rutan-
Florence M. Carter; Note: another record has
him born in 1890; GSNJ

Olive Rutan - **Olle** b 1822 p/Abraham Rutan-Olive
Burt of Washington Co.;m James Davis; MAR;
RICR

Olive Augusta Rutan - p/Joel Rutan-Katherine
Smith m Edgar Lemont Van Etten at Milford,

Pike Co. in 1873; Note: a record exists that
dates the wedding in 1851; CoMR; ROOTSW

Oliver Rutan - b 1862 p/John Rutan-Sarah _____
of Prosperity; he moved to KS (see KS listing) LDS; GSNJ

Owen Rutan - (1898-1977) p/Forest Rutan-Elizabeth McGlumphy m (1) Hazel Myers dc 1938 (2)
Rose _____ b 1915 about 1938; he owned a bar
and later bought a farm in Claysburg PA where
he died (see Charles O. Rutan, above) GSNJ;
SSA

Paul Rudolphus Rutan - (1904-1979) p/Charles F.
Rutan-Minnie Chambers m Bertha Jane Carmich-
ael b 1909 in 1930; he was a school teacher
and they lived in Rogersville; Note: PSAR:
286 has 1935 as the year of their marriage;
GSNJ; PSAR; CoMR; SSA

Peter Retan - (1770-1852) he is bur at Millerton
Cem, Jackson Twp, Tioga Co. (cemetery records) WTWP

Peter Ruton - resident of Newton Twp, Luzerne
Co.; 1850C

Peter Ruton - resident of Athens Twp, Bradford
Co.; 1860C

Peter C. Rutan - (1808-1896) m Maria Compton
(1806-1887) they were from NJ; he was a farmer in Athens Twp, Bradford Co. in 1860 (see
Northeast listing) 1860C; JS; GSNJ

Phoebe Rutan - b 1828 p/Abraham Rutan-Olive Burt
of Washington Co.; m Elza Archibald; RICR;
MAR

Phoebe Rutan - (c1843-1907) p/Samuel Rutan-
Elizabeth Jones of Washington Co.; m James
Hendershot (1842-1917); Note: there is anoth-
er record that has 1856 as her birth year;
CoMR; 1850C

Phoebe J. Rutan - (1844-1855) p/Samuel Rutan-
Elizabeth _____; she is bur at Mt. Herman
Baptist Cem, Washington Co. (cemetery records
but see prior entry)

R.H. Rheutan - foreman, Erie City Iron Works,
Erie, 1891; CDIR

Ralph L. Rutan - (1906-1970) p/Frank M. Rutan-
Rosa A. McClintock m Margaret Walker in 1941;
he was a coal miner born in Time, Greene Co.;
he served in the Air Corps in WWII; he died
in Washington and is bur at Forest Lawn Cem,
Washington Co.; CoDR; GSNJ; SSA; 1920C

Rebecca Rheutan - (1794-1878) she is bur at

Pfoutz Valley United Brethren Cem, Greenwood
Twp, Perry Co. (cemetery records)

Rebecca Rutan - (1815-1876) p/Abraham Rutan-Olive Burt of Washington Co. m Thomas Hill (see
OH listing) MAR; ROOTSW

Retha Rutan - (1903-1990) p/John Rutan-Anna
Foster m James A. Victor b 1903; she died in
Uniontown Fayette Co.; ROOTSW

Richard Rutan - p/Harry M. Rutan-Nellie H. Miller (from his brother James' Obit)

Richard Austin Rutan - (1864-1933) p/Daniel
Rutan-Sarah Wynso m Sarah E. Gunn (1873-1947)
in 1893; both are bur at Highland Cem, Cameron, Marshall Co. WV (cemetery records) GSNJ

Richard Byron Rutan - (1929-1929) p/Byron E.
Rutan-Ella Trowbridge; ROOTSW

Robert Rutan - bc 1848 p/Stephen P. Rutan-Rebecca W. French; 1850C

Robert Retan - b 1873 m Lucy _____ b 1882; they
were born in NY and were living in Mt. Carmel
Northumberland Co. in 1910; 1910C

Robert Eugene Rutan - (1914-1998) p/Hancle Rutan
-Gay McCracken m (1) Edith Leppert d 1968 (2)
Florence Crouch in 1970 at Washington; he was
born in Sycamore, served in WWII and was a
meter-reader for the Columbia Gas Co. (from
his Obit in the *Pittsburgh Post-Gazette*

Robert Harley Rutan - (1896-1959) p/Theodore
Rutan-Mary Roupe m Ada Luella Fitch (1899-
1991) in 1919; he died in Tulare CA; 1900C;
GSNJ; CADRI

Romney George Rutan - (1891/2-1968) p/Alfred B.
Rutan-Johanna Mankey m Cora Cynthia Finley at
Nineveh in 1917; he died in Penns Hills, All-
egheny Co.; SSA; 1900C; GSNJ; CoMR

Ross Rutan - p/Daniel Rutan-Martha Dille; he was
apparently a CW soldier who died of disease
while in service, however no record has been
located; he may be William Rutan, see below)
GSNJ; CRC; USARCH

Samantha Rutan - bc 1858 p/John Rutan-Sallie
Winget of Morris Twp, Greene Co.; LDS

Samuel Rutan - (1754-1840) p/Abraham Rutan of
New Providence, Morris Co. NJ; m Elinor Bedell (1759-1842) in NJ in 1778; he was a RW
soldier who moved to Washington Co. in 1791;
he lived there for the remainder of his life;
LITT; PSAR; MEACH; 1800C

Samuel Rutan - m Mary Teeple (1794-1824) she was

born in Washington Co.; ROOTSW

Samuel Rutan - d 1818 p/John Rutan-Catherine
_____ of Westmoreland Co. (George A. Rutan)
MEACH

Samuel Rutan - (1804-1883) p/Jacob Rutan-Elinor
Sayres; m (1) Elizabeth Jones (1808-1862) (2)
Sarah Lois Hart Dunlap (1827-1881) in 1868;
Sarah was born in Bucks Co.; he was a broom-
maker of Washington Co.; Samuel and Sarah are
bur at Upper Ten Mile Cem, Prosperity, Wash-
ington Co.; Elizabeth is bur at Mt. Herman
Baptist Cem; Note: Sarah's daughter, Mary D.
Adams, m Samuel's son Daniel (see above) (Bev
Todd) (cemetery records) GSNJ; 1850C; ROOTSW

Samuel Rutan - m Mary Hampton; ROOTSW

Samuel Rutan - d 1818 p/Nicholas H. Rutan-Mary
_____ of Rostraver Twp, (McKeesport) Westmoreland Co.; MEACH; LDS; GSNJ

Samuel Rutan - m Mary Finley; they lived in
Rostraver Twp, Westmoreland Co.; she m (2)
Samuel Davis and she may have died in 1819
("History of the Old and New Monongahela")

Samuel Rutan - resident of Litchfield, Bradford
Co.; 1840C

Samuel Rutan - b 1834 p/John Rutan-Jane Davis of
Washington Co.; m Anna Elliot; moved to Homer
IL; Note: at least one record has 1824 as his
birthyear; CRC; MCRC; GSNJ

Samuel Ingraham Rutan - (1866-1916) p/Daniel
Rutan-Sarah Wynso of Greene Co.; m Florence
Mae Carter (1870-1945) in 1888; 1880C; GSNJ;
1900C

Samuel J. Rutan - (1877-1943) p/Frank M. Rutan-
Ellen V. Carter; he is listed as **Samuel F.**
Rutan, a glass-maker in the Washington city
directory for 1914; 1900C; GSNJ; CDIR

Sarah Rutan - (1813-1870); probably the daughter
of Jacob Rutan-Elinor Sayres; GSNJ

Sarah Rutan - (1835-1910) p/Daniel Rutan-Lucy
Compton m Henry W. McMullen (1828-1909); she
is bur at Prompton Cem, Wayne Co. (Peter
Quigg; 1850C; MCRC

Sarah Rutan - b 1839 m George W. Arnold b 1839
by 1866; he was born in KY; they lived in IA
and NE; she was the widow of a Rutan; LWEB

Sarah Rutan - m Cephas D. Sanders b 1845 in
Amity, Washington Co.; ROOTSW

Sarah Ann Rutan - (1845-1925) p/Israel Rutan-
Elizabeth McGlumphy m John Warren Beabout

(1859-1913) of Morris Twp, Greene Co. prior
to 1894; Note: there is uncertainty as to her
birth year, it may be 1854 or 1856; ROOTSW;
GSNJ; CoMR; LDS

Sarah McNay Rutan - (1781-1817) p/Samuel Rutan-
Elinor Bedell m William Clutter (1772/5-1843)
in 1803 at Washington Co.; he was born in NJ;
she died in Amwell Twp, Washington Co. and
they are bur at Mt. Herman Baptist Cemetery
(Bethel Nagy) ROOTSW

Selah Rutan - Cela (1830-1902) p/Samuel Rutan-
Elizabeth Jones m (1) Amy Ewing d 1863; (2)
Alice Hafenwhite (1842-1924); Selah was born
on Long Island NY, a farmer in Morris Twp,
Washington Co.; they are bur at Upper Ten
Mile Cem, Prosperity (cemetery records) GSNJ;
1850C; 1900C; CoDR

Stephen P. Rutan - (1811-1864) he is erroneously
enumerated as **James** Rutan in the 1850C; he
was born in MD; m Rebecca Welch French and
moved to MI (see MD and MI listings) MEACH

Susan Rutan - b 1839 p/Daniel Rutan-Lucy Compton
of NJ; 1850C

Sylvia Pearl Rutan - (1893-1985) p/Albert B.
Rutan-Johanna Mankey m Leroy Wolfe Breese
(1891-1981) in 1914; GSNJ; CoMR; ROOTSW

Theodore Rutan - (1873-1938) p/George Rutan-
Rachel Ewing m Mary Roupe (1874-1947) in
Morris Twp, Greene Co.; 1880C; GSNJ; 1900C

Thomas D. Rutan - d 1944; Seaman, 2nd Class,
U.S. Navy, WWII, missing-in-action; his name
appears on the WWII memorial at the Manila
American Cemetery, Ft. William McKinley, Republic of the Philippines; USARCH

Thomas Duane Rutan - p/Harry M. Rutan-Nellie H.
Miller (from his brother James' Obit) (see
prior entry)

Thomas Franklin Rutan - (1872-1955) p/Selah
Rutan-Alice Hafenwhite m Ida Lauria McCollum
(1876-1962) in 1900; they were living in
Greene Co. in 1920; Note: he is called **Frank**
Rutan in the 1920C; both are bur at Upper Ten
Mile Cem, Prosperity (Donna Mohney) but
another record says Beulah Cem; the records
of the Harmony Presbyterian Church of Wood
Ridge says that they wed in 1897; GSNJ; LDS;
1920C

Viola Rutan - b 1892; she was a "servant" in the
Moore household of Munhall, Allegheny Co.;

1910C

Walter Rutan - (1904-1981) of Aleppo Twp, Greene
Co.; SSA

Warren K. Rutan - b 1855 p/Joel Rutan-Katherine
_____ of Pike Co.; m Marietta D. "Ettie" _____
b 1856; they were living in Wayne Co. in 1910
1860C; 1910C

Weir Rutan - (1849-1941) p/John Rutan-Susanna
Van Dyke m (1) Anna Mary Wright (1847-1884)
in 1870 (2) Mary Elizabeth Sanders Simpson
(1852-1945) they were living in Morris Twp,
Washington Co. 1900-1920 (Pat Brand) CRC;
1850C; GSNJ; 1900C; 1920C

Wilbert Rutan - p/Harry M. Rutan-Nellie H. Miller (from his brother James' Obit)

William Rutan - b 1852 p/Peter Rutan-Maria Compton of Bradford Co.; Note: in one record he
is called **Wilber** Rutan (see Northeast listing) 1860C; LDS

William Rutan - (1844-1864) p/Daniel D. Rutan-
Martha Dille; CW soldier, 140th PA Infantry;
died of disease in Washington DC; bur at Arl-
ington National Cem; (Info from his CW pens-
ion file); Note: CRC has him the son of John
Rutan-Jane Davis and that he was killed at
Gettysburg; he may be **Ross** Rutan, see above;
GSNJ; CRC; SQHS; USARCH; VA

William Rutan - (1772-1845) p/John Rutan-Catherine _____ of Bellevernon, Westmoreland Co.; he
moved to Champion Twp, Warren, Trumbull Co.
OH about 1805 (see OH listing) MEACH

William Rutan - b 1867; he was living with his
son-in-law, Joseph E. Goss at North Braddock,
Allegheny Co. in 1910; 1910C

William Addison Rutan - (1872-1957) p/Joseph
Addison Rutan-Annie Eliza Day m Margaret E.
McVay (1869-1921) MCRC; 1900C; GSNJ

William Austin Retan - (1824-1864) p/Joseph B.
Retan-Hannah _____ m (1) Hulda Evans of Wells
Twp in 1852 (2) Bathiah Frost (1827-1862) (3)
Lucretia Warner (1833-1901) Bathiah was from
Carmel NY and she, Lucretia and William are
bur at Millerton Cem (see Austin in the
Northeast listing) 1860C; WTWP

William M. Rutan - b 1846 p/Stephen P. Rutan-
Rebecca W. French of Fayette Co. (see MD and
MI listings) 1850C; MEACH

William T. Rutan - d 1996 in Erie Co.; ROOTSW

Willis Raymond Rutan - m Josephine ?McClesky

(Kim Enfield)
Wray Lester Rutan - b 1905 p/Frank M. Rutan-Rosa
McClintock; Note: he is listed as **W. Raymond**
Rutan, a bookkeeper in Washington in the city
directory for Washington in 1914; he lived in
Bloomingdale OH; GSNJ; CDIR; ROOTSW
Zanna E. Rutan - **Zenna** b 1894 p/Richard A.
Rutan-Sarah E. Gunn m Ray E. McCracken; GSNJ;
1900C
Zelma Rutan - b 1898 p/Theodore Rutan-Mary Roupe
(see Hazel Gelma Rutan, above) 1900C

S O U T H   C A R O L I N A

Malzie Reton - m Joshua Goodwin (1805-1884) of
Pickens Co. in 1849; she was alive at Tignol,
Wilkes Co. GA in 1884 (William & Mary College
Supplement Quarterly Historical Magazine, vol
8)

S O U T H   D A K O T A

A.P. Rutan - farmer in Chamberlain 1925-1932
(Brule Co. telephone directories) (see next
entry)
Alfred Peter Rutan - m Lena Peterson
Alva Rutan - resident ot Twp 119, Faulk Co.;
1885C
Amos George Rutan - (1895-1940) p/John T. Rutan-
Caroline Olson of Lyman Co.; m Ann Catherine
Geditz (1903-1978) at Ipswich; he served in
the U.S. Navy in WWI and after the War was a
butcher in Chamberlain where they lived; he
is bur at Riverview Cem ("History of Brule
County", 1976) SSA
Calvin Rutan - bc 1853 in NY; laborer in Canton
Twp, Lincoln Co. in 1880; 1880C
Carl Edwin Rutan - (1892-1966) p/John T. Rutan-
Caroline Olson of Lyman Co.; m Frances O.
_____ (1895-1988) they are bur at Riverview
Cem (Jones County WWI Registrations) (cemet-
ery records) (Michael Rutan) LWEB; 1880C;
SDBI
Eva Rose Rutan - (1905-1980) p/Alfred P. Rutan-

Lena Peterson m Morris Dow Eatherton
(1905-1973); they lived in Chamberlain and
she died in OR (Roxanne Johnson)

Frances O. Rutan - (1895-1988) probable p/John
T. Rutan-Caroline Olson; she is bur at Riverview Cem (cemetery records)

George W. Rutan - owner of a sporting and auto-
mobile goods store in Watertown, Codington
Co.; CDIR

Gladus Rheutan - born in IL; resident of Dead-
wood, Lawrence Co.; 1900C

J.C. Rutan - mentioned in "Early History of
Brown County, South Dakota" p 114

J.E. Rutan - purchased land in 1883 (McCook Co.
land records)

Jessie May Rutan - b 1890 p/Alfred Peter Rutan-
Lena Peterson m _____ Becker; she was born in
Lyman Co.; (Roxanne Johnson) SBDI

John Thomas Rutan - (1855-1919) m Caroline L.
Olson (1859-1906) they lived in Chamberlain,
Brule Co. and are bur at Riverview Cem (cem-
etery records) ("History of Brule County")

Lena C. Rutan - (1880-1951) she is bur at Riverview Cem (cemetery records)

Peter Rutan - (1861-1945) landowner in Lyman Co.
in 1901; he is bur at Riverview Cem (Lyman
Co. land records) (cemetery records)

Rebecca J. Rutan - bc 1842 p/Henry Lane Rutan-
Mary Guy of Trumbull Co. OH; m William Henry
McVay (1839-1907) of Pittsburgh at Yankton in
1866; he was a banker; she later lived in
Portland OR ("Kansas and Kansans" 4:1871)
LDS

Robert Wayne Rutan - (1925-2001) p/Amos G. Rutan
-Ann C. Geditz; his Obit appeared in the
Chamberlain Daily Republic, 10 Nov 2001

Richard Peter Rutan - (1927-1996) p/Amos G. Rutan-Ann C. Geditz m Betty Olson b 1933 of Kimball; his Obit appeared in the *Chamberlain-
Oacoma Register* (Roxanne Johnson) SSA

William Rutan - (1899-1966) p/Alfred Peter Rutan
Lena Peterson; he was born in SD and died in
Long Beach CA (Roxanne Johnson) SDBI; SSA

William Rutan - resident of Chamberlain in 1925
(Chamberlain telephone directory)

William Rutan - he purchased land in Steele Co.
in 1884 (Steele Co. land records)

TENNESSEE

Bernard Chester Ruton - m Myrtle L. Peek in 1897 at Manchester, Coffee Co.; ROOTSW

H. Rutan - resident of District 7, Van Buren Co. in 1891 (from voter list) LDS

Nancy Ruton - m Thomas Conway, Sr. in Green Co. in 1792; Note: she may have been born Nancy Rector; CoMR; LDS; ROOTSW

W.L. Rutan - resident of District 13, Roane Co. in 1891 (from voter list)

TEXAS

Adele L. Rutan - d 1932 in Liberty Co.; BIOG

Adeline Rutan - d 1965; a widow who died in El Paso Co.; CoDR

Andreas M. Rutan - d 1950 in Harris Co. (see MN listing) BIOG

Anna M. Rutan - d 1920 in Harris Co.; BIOG

Anne Rutan - m Jack England; their daughter born in Brazoria in 1946; CoBR

Cecil Lee Rutan - d 1909 in Bastrop Co.; BIOG

Donald R. Rutan - he was born in IN and died in Hildago Co.; CoDR

Edward Adell Rutan - d 1915 in Bastrop Co.; BIOG

Edward C. Rutan - a clerk in Houston in 1917; (see next entry) CDIR

Edward Cecil Rutan - d 1936 in Harris Co.; BIOG

Garniah S. Reton - m J.N. Weed at Van Zandt Co. in 1867; CoMR

Hilda M. Ruttan - (1924-1993) she is bur at Ft. Sam Houston National Cemetery, Bexar Co. (cemetery records)

James Rutan - resident of Houston, 1890-91; CDIR

James L. Rutan - d 1950 in Harris Co.; BIOG

James M. Rutan - bc 1842, CW soldier, he served with the 23rd Texas Cavalry (CSA) (information from his service file) USARCH; ACPL

John A. Rutan - b 1889; BIOG

Joe L. Rutan - (1918-2000) of Port Arthur; he died in Stockton CA (his Obit appeared in the *Stockton Record*, 9 May 2000)

Mabel F. Retan - (1909-1987) she died in Cameron Co.; TXDR

Margaret Rutan - (1893-1980) m Lloyd N. Merriman

(1895-1973) he was a Sergeant, U.S. Army;
they lived in Galveston and are bur at the
Houston National Cemetery (cemetery records)
Norma D. Rutan - d 1965; a widow who died at
Bexar Co.; CoDR
Thomas Retan - (1906-1977) he lived in MI and in
Brownsville; SSA
Wilton Rutan - b 1895 (see OH listing) BIOG

U T A H

Jack Rutan - b 1893; he lived in Kaysville,
Davis Co.; LDS
Lamont Rutan - (1906-1979) m Ellen Robertson
(1923-1983) in 1942; ROOTSW
Ruth Rutan - b 1887 m Harvey Greenwood (1883-
1967) in 1934; they were both born in American Fork; LDS

V I R G I N I A

Daniel Rutan - resident of the 36th District,
Monongalia Co.; 1850C
David Ruton - resident of Preston Co.; 1850C
Donald Everett Rheutan - (1896-1981) p/Isaac
Rheutan-Gertrude Everett of Worcester MA m
(1) Leila Allen Carroll (2) Jennie _____
(1902-1981) he was a graduate of Virginia
Military Institute, Class of 1917; he lived
in Richmond; CRC; SSA
Edmund Ruton - RW soldier, member of the 10th
Regiment, Continental Line (Gwathmey)
Elva Hogstrom Rutan - (1909-1995) of Staunton
(Obituary Daily Times)
James Rutan - d 1852; he was a RW soldier from
Buckingham Co.; m Eliza McCormick; LIZR
John Rutan - RW soldier from Bedford Co.; LIZR
Millie Routon - m Thomas Millican in Bedford Co.
in 1780 ("Some Virginia Marriages", v23)
Richard DeWitt Rheutan - (1904-1977) p/Isaac
Rheutan-Gertrude Everett; he lived in Rich-
mond and died in Ft. Lauderdale FL; SSA; GSNJ

W A S H I N G T O N

Abraham D. Rutan - a blacksmith in Seattle in
1910: CDIR
Adelbert B. Rutan - a laborer in Seattle in 1910
he lived with Abraham D. Rutan; CDIR
Charles A. Rutan - a laborer in Seattle in 1910;
he lived with Abraham D. Rutan; CDIR
Charles Augustus Rutan - (1888-1931) he is bur
at the Masonic Memorial Park, Tumwater (cem-
etery records) (see prior entry)
Charles F. Rutan - b 1856 in MA; he was a resid-
ent of Spokane in 1900; 1900C
Dollie Rutan - (1892-1892) p/William H.H. Rutan-
Cervilla M. Wiley; she was born and died at
Sprague (Kim Vierra)
Edythe Mae Rutan - (1894-1948) she is bur at the
I.O.O.F. Cem, Olympia; ROOTSW
Ferdinand Nelson Ruttan - (1889-1931) p/David J.
Rutan-Ida _____ m Ethel Maverite McIlroy
(1884-1960) at Hastings, Ontario in 1907; he
died in Seattle; RUTT
Hawley Rutan - (1901-1971) he lived in CA and
Seattle; SSA
Iza R. Rutan - living with Abraham D. Rutan in
Seattle in 1910; CDIR
Jennie Isabel Rutan - (1888-1974) p/William H.H.
Rutan-Cervilla M. Wiley m David Murl Riddle
(1883-1978) she was born in Sprague WA and
died at Carstairs, Alberta; he was born at
Ida Grove, IA and died at Didbury, Alberta
(Kim Vierra)
Leon Rutan - (1891-1964) he was a laborer in
Seattle in 1910 living with Abraham D. Rutan;
he later lived in Brier, Snohomish Co.; CDIR;
SSA
Morton L. Rutan - a bookkeeper in Seattle in
1910 (see KS listing) CDIR
Norman Gerald Rutan - (1902-1966) m Jettie
Czerney (1905-1989) ROOTSW
Otis Artmun Rutan - (1921-1994) m Betty Jean
Stewart (1921-1974) his Obit appeared in the
Seattle Post-Intelligencer, 24 May 1994; LDS;
SSA
Temby A. Rutan - (1883-1966) a plasterer in 1910
in Seattle living with Abraham D. Rutan; he
later lived in Bitter Lake, King Co.; CDIR;
SSA
Theodore William Rutan - (1913-1951) p/Charles
O. Rutan-Lieucetta F. Miller; he was born in
Carstairs, Alberta and died at Medicine Lake

WEST VIRGINIA

Ada Rutan - b 1897 p/Thomas B. Rutan-Susan E.
Steele; 1920C

?Alen J. Rutan - **Olen** b 1894 p/Mitchell Rutan-
Ella Staniford; he was a WWI soldier at Camp
Greenleaf GA in 1918; he was living with his
parents in 1920 (Marshall County WWI Volunteers) 1920C

Alice Ruton - b 1899; a resident of Kanawha Co.;
1920C

Arlington Roosevelt Rutan - **Arlie** (1901-1980) p/
Mitchell Rutan-Ella Staniford; he died in
Orange Co. CA; CADRI

Angie Rutan - m Denver F. Yoho and later divorced ("Yoho Recollections" in the *Putnam Democrat*) (see PA listing)

Bertie B. Rutan - (1915-2000) p/Elzie Rutan-Florence Richmond m Herbert Matthews; she lived
in Moundsville; her Obit appeared in the
Wheeling News-Register, 14 Feb 2000 (Paul R.
Rutan) 1920C; MEACH

Bessie P. Rutan - (1895-1900) p/Mitchell Rutan-
Ella Staniford; she is bur at Shiloh Cem,
Saunders, Putnam Co. (cemetery records)

Betty Jane Rutan - (1927-2000) she was the widow
of a Rutan; she died at Hurricane WV and is
bur at Shiloh Cem; her Obit was in the *Charleston Daily Mail*

Carolina P. Rutan - p/John H. Rutan-Caroline
Minor (see Lina Pearl Rutan, below) CRC

Cashes Earl Rutan - (1887-1973) p/John H. Rutan-
Caroline Minor m Bertha Rush (1893-1987) in
1915; they lived in Red House, Putnam Co.;
he died in So. Charleston; they are bur at
Macedonia Cem, Wetzel Co.; Note: RUDR has him
(1888-1974) SSA; USARCH; RUDR; RICR

Catherine D. Rutan - bc 1835 p/Daniel Rutan-Anna
_____ ; 1850C

Clarice Maye Rutan - (1917-2000) m _____ Van
Syoc; she lived in Moundsville; her Obit was
in the *Wheeling News-Register*, 27 Mar 2000

Delmar Rutan - p/Sylvester F. Rutan-Keziah Mason
m Betty Jo _____ ; ROOTSW

Dessie Emaline Rutan - (1906-1919) p/Elza Rutan-

Florence V. Richmond of Red House, Putnam Co. she is bur at the Methodist Chyd, Pleasant Ridge, Marshall Co. (cemetery records) LDS

Dock Rutan - (1886-1960) p/John H. Rutan-Caroline Minor m Eva A. Postalwait b 1895 in 1913; Note: Andi Wilson has him born in 1885; RUDR; USARCH; 1920C

Dorothy M. Rutan - (1915-1976) probably the wife of James O. Rutan (see below) she is bur at Shiloh Cem. Putnam Co. (cemetery records)

Edith Rutan - b 1906 p/Thomas B. Rutan-Susan E. Steele; 1920C

Edna Rutan - b 1883 (see Maria Edna Rutan, below)

Edna Rutan - b 1914 p/Elzie Rutan-Florence V. Richmond; 1920C

Elza A. Rutan - **Elzie** (1874-1949) p/John H. Rutan-Caroline Minor of Adaline, Marshall Co. m Florence V. Richmond (1877-1953) at Adaline in 1897; he died at Glen Dale, Marshall Co.; they are bur at the Methodist Chyd, Pleasant Ridge, Marshall Co.; 1880C; LDS; ROOTSW; 1920C

Emma J. Rutan - resident of Franklin Twp, Marshall Co.; 1870C

Emma Jane Rutan - (1865-1943) p/John H. Rutan-Caroline Minor; she was living with her parents in 1920; she is bur at the Methodist Chyd, Pleasant Ridge, Marshall Co.; 1880C; LDS; RUDR; 1920C

Ernest Rutan - (1900-1976) p/Elza Rutan-Florence V. Richmond of Marshall Co.; m Mabel Richmond (1903-1928) they are both bur at the Methodist Chyd, Pleasant Ridge, Marshall Co. (cemetery records) SSA; 1920C

Eva Mae Rutan - (1913-1967) p/Henry B. Rutan-Austa Rine m Joseph Harrison Knapp; ROOTSW

Feeby Rutan - (See Phoebe L. Rutan, below) LDS; 1880C

Hazel Lucreta Rutan - (1896-1909) p/Elza Rutan-Florence V. Richmond; she is bur at the Wade Chapel Chyd, near Red House, Putnam Co. (cemetery records) LDS

Henrietta Chambers Rutan - mentioned in her father's 1851 will in Marshall Co.; ROOTSW

Henry Bruce Rutan - (1880/82-1954) p/John H. Rutan-Caroline Minor m Austa Josephine Rine (1895-1977) in 1918; they are both bur at Shiloh Cem, Putnam Co.; Note: Rick Rutan calls her Ostie Ryan; USARCH; RUDR; RICR; 1920C

Hobert Rutan - b 1903 p/Thomas B. Rutan-Susan E. Steele; 1920C

Howard W. Rutan - (1919-1979) probable p/Henry B. Rutan-Austa J. Rine; he is bur at Shiloh Cem, Putnam Co. (cemetery records)

Hugh Elwood Rutan - (1915-1981) p/William Rutan-Frances P. Bonar; he died in Akron OH (Andi Wilson)

Icy Pearl Rutan - (see Pearl Rutan, below)

Irene Josephine Rutan - p/Henry B. Rutan-Austa J. Rine m Ernest Clayton Lyons in 1944; ROOTSW

Ivor Gardner Rutan - p/James Leslie Rutan m Shirley Hershey; ROOTSW

Jacob H. Rutan - (1909-1909) probable p/Elza Rutan-Florence V. Richmond; he is bur at Wade Chapel Chyd, near Red House, Putnam Co. (cemetery records)

James Dudley Rutan - (1870-1952) p/John H. Rutan -Caroline Minor; LDS; 1880C

James O. Rutan - b 1915 he is bur at Shiloh Cem, Putnam Co. (see Dorothy M. Rutan) (cemetery records)

John Rutan - (1886-1970) he died in Colerain, Belmont Co. OH; SSA

John Alva Rutan - b 1921 p/Cashes Rutan-Bertha Rush of Red House; m Ruby Irene Kersey b 1921 in 1936; RICR

John Hannon Rutan - (1832-1920) p/Abraham Rutan-Olive Burt of Washington Co. PA; m Caroline Minor (1844-1934) of VA in 1860 at Glen Easton; he was a CW soldier serving in the 17th West Virginia Infantry; he was born in Knox Co. OH and lived in Rosby's Rock, Lynn Camp and Millsboro WV; he died in Kausooth (from his CW pension file) they are bur at the Methodist Chyd, Pleasant Ridge, Marshall Co.; her Obit appeared in the *Wetzel Republican*, 9 Mar 1934; RICR; 1870C; 1880C; USARCH; ACPL; 1890C; 1920C;

John L. Rutan - b 1887 m Carrie H. _____; they were residents of Marshall Co.; 1920C

Laura Edna Rutan - b 1905/08 p/Thomas B. Rutan-Susan E. Steele of Red House, Putnam Co.; m Truman Guthrie Hill in 1930; LDS

Lina Alice Rutan - b 1884 p/Mitchell Rutan-Ella Staniford of Red House, Putnam Co.; LDS

Lina Purl Rutan - (1888-1962) p/John H. Rutan-Caroline Minor m (1) William Baker (2) Sam Rush; she was living with her parents in 1920 RUDR; 1920C; USARCH

Lindsay Rutan - (1903-1996) p/Elzie Rutan-Florence V. Richmond; he lived in Ft. Myers FL; 1920C; SSA

Lula May Rutan - b 1908 p/Elzie Rutan-Florence V. Richmond of Red House, Putnam Co.; 1920C; LDS

Lulu E. Rutan - (1925-1925) p/Ernest Rutan-Mabel Richmond; she is bur at Pleasant Ridge Cem, Marshall Co.; ROOTSW

Maradith Dale Rutan - p/Sylvester F. Rutan-Keziah Mason m Gracey R. Hill; ROOTSW

Marcellus Rutan - b 1849 p/Daniel Rutan-Anna ?Devoll; TDR

Maria Edna Rutan - b 1883 p/John H. Rutan-Caroline Minor m Marion Dennis Williams in 1906; USARCH; RUDR

Martha A. Rutan - bc 1814 p/Daniel Rutan-Anna ?Devoll; 1850C

Mary Rutan - b 1917 p/Elzie Rutan-Florence V. Richmond; 1920C

Mary Bertie Caroline Rutan - p/Henry B. Rutan-Austa Rine m Ernest Homer Kessel in 1938; ROOTSW

Melba Rutan - p/Sylvester F. Rutan-Keziah Mason m (1) Raymond Leroy Bye (2) John I. Stafford; ROOTSW

Mitchell Rutan - (1861-1951) p/John H. Rutan-Caroline Minor m Ella A. Staniford (1859-1934) in 1884; they were living in Marshall Co. in 1920; they are both bur at Fairview Cem, Moundsville, Marshall Co.; Note: LDS has him born in 1865; his father's CW pension file says 1862; 1880C; USARCH; RUDR; 1920C

Nora E. Rutan - b 1886 p/Mitchell Rutan-Ella Staniford m Clarence T. (Clem) Montgomery b 1882 in 1906; he was born in Tyler; ROOTSW; MEACH

Opal Rutan - (1930-1998) m Harry Dotson; she is bur at Shiloh Cem, near Red House (her Obit was in the *Charleston Daily Mail*, 25 Dec 1998)

Opal V. Rutan - m Myrl S. Wood (1915-1999) he was a log-cutter; they are bur at Salem Cem, Glen Easton, Marshall Co.; his Obit was in the *Moundsville Daily Echo*, 11 Mar 1999; CoDR

Oscar Hollis Rutan - **Hollis** (1897-1979) p/Mitchell Rutan-Ella Staniford m Angela Gertrude Baker (1899-1925) of St. Joseph, Marshall Co. he lived in IN and died in Hollywood CA; LDS; CoMR; SSA

Pearl Rutan - **Icy Pearl** (1897-1974) p/Thomas B. Rutan-Susan E. Steele of Red House, Putnam Co.; m Frank Allen Martin (1900-1985) he was born in Kanawha Co.; she is bur at Tyler Mountain Memorial Gardens, Cross Lanes, WV (Andi Wilson) 1920C

Phoebe Lude Rutan - (187 8-1918) p/John H. Rutan-Caroline Minor m George E. Harlan in 1899 in Wetzel Co.; she is bur at Washington PA (Resner Funeral Home of Brook Co. WV) Note: per Rick Rutan her name was **Phoebe Lula Odessie** Rutan

Ralph Eugene Rutan - p/Leslie Rutan m Mada Martin in 1948; they divorced in Greenup, Greenup Co. KY; ROOTSW

Romaine Beatrice Rutan - (1917-1973) p/William Rutan-Frances P. Bonar of McMechen, Marshall Co.; she died in Los Angeles (Andi Wilson)

Rosa Rutan - b 1912 p/Thomas B. Rutan-Susan E. Steele; 1920C

Ruby Sharon Rutan - p/Sherman M. Rutan-Alice Hatfield m Lee Eugene Russell; ROOTSW

Ruth Rutan - b 1910 p/Thomas B. Rutan-Susan E. Steele; 1920C

Sherman Rutan - b 1897, a nephew of Cashes Rutan he was living in Red House, Putnam Co. in 1920 (see OH listing) 1920C

Sherman Lee Rutan - p/Sherman M. Rutan-Alice Hatfield m Linda Bartley; ROOTSW

Simeon Albert Rutan - (1901-1909) p/Elza Rutan-Florence V. Richmond; he is bur at the Wade Chaple Chyd, near Red House, Putnam Co. (cemetery records)

Sylvester Franklin Rutan - (1899-1926) of Marshall Co.; m Keziah Kay Mason (1900-1973) he was born in Confidence, Putnam Co. and died in Sebring, Mahoning Co. OH; he is bur at Grandview Cem, Sebring; she died at Downey or Compton CA and is bur at Rose Hill Cem, Whittier (see OH listing) ROOTSW

Thomas Benton Rutan - (1868-1961) p/John H. Rutan-Caroline Minor m Susan E. Steele (1872-1951) in 1896; they were living in Putnam Co. in 1920 and both are bur at the Steele Cem,

Red House (Andi Wilson) LDS; 1870C; 1880C;
RUDR; 1920C

Thomas Earl Rutan - (1921-1968) probable p/Henry
B. Rutan-Austa Rine; he is bur at Shiloh Cem,
Putnam Co. (cemetery records)

Tressie Diana Gladys Rutan - p/Sherman M. Rutan-
Alice Hatfield m Carl Birtcher; ROOTSW

Velma Gertrude Rutan - (1921-1977) p/Henry B.
Rutan-Austa Rine m Pearl Franklin Cochrane;
ROOTSW

Walter L. Rutan - (1927-1999) p/Clyde H. Rutan-
Mabel M. Balch m Lois Webb; he died in
Springfield, Clark Co. OH; ROOTSW

Wilda Rutan - b 1912 p/Elza Rutan-Florence V.
Richmond m _____ Johnson; 1920C; MEACH

William Rutan - (1860-1860) p/John H. Rutan-Caroline Minor; he died in Marshall Co.; RUDR

William Rutan - d 1866 in Ohio Co.; CoDR

William Rutan - CW soldier, Pvt., 12th West Virginia Infantry (Civil War Muster Rolls)

William C. Rutan - (1891-1966) p/Mitchell Rutan-
Ella Staniford m Frances Pearl Bonar in 1912
at Moundsville, Marshall Co.; they were living in Akron OH in 1920; he died there; Note:
one record has him William B. Rutan; 1920C;
LDS; ODI

William Elias Rutan - (1899-1985) m Gusta May
Jacobs (1906-1953) at Oakland MD in 1923;
they lived in Grafton, Taylor Co.; ROOTSW;
SSA

W I S C O N S I N

Amanda Ruttan - p/Jacob Ruttan-_____ Livingston
of Kingston, Ontario; m Willis S. Warner;
they lived in Dallas WI

Arthur Ruttan - (1901-1976) of Milwaukee; SSA

Blanche Ruttan - (1902-1966) m _____ Mecklenburg
she lived in Milwaukee, served in the U.S.
Army and is bur at Wood National Cemetery,
Milwaukee (cemetery records)

Charles Ruttan - b 1858 m Mary _____ b 1867 in
MI; they were living in Sampson Twp, Chippewa
Co. in 1910; 1910C

George William Rutan - p/George W. Rutan-Nell
_____ m Florence Mildred Hemminger (1920-
1992); he was born in Withee, Clark Co. and
died in AZ; BFH; ROOTSW

Gulbrand Reton - he acquired land in 1893 (state land records)

Hattie Ruttan - b 1899 p/Charles Ruttan-Mary _____ of Chippewa Co.; 1910C

Ida Rutan - a domestic living in Washburn Twp, Bayfield Co,; 1910C

John Rutan - bc 1820 m Susan _____ bc 1820; John was born in OH; Susan in PA; he was a "land-lord" who lived in Buena Vista Twp, Richland Co.; he served as county clerk; 1850C; 1855C ROOTSW

John Rutan - acquired land in Richland Co. in 1852 (see prior entry) (state land records)

John Reton - acquired land in 1893 (state land records)

John Ruton - resident of Ixonia, Jefferson Co.; 1850C

Minnie Ruttan - she was born in WI; ROOTSW

Niels E. Reton - m Alice Marion Chaflin (1856-1947) in 1887 at Stevens Point; they were living there in 1900; she m (2) Robert Charles Ord in San Diego in 1915 and she died in Los Angeles; ("Genealogy of the Chaflin Family" AGBI; CADRI; ROOTSW

Peter H. Ruttan - resident of Cadiz Twp, Green Co.; 1910C

Sada Ruttan - b 1897 p/Charles Ruttan-Mary _____ of Chippewa Co.; 1910C

Willmet S. Ruttan - probably Wilmot S. Ruttan (see Canada listing) he was a teamster in Superior, 1891-1892; CDIR

L O C A T I O N   U N C E R T A I N

A.S. Rutan - U.S. Navy, a member of the crew of the battleship U.S.S. New Jersey ("Aboard the Great White Fleet, 1907")

E.J. Rutan - U.S. Navy, a member of the crew of the store-ship U.S.S. Glacier ("Aboard the Great White Fleet, 1907")

Hannah Rutan - bc 1811 m Samuel Marrs (1796/98-1895) about 1824; ROOTSW

Kathleen Rutan - m Samuel F. Cunningham bc 1890 ROOTSW

R. Rutan - U.S. Navy, a member of the crew of the battleship U.S.S. Georgia ("Aboard the Great White Fleet, 1907")

Roy Rutan - m Florence Cholette b 1917; ROOTSW

Wesley Rutan - m Mildred Cholette b 1915; ROOTSW

Cross Reference

Abbot,	Ida	M.		35
Abbot,	Mary			35
Abbot,	Mary	Elizabeth	Jane	123
Ables,	Augustus			180
Ackerman,	Dorothy			77
Ackerman,	Frank	Irving		51
Ackerman,	Helena	(Ellen)		65
Ackerman,	Isaac	P.		84
Ackerman,	Jantjie			17
Ackerman,	Maria			40
Adams,	Grace			196
Adams,	Marietta			109
Adams,	Mary		236	
Adams,	Milton			68
Adams,	Orson	L.		50
Adams,	Sarah			98
Adkinson,	John			111
Aggear,	Elizabeth			65
Alberson,	Melinda	Carolyn		111
Alderman,	Dean			136
Allan,	Daniel	J.		99
Allen,	Roseida			193
Allen,	Theora	V.		198
Allensworth,	Lewis	H.		210
Allison,	Alice			43
Allison,	George	W.		160
Allison,	John	M.		249
Anderson,	Clarence	Vernon		239
Anderson,	Margaret	Frances		243
Andrews,	Charles	R.		79
Andrews,	Charles	Williams		223
Anthony,	Peter			159
Anway,	Willis			191
Applegate,	William			119
Archibald,	Elza			251
Armstrong,	Edna			53
Armstrong,	Edna	W.		136
Armstrong,	Nenon	Margaretta	Louisa	132
Arnold,	George	W.		253
Arthur,	Melissa			40
Attkinson,	Cyrus	J.		160

Ault,	William	Henry	161
Austin,	Frank	Lee	78
Ayers,	Kate		24
Ayers,	Ora		152
Ayrhart,	Jennie		36
Babcock,	Jennie	A.	105
Babcock,	Lucy	Pendleton	92
Bacon,	Menville	Almarion	182
Bailey,	James	Dade	30
Baillie,	Sarah	M.	128
Bailor,	Charles	O.	160
Bain,	Sarah		144
Baker	William		264
Baker,	Angela	Gertrude	265
Baker,	George	Otto	180
Baker,	Hannah		5
Baker,	Hazel		26
Baker,	James		81
Baker,	Margaret		10
Baker,	Sheridan		215
Balch,	Mabel	Mae	213
Baldwin,	Lucky"		121
Ball,	Esther	Salle	88
Ball,	Frances	Maria	58
Ball,	Helen	M.	88
Ball,	Mary		143
Bambarger,	Ivan		246
Banker,	Annie	Eliza	72
Banks,	Sarah	J.	143
Banta,	Margaret		19
Barberie,	Andrina		127
Barberry,	Zoa		192
Barker,	Arnold		219
Barnes,	Mary	Caroline	63
Barnheisel,	John		212
Barr,	Levi		148
Bartevian,	V.	R.	198
Bartley,	Linda		265
Bates,	Daniel	Nichols	32
Bauer,	Grace		89
Bauter,	Margaret		73

Bissell,	Mary	Louisa/Laura	34
Bixler,	Sarah		154
Black,	John	A.	248
Black,	Sarah		102
Blauvelt,	Andrew	John	33
Blauvelt,	Helena		9
Blauvelt,	Jane		12
Blauvelt,	Joseph	Edgar	75
Block,	Emil		38
Blume,	Fritz		84
Bolden,	J.	M.	142
Bollinger,	Benjamin	Albert	212
Bonar,	Frances	Pearl	266
Bond,	John	F.	90
Bonham,	Katherine	L.	159
Boone,	Ida	M.	53
Boone,	Ida	M.	136
Boor,	Lovinya	K.	203
Bord,	Caterina		7
Bord,	Jannetje		16
Borland,	Marion		97
Borton,	John	Curtis	135
Boucher,	Robert	Mant	130
Bounsall,	George		82
Bower,	Mary		133
Boyd,	Charles	B.	237
Boydell,	Dorothy		60
Boyes,	Susan		44
Brace,	Helen		27
Bracklin,	Ila		111
Bradford,	Mary	C.	22
Bradner,	Harry		28
Bradshaw,	Mabel	Cassandra	113
Brawn,	Regina	Clara	62
Brazee,	John		37
Brazelton,	Eunice		162
Breese,	Amelia	M.	66
Breese,	Leroy	Wolfe	254
Breese,	Squire	Whitaker	44
Bremer,	Arthur		49
Brigge,	Elsie		76

Bright,	William	H.	161
Brinkerhoff,	Christian		84
Britchford,	Lillian		55
Brock,	Ellen		154
Brockman,	Anna		224
Broderick,	Frederick		104
Brooks,	Dorothy		62
Brooks,	Hannah	Bertha	134
Brouwer,	Jannitje		6
Brower,	Antye	Nix	5
Brower,	Jannitje		5
Brower,	Rachel		21
Brower,	Sarah	Ellen	35
Brower,	Isaac		3
Brown,	Annie	L.	89
Brown,	Della	Elvira	35
Brown,	Edgar		153
Brown,	Elias	Clapp	130
Brown,	Harriet	P.	177
Brown,	Hilda	J.	124
Brown,	Josie	B.	164
Brown,	Mary		19
Brown,	William	F.	148
Bruckhart,	John	Franklin	224
Brundage,	Catherine	H.	30
Brunskill,	Ina		121
Bruyn,	Maria		19
Bryant,	Olive	L.	144
Buchner,	Charles	Edward	202
Budd,	Joshua		84
Bull,	Laura	H.	72
Bumgardner,	Margaret		214
Bunnell,	Alfred	Ranney	26
Burch,	Francis	Jeffrey	131
Burgess,	Naaman		149
Burkacky,	Helen	M.	38
Burley,	Emma	Pauline	39
Burley,	Emma	Pauline	124
Burnett,	Harriet		61
Burnham,	Ethelyn		217
Burns,	Hugh		211

Burns,	Martha	K.		154
Burt,	Magdeline			178
Burt,	Olive			233
Buss,	Oscar			170
Button,	Leroy			228
Bye,	Raymond	Leroy		264
Cadman,	Phily	Ann		188
Cadman,	Sarah	Melissa		134
Cahill,	Marion			52
Cahill,	Rita			55
Caldwell,	Abraham			8
Caldwell,	John	J.		9
Caldwell,	Lucinda			225
Calhaun,	Samuel			187
Calhoun,	Lucy			25
Cameal,	Emily			128
Camp,	Julius			99
Camp,	Moses			15
Campbell,	Harlan			207
Campbell,	Mary			119
Canham,	Harriet	M.		206
Caniff,	Joseph	Brant		129
Caniff,	Levi			123
Cantwell,	Josephine	Margaret		227
Carlisle,	Christie	Worth		213
Carlock,	Abraham			28
Carman,	Christiana			126
Carman,	Eunice			70
Carman,	Frank			39
Carmer,	Henry	W.		60
Carmer,	Maria	Louisa		79
Carmichael,	Bertha	Jane		251
Carpenter,	Frances	Ann	Force	215
Carpenter,	John	Truesdell		46
Carpenter,	W.	Bentley		248
Carr,	Andrew	Jackson		162
Carr,	Vincent			85
Carroll,	Leila	Allen		259
Carter,	Ellen	Virginia		239
Carter,	Florence	Mae		253
Carter,	Ollie	G.		160

Case,	Anna	Elizabeth	24
Cash,	Cora	Viola	172
Cassidy,	Delina		41
Cassidy,	Elizabeth	Jane	41
Catron,	Homer	Benjamin	203
Cauldwell,	Jane		5
Cavanaugh,	Louisa	M.	170
Caylor,	George	Manual	144
Chadwick,	Reefa		157
Chaflin,	Alice	Marion	267
Chambers,	Anna		145
Chambers,	Minnie	Alberta	236
Chandler,	Minnie		153
Chant,	Mary		24
Chapman,	Mary	Lee	219
Cheever,	Laura	A.	230
Cholette,	Florence		267
Cholette,	Mildred		268
Christopher,	Catherine		34
Chubb,	Melissa		178
Church,	Denver	Samuel	113
Clabaugh,	Delwin		136
Clapp,	Margaret		127
Clapp,	Robert		126
Clark,	Charles	T.	158
Clark,	Edward	Willeby	36
Clark,	Frances	Adelaide	114
Clark,	Hannah	Jane	172
Clark,	Hannah	J.	229
Clark,	John	M.	57
Clark,	Phoebe		43
Clerihew,	William		85
Clifford,	Harmon		84
Clutter,	Robert	Lee	249
Clutter,	Selah		247
Clutter,	William		242
Clutter,	William		254
Coburn,	Martha	Lee	224
Cochrane,	Pearl	Franklin	266
Cody,	Jesse		52
Coeyman,	Peter	Lucas	3

Coffman,	Emma	Retta	158
Coffman,	William	Casper	168
Cogle,	Elbert		160
Cole,	Chester	Enos	100
Cole,	Green		75
Cole,	Jacob		68
Cole,	Parsells		83
Cole,	Spencer	H.	75
Coleman,	Joel		78
Coles,	Elizabeth		73
Collacott,	Ika	Moselle	181
Collier,	Paul		158
Collins,	Ellis	E.	33
Collum,	Axton		150
Colman,	Leo		223
Colsher,	Martha	Alta	157
Colvin,	Jeanette		138
Colwell,	Hannah		214
Colwell,	Peter	Edgar	223
Combs,	Sarah		153
Combs,	Susan	R.	162
Comer,	Emily		144
Compton,	Lucy		39
Compton,	Mariah		92
Concklin,	David		15
Conklin,	Charles		83
Conklin,	Kate	L.	52
Conklin,	Laura	Hulse	72
Conklin,	Lauretta		24
Conklin,	Mary	Alice	37
Conley,	James	B.	249
Connet,	Eugene	Virginius	100
Conover,	Urania		65
Conrow,	Anna	Louise	173
Conway,	Thomas		258
Cook,	Julia	Ann	156
Cook,	Peter	Napoleon	193
Cooman,	Peter		4
Coomber,	George	F.	202
Coon,	Catherine		11
Cooper,	Samuel	A.	101

Cooper,	Sarah	Edna		167
Corneal,	Emily			128
Cornell,	William	Olen		182
Corselius,	Charity			17
Cortright,	Martha			47
Cortwright,	Charles			58
Corwith,	Sarah			95
Cosby,	Martha	Evelyn		204
Coss,	Anna			2
Coss,	Margaret			2
Costello,	George	Daniel		194
Coulter,	James	D.		159
Coulter,	Lydia	B.		157
Courter,	Ann			2
Courter,	Mary			19
Courter,	Sarah			61
Covert,	Dennis	T.		186
Cowles,	Clara	Jane		56
Cowley,	Elizabeth			70
Cox,	Ben	F.		111
Cox,	Eliza	McNeely		243
Cox,	Rachel			21
Coykendall,	Juliette			78
Cracraft,	Abner			210
Cracraft,	Sarah			120
Crandle,	Mattie			169
Crawford,	Anna	Verna		166
Crawford,	Easter			100
Crawford,	Emma	Jane		116
Crawford,	John	C.		217
Crego,	Elizabeth			220
Crews,	Charles	Benton		171
Cromer,	Mary	Catherine		93
Crone,	Alva			86
Croscroft,	Deborah	R.		222
Crouch,	Florence			252
Cryderman,	Annie	M.		129
Cuckler,	William	Jennings	Bryan	205
Culley,	Barbara	Lucilla		161
Cunningham,	Sam			212
Cunningham,	Samuel	F.		267

Curry,	Mary			66
Cymer,	Susan			6
Czerney,	Jettie			260
Dailey,	John	Lindeman		47
Dailey,	Minerva	Sloan		156
Dainard,	Mary	Ellen		133
Dake,	Samuel	W.		184
Danielson,	Crist			169
Danley,	Lucilia			56
Davenport,	Catherine			146
Davenport,	June	Claire		186
Davidse,	Engletje			16
Davidson,	Hester			58
Davis,	Alberta			169
Davis,	Dorothy	Marie		74
Davis,	Gertrude			250
Davis,	James			250
Davis,	Jane			244
Davis,	Mary	Jane		131
Davis,	Nancy			124
Davis,	Olive	Z.		139
Davis,	Thomas	Demarest		85
Day,	Annie	Eliza		245
Day,	Daniel	Harry		150
Day,	Helen	Louisa		179
Day,	Orlando	E.		239
De Forest,	Sarah			1
DeCamp,	Rachel			228
Decker,	Elizabeth			50
Decker,	Isaac			249
Decker,	Lewis			64
Demarest,	Julian			20
DeMille,	James	A.		125
Denninger,	May			62
Dennis,	John			216
Dennison,	Marion	B.		39
Depew,	Alice	Angelica		102
Depue,	Sate	Lyon	Tousley	88
Depue,	Timothy			103
Dewey,	Charlotte			21
Dewey,	Frances			202

Duetta,	Martha	A.		34
Duetta,	Martha	Ann		103
Duff,	Rosina	B.		39
Dulmager,	Addie	M.		26
Duncan,	Magdalena			73
Duncan,	Rebecca			235
Dunham,	Elizabeth			102
Dunlap,	Sarah	Lois	Hart	253
Dunn,	Earl	D.		78
Dunn,	Warren	H.		45
Dunning,	Julia	A.		107
Dupuw,	Elizabeth			1
Durand,	Arthur	Judson		143
Durbin,	George			214
Dutech,	Joseph			120
Duval,	Thomas	Jefferson		176
Dyer,	Edith	Gwendolyn		230
Dyer,	Elizabeth			180
Dykes,	Nancy			137
Eakins,	Robert			81
Earl,	Barnabas			8
Early,	Blanche	Edna		35
Eatherton,	Morris	Dow		257
Eberhart,	Samuel			226
Ebersole,	Anna	Hewitt		214
Eccles,	Florence			22
Edgeton,	Amanda			234
Edmonson,	Thomas			173
Edmonston,	Mary			53
Edwards,	Rozella			65
Egner,	Susanna			220
Eighmey,	Zealiah			43
Eiseler,	Katherine			109
Eisenbice,	Peter			158
Ekings,	Elizabeth	White		96
Elder,	Mary	Virginia		146
Elder,	Roxie	Goldie		166
Elliot,	Anna			253
Ellis,	Suzanne			211
Ellmaker,	Sarah			219
Elmer,	Hadassah			245

Elmes,	Abigail	Caroline	245
Elset,	Joanna		1
Elston,	Corcelia	Elizabeth	31
Elwell,	Nellie		49
Emmons,	Catherine		73
Emmons,	Catherine		190
Emmy,	David		15
Emonce,	Victoria	L.	121
Emory,	D.	Boyd	244
England,	Jack		258
Engleman,	Amelia		55
Enolm,	Alma	Alexandra	89
Enolm,	Alma		232
Enos,	James		17
Erickson,	Catherine		113
Estes,	Cecelia	A.	186
Evans,	Hulda		105
Evans,	Walter	Adam	98
Everett,	Gertrude	Rich	65
Everett,	Sarah	Jane	98
Ewart,	Samuel		244
Ewing,	Amy		254
Faddis,	Anne	J.	199
Fane,	Harry		165
Farber,	William		45
Farley,	Mary	Jane	124
Farnsworth,	Mary	Emily	218
Farr,	Lee		242
Faubion,	Nettie		205
Fehlhaber,	Lydia		221
Fellow,	Hettie		5
Feloy,	Anna		165
Fenton,	Mabel	Florence	175
Ferguson,	Mila		211
Ferguson,	Peter		134
Finch,	Samuel		195
Finch,	Willis	E.	143
Finley,	Cora	Cynthia	252
Finley,	Mary		253
Fisher,	Simon		209
Fitch,	Ada	Luella	252

Fitzgerald,	Mary	Louisa		98
Fitzsimmons,	Anna			4
Flaherty,	Frances	Josephine		126
Flanagan,	Katherine			60
Flanders,	Willie	J.		51
Flannery,	Geraldine			193
Fleming,	Martha			239
Flewwellin,	George	Whitney		68
Flora,	Charles			95
Flournoy,	Labon	Scott		137
Flynn,	Mary			61
Fogelsong,	John			210
Folts,	Lovina	Louisa		39
Ford,	Nillah	Idell		120
Fordham,	Ardelia			179
Fornote,	Sally	Anne		73
Forsythe,	Robert			46
Foshier,	Elizabeth			16
Foster,	Anna			221
Foster,	William	W.		150
Fouser,	Mary			146
Fowler,	Emily	E.	A.	177
Fowler,	Mildred			135
Fox,	Catherine			66
Fox,	Clarabelle			174
Fox,	Clarence			26
Fox,	Elizabeth			178
Fox,	Helena	Jennie		191
Fox,	Jonathan			67
France,	Hiram			33
Franklin,	Gertrude			26
Frazee,	Samuel			13
Frazee,	Elisha			15
Frazer,	Hannah			13
Freeman,	Ira			42
Freeman,	John			128
Freeman,	Mary	Jane		225
Freeman,	Ira			214
Freiberger,	Joseph	Alexander		193
French,	Rebecca	Welch		177
Frost,	Bathia			30

Frost,	Martha	(Maria)	12
Frost,	Phebe	A.	246
Fruits,	William	Jason	159
Frye,	Stewart	Edward	250
Fuller,	Joseph	A.	174
Funay,	George		150
Fury,	Amanda	J.	143
Fury,	George		150
Gallagher,	Edward	George	203
Gallagher,	Eliza	J.	126
Gallagher,	Grace	V.	121
Gamble,	Archibald	J,	58
Gardiner,	Hermanus		14
Gardner,	Annie	H.	127
Gardner,	Frank	R.	125
Garrabrant,	Hannah		20
Garrabrant,	Letitia		27
Garrison,	Rachel		1
Gaulin,	Edna	Rose	186
Gault,	James	A.	27
Gault,	James	Andrew	239
Gaylord,	Ethelyn		70
Gaylord,	Josephine	E.	235
Geary,	Wilfred		211
Geditz,	Ann	Catherine	256
Geer,	Nancy		164
George,	Willie	Lee	137
Gibson,	Ray		28
Gibson,	Samuel		98
Gilbert,	Clara	A.	145
Gilbert,	Clara	A.	231
Gill,	Edna	Alberta	208
Gill,	Lovina	E.	198
Gillam,	Hannah		121
Gilmore,	Robert		225
Gilson,	Solon		212
Goad,	Marie	Emma	161
Gobrecht,	Faye		222
Godbold,	Amy		89
Goetschius,	John	Zabriskie	33
Goforth,	Irene		116

Golden,	Bertha	Mae	154
Golden,	Charles		160
Goldsmith,	Sydney		55
Good,	Jacob	R.	194
Goode,	John	G., Jr.	28
Goodwin,	Joshua		256
Gordon,	Elvira	Eloise	122
Gordon,	George		159
Gore,	John		170
Goss,	Joseph	E.	255
Goudy,	Marie	Elizabeth	194
Gould,	George E.		51
Gould,	Jacob	Clair	79
Graham,	Murtilla	T.	232
Grant,	Mary	Esther	133
Gray,	Mary	Elizabeth	29
Gray,	Ruth	A.	120
Green,	Mary	Ohlmann	231
Green,	Mattie	Eliza	102
Greene,	Franklyn		46
Greenwood,	Harvey		259
Griffin,	Georgianna		214
Griffis,	Elizabeth	Content	124
Griffis,	Elizabeth	Maria	132
Griffith,	Mary		230
Grim,	Mary	Alice	243
Grimmon,	Robert		132
Grinnage,	Elmer		233
Groff,	John	Peter	223
Grove,	Claudie		146
Grove,	Vernon	G.	183
Guile,	Elizabeth	Angeline	76
Gunderman,	Joanne		213
Gunn,	Rosella		206
Gunn,	Sarah	E.	252
Hackett,	Eliza		61
Hadlock,	Emma	R.	172
Hafenwhite,	Alice		254
Haight,	Jeremiah	K.	67
Haight,	Rhoda	Bathsheba	124
Haines,	Daniel		187

Haldane,	Andrew	P.		59
Hall,	Lola			159
Hall,	Ora			153
Hall,	Robert	D.		153
Hall,	Ruth	Imogene		164
Halliday,	Bernard			68
Halliman,	Luella			41
Halliman,	Luella	D.		154
Hammond,	Emily	M.		90
Hampton,	Mary			239
Hampton,	Mary			253
Haner,	Carl			102
Haney,	Jane			23
Hardy,	Mary	E.		31
Hardy,	Mary	Louise		71
Hare,	Henry	Darling		85
Haring,	Margaret			10
Harlan,	George	E.		265
Harpel,	Margaret			129
Harper,	Aaron			165
Harper,	Frances			121
Harper,	Henry	Isaac	Raymond	48
Harris,	Charles	S.		193
Harris,	Francis	M.		145
Harrison,	Mary	Louise		129
Harshman,	Freda	Melvina		148
Harshman,	Freda	Melvina		158
Hart,	Emma	Mary		168
Hart,	Jeanette	(Janet)		92
Hartley,	John			33
Harvey,	Delilah	Margaret		152
Harvey,	Frances	Cecile		231
Hatfield,	Alice			228
Hatfield,	Earl			155
Hatt,	Henrietta			71
Hatt,	Polly			18
Hatton,	Horace			210
Haven,	Guy			192
Hazard,	Hannah	Maria		108
Hazard,	Laura	Louisa		109
Hazel,	Jacob			224

Hazel,	Mary		176
Hazelton,	Eliza	Jane	178
Hazen,	David		22
Hazen,	Susannah	Coss	2
Headley,	Ethel	Loretta	218
Heavlin,	Mary	Matilda	164
Heazle,	Jacob		224
Hedden,	Stephen		3
Helling,	Susanna		11
Helmich,	Peter		9
Helvy,	Betty		173
Hemminger,	Florence	Mildred	266
Hendershot,	Eva		235
Hendershot,	James		251
Hendron,	William		125
Hennessey,	Annie	H.	37
Hennion,	David		94
Hensley,	Schell		174
Hepp,	Henrietta		55
Herbaugh,	Henrietta	L.	113
Hershey,	Shirley		263
Hewet,	John		76
Hewy,	Samuel		63
Hiatt,	Martha		147
Hibschman,	Perry		158
Hicks,	Harriet		23
Hicks,	Mary		106
Higginbottom,	Thomas		91
Highley,	Vera	M.	175
Hight,	Iretta	M.	184
Hilborn,	Charles	Newton	190
Hill,	Emma	E.	180
Hill,	Gracey	R.	264
Hill,	Laura	Marie	212
Hill,	Lester		89
Hill,	Letha		174
Hill,	Thomas		226
Hill,	Truman	Guthrie	263
Hinkle,	Elizabeth	Hill	187
Hinkley,	Samuel	J.	192
Hinman,	Harriet	E.	23

Hinton,	Ona	Mabel		214
Hoff,	Tobias			177
Hoff,	Willem			8
Hole,	Rachel			13
Holland,	William			111
Holmer,	Anna			61
Holmes,	Louise	H.		174
Hood,	Clyde	E.		43
Hooey,	Samuel			63
Hopper,	Amanda	Lavinia		107
Hopper,	Emma	Jane		107
Hopper,	Melvina	(Wyntje)		2
Horner,	Edward	Day		207
Horner,	Ida	F.		206
Horner,	Ira	S.		205
Hoss,	Faye	Etta		115
Hough,	Rebecca	Jane		93
Houston,	Louper			141
Howe,	Barbara	Ellen		131
Howe,	Delbert			48
Howe,	James			16
Hoye,	William	Waller		176
Hoyt,	Mary	Young		23
Hubbard,	Emmaline			103
Huff,	Henrietta			71
Huggins,	Thomas			223
Hughes,	John	W.		155
Hull,	Dorothy			76
Hulse,	Harriet	A.		90
Humes,	Nellie	Louise		44
Hunt,	David	O'Connell		78
Hunt,	Edith			128
Hunt,	Jennie	A.	Babcock	105
Hupp,	Louisa	Pernetta		157
Hursh,	Maria	DePue		92
Hurtt,	Aaron			155
Hussey,	James			209
Huston,	Myra			106
Huyck,	Elizabeth			215
Huyler,	John			14
Huyler,	John			80

Hyde,	Benjamin	Henry	142
Ike,	Harry	A.	97
Inslee,	Phineas	J.	9
Inslee,	Phineas	J.	57
Ireland,	Sarah	Jane	190
Irland,	Lyman		181
Irvin,	Roy		206
Jackson,	Celia		161
Jackson,	Ethel	Elizabeth	108
Jackson,	Nancy	Ann	227
Jackson,	Pauline	M.	146
Jacobs,	Fidelia		178
Jacobs,	Gusta	M.	266
Jay,	Eliza	Jay	191
Jenkins,	Ethel	M.	153
Jenkins,	Russell	J.	149
Jerbus,	Ann	Maria	106
Johnson	A.	Marshal	244
Johnson,	Betty	Jean	143
Johnson,	Condrance	(Candace)	52
Johnson,	Joseph		153
Johnson,	Joseph	H.	159
Johnson,	Myron		205
Johnson,	Sidney	S.	203
Johnson,	Wilber	L.	160
Johnson,	William	Henry	181
Joline,	William		4
Joline,	William		13
Jolley,	Ida	Cloe	164
Jones,	Abram		194
Jones,	Beulah		111
Jones,	Elizabeth		253
Jones,	Joseph		48
Jones,	Margaret	B.	66
Jones,	Mary		126
Jones,	Roy		111
Joralemon,	Sarah		20
Jordan,	Alice		95
Joseph,	J.		151
Juno,	William	Henry	181
Kadel,	Lillian	L.	70

Kasine,	Rachel		2
Keegan,	Annie	F.	108
Kelder,	Anna		92
Kelly,	Adelaide		38
Kelly,	John		170
Kelly,	Mary	Agnes	171
Kennedy,	Nelson	A.	197
Kenyon,	Charles		167
Kenyon,	Charles		174
Kern,	Elizabeth	M.	50
Kerr,	Howard		199
Kersey,	Ruby	Irene	263
Kershaw,	Harry		160
Kessel,	Ernest	Homer	264
Kimball,	Angeline	Lucy	214
King,	Mabel		182
King,	William	Michael	140
Kingsland,	Rachel		10
Kingsland,	Theodore		33
Kirby,	Edward	Lee	229
Kiritz,	Henrietta		78
Kirkpatrick,	Jane		127
Kirkwood,	William	W.	219
Kittle,	Robert	Grist	64
Klug,	William	J.	91
Knapp,	George	Parcell	247
Knapp,	Joseph	Harrison	262
Knapp,	Myrtle	Aldrich	70
Knapp,	Sarah	J.	45
Knight,	Allen	S.	63
Knight,	Mary	Ann	122
Knowles,	William	Emery	181
Kosier,	Hulda		194
Kramer,	Adolph		210
Kramer,	Mary	Thanks	219
Krause,	Elizabeth	J.	234
Kreider,	George	W.	211
Kuhn,	Mildred		233
Kymer,	Susan		6
Ladd,	William	G.	80
Lafara,	Orville		152

Laid,	Susan		129
Lake,	Elizabeth		11
Lakestream,	Lucille	Winifred	87
Lamkin,	William	B.	194
Lane,	Asa		236
Lane,	Sarah	Elizabeth	49
Lang,	Helen		49
Lang,	James		167
Lapp,	Ann	Preston	180
Lasell,	Fred		185
Lathrop,	Arthur		33
LaTourette,	John	Hillikin	81
Laurence	Jane	Ann	195
Lawrence,	Hester		178
Layton,	Isaac		81
Leach,	John		182
Lederer,	George		88
Lee,	Cora	I.	147
Lee,	Jennie		36
Lehr,	Melba	(Melva)	106
Lemen,	Noah	A.	153
Lemons,	David		233
Lemy,	Polly		69
Lepper,	Catherine		71
Leppert,	Edith		252
Lewis,	Charles		160
Lewis,	Sylvanus		155
Lighter,	Mildred	Lenora	246
Likens,	Frank		117
Lilly,	Jonathan		69
Lines,	Conrad		5
Lippincott,	Dorothea	P.	150
Litts,	Mary Ann		56
Livingston,	Henry		127
Lloyd,	Elmida	Margaret	127
Lobdell,	Chloe		9
Lockhardt,	Lydia	Windsor	205
Lodge,	Harry		136
Logan,	Francis		160
Logston,	Mary		209
Loiselle,	Fred		185

Lombard,	Mabel	Maud			179
Long,	Mary				131
Longwell,	Lewis	B.			94
Longwell,	Mehetabel	(Hettie)			91
Longwell,	Susan	Elizabeth			68
Longwell,	Zylla				27
Lord,	Cara	Estelle			87
Lounsbury,	William				101
Love,	Elizabeth				125
Lowe,	Cynthia	Victoria			128
Lowe,	James	Byron			123
Lowe,	Roy	E.			205
Ludlow,	Jeanne		May		31
Luff,	Ida				87
Lynde,	Edith	Lorraine	(Todd)		51
Lyon,	Emma				90
Lyons,	Eleanor				214
Lyons,	Ernest	Clayton			263
Mabie,	Jenny				16
Mabie,	John				16
Mager,	Lillian				69
Magruder,	Mary	Ann			229
Malcolm,	Sarah				124
Malcolm,	William				125
Mallette,	James				141
Manee,	Annie				107
Mangel,	Johannes				14
Mankey,	Johanna				233
Mankey,	Pauline				233
Manly,	James				229
Manning,	Sarah				11
Mansfield,	Sarah	Isabel			100
Mansfield,	Sarah	Jane			173
Marble,	James	L.			192
March,	Ella	R.			76
Markert,	Grace	Helen			67
Markle,	Frank				30
Markley,	Elizabeth	Stough			225
Marks,	Irene				64
Marks,	Sarah	Elizabeth	Bard		131
Marlatt,	Rebecca	Ann	Stringer		188

Marley,	Alliene	Nichols	73
Marquis,	Samuel		224
Marrs,	Mahala		150
Marrs,	Samuel		267
Marsh,	Mildred	K.	215
Marsh,	Sarah	Elizabeth	89
Marshall,	Carolyn	Elizabeth	179
Martin,	Agnes		174
Martin,	Cornelius	S.	85
Martin,	Fannie	L.	74
Martin,	Flora	S.	228
Martin,	Frances	L.	93
Martin,	Frank	Allen	265
Martin,	Lovinia	S.	228
Martin,	Mada		265
Martin,	Rice		195
Martin,	Robert	A.	45
Martin,	Sarah		55
Martin,	William		136
Mason,	Keziah		217
Mason,	Keziah	Kay	265
Mason,	Tempa	Almeda	174
Mastin,	Ernest		125
Mather,	Cornelia		54
Mathis,	Thomas		68
Matthew,	Thomas	E.	16
Matthews,	Beulah	Mae	205
Matthews,	Herbert		261
Matthews,	Raymond	Alfred	207
Matthews,	Thomas	Elmes	130
Mattox,	David		215
Mattox,	Mary	A.	6
Mattox,	Michael		15
Mattox,	Michael		83
Maxwell,	Gertrude		94
Maxwell,	Venus		215
May,	Fannie		23
May,	Mary	E.	194
Maybee,	Amanda		134
McAllister,	John	C.	90
McArnt,	Cecil		101

McPherson,	Gladys	V.	131
McVay,	Margaret	E.	255
McVay,	William	H.	226
McVay,	William	Henry	257
Mead,	Tryphena		21
Mead,	Tryphena		198
Mears,	Lucille		140
Mecray,	Harry	Souder	42
Medinger,	Frank		207
Meeker,	Abigail		19
Meeker,	Rachel		19
Melber,	Harry		29
Mentzer,	Frank	D.	210
Mercer,	Leon	A.	187
Merkle,	Elizabeth		104
Merriman,	Lloyd	N.	258
Merring,	Amzi		28
Metcalf,	Lucille		124
Meyer,	Evelyn	Wilson	112
Meyer,	Hannes		14
Meyers,	Cornelius		14
Meyers,	George		49
Meyers,	Jane		98
Meyers,	Mahala		150
Meyers,	Matilda	Anetta	172
Millar,	Ida		172
Miller,	Charles	M.	192
Miller,	Fairy	W.	157
Miller,	Francis		160
Miller,	Gretta	Belle	245
Miller,	Harriet		166
Miller,	Hattie		216
Miller,	Hazel	Nellie	241
Miller,	John		4
Miller,	Lieucetta	F.	164
Miller,	Lottie	C.	210
Miller,	Matilda	Jane	129
Miller,	Maude	M.	163
Miller,	Minnie		129
Miller,	Olive	C.	60
Miller,	Ruth	E.	154

Miller,	William			86
Millican,	Thomas			259
Mills,	Esther			16
Mills,	Zella	Blanche		146
Minor,	Caroline			263
Mintz,	Levina	Ann		129
Mitchell,	James			186
Mitchell,	Margaret	A.		249
Mitchell.	Josephine	Marie		34
Mizon,	Mabel	Victoria		131
Moffit,	Nancy			220
Montgomery,	Clarence	T.	("Clem")	264
Moody,	Clarissa			31
Mooney,	Joseph	J.		224
Moore,	Della			140
Moore,	Joseph			177
Moore,	S.	B.		149
Moore,	Samuel	Thomas		13
Moore,	Sarah			5
Moore,	Sarah			177
Morehouse,	Inez	Reynolds		220
Morehouse,	Milton			199
Morgan,	Mabel			150
Morris,	George			192
Morris,	Jack			242
Morris,	Mahala			151
Morrison,	Clarence			241
Morrison,	James			197
Moss,	Mary	Emma		236
Mount,	Richard			18
Mountainee,	Mary	Ann		130
Mullenax,	Grant	P.		145
Mulligan,	Rose	Ellen		29
Munn,	Lovinia	A.		62
Murphy,	Benjamin			45
Murphy,	John			223
Murphy,	Joseph			44
Murphy,	William	Arthur		128
Murray,	Anthony			217
Murray,	Molly			236
Murray,	Robert			130

Myers,	Amzi		157
Myers,	George		63
Myers,	Hazel		251
Nanny,	Geneva		105
Napier,	Nila	Mae	154
Nash,	George	R.	145
Nearing,	Linn	M.	83
Neary,	Lillian		63
Needham,	Donald		126
Needham,	Jean	Adeline	184
Neidinger,	Lucy	M.	104
Nelson,	Estelle		181
Nelson,	Margaret		219
Newel,	Edith		165
Newell,	Frank	Linford	28
Newman,	Belle		240
Newton,	Dency	Hull	127
Niccols,	Louisa	A.	208
Nichols,	Rose		38
Nichols,	Samuel		225
Niver,	Eva	A.	183
Norman,	Phoebe	Emma	134
Novell,	William	Walter	85
Nummo,	Imo		179
Ochs,	John	Lewis	173
Ogden,	Jonathan		143
Olson,	Betty		257
Onderdonk,	Rem		9
Ord,	Robert	Charles	267
Osborne,	Samuel		125
Osenbaugh,	Sarah	Jane	36
Osgood,	Janna		45
Outwater,	Daniel		132
Outwater,	Peter		126
Outwater,	Susanna		125
Padgett,	C.	F.	137
Page,	Raymond	B.	185
Paine,	Lucy	Emma	32
Paine,	Lucy	E.	75
Pake,	Mary	Ann	134
Palme,	Marianne		29

Palmer,	Elsie	M.	136
Palmer,	Matilda		126
Parier,	Peter		139
Parish,	Orin	A.	195
Parker,	Maria	J.	54
Parker,	Roland		246
Parker,	William		242
Parks,	Rebekah		26
Parr,	Phoebe		42
Parrot,	Thomas		19
Parsells,	Stephen		33
Partridge,	Catherine	B.	187
Partridge,	John	Willet	193
Partridge,	Katherine	Sears	55
Patch,	Zula	Avadelle	191
Patrick,	Jared		46
Patrick,	Ransom		229
Patterson,	Robinia		229
Patton,	David		228
Paul,	Mary	J.	240
Paulsen,	Hattie		232
Payne,	Marie		159
Peacock,	Joseph	Brantley	111
Pearce,	Clarence	Eugene	119
Pearcy,	George	Vernon	151
Pearson,	Hannah		176
Peart,	Naomi	Belle	168
Peek,	Myrtle	L.	258
Peel,	Xeripha	Johnette	138
Pegg,	Clark		158
Pegg,	Phebe		158
Pelton,	Alexander		9
Pennel,	Lucy	A.	180
Penny,	John		14
Pepe,	Tina		108
Perras,	Beatrice	J.	132
Perry,	Anna		71
Perry,	Harriet		41
Perry,	Louise		156
Perry,	Phyllis	Ernestine	226
Peter,	Paralee		114

Peters,	Alice	Almira	128
Peters,	Elaine		219
Peterson,	Lena		256
Petilon,	Marie		1
Petry,	Harvey	Clement	223
Pettit,	James		242
Petty,	Virginia		114
Phegley,	Emma		157
Phelps,	Mary	Ann	23
Phillips,	John		78
Phillips,	William		228
Pier,	Johannes		20
Pier,	Thomas		14
Pierson,	Stephen		3
Pinkney,	Clara	P.	54
Pinrod,	Martin	W.	157
Pittenger,	Mary	E.	31
Pittman,	William	H.	224
Poe,	Andrew		8
Pond,	Arthur	J.	199
Poole,	Atlas	Frank	202
Porter,	Peter		139
Porter,	Seth		190
Porterfield,	Marybelle		240
Post,	Isaac		51
Post,	Isaac		100
Postalwait,	Eva	A.	262
Potes,	George	A.	194
Potter,	Catherine		203
Potter,	Mary	J.	31
Powell,	Norman		68
Powell,	Norman		89
Power,	Alice		144
Power,	Samuel		14
Powers,	Alice		189
Powers,	Eva	V.	196
Powers,	Joseph	T.	4
Preble,	Charles	E.	222
Predmore,	Mary		10
Predmore,	Reuben	Randolph	90
Price,	Edward	Valentine	81

Price,	J.	Bernice		222
Price,	Jefferson	H.		48
Pringle,	Margaret			127
Pryor,	Mary	Belle		237
Puckney,	Willard			45
Puff,	James			45
Pullen,	George	Jay		180
Pullen,	John			85
Putnam,	F.	Estelle		200
Putnam,	Georgia	A.	E.	201
Quackenbush,	Abraham			11
Quackenbush,	Arthur			79
Quackenbush,	Jacomyntje			13
Quick,	Ella	Van Sickle		107
Quick,	Esther			69
Quigley,	James			138
Ragen,	Elmer			169
Rahn,	Delores			222
Rankin,	Eliza	Jane		123
Ratts,	Benjamin	G.		156
Raynor,	Samuel			46
Rector,	Nancy			258
Reddick,	Nancy			133
Redmen	Andrew	Jackson		151
Redmen,	Anna			149
Reed,	George	Washington		148
Reid,	Abigail	Jane		132
Reilly,	Raymond			47
Requa,	Eliza	Ann		72
Requa,	James			15
Requa,	James			77
Reynolds,	Carrie	M.		145
Reynolds,	Eleanor			70
Reynolds,	Elizabeth			237
Reynolds,	Sarah	Jane		186
Rhodes,	Catherine	Anne		23
Rhodes,	Jonas	W.		32
Rice,	Adelaide	L.		108
Richardson,	Caroline	Martha		125
Richardson,	Daniel	S.		179
Richardson,	Elwood			192

Richardson,	Frank			149
Richardson,	Samuel			82
Richman,	Marshal	Harvey		207
Richmond,	Florence	V.		262
Richmond,	Mabel			262
Rickert,	Nicholas			25
Rickey,	Martha			150
Riddle,	David	Murl		260
Riddle,	Mary			176
Riker,	Cora	B.		186
Riley,	Margaret			136
Rine,	Austa	Josephine		262
Roberts,	Alberta	Elizabeth		126
Roberts,	Clarence	H.		196
Roberts,	Mary	Elizabeth		163
Roberts,	Thomas			8
Robertson,	Ellen			259
Robertson,	Florence	Elizabeth		76
Robinson,	Charry	Alice		230
Robinson,	Effie			213
Robinson,	Esther			178
Robinson,	Jacob	Howard		166
Roblin,	Fanny			131
Roblin,	Owen			130
Rockafellow,	Anna			56
Rockefeller,	Mida			56
Rodick,	James			208
Roe,	Lucetta		May	62
Roger,	Ruth			156
Rogers,	Alexander	Hubert		132
Roll,	John			14
Roll,	Matthias			15
Rollison,	Charlotte	A.		40
Rollison,	Horace	J.		94
Romaine	Ralph	Benjamin		3
Roof,	James			221
Rooney,	Matilda			235
Roosa,	Mary	E.		36
Rose,	Andrew	J. A.		42
Rose,	Ida		May	87
Rosenbrock,	Anna	E.		204

Ross,	Julia		109
Roth,	Eugene		57
Rotherie,	William		18
Roupe,	Mary		254
Roushon,	Belle		34
Roushorne,	Sarah	Ann	132
Rowe,	Mary	Brown	123
Rowe,	Mary	Brown	165
Rowinsky,	George	Andrew	159
Rowinsky,	George	Andrew	223
Roy,	Stephen		20
Royster,	Hubert		238
Rozell,	Ethel		197
Rozell,	Orphy		133
Rozell,	Orphy		197
Ruble,	Eliza	Ellen	167
Rummel,	John	C.F.	7
Rumph,	William	Thomas	155
Runcie,	Hiram	E.	207
Rundell,	Munsell		83
Rush,	Bertha		261
Rush,	Sam		264
Rusk,	Nancy		220
Russell,	Caty		41
Russell,	Lee	Eugene	265
Ryan,	C.	E.	249
Ryan,	George	E.	47
Ryder,	Martha	A.	132
Ryerson,	Peter	Nicholas	78
Sacks,	Ida	M.	175
Saleture,	Margaret	A.	230
Sammons,	Sylvia	S.	65
Sample,	Martha	Jane	188
Sanders,	Cephas	D.	254
Sanders,	Daniel		236
Sandusky,	Harmon	Wynn	173
Sapp,	Elsie		140
Sarine,	Nicholas		93
Saunders,	Maria	Antoinette	133
Sayer,	Alice		108
Sayre,	Mary		10

Sayre,	Nancy	J.	49
Sayre,	Sarah	J.	26
Sayres,	Elinor		242
Sayres,	Mary		242
Scales,	Elizabeth		152
Schlee,	Katherine		52
Schneider,	Frances		50
Schrey,	Oscar		173
Schworm,	John	W.	162
Scofield,	Frank	A.	178
Scott,	Jacob		226
Scott,	Joseph	L.	219
Scott,	Sarah	E.	153
Scrafford,	Myra		52
Scully,	James		122
Seaman,	Ida		105
Seapy,	Amanda		143
Sears,	Stephen	James	63
Sebring,	Bessie		155
See,	Mary	Ann	122
See,	Sarah	E.	92
Seely,	Adeline		246
Seitler,	Carolina	(Lena)	52
Seltzer,	Susan		221
Senior,	Mary	Semer	99
Sering,	Bessie		155
Shafer,	Peter		144
Shaffer,	John	H.	101
Shahan,	Reuben		177
Shakespeare	Clarence		247
Shamp.	Isaac		224
Shane,	Josie		162
Shannon,	Paul		144
Share,	Mary	E.	92
Sharp,	Isaac		125
Sharpe,	Priscilla	Ann	149
Sharpless,	Ethel	L.	140
Shaw,	Emma	Jane	25
Shay,	Abby	Ann	48
Shay,	Lois	Arminda	42
Shearer,	John	P.	143

Shearer,	Mary	Ann		130
Sheels,	Fanny	O.		36
Shepherd,	Arthena			161
Shepler,	Matthias			238
Sherer,	Greta			67
Sherer,	James	Edward		233
Sheridan,	Margaret	Ellen	(Nellie)	59
Sherley,	Rosaleta			175
Sherman,	Jane			91
Sherman,	Violet			35
Sherwood,	Anna	E.		194
Shipman,	Hannah			3
Shivers,	Hannah			221
Shode,	Charles	B.		217
Shoemaker,	Anna			10
Shoemaker,	Moses			92
Shuart,	Rachel			69
Shuler,	Grover	C.		162
Shurley,	Martha			124
Shy,	Ida			230
Sickles,	Elizabeth			17
Sigafoos,	Mabel	Diana		36
Simonson,	Joseph			3
Simpson,	Georgiana			136
Simpson,	Mary	Elizabeth	Sanders	233
Simpson,	Mary	Elizabeth	Sanders	255
Simpson,	Simeon			20
Sinai,	Rose			114
Sisson,	Dora	A.		78
Sisson,	Fred	Edmund		57
Skinner,	Francis	Cornelius		59
Skinner,	Lewis	Edgar		46
Skinner,	Thankful			91
Slack,	Mary	Eliza		128
Slicer,	Eleanor			176
Slidell,	Joshua			14
Sloot,	Jemima			131
Sloot,	Michael			131
Smedley,	Harriet			189
Smith	Clinton	H.		83
Smith,	Althea	Edwards		89

Smith,	Caroline		123
Smith,	Catherine		22
Smith,	Catherine	Ann	69
Smith,	Charles	Edgar	133
Smith,	Clayton	Tilton	152
Smith,	Cora	C.	38
Smith,	Edgar	C.	100
Smith,	Eliza	Jane	86
Smith,	Ellen	J.	206
Smith,	Gotlieb		224
Smith,	Henry		101
Smith,	James		170
Smith,	Leonard		103
Smith,	Lucille	M.	185
Smith,	Margaret		11
Smith,	Martha	Elnora	36
Smith,	Martin	M.	49
Smith,	Mary	E.	63
Smith,	Perry		248
Smith,	Rachel		130
Snepp,	Eva	M.	159
Snider,	Raymond	H.	145
Snook,	Edward	P.	25
Snow,	Prince		33
Snyder,	Ada		71
Snyder,	John	J.	84
Soey,	Mary	Virginia	144
Sornberger,	Mary	Augusta	90
Soules,	Cora	Varney	186
Spangenburg,	Sarah	E.	93
Spencer,	Eve	Ann	221
Spencer,	George		155
Spencer,	Isabel	Mae	116
Spier,	Barney		11
Spier,	Johannes	Teunisse	20
Spier,	Thomas	Teunisse	14
Spigelmoyer,	Minnie	Gertrude	230
Sprague,	John		100
Sprague,	John	L.	102
Sprout,	Joanna	M.	240
Squier,	Moses		234

Squire,	Thomas		223
Stafford,	John	Ivan	119
Stafford,	John	I.	264
Stager,	Rachel	Elizabeth	32
Stagner,	Stella		163
Stanaback,	Grace	Bell	106
Standerwick,	Alice		103
Staniford,	Ella	A.	264
Starnaman,	Clarence	Hamilton	250
Starr,	Charlotte	Crosby	53
Stearns,	Rhoda	Arvilla	116
Steel,	Margaret		21
Steel,	Mary		128
Steele,	Susan	E.	265
Steffy,	Lula	F.	147
Stegg,	Isaac		19
Steinbeck,	Susan		45
Stephen,	Ida		126
Stephens,	Eliza		152
Stephenson,	Willard	L.	154
Sterling,	Martin	M.	239
Stetser,	Albert		135
Stevenson,	Alice		199
Stevenson,	Elsie	M.	108
Steward,	Joseph		30
Stewart,	Betty	Jean	260
Stewart,	Elmer	A.	223
Stewart,	Sarah	Maria	22
Steyer,	Tressa	Arela	219
Stinnett,	Arthur		184
Stinson,	Mary	Ann	128
Stivers,	Sharon	Montez	164
Stone,	Christiana		156
Stone,	Ira		194
Stone,	Louisa		130
Stone,	Olive	A.	182
Storm,	Susanna		12
Storms,	Mary		2
Stoughtenburg,	Maria		19
Stoughton,	Iona	Edell	158
Stradworthy,	Alice		108

Stradworthy,	Alice		198
Strang,	William	T.	80
Stratton,	Mary	Etta	43
Strickland,	Ettie	Louise	139
Struble,	Jacob		20
Struble,	John		94
Stump,	Goldie		240
Sturr,	Daniel		4
Sturr,	Henry	S.	43
Stygall,	Edith	A.	196
Summers,	Frank	E.	162
Swackhammer,	Alida		39
Swain,	Thelma		232
Swainson,	Catherine	R.	54
Sweeney,	Charles	Anthony	88
Sweetland,	Lyman		173
Swick,	John		93
Swick,	Joseph	M.	84
Swick,	Josiah		94
Swiger,	Perlie		233
Switzer,	Edith	Elizabeth	128
Switzer,	John		133
Switzer,	Lorenzo		125
Switzer,	Peter		132
Symington,	George		49
Tanger,	Miriam		37
Tarbox,	David		83
Taunton,	Mary	Elizabeth	141
Taylor,	Clarinda	Phoebe	177
Taylor,	Ellen		236
Taylor,	Emma		149
Taylor,	Mary	Ann	127
Taylor,	Sarah	J.	147
Teague,	Curtis		153
Tedford,	George	A.	223
Teeple,	Mary		252
Teeples,	John	S.	193
Teeter,	Philip		28
Teeter,	Verna	Adella	186
Tenant,	Etta		126
Terpening,	Alta	Mae	191

Terry,	Elsie			60
Terry,	Richard	Allison	Lain	74
Terwiliger,	Elsa	Ann		38
Thomas,	Marie			245
Thomas,	Mary			103
Thompson,	George			217
Thompson,	Isaiah			130
Thompson,	Nancy			147
Thompson,	Nancy			245
Thompson,	Sarah			17
Thomson,	Hugh	C.		125
Thorbahn,	Joan	Alice		90
Thorsen,	Valda			169
Tiley,	Hazel			212
Tilley,	Hazel			34
Tilley,	Tina			205
Tillingast,	Harry	C.		170
Timms,	John	H.		189
Timms,	Philip	S.		70
Tinsman,	Abigail			24
Titman,	Elizabeth			80
Titman,	Elizabeth			247
Titus,	Andrew			83
Todd,	William			136
Toers,	Johannes			8
Tompkins,	Gertrude	Mae		113
Townley,	Adam			125
Townsend,	Flora			73
Traffer,	George			141
Transo,	Hiram			48
Travis,	Julia	A.		113
Traynor,	Alice			108
Trimble,	Ruby	Anna	Lee	175
Trowbridge,	Ella			235
Truesdell,	John	Giveans		57
Tubbs,	Josephine			122
Tullus,	Wingate			223
Turner,	Harold			143
Tuttle,	Lucius			76
Underwood,	Alpheus	Hugh		218
Uren,	William			235

Usher,	Frances		17
Utter,	Carlos	A.	67
Utter,	Violet		97
Valentine,	Catherine	Mariah	79
Valleau,	Hettie		5
Van Alen,	Catherine		38
Van Blarcom,	Nicholas		16
Van Dewater	Peter		4
Van Dyke,	Susannah	Meek	244
Van Etten,	Edgar	Lemont	250
Van Gelder,	John		15
Van Gelder,	Sarah		1
Van Gelder,	Tobias		3
Van Giesen,	Sarah		62
Van Horn,	Aaltje	(Prevost)	12
Van Horn,	Thomas		8
Van Houten,	Claartje		5
Van Houten,	Garrabrant		16
Van Houten,	Helmerich		9
Van Kuren,	Sarah		198
Van Orden,	Anna	Maria	70
Van Orden,	Matthew		8
Van Orden,	Thomas		14
Van Riper,	Peter		28
Van Riper,	Peter		84
Van Sickle,	Samuel		17
Van Sicle,	Rosetta		134
Van Tassel,	Aeltie		1
Van Valer,	Jacob		75
Van Wart,	Rachel		21
Vanalstrom,	Perry		156
Vanderbeek,	Abraham		20
Vanderbeek,	Lydia		2
Vanderbeek,	Rachel		11
Vanderhoef,	Geertruy		17
Vanderhoff,	John		60
Vanderhoof,	Emma	A.	72
Vanderlinden,	Matthew		8
Vandervoort,	Hattie		190
Vandewater,	Catherine		18
Vanluven,	Eliza		134

Vanover,	Margaret			36
Vanvoorhees,	John	W.		13
Varner,	Margaret			217
Vasey,	M.	K.		208
Vermilye,	Joanna	Maria		31
Vermilyea,	William			132
Vermule,	Adeline			25
Victor,	James	A.		252
Vincent,	Louisa	(Southard)		124
Vinton,	Percy			25
Vogel,	Marguerite	E.		44
Vogenberger,	Frank	Conrad		216
Voorheis,	Katherine	M.		187
Waddle,	Freeman	G.		162
Wade,	Joseph			27
Wager,	Elizabeth			95
Wagershutz,	Janet			184
Waggoner,	Henry			155
Waggoner,	Raleigh	B.		154
Wagner,	Henry			155
Wagner,	William	H.		64
Wahl,	Charles	Wilbur		138
Wakefield,	Rosa	Baker		76
Walker,	Elizabeth			129
Walker,	John			212
Walker,	Margaret			251
Walker,	William	Jackson		58
Wallace,	Leon	A.		187
Wallace,	William			83
Wallow,	Minnie			24
Walls,	Margaret			136
Walsh,	Alice	R.		66
Walsh,	John	Howard		165
Walters,	Annie	G.	Carnahan	127
Walz,	Dorothy			61
Ward,	Frank	Clay		165
Ward,	Walter			160
Ware,	Laura	Elmer		110
Warford,	Benjamin	Hill		105
Warner,	Luther	F.		27
Warner,	Marguerita	A.		188

Warner,	Willis	S.	123
Warren,	Catherine	Margaret	225
Wascher,	William	C.	146
Watkins,	Carrie		247
Watson,	Jack	Edward	158
Watson,	Mary		225
Wattson,	George		166
Way,	Joseph		28
Weaver,	Alna		185
Webb,	Lois		266
Webb,	Mary		177
Webb,	Sally	Ann	12
Webb,	Schuyler	S.	213
Webbers,	Hillegond		7
Weed,	Edith	Avalda	244
Weed,	J.	N.	258
Weekly,	Mary	Lavina	155
Welch,	Ann		73
Welch,	Edward		25
Welch,	Jacob		61
Welch,	Rebecca		177
Weller,	Emilie		55
Welling,	Jesse		247
Wells,	Ada		77
Wenman,	Effy		3
Werly,	Henry	C.	88
West,	Charles	A.	122
West,	Thomas		50
Wheeler,	Roy	Edwin	130
Whicker,	Chauncey	D.	146
Whisman,	Howard		153
Whisman,	Leila		156
Whitaker,	Harry	Osborn	225
White,	Charlotte		142
White,	Helen	C.	234
White,	Lydia	Catherine	188
Whitfield,	Henry	Monroe	46
Whitt,	J.	Harold	210
Whysong,	Alletta	Bell	162
Wiggins,	Gertrude	Valeria	173
Wiggins,	L.	D.	203

Wilcox,	Caroline			155
Wilcox,	Marie			109
Wilcox,	William	M.		150
Wilder,	Levi			93
Wildrick,	Raymond	G.		135
Wiley,	Cervilla	Medora		172
Wiley,	Henry			171
Willhauck,	Mary	Agness		182
Williams,	Albert	L.		59
Williams,	Amos			51
Williams,	D.	A.		233
Williams,	Eliza			111
Williams,	John	Beatty		226
Williams,	Lavinia	L.	(Vinnie)	59
Williams,	Marion	Dennis		264
Williams,	Nathan	B.		228
Willour,	Forest	E.		208
Willson,	Nelson	J.		82
Wilson,	Angeline	Corzette		247
Wilson,	Burton			88
Wilson,	Elizabeth	Mae		34
Wilson,	Fred			28
Wilson,	Fred			68
Wilson,	Genevieve	Lita		112
Winant,	James	Johnson		85
Windsor,	Lydia			205
Winfield,	Bartlett	C.	(Barton)	94
Winget,	Sallie			244
Winne,	Hannah			20
Winston,	Sepronah			21
Winters,	Hannah			107
Winters,	Lizzie			153
Wise,	Alvin	R.		237
Withers,	Eva	L.		138
Wood,	Frances	Jane	Mary	123
Wood,	J.	Roscoe		50
Wood,	Joseph	A.		160
Wood,	Myrl	S.		264
Wood,	Nellie	M.		105
Wood,	Robenia			230
Woodbury,	Lydia	Lizzie		60

Woodhull,	Charles	Howell	75
Woodrum,	Irvin	L.	216
Woods,	Lester		207
Woodward,	Henrietta	Grace	116
Wright,	Anna	Mary	255
Wright,	Annie	M.	233
Wright,	Charles		111
Wright,	Cordelia	Edith	247
Wright,	Cornelius	Morford	167
Wright,	Dean	C.	193
Wright,	Elizabeth	M.	54
Wright,	Howard	E.	80
Wright,	Mary		227
Wyatt,	John	A.	99
Wyatt,	Martha		203
Wynso,	Sarah		236
Yoho,	Denver	Franklin	234
Young,	Elizabeth		109
Young,	Mary	A.	89
Young,	Mary	A.	131
Young,	Violetta		69
Young,	W.	H.	232
Young,	William		58
Young,	William	Edward	87
Yount,	William	C.	160
Zabele,	George	Grant	51
Zabriskie,	David	Christie	43
Zebriskie,	Keziah	Eve	40
Zoch,	Carl		136

SOURCES

1790C	1790 federal census
1855C	1855 state census
AAR	Genealogy of Abraham A. Rheutan
ACOHS	Ashland Co. Ohio Historical Society
ACPL	Allen Co. IN Public Library
ADRC	Acquackanonk (Passaic) Reformed Church
AFH	Ackerman Family History
AGBI	American Genealogical Biographical Index
ARMS	Armstrong, "Pioneer Families"
ARWPF	American Revolutionary War Files
BARB	Barber, NYGBR Index
BAYL	Baylis, "History of Richmond County"
BCGI	Bergen Co. NJ Grave Inscriptions
BCMR	Bergen Co. Marriage Records
BCPHAS	Bradford Co. PA Historical Society
BDC	Brooklyn NY Death Certificate
BFG	Blauvelt Family Genealogy
BFH	Blauvelt Family History
BHS	Brooklyn Historical Society
BIOG	Texas Biographies
BLM	Bureau of Land Management
BOGGS	Information from Ruth Ann Boggs, Austin, TX
BPL	Brooklyn Public Library
BRVC	Branchville NJ Cemetery Records
CABRI	California Birth Records Index
CADRI	California Death Records Index
CAREY	Information from Richard Carey, Middletown, NY
CAROHS	Carroll Co. OH Historical Society
CBRF	Culver Brook Restoration Foundation Report on the Rutan Cabin
CCNEW	Columbia Centinel Newspaper of Newark, NJ
CCPL	Champaign Co. OH Public Library
CDAR	DAR application of Eleanor J. Carry
CDIR	City/County Directory
CHEMHS	Chemung Co. NY Historical Society

CIMB	Information from Michele A. Cimbala, Silver Spring, MD
CMAC	Grenville Mackenzie Records
CMOR	Morris Co. NJ Cemetery Records
CoBR	County Birth Records
COCHS	Cortland Co. NY Historical Society
CoDR	County Death Records
CoMR	County Marriage Records
CRAWN	Crawn Files, Sussex Co. NJ Historical Society
CRC	Clinton Rutan Collection, New Jersey Historical Society
CVAN	Information from Carol Van Buren, Westtown, NY
CVHM	Connecticut Valley Historical Museum
CVMR	Connecticut Valley Marriage Records
CWW	Canadian Who Was Who
DARLDC	DAR Library, Washington, DC
DARP	DAR Patriot Index
DAVIS	Bergen Co. NJ Deed Records
DFH	Demarest Family History
DMD	Information from Diane Miller Devido
DRCNYC	Dutch Reformed Church, New York City
DRCSHP	Dutch Reformed Church, Stone House Plains (Bloomfield) NJ
EARDP	William A. Eardeley Papers, Brooklyn Historical Society
ECDR	Essex Co. NJ Death Records
ECMR	Essex Co. NJ Marriage Records
EG	Information from Elsie Garris, Newton, NJ
EOVB	Probate Papers, Estate of Virginia Broderick, Queens Co. NY
EVG	Everton's Genealogical Helper
FER	Information from Frank E. Rutan, St. David's PA
FH	"The Rutan Family in America", Herbert Fisher
FLDI	Florida Death Index
FMLWT	Flower Memorial Library, Watertown, NY
GAR	Information from George A. Rutan, Palmdale, CA

	New York Herald
MAR	Information from Martha Colsher Rutan
MAV	Information from Donald Mavros, Village Historian, Unionville, Orange Co. NY
MCRC	Information from Arthur C. Rutan of Corning NY compiled by his mother Mary Cromer Rutan
MCNF	Methodist Church, Newfoundland NJ
MCNY	New York State Marriage Certificate
MCOPC	Morgan Co. IN Public Library
MDI	Michigan Death Index
MEACH	Information from J. Robert Meachem of West Palm Beach, FL
METC	Information from Frank and Martha Metcalf Of Orchard, MA
MHAWS	Information from Marjorie Haws, Magnolia, IL
MHILL	Information from Michael Hill, Walnut Creek, CA
MMI	Michigan Marriage Index
MNDCI	Minnesota Death Certificate Index
MRCL	Mansfield-Richland, OH County Public Library
MRUT	Information from Michael Rutan-Heningham Of Bangor, ME
MZB	Maria Zabriskie Diary
NCDI	North Carolina Death Index
NCPL	New City, Rockland Co., NY Public Library
NDIR	City Directory, Newark NJ
NEHGS	New England Historic Genealogical Society, Boston
NGS	National Genealogical Society
NJBI	New Jersey Biographical Index
NJCW	"New Jersey in the Civil War"
NJG	"New Jersey Genesis"
NJHS	New Jersey Historical Society
NJW	New Jersey Wills (part of the N.J. Archives)
NKG	Nicholas Knapp Genealogy
NPL	Newark, NJ Public Library
NSDAR	National Society Daughters of the

GDAW	Information from Gladys Rutan Daw, Crystal River, FL
GENEX	Genealogical Exchange Magazine, May 1904
GKB	Information from Georgia K. Bopp
GMNJ	The Genealogical Magazine of NJ
GSBC	Genealogical Society of Bergen Co. NJ
GSNJ	Genealogical Society of NJ
HACHS	Hackettstown NJ Historical Society
HDRC	Hackensack NJ Dutch Reformed Church
HKING	Information from Herb Kingsland, Hollywood, CA
HONEY	Honeyman, "History of Union Co. NJ"
HOYE	"The Hoyes of Maryland"
IBRI	Indiana Birth Records Index
IMI	Illinois Marriage Index
JAS	Information from Jonathan A. Smith
JRB	Information from Janet Rutan Bowers of Ft. Lee, NJ
JN	Information from Jean Newman, Geneseo, IL
JS	Information from Jean Sproul of Long Valley, NJ
KCH	Kent County History (Michigan)
KFH	Kingsland Family History
KKI	KindredKonnections
LDS	Records of the Church of Jesus Christ and Latter Day Saints, primarily the IGI
LEE	Information from Candy Lee
LINT	Reid, "The Loyalists in Ontario"
LISTAR	Long Island Star, a newspaper in Brooklyn Prior to the Civil War
LITT	Little, "Genealogies of the First Settlers of Passaic Valley, N.J."
LIZR	Information from Liz Rutan, Easton, PA PA
LLC	Loyalist Lineages of Canada
LVLC	Longville Cemetery, Vernon, Sussex Co., NJ
LWEB	Information from Lola Weber, Longview, WA
MACK	"Families of the Colonial Town of Philipsburgh"
MAHER	Index of Marriages and Deaths in the

	American Revolution
NYBC	State of New York Birth Certificate
NYCBC	City of New York Birth Certificate
NYCMM	"New York City Methodist Marriages"
NYEP	New York Evening Post
NYGBR	New York Genealogical and Biograph- ical Society
NYHS	New-York Historical Society
NYMC	State of New York Marriage Certif- icate
NYT	New York Times
NYTO	New York Times Obituary
OAR	Official Army Register
OCD	Orange County NY Directory
ODI	Ohio Death Index
OKAFL	Okaloosa Co. FL Marriage Records
ORDI	Oregon Death Index
PAARCH	Pennsylvania Archives
PATB	Information from Pat Brand, Hastings, NE
PCHS	PCHS Newsletter
PCHSB	Mattie Bowman Collection, Passaic Co. Historical Society
PCHSP	Family Sheets, PCHS
PCHSQ	Quackenbush Collection, PCHS
PCTU	Presbyterian Church at Turkey (New Providence) NJ
PDRC	Paramus NJ Dutch Reformed Church
PERSI	
PJPL	Port Jervis NY Public Library
PJUGO	Port Jervis Union Gazette
PNJHS	"Proceedings of the N.J. Histor- ical Society"
POCGS	Predmore Collection, Orange Co., NY Historical Society
POV	Information from Barbara J. Povalac
PPDLN	Perlee Papers, Dennis Free Library, Newton NJ
PSAR	Records of the Sons of the American Revolution of Pennsylvania
PUH	Information from the Town Historian, Town of Pulteney, Steuben Co., NY
QCDI	Queens Co. NY Death Index

QFH	Quackenbush Family History
RCFL	Reton Cemetery, Ft. Lee, NJ
RER	Information from Robert E. Rutan, Mansfield, OH
RICR	Information from Richard F. Rutan, Taylors, SC
ROOTSW	Rootsweb, Internet Genealogy website
RRET	Information from Robert Reton
RUDR	Information from Irvin E. Rutan, Columbus, OH
RUTT	Henry N. Ruttan, "A Part of the Family of Ruttan"
SCDR	Sussex Co. NJ Death Records
SCMR	Sussex Co. Marriage Records
SDRC	Schraalenburgh (Dumont, NJ) Reformed Church
SFH	Sayre Family History
SIHS	Staten Island Historical Society
SLHOLOW	Perry, "The Old Dutch Burying-Ground of Sleepy Hollow"
SQHS	Susquehanna Co.PA Historical Society
SRDC	Saddle River Reformed Church
SRDRC	Second River (Belleville) Reformed Ch
SSA	Records of the Social Security Admin
STICK	Stickney, "Old Sussex Families of the Minisink Region"
STUCHS	Steuben Co. NY Historical Society
SUSESS	Brown, "Warren and Sussex Estates"
SXHS	Sussex Co. NJ Historical Society
TAPDRC	Tappan NY Reformed Church
TCCI	Trumbull Co. OH Cemetery Inscriptions
TDR	Information from Thomas D. Rutan, Grove City, OH
TDRC	Totowa NJ Reformed Church
TMR	Information from Thomas M. Rutan, Lake Jackson, TX
TXDR	Texas Death Records
USARCH	U.S. Archives
VA	Office of Veterans Affairs
VHFH	Van Houten Family History
VIRUT	Information from Viola Rutan, Henderson NV

VWR	Vernon W. Ruttan, "Some Ruttan Family History"
WCCL	Citizens Library, Washington PA
WCHS	Washington Co. PA Historical Society
WENP	Wenman Papers, Brooklyn Historical Society
WHIT	Information from Betty Ewing Whitmer, Navarre OH
WPCC	Citizens Library, Washington PA
WSIM	Information from Warren Simmons
WTWP	Wells Twp., Bradford Co. PA Vital Records
WWW	Who Was Who
WYCK	Wyckoff Cemetery, Wyckoff, Bergen Co., NJ
YRR	Information provided by Yvonne Rutan Reed, Alexandria, VA
ZAB	Zabriskie Family History

BIBLIOGRAPHY

Ackerman, Herbert S. (compiler) Hackensack
Reformed Church Records 1801-1886, typesript
Ridgewood, NJ 1943

Ackerman, Herbert S., Van Houten Family History,
typescript, Ridgewood NJ, 1945

Anson, Shirley V. and George A. Badgely, Index of
the Commemorative Biographical Record of Dutchess
County, N.Y., The Reporter Co., Walton NY 1991

Avery Obituary Index of Architects and Artists,
G.K.Hall & Co., Boston, 1963

American and English Genealogies in the Library of
Congress, GPC Baltimore, 1967

Armstrong, William C., Pioneer Families of North-
western New Jersey, Hunterdon House, Lambertville
N.J., 1979

The American Genealogical-Biographical Index,
Godfrey Memorial Library, Middletown, CT 1988

Baird, Charles W., History of the Huguenot Emig-
ration in America, 1885; Regional Publishing Co.,
Baltimore, repr 1986

Banta, Theodore M., Sayre Family History, De Vinne
Press, New York, 1901

Barber, Gertrude, Surname Index to the New York
Genealogical and Biographical Record

Barber, Gertrude (compiler), Index to the Letters
of Administration of New York County 1743-1875,
privately printed, 1951

Barber, John W. Historical Collections of N.J.
Past and Present, published by subscription, New
Haven CT, 1868

Baughman, Abraham J., <u>A Centennial Biographical</u>
<u>History of Richland County, Ohio</u>, The Lewis Pub-
lishing Co., Chicago, 1901

Bausman, Rev. Joseph H., <u>History of Beaver County</u>
<u>Pennsylvania</u>, The Knickerbocker Press, New York,
1904

Bayles, R.M. (ed), <u>History of Richmond County</u>
<u>(Staten Island) New York</u>, L.E. Preston & Co. New
York, 1887

<u>Bergen County Panorama</u>, Works Progress Administ-
ration, Hackensack NJ, 1941

<u>Biographical and Genealogical History of the City</u>
<u>of Newark and Essex County, N.J.</u>, Lewis Publish-
ing Co., N.Y. and Chicago, 1898

Bowen, Clarence W., <u>History of Woodstock, Conn-</u>
<u>ecticut</u>, The Plimpton Press, Norwich, MA, 1935

Bowman, Fred Q., <u>10000 Vital Records of Eastern</u>
<u>New York, 1777-1834,</u> GPC, Baltimore, 1987

Boyer, Carl 3rd, <u>Ships' Passenger Lists New York</u>
<u>and New Jersey 1600-1825,</u> Newhall CA :the Compil-
er, 1978

Boyer, Charles S., <u>Early Forges and Furnaces in</u>
<u>New Jersey</u>, University of Pennsylvania Press,
1931

Brown, Virginia Alleman, <u>Warren County, N.J.</u>
<u>Abstracts of Divisons and Partitions, 1825-1946</u>,
privately printed, 1978

Brown, Virginia Alleman, <u>Abstracts of Divisions</u>
<u>of Warren and Sussex County Estates</u>, Clearfield
Co., Baltimore, 1992

Brown, Virginia Alleman, <u>Abstracts of Essex Coun-</u>
<u>ty N.J. Partitions and Divisions of Estates,</u>
<u>1793-1881</u>, privately printed, Washington, NJ 1981

Brown, Virginia Alleman, <u>Morris County Heirs to</u>
<u>Estates, 1785-1900</u>, Clearfield Co., Baltimore,
1984

Brown, Virginia Alleman, Abstracts of Essex County, N.J. Partitions and Divisions of Estates, 1793-1881, privately printed, Washington, NJ 1981

Bunnell, Paul J., The New Loyalist Index, Heritage Books, Inc. Bowie, MD, 1989

Burnett, Robert B., Belleville Historical Highlights, 1839-1989, Belleville 150th-Anniversary Committee, Belleville, NJ, 1991

Burrows, Edwin G. and Mike Wallace, "Gotham, A History of New York to 1898", Oxford University Press, New York, Oxford, 1999

Carman, Harry J. & Arthur W. Thompson, A Guide to the Principal Sources for American Civilization 1800-1900, Columbia University Press, New York, 1960

A Census of Pensioners for Revolutionary or Military Service, Blair & Blair, DC 1841, GPC Baltimore, repr 1965

Clemens, William Montgomery, American Marriage Records Before 1699, GPC Baltimore, 1977

Coldham, Peter Wilson, The Complete Book of Immigrants, 1661-1699, GPC, Baltimore, 1972

Coldham, Peter Wilson, American Loyalist Claims, National Genealogical Society, Washington, DC, 1980

Cleveland, Edmund James and Horace Gillette Cleveland, The Genealogy of the Cleveland and Cleaveland Families, Case, Lockwood & Brainard Co., Hartford CT, 1899

Clute, J.J., Old Families of Staten Island, (1877) Clearfield Co., Baltimore, repr 1990

Cole, Rev. David (ed) History of Rockland Co., J.B. Beers & Co., New York, 1884

Cole, Rev. David D., First Record Book of the Old Dutch Church at Sleepy Hollow, Yonkers Historical Society, Yonkers, NY, 1901

Coleman, Charles, <u>The Early Records of the First Presbyterian Church of Goshen, N.Y. from 1767 to 1885</u>, (1934), Clearfield Co., Baltimore, repr 1990

<u>The Colonial Graves of the Presbyterian Church at New Providence, N.J.</u>, April 1990

Crumrine, Boyd, (ed) <u>History of Washington County, Pennsylvania</u>, L. H. Everts & Co. Philadelphia, 1882

Dandridge, Danske, <u>American Prisoners of the Revolution</u>, 1911, GPC Baltimore, repr 1967

DAR Patriot Index, <u>National Society of the DAR</u>, Washington, DC 1966

DeLancey, Edward F. (ed), <u>Muster Rolls of New York Provincial Troops, 1755-1764</u>, Collection of the New-York Historical Society, New York, 1891

<u>The Demarest Family,</u> Demarest Family Assn, Hackensack, NJ, 1964

Deming, Judson Keith, <u>Genealogy of John Deming</u>, Matthis-Mets Co., Dubuque, IA, 1904

<u>Dictionary of Canadian Biography</u>, Univ. of Toronto Press, Toronto, 1987

Dilts, Bryan Lee, <u>1890 New York Census Index of Civil War Veterans and Their Widows</u>, Index Publishing, Salt Lake City, 1984

Dornbusch, C.E., <u>Military Bibliography of the Civil War</u>, New York Public Library, 1961

Dubois, Kathryn Phillips, <u>Old Wills of Bergen County, N.J.</u>, David Demarest Chapter, NSDAR, 1954

Eckley, H.J. and William T. Perry, editors <u>History of Carroll and Harrison Counties, Ohio</u>, Lewis Publishing Co., Chicago and New York, 1921

Falk, Byron A. Jr. and Valerie R. Falk, <u>Personal Names Index to the New York Times Index,</u> Roxbury Data Interface, Succasunna, NJ, 1981

Fernow, Berthold, <u>Calendar of Wills Recorded by</u>

the County Clerk at Albany, 1626-1836, GPC, Baltimore, 1967

Filpy, P. William, Passenger and Immigration Lists Bibliography, 1538-1900, Gale Research Co., Detroit, 1988

Filpy, P. William and Mary K. Meyer Passenger and Immigration Lists Index, Gale Research Co., Detroit, 1981

Fisher, William Scott (compiler) New York City Methodist Marriages, 1785-1893, Picton Press, Camden ME, 1994

Foley, Janet Wethy, Early Settlers of New York State, 1934, GPC, Baltimore, repr 1993

Foster, John Y., N.J. and the Rebellion, Martin R. Dennis & Co., Newark NJ, 1968

Frank, Henrietta, Richland County Wills Records of Administration 1813-1826, pp undated

Gannon, Peter Steven (ed) Huguenot Refugees in the Settling of Colonial America, The Huguenot Society of America, NY

Genealogical Exchange, May 1904

Genealogical Index of the Newberry Library of Chicago, G.K. Hall & Co., Boston, 1960

Genealogical Magazine of New Jersey, Vols.2-50; 1927-1976

Gibbs, Whitfield (ed), One Hundred Years of the Sussex Register, 1813-1913, Newton, NJ 1913, Heritage Books, Bowie MD, repr 1992

Graham, Albert Alexander, History of Richland Co. Ohio, A.A. Graham & Co., Mansfield, OH, 1880

Gwathmey, John H., Virginians in the Revolution, Baltimore, GPC, 1979

Haines, Alanson Austin, "History of the 15th Regiment, New Jersey Volunteers", Jenkins & Thomas, New York, 1883

Hatcher, Patricia Law, Abstracts of Graves of Revolutionary Patriots v.3, Pioneer Heritage Press, Dallas, TX, 1988

Hatfield, Rev. Edwin, History of Elizabeth, New Jersey, Carlton and Lanahan, New York, 1868

Headley, Russel, History of Orange County, NY, Van Deusen & Elms, Middletown NY, 1908

Heitman, Francis B., Historical Register of the Officers of the Continental Army During the War of the Revolution, GPC, Baltimore, 1967

History of Beaver County, Pennsylvania, A. Warner & Co., Philadelphia and Chicago, 1888

History of Morris County, New Jersey, W.W. Munsell & Co., New York, 1882

History of Trumbull and Mahoning Counties, H.Z. Williams & Bro., Cleveland, 1882

Historical Collections of the Mahoning Valley, Mahoning Valley Historical Society, Youngstown, OH, 1876

Hoff, Henry B. Genealogies of Long Island Families, GPC, Baltimore, 1967

Hoff, Henry B. Long Island Source Records, GPC, Baltimore, 1987

Holmes, Lois and Holly H. Newcomb, Historic Structure Report/Historical Data: The Rutan Log Cabin, Frankford Twp, Sussex County, N.J., Culver-Brook Restoration Foundation, Branchville NJ, 1986

Honeyman, A. Van Doren, History of Union County, 1664-1923, Lewis Publishing Co., New York & Chicago, 1923

Hoskins, Barbara, compiler, Men From Morris County, N.J, Who Served in the American Revolution, The Joint Free Library of Morristown and Morris Township, Morristown, NJ

Howard, Henry W. B., _History of the City of Brooklyn_, Brooklyn Daily Eagle, Brooklyn NY, 1893

Hoye, Capt. Charles E., _The Hoyes of Maryland_, Sincell Printing Co., Oakland MD, 1942

Index of American Genealogies, Joel Munsell's Sons, Albany, 1900

Index of the Official Register of the Officers and Men of New Jersey in the Revolutionary War, The Historical Records Survey, Works Projects Administration, Newark NJ 1941

Index to Massachusetts Soldiers, Sailors and Marines in the Civil War, Wright & Potter Printing Co., Boston, MA, 1937

Index to the Marriage Records of the Reformed Dutch Church in New Amsterdam and New York, privately printed, New York, 1890

Jackson, Ronald Vern (ed), _Index to Military Men of New Jersey, 1775-1815_, Accelerated Publishing Co., Bountiful UT, 1977

Jacobus, Donald Lines, _Index to Genealogical Periodicals_, GPC, Baltimore, 1962, 1963, 1967

Jones, Edward Alfred, _The Loyalists of New Jersey_, Gregg Press, Boston 1972

Kaminkow, Marion J., _A Complement to Genealogies in the Library of Congress_, Magna Carta Book Co., Baltimore, 1981

Keegan, James J., _A Rutan Family Index_, Heritage Books Inc., Bowie MD, 1996

Keegan, James J., _A Second Rutan Family Index_, Heritage Books, Inc., Bowie MD, 1997

Kelly, Arthur C.M., (compiler) _Marriage Notices from Dutchess County , N.Y. Newspapers, 1826-1851_, Kinship, Rhinebeck, NY 1983

Kelly, Arthur C.M., (compiler) _Vital Records of the Protestant Dutch Reformed Church at Acquack-_

anonk, N.J., 1727-1816, The Holland Society, Rhinebeck, NY

Knapp, Alfred Averill, Nicholas Knapp Genealogy, pp, Winter Park, FL, 1953

Koehler, Albert F., The Huguenots, or Early French in New Jersey, Clearfield Books, Baltimore, 1992

Lart, Charles E., Huguenot Pedigrees, GPC, Baltimore, 1967

Lawton, Mrs. James M., compiler, Family Names of Huguenot Refugees to America (1901) GPC Baltimore, repr 1963

Leary, Peter J., Essex County, N.J. Illustrated, Hardham Press, Newark NJ, 1897

Leiby, Adrian C., The Early Dutch and Swedish Settlers of New Jersey, D. Van Nostrand Co. Princeton, NJ, 1964

Leiby, Adrian C., The Revolutionary War in the Hackensack Valley, Rutgers U. Press, New Brunswick, NJ, 1962

Leiby, Adrian C., The Huguenot Settlement at Schraalenburgh, Bergenfield Free Library, Bergenfield, NJ 1964

Leiby, Adrian C., The United Churches of Hackensack and Schraalenburgh, N.J., 1686-1822, Bergen Co. Historical Society, River Edge NJ, 1976

Littel, John, First Settlers of Passaic Valley, N.J. 1852, GPC, Baltimore, repr 1976, 1981

Mackenzie, George Norbury, Colonial Families of the United States of America, 1920, GPC, Baltimore, repr 1966

Maher, James P., Index to Marriages and Deaths in the New York Herald, 1835-1855, GPC, Baltimore, 1987

Martin, Yvonne E., Marriages and Deaths from Steuben County NY Newspapers 1797-1868, Heritage Books, Inc., Bowie MD, 1988

Mather, Frederick Gregory, Refugees of 1776 from Long Island to Connecticut, Albany 1913, GPC, Baltimore, repr 1972

McMann, Evelyn de R. (editor), Canadian Who's Who, Univ. of Toronto Press, Toronto, 1986

Middleton, Evan P., A Centennial Biographical History of Champaign County, Ohio, Lewis Publishing Co., New York & Chicago, 1902

Muster Rolls of the Regiments of the State of New York, Weed Parsons & Co.. Albany, 1866

The National Cyclopedia of American Biography, James T. White & Co., Clifton, NJ, 1984

Names of Persons For Whom Marriage Licenses Were Issued-Province of New York to 1784, Weed, Parsons & Co., Albany, 1860

Nelson, William, New Jersey Marriage Bonds, GPC, Baltimore, 1967

Nelson, William, New Jersey Marriage Records 1665-1800, GPC, Baltimore, 1982

Nelson, William, History of the Old Dutch Church at Totowa, Press Printing and Publishing, Paterson, NJ, 1892

Nelson, William, The First Presbyterian Church of Paterson, N.J., Call Printing and Publishing Co., Paterson, NJ, 1893

Nelson, William, The Van Houten Manuscripts, pp Paterson, NJ, 1894

New Jersey in the Civil War, Office of the Adjutant General, John L. Murphy Printer, Trenton, NJ, 1876

New York Genealogical and Biographical Record, 1986-1994

New York in the Revolution, James A. Roberts, Comptroller, Brandon Printing Co., Albany, 1898

Nichols, Mary J.G. and Leona N. Nichols, A History of the Descendants of Jean Guenon of Flushing, Long Island, A.W. Hendricks & Co., Brooklyn 1906

Norton, James S., New Jersey in 1793, Everton Publishers, Logan UT 1973

O'Callaghan, Edmund Bailey, Lists of Inhabitants of Colonial New York, GPC, Baltimore, 1979

O'Callaghan, Edmund Bailey, General Index to the Documents Relative to the Colonial History of the State of N.Y., Weed, Parsons & Co. Albany, 1861

Palmer, Gregory, Biographical Sketches: Loyalists of the American Revolution, Meckler Publishing, Westport/London, 1984

Pennsylvania Archives, Harrisburg Publishing Co. Harrisburg, PA, 1907

Periodical Source Index, Allen County Public Library, Genealogy Dept., Fort Wayne, IN, 1972

Perry, William Graves, The Old Dutch Burying Ground of Sleepy Hollow, Rand Press, Boston 1953

Phisterer, Frederick (compiler) New York in the War of the Rebellion, D.B. Lyon & Co., Albany, 1912

Platt, Charles D., Dover History, M.C. Havens, Dover, N.J., 1914

Pomfret, John E., Colonial New Jersey --A History, Charles Scribner's Sons, New York, 1973

Pomfret, John E., The New Jersey Proprietors and Their Lands, D. Van Nostrand & Co. Inc., Princeton, NJ, 1964

Proceedings of the New Jersey Historical Society, Newark, N.J.

"Progressive Men of Western Colorado", A.W. Bowen & Co., Chicago, 1905

Pyne, Henry Rogers, "Ride to War, A History of the 1st New Jersey Cavalry", Rutgers Univ. Press, New Brunswick, N.J., 1961

Randolph, Howard S.F. and Russell Bruce Rankin
Paramus, Bergen County, N.J. Reformed Dutch Bapt-
isms, Newark, 1935

Reaman, George Elmore, The Trail of the Huguenots
in Europe, the United States, South Africa and
Canada, GPC, Baltimore, 1966

Reamy, Martha and Bill, compilers, Pioneer Families of Orange County, undated, privately printed

Records of the Town of Newark, NJ, New Jersey
Historical Society, Newark, 1864

Records of Officers and Men of New Jersey in Wars
1791-1815, Office of the Adjutant General, Gazette
Publishing Co., Trenton, NJ, 1909

Reid, William D, The Loyalists in Ontario, 1973,
GPC, Baltimore, repr 1994

Richland County, Ohio Cemetery Records, The Richland Co. Chapter of the Ohio Genealogical Society,
pp, undated

Reynolds, Helen Wilkinson (compiler) Marriages and
Deaths Published in Poughkeepsie Newspapers, 1778-
1825, Gateway Press, Baltimore, 1982

Ross, Peter, A History of Long Island, Lewis Publishing Co., New York and Chicago, 1902

Ruttan, Henry Norlunde, A Part of the Family of
Ruttan, 1590-1986, Emery Publishing, Ottawa, 1986

Ruttenber, E.M. and L.H. Clark, History of Orange
County, NY, 1881, Heart of the Lakes Publishing,
Interlaken, NY, repr 1980

Sabine, Lorenzo, Loyalists of the American
Revolution, 1864 GPC. Baltimore, repr 1974

Sawyer, Ray C. (ed), N.J. Death Notices as Published in the Christian Intelligencer of the
Reformed Dutch Church 1830-1871, 1932

Sawyer, Ray C. (ed) Marriages as Published in
the Christian Intelligencer of the Reformed Dutch
Church 1830-1871, 1932

Sawyer, Ray C. (compiler) <u>Gravestone Inscriptions</u>
<u>of Trinity Cemetery, New York City, N.Y.</u>, pp 1931

Sawyer, Ray C., <u>Abstracts of Wills for New York</u>
<u>County 1818-1823</u>, privately printed, 1935

Scott, Kenneth, <u>Coroner's Reports NYC 1823-1842</u>,
Collection of the New York Genealogical and
Biographical Society, NY, 1989

Scott, Kenneth, <u>NYC Court Records, NYC Court of</u>
<u>Quarter Sessions, 1760-1797</u> National Genealogical
Society, DC, 1983

Scott, Kenneth, <u>NYC Court Records, NYC Court of</u>
<u>General Sessions, 1797-1801</u>, National Genealogical
Society, DC, 1988

Scott, Kenneth, <u>Genealogical Data from the New</u>
<u>York Post-Boy, 1743-1773</u>, National Genealogical
Society, DC, <u>1980</u>

Scott, Kenneth, <u>Genealogical Data from New York</u>
<u>Adminisration Bonds, 1753-1799</u>, Collections of the
NYGBS, NY, 1969

Scott, Kenneth, <u>Marriages and Deaths from the New</u>
<u>Yorker, 1836-1841</u>, National Genealogical Society,
DC, 1980

Scott, Kenneth, <u>Early New York Naturalizations:</u>
<u>Abstracts From Federal, State and Local Courts,</u>
<u>1792-1840</u>, GPC, Baltimore, 1981

Scott, Kenneth <u>New York Marriage Licenses,</u>
<u>1639-1706</u>, NYGBR Jan and April 1967

Scott, William W.,(Compiler), <u>Index to the</u>
<u>Acquackanonk Church Records Published in the</u>
<u>Church Tablet</u>, pp, Passaic, NJ. 1941

Scott, William W., <u>History of Passaic and Its</u>
<u>Environs</u>, Lewis Publishing Co., New York and
Chicago, 1922

Shaw, William H., <u>History of Essex and Hudson</u>
<u>Counties N.J.</u>, Everts & Peck, Philadelphia, 1884

Sinclair, Donald A., _A New Jersey Biographical Index_, GPC, Baltimore, MD, 1993

Simon, Joel R. (compiler), _1866 Brooklyn Marriage Index_, privately printed, Oceanside, NY 1993

Smith, Thelma E.(compiler), _An Index to the Parish Registers of St. Paul's Church, Flatbush (1904-1923)_, pp, Brooklyn NY, 1974

Snell, James P. (compiler), _History of Sussex County, N.J._, Genealogical Researchers, Washington, NJ, repr 1981

Snell, James P. (compiler), _History of Sussex and Warren Counties, N.J._, Everts and Peck, Philadelphia, 1881

Skemer, Don C. and Robert C, Morris, _Guide to the Manuscript Collections of the N.J. Historical Society_, Newark, 1979

Stapleton, Rev. A., _Memorials to the Huguenots in America_, 1901, Clearfield Co., Baltimore repr 1974

Stickney, Charles Edgar, _Old Sussex Families of the Minisink Region_, Genealogical Researchers, Washington, NJ, repr 1988

Stiles, Henry R., _History of the City of Brooklyn, N.Y._, published by subscription, 1869

Stiles, Henry R., _History of the County of Kings and the City of Brooklyn_, W.W. Munsell & Co., New York, 1884

Stiles, Pence LaFayette, _History of the Stiles Family in Kentucky and Missouri_, W. T. Hawkins, Lebanon, KY 1896

Stryker-Rodda, Harriet, _Some Early Records of Morris County, N.J. 1740-1799_, Polyanthos, New Orleans, LA, 1975

Stryker-Rodda, Kenn, _Revolutionary Census of New Jersey_, Polyanthus, Cottonport, LA, 1972

Stryker-Rodda, Kenn, _Digging for Ancestors in the Garden State_, The Detroit Society for Genealogical

Research, Inc., Detroit, 1970

Taylor, Alan, "American Colonies", Viking-Penquin,
New York, 2001

Troy, Ann A. (editor), Nutley Yesterday-Today, The
Nutley Historical Society, Nutley, NJ, 1961

Upton, Harriet Taylor, A Twentieth Century History
of Trumbull County, Ohio, Lewis Publishing Co.,
Chicago, 1909

Versteeg, Dingman and Thomas Vermilye, Jr. (eds.)
Bergen Records, Records of the Reformed Protestant
Dutch Church of Bergen, N.J. 1666 to 1788, Clear-
field Co., Baltimore, 1976

Virkus, Frederick A., Immigrant Ancestors, GPC,
Baltimore, 1963/1976

Virkus, Frederick A., The Abridged Compendium of
American Genealogy, v.VI, (1937), GPC, Baltimore,
repr 1987

Wallace, William Stewart, The United Empire
Loyalists, 1922, Gregg Press, Boston, MA, repr 1972

War of the Rebellion Index, Government Printing
Office, Washington, DC, 1901

Watts, Ralph M., "History of the Underground Railroad in Mechanicsburg, Urbana", Champaign Co.
Historical Society, no date

Wells, Robert V., The Population of the British
Colonies in America before 1776, Princeton Univ.
Press, 1975

Westervelt, Frances A. (editor) Bergen County, N.J.
Marriage Records, privately printed, Maywood, NJ,
1946

White, Virgil D. (transcriber) Index to War of 1812
Pension Files, The National Historical Publishing
Co., Waynesboro, TN, 1992

Whittemore, Henry, The Founders and Builders of the
Oranges, L.K. Hardham Co., Newark, 1896

Worden, Jean D., _New York Genealogical and Biographical Record, Master Index 1870-1982_, privately printed, Franklin, OH. 1983

Wright, Esther Clark, _The Loyalists of New Brunswick_, Moncton Publishing Co, Ltd, Moncton, N.B., Canada, 1955

Zabriskie, George Olin, _The Zabriskie Family_, privately printed, 1963

www.ingramcontent.com/pod-product-compliance
Lightning Source LLC
Chambersburg PA
CBHW070551270326
41926CB00013B/2278